Operation
Esther

Operation
Esther

Opening the Door for the Last Jews of Yemen

by

Hayim Tawil
with Steven Miodownik
and contributions by Pierre Goloubinoff

BELKIS PRESS

The publication of

Operation Esther

was made possible in part by a generous donation from

HARRY EPSTEIN

in honor of his parents

EDWARD AND ELLI

The glory of children are their parents
(Proverbs 17:6)

BELKIS PRESS, 24 Bennett Ave, Suite 24B, New York, NY 10033

For

Esther Tawil, z"l

Laurie Johnson, in memoriam

Dalia Tawil, long may she live

On account of the righteous women of that
generation Israel was redeemed from Egypt
(Babylonian Talmud, Sotah 11b)

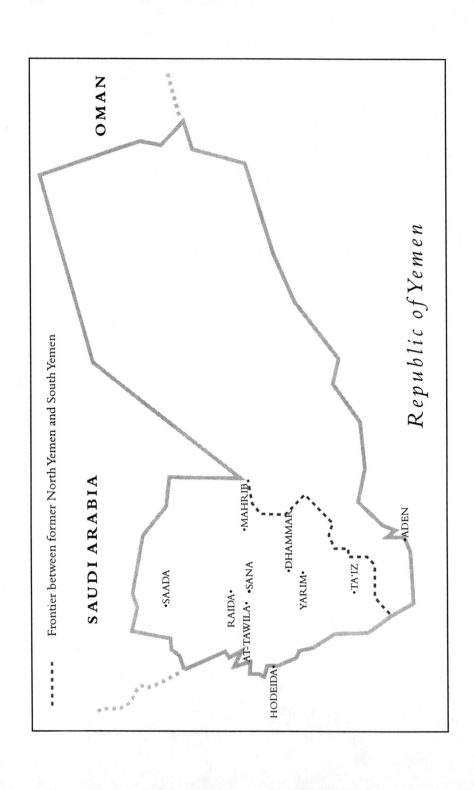

OMAN

SAUDI ARABIA

Republic of Yemen

- - - - - Frontier between former North Yemen and South Yemen

•SAADA

RAIDA•

AT-TAWILA• •SANA

•MAHRIB

•DHAMMAR

YARIM•

•TA'IZ

HODEIDA•

•ADEN

Contents

Introduction: When Democracy Works   1
Acknowledgments   6
Prologue: Missing the Magic Carpet   7

Part One

1   From Jerusalem to Sanaa   23
2   Families Torn Apart   45
3   "You Must Go To America!"   65

Part Two

4   Meeting at Stern College   87
5   Mr. Smith Goes to Washington   111
6   Journey Back in Time   129
7   "Operation Esther"   147
8   A State Visit from President Salih   167

Part Three

9   "Whoever Saves One Life"   183
10   "We're Already in the Sky"   203
11   Declarations and Demands   219
12   Stepping into History   237
13   From Sanaa to Jerusalem   255

Epilogue   277
Appendix   289
Bibliography   333
Index   335

Brief Chronology

25 B.C.E.	Roman expeditionary force under Aelius Gallus sent to Yemen
c. 550 C.E.	King of Himyar adopts Judaism.
632	Death of Muhammad.
1172	Maimonides *Iggeret Teiman* (Epistle to Yemen).
1618	British trading post established at Mocha.
1619	Birth of Jewish poet Shalom Shabbazzi at Shabez.
1676–79	Decree ordering destruction of Synagogues and expulsion of Jews to Mauza
1839	British take Aden.
1846	Anti-Jewish "Latrine" Law.
1871	Sanaa blood libel.
1906	Anti-Jewish legislation enacted by Imam Yhia.
1918	End of Ottoman control of Yemen.
1918	State of Israel established; Operation On Eagles' Wings (Magic Carpet) airlifts Jews of Yemen to Israel.
1962	Yemen Arab Republic (North Yemen) established; civil war begins; travel restrictions against Jews of Yemen.
1967	Six-Day War; British withdrawal from Aden; People's Republic of Southern Yemen. (South Yemen) established.
1970	End of civil war; South Yemen becomes People's Democratic Republic of Yemen.
1979	Renewed fighting between North and South Yemen.
1990	Reunification of Yemen.

Introduction

Hinda Zindani is a middle-aged Israeli woman, brought into this world, like her brother, Massoud, on the matted floor of an ancient stone house in a tiny village in the Amlah region of Yemen, in the southern part of the Arabian Peninsula. There, among the ramshackle homes and rocky fields and dirt roads of a Jewish village, she inherited the rich traditions of a people whose presence in Yemen dated back to the time of King Solomon almost three thousand years before; she learned ancient customs and messianic yearnings that had been meticulously preserved over the millennia. But suddenly there arose from the ashes a tiny Jewish state, somewhere to the northwest, across the vast Arabian Desert, so Hinda Zindani left Yemen, along with tens of thousands of other Jews, and set out for the Land of Israel. Massoud, too young, remained behind. So did her mother, her father, and her other brothers. Indeed, although the world mistakenly believed that Yemen's Jews had all been transported to Israel by the planes of Operation Magic Carpet, writing finis to the long history of Jewry on the southern tip of the Arabian Peninsula, several thousand had, in fact, remained behind. And when the doors of emigration closed in 1962, they were trapped, not to be heard from again, whether by mail or by telephone. Hinda had been orphaned, though her parents and brothers were still alive.

In consequence of these events, the Zindani family, like scores of others, was divided, living in two nations officially at war with each other, denied the curative company of their own flesh and blood, robbed of basic human rights, prevented by politics from even knowing whether parents or siblings were still alive or if their deaths should be mourned. Either way, their existence had been erased from the record books, though not from memory. And all attempts to

1

reunite the divided families of Israel and Yemen resulted in failure.

Twenty-eight years passed. And then . . . some American citizens got the call. Contrary to what any reasonable person might have expected, they persuaded the United States government to involve itself in this unfortunate human drama.

Yosef Levy is an ordinary guy: married, two grown children, a modest home in Brooklyn his home of thirty years. A teacher by profession, short in stature, gentle in demeanor, Yosef Levy has never run for office or held an elected position. He isn't comfortable standing in front of a microphone with camera bulbs flashing, has no desire to make a spectacle of himself, doesn't wear finely tailored Italian suits and speak with the glad-handing flourish that wins and holds an audience's attention. One would not expect to find Yosef Levy in the nation's capital helping to craft United States foreign policy, or traveling across the world on a mission for the Department of State. Such activities are the province of public figures and politicians, not of private citizens. Ordinary people don't operate on so grand a scale, mounting lobbying campaigns, persuading the United States to flex its mighty muscles, changing lives as a result.

Or can they?

Can ordinary Americans, unschooled in high-stakes diplomacy and the art of politics, make a difference?

This is the story of some private citizens, Yosef Levy among them, who weren't satisfied to leave things in the hands of bureaucrats and government officials. It is a tale of the remarkable success they achieved when they decided to take action when they learned that Washington was not adequately addressing a human rights issue that should have been a concern to all right-thinking people. It tells how these ordinary folks corrected the problem with the help of their congressional representatives, providing a supreme example of "Track II Diplomacy," in which professional diplomats and citizens at large collaborate on foreign policy initiatives.

In telling this tale, *Operation Esther* chronicles the nearly fifteen years of activity that won freedom of emigration for the tiny population of Jews isolated in the desert wasteland that is northernmost Yemen. Along the way, it acquaints the reader with the whirlwind of political and religious issues that have a bearing on American policy in the Middle East. It describes the monumental coalescing of governments, human rights advocates, political action organizations, and private persons that produced the rescue effort. Finally, it introduces one of the world's oldest and most fascinating Jewish communities.

To fully appreciate the significance of Yosef Levy's accomplishments, one must become fluent, if not immersed, in the history and culture of the Jews of Yemen. So *Operation Esther* opens with their story. You will enter their world via Operation Magic Carpet, the airlift that brought most of Yemeni Jewry to the Holy Land upon the State of Israel's birth in 1948. Next, you will meet the Jews who remained in Yemen, and finally the American citizens who rescued them by establishing contacts with Congressmen and other "bigs" in Washington and with officials in Yemen itself, eventually traveling to the southern tip of the Arabian Peninsula as emissaries of the State Department. Among these crusaders were some several colorful characters who almost seem to have been lifted from the pages of fiction: a black Southern Baptist-turned-Jew imprisoned in Yemen as an Israeli spy, a Swiss botanist trekking the country at his own expense, a whole cadre of brilliant individuals in Washington and Sanaa, Yemen's capital.

The narrative in this volume provides a basis for analyzing the performance and positions of America's myriad Jewish organizations, both political and philanthropic. Along with the largest Jewish population in the world, the United States is home to federations of all types that wield great power on Capitol Hill and in the State Department and White House. Why did the influential men and women who run these organizations, Jewish professionals at ease in the highest circles, fail to win the Jews of Yemen their freedom, leaving the job for the likes of Yosef Levy and company? And what of the Israeli government and the Mossad, its celebrated intelligence agency: what did they do, and why were their maneuvers overshadowed by Washington's?

The Jews of Yemen were a people in whose souls was etched a special capacity for scholarship and piety, and for messianic longings, a reverence for Zion. For almost three thousand years they had been patiently awaiting their return to Zion, an event, in the minds of many, that would occur at the end of days and not by human agency. Resettling the Jews of Yemen in another country of the Diaspora would have missed the point; they were yearning for redemption, and to their way of thinking redemption could only be found in the Land of Israel. Thus Yosef Levy and his friends had to proceed carefully and with great delicacy, for in the first place, the messianic era has obviously not yet arrived, and in the second, Yemen and Israel were officially at war.

On a more practical level, *Operation Esther* is a lesson in democracy, showing that Everyman, without vast financial resources and the assistance of professional lobbyists, can win the attention of the people he elects to high office. According to Richard Schifter, former Assistant Secretary of State for Human Rights and Humanitarian Affairs, the inexperienced few injected order and coherence "into a situation in which there was turmoil and confusion." Their work was "highly regarded by the United States Government, both by the State Department and by members of Congress." David Ransom, former Arabian Peninsula chief in the State Department, noted that their effort was "multilateral, requiring endless contacts between groups and officials who did not always see eye to eye on tactics or even ends. [They] melded [their] concerns with those of the existing diplomatic situation and put forward programs and agendas which were the basis for unprecedented successes in dealing with an isolated and uncertain community of Jews who had long been out of touch with their brothers in America. A splendid example of Americans who sets out to do privately good works which governments cannot always manage." In the pages of *Operation Esther*, you will meet these heroes.

Finally, this book is a window on the day-to-day operations of the U.S. State Department, of America's ambassadors and embassies abroad, of famous human rights leaders and foreign policy decision-makers. Here is the story of ranking government officials who opened up the diplomatic process to the inexperienced and unimportant, to ordinary people. Why? Because sometimes ordinary

American citizens can do what Washington can't.

Just ask Hinda and Massoud Zindani. You'll find them both in Israel now, with their mother and father. And ask Yosef Levy. You'll find him back in his modest apartment in Brooklyn, once again teaching students and leading a normal life.

Hayim Tawil
October 15, 1997

Acknowledgments

ICROJOY would like to extend many thanks for moral and spiritual support to the following colleagues: Professor Haym Soloveitchik, Rabbi Hershel Schachter, Rabbi Moshe Shamah, Rabbi Eliyahu Ben Haim, Rabbi Eliezer Havivi, Rabbi Allen Londy. Likewise we owe a debt of gratitude to our dear friends Murray Hammerman, Peter Merker, Bob and Tamsin Wolf, Alfred Gruenspecht, Nathan Hilu, David, Dani and Alan Shedlo, Tehilla Rieser, Shoshana Arrowood, Peter Weinstein, Ashley Lazarus, J. J. Gross and Aryeh Jesselson.

To Dalia Smerka, Janice Levy and Cohi Goloubinoff and Marie Wolf who continuously supported their husbands' human rights activities on behalf of the Jews of Yemen.

Special thanks to Michael Steinhardt, Bill Gross, Roni Ben Nun and Harry Epstein for their generous assistance.

To Isaac and Bonnie Pollak who championed the cause of the plight of the Jews of Yemen since the founding of ICROJOY in 1989.

Our efforts in Yemen would never have succeeded without the assistance and goodwill of many members of the United States government and the government of the Republic of Yemen. To them we extend our heartfelt gratitude for all their efforts.

Sincere thanks to Robert Milch and to my friend and colleague Professor Richard White for their help and advice concerning the publishing of Operation Esther.

Operation Esther could have not been successfully executed without the continued support of my two children Aryé and Taphat and especially my wife Dalia who dedicated four years of her life to this noble cause.

HT

Prologue

Two thousand miles south of Jerusalem, and three thousand years after the era when it first became the capital of Israel during the reigns of David and Solomon, the Jews of Yemen were boarding the man-made eagles that would spirit them away to the Holy Land. Cocooned for so long in the most isolated of exiles, they had breathed the promise of redemption from the sky while fiercely preserving their traditions amidst a sea of Arab neighbors. And now, at last, they were returning to the fount of their traditions, with permission from the ruler of Yemen himself. The year was 1949, and Imam Ahmad ibn Yhia Hamad-a-Din, perceiving a divine hand at work, had reluctantly decided to contribute to the ingathering of Zion's exiles precipitated by the birth of the State of Israel.

The Jews of Yemen had first learned of the new Jewish state, and its heroic struggle to preserve its precarious existence, when the Yemen government began recruiting some of their Arab neighbors into the negligible military force it would be sending to Palestine to help drive the Jews there into the sea. Contrary to all expectations, the Jews of the harried State of Israel defended and even extended their territory, defeated their Arab adversaries, and emerged victorious from the War of Independence. With the new state firmly established, the call went out for the fifty thousand exiles in Yemen to come home at last.

And the Jews of Yemen responded with a zeal bred by centuries of separation. Before their magic carpet flight could begin, they had to trek from their rural villages in the back country to the port of Aden on the tip of the Arabian Peninsula. Marching southward, the Jews abandoned their neighborhoods in the capital, Sanaa, and emptied their villages surrounding the mud-walled town of Saada.

Lugging their possessions on their backs as did their forefathers before them, they arrived in Aden from Taiz, and from Dhammar, and from sun-beaten outposts in wadis and valleys all along the uncharted Saudi Arabian border to the north. They came from the district of Hidan Asham, and from the villages of al-Shaghadra and Barat, and from the sheikh-ruled Hashid region. They vacated their two-story houses north of Yarim and abandoned their shops in the suqs of al-Hajjar and al-Gauf and Arhab.

The Jews of Yemen were in a hurry. Legend said that once, long before, they had failed to heed the call of redemption when Ezra the Scribe had urged them to return to Jerusalem after the end of the Babylonian Exile in the sixth century B.C.E. In consequence, so it was told, they had been cursed and made to suffer the cruelest and most bitter exile of all. Ever after, few Yemeni Jews would ever name their sons "Ezra." If their ancestors had responded to his plea, they would have ended a Jewish presence in Yemen that was ancient even in Ezra's time. According to many Yemeni historians, it was none other than King Solomon who was responsible for the existence of Jewish life in Yemen. Piqued by a visit to Jerusalem by the Queen of Sheba and her opulent entourage, the wisest of all men set his eyes on the riches of his neighbor to the south. The Queen's tributes of spices, gold, and precious stones bespoke a region of vast economic opportunity.

Its lofty mountains bordering the Red Sea to the west, Yemen, as Solomon would learn, was blessed with a natural wall within which to trap the wet clouds of the monsoon rolling in from the Indian Ocean to the south and east. The water provide by the annual summer rains, stored through a sophisticated system of dams and cisterns, made it possible for Yemen's farmers to cultivate their verdant terraces. Profitable trade by sea could be pursued by way of the Tihama, a sandy, narrow coastal plain that gave way to a dry, hilly plateau rising more than 10,000 feet. Yemen would become known to the Greeks and Romans as Arabia Felix, "Fortunate Arabia."

This green island in the middle of a desert was home to certain plant products that were in great demand, frankincense and myrrh. These valued spices were important ingredients in the incense used in the religious rites of virtually every country. In Egypt, frankincense and myrrh were essential to the compounds prepared for embalming and mummifying the dead. Moreover, there and everywhere else, spices was also used for cooking, fumigating, perfumes, and anointing. In addition to obtaining a supply of frankincense and myrrh for his new Temple in Jerusalem, Solomon apparently hoped to become a major player in the lucrative spice trade. With Solomon, in effect, as her partner on the Mediterranean coast, conveniently situated just north of Egypt, the Queen of Sheba would benefit from having a "distributor" with access to markets far beyond her borders.

Spices were costly because passage on the Frankincense Road was prohibitive. The toll charged by the Sabians, who controlled the route across the Arabian Desert, made the frankincense worth a thousand times more at the port of Gaza, the northern tip of the road, than at its harvesting from the bushes on which it grew in southeastern Yemen. Civilizations of tremendous wealth were sprouting and flourishing in the area of Ophir, and the king of Israel thirsted to participate in its commerce. An economic partnership had been born.

Thus Jewish contacts with Yemen began during the reign of Solomon, and Jews began to settle in Yemen throughout the period of the First Temple, first arriving as emissaries and merchants, perhaps, but eventually establishing permanent residence for business and other purposes. Jews continued to live in Yemen after the First Temple's destruction, in the time of Jesus, and during the last days of the Second Temple. The Jewish communities of Yemen thrived in the era of the Kingdom of Himyar. Jewish life continued in the lifetime of Muhammad and after Yemen's acceptance of Islam in the mid-seventh century, during the centuries of theocratic rule by imams, and later, under the Ottoman Turks.

Isolated as time slowly passed, as their brothers and sisters contended with the Greeks and the Romans, with Crusades and pogroms, with the Chmielnickis and Hitlers who added their malevolent contributions to Judaism's history of tears, Yemen's Jews lingered in the world of Solomon. Ever-faithful to their religion, they fastidiously preserved their Hebrew names and their long, flowing garments. Eating was still done cross-legged on a matted floor, and the menu hadn't changed in millennia: communal platters of breads, thick dips, and vegetables remained a staple of their diet. Their fathers had taken multiple wives and had written of plagues of locusts that devoured years of sustenance.

Mysticism and the Kabbalah were etched into the annals and hearts of the Jews of Yemen. Alone among the world's Jews, who in other places and climes communicated in Yiddish, Ladino, or the language of the land, they looked back on an uninterrupted tradition of spoken as well as written Hebrew. Their young were still taught Aramaic, and they lived in a world without printing presses. Upon acquiring the skill of writing, their boys would sit and copy by hand the sacred texts that would one day comprise a lifelong library: the *Tafsir*, Saadiah Gaon's translation of the Torah into Arabic, the *Tijan*, an authoritative ancient guide to Hebrew grammar, the *Tiklal*, the prayer book, and an anthology of poetry called *Diwan*. Most precious of all was the *Taj*, or "Crown," which in parallel columns presented Hebrew text of the Torah side by side with the *Tafsir*. And some of their scrolls contained a third column for the ancient translation of the Torah into Aramaic by Onkelos. Truly a People of the Book, the Jews of Yemen had survived exile only by remaining loyal to their spiritual heritage and their modest library of literary treasures. But their centuries of seclusion provided fertile soil for a long series of false messiahs who peppered their history, stirring up the people and often wreaking havoc. Steeped in eschatology, Yemenite Jewry adhered strictly to tradition while conjuring up visions of the end of days.

Remembering Zion was part of daily life; hope for immediate redemption permeated their prayers and studies, their songs and celebrations. The walls of Yemeni Jewish homes remained unfinished, mute testimony to the incompleteness of Jewish life in exile. Musical instruments were banned forever, because The Holy Temple lies destroyed. Shall I exult in my perfect abode when God's presence has no home? Shall I rejoice with flute and harp when the symphony of the Levites has been silenced? At weddings, the women, and only the women, were permitted to make a joyful noise with tambourines and timbrels. But at the climax of ceremony, ash would be placed on the forehead of the proud bridegroom. If I forget thee, O Jerusalem . . .

The Temple's progeny, the synagogue, became the spiritual and social center of Yemeni Jewry, the setting for prayer, education, and celebration. The Sabbath day was dedicated almost exclusively to prayer and Torah study. While the son's religious and cultural education was entrusted to the father, as the Talmud prescribes, young boys were often dispatched to *heder* at the synagogue to learn with the *mori*, "master," and other friends. In the home, the mistress of the household was also its Angel of Peace, shielding her son from the wrath of his disciplinarian father. She was also mentor to her daughters, who spent their formative years by their mother's side, preparing for the rigors of family life.

The Jews of Yemen, though isolated from world Jewry, played a significant role in Yemen's history. They played an important part in the land's intellectual and economic evolution, and in pre-Islamic times some even belonged to its upper classes. In the third and fourth centuries of the common era, Yemen's Himyari Jews kept in close contact with the academies and religious authorities in Tiberias and the Galilee, sometimes sending their dead there to be buried, as is attested by inscriptions discovered at Beit Shearim. The Himyarite era was a glorious time when the monotheistic spirit emanating from the Jews profoundly influenced their non-Jewish neighbors. The Himyars found Jewish customs and beliefs appealing, and many of them, including members of the country's aristocracy, converted to Judaism. This trend culminated during the reign of King Dhu Nuwas (518 to 525), who declared Judaism the state religion.

In the seventh century, with the advent of Islam, the status of the Jews of Yemen declined dramatically. Under the Pact of Omar, which for many centuries defined the relationship between the Muslim overlords and the indigenous Jewish and Christian populations of the countries they conquered, the two peoples of the book were allowed to practice their respective religions. But along with this freedom came certain conditions that emphasized their inferior status. Under Islamic domination, the Jews had to pay a progressive head tax, *al-gizya*, and in return were granted the status of protected citizens, *ahl-dhimmi*, in the Muslim polity. Other discriminatory regulations passed by Caliph Omar prohibited the construction of new synagogues and the renovation of old ones. Moreover, Jews were not allowed to pray aloud or to live in houses higher than those of their Muslim neighbors. The horse, as the chosen mount of warriors and noblemen, was prohibited; Jews were only allowed to ride donkeys, but not astride— by law they had to keep both legs on one side. Moreover, no Jew could sport a *jambiya*, the ornate J-shaped dagger worn at the hip of Yemeni men as a sign of masculinity.

For centuries, the Jews of Yemen lived as artisans and merchants, working as silversmiths, tin-cutters, tailors, weavers, and potters. They made such products as gunpowder or leather goods while the Arabs tilled the soil and toiled in Yemen's agriculture. By monopolizing such craft, the Jews of Yemen carved out a satisfactory niche for themselves, a lifestyle that guaranteed their survival in this isolated corner of the world despite the many constraints and restrictions imposed upon them.

Throughout the Middle Ages the Jews of Yemen maintained contacts with Jewish communities in Babylon and Egypt, Syria and Palestine, North Africa and Spain. They helped to support the talmudic schools of Babylonia, and the sages to the north reciprocated by bestowing the title of *nagid*, "prince," on distinguished Yemeni scholars. Later, Saadiah Gaon's Arabic translation of the Torah became part of the Yemenite heritage, and the prayers and poems he composed for the Sabbath subsequently passed down from generation to generation. In the twelfth century, a false messiah made his appearance, enjoying a following among both Jews and Muslims, and ultimately forcing his Jewish acolytes to embrace Islam when his claim was proved spurious. In their hour of need the Yemeni Jews turned to their greatest hero, the great sage Moses Maimonides, for advice on how to recognize the true Messiah. The answer he sent them from Cairo in 1172, known as the *Iggeret Teiman*, ("Epistle to Yemen"), is still regarded as one of his most important works.

While the long era in which their Ashkenazi brothers could never regard any home as permanent, because they were so frequently expelled by one or another of Europe's kings and queens, the Jews of Yemen remained in Yemen. Scattered in hundreds villages, they faced famine, crop failure, and plague. And then, in 1676, after a bloody Turkish attack, Imam Ahmad bin Hassan ibn al-Imam al-Qasim came to power. Proclaiming Yemen "consecrated ground," he reversed the long-standing policy of begrudging religious tolerance, declaring it impossible for two faiths to exist side by side on Arab soil. The imam forced many of the country's Jews to become Muslims, prohibited the Jewish trade in wine and arrack, and banned both synagogue construction and communal prayer.

A mass exodus from Sanaa took place in 1679 after the appearance of Shabbetai Zevi, the most infamous of the many false messiahs produced by Judaism over the centuries. His elated Yemeni followers took to the dusty streets of Sanaa to sing and dance with Torah scrolls, heralding the redeemer's arrival at last. But when the would-be savior became a Muslim, the Jews of Yemen were devastated, and to make matters worse, the imam expelled them from Sanaa and from the central and southern highlands to Mauza on the Red Sea coast, plunging them into the bloody Exile of Mauza. In a three-year span, two-thirds of Yemen's Jewish population perished. This left the entire country bereft of craftsmen to fashion jewelry and new tools and repair old ones. So the imam's loyal Arab subjects beseeched their leader to reverse the exile. The Jews reentered Sanaa to find their Great Synagogue transformed into the *Masgid al-Gala*, the Mosque of the Banished; their mikveh was now the *hammam al-gala*, the public bathhouse. These humiliations were followed by years of decrees, epidemics, and tribal warfare always disastrous to Jews; in 1871 there was even a blood libel in Sanaa.

But now, in the year 1948, a different imam had given the Jews permission to leave! Tens of thousands of Jewish craftsmen and shopkeepers, a large proportion of the country's lower middle class, liquidated their belongings, creating a massive sell-out. As prices plummeted, the Jews' lucky Arab neighbors received unprecedented bargains on stores, houses, tools, and animals. Deeply convinced that in the new kingdom of Israel they would need no earthly goods to sustain their existence, the Jews settled for a tenth of the price for most of their worldly possessions before embarking on the perilous journey south to Aden. They relinquished items that couldn't be sold, burying the Torah scrolls and prayer books that were too heavy to be transported through the desert to the airstrip where the planes of Operation Magic Carpet were waiting.

During the long centuries of exile, the Jews had prayed for an abrupt and dramatic end to their existence in Yemen, a time when their triumphant remnant would return to the Holy Land on the wings of eagles, as foretold by the prophets. Now, at last, those magical harbingers of the messianic era, their coming for so long merely the babble of ancient kabbalists kindling the fires of hope in people's hearts, rested on the Aden tarmac emitting horrific roars and leaking oil, their talons scarred after many consecutive days and nights of flight broken only by stops to pick up and discharge passengers. These were not the graceful, mighty birds whose images were woven into the dreams of generations of isolated Yemeni Jews through words of prophecy preserved in the yellowed pages of sacred texts; no, a bevy of battered C–47 cargo planes and exhausted pilots provided by the nascent State of Israel would have to do.

As each plane's human cargo spilled onto Israeli soil, the massive ramifications of Operation On Eagles' Wings, or Magic Carpet, as it came to be known colloquially, became clearer. Over forty thousand Jews had been introduced almost overnight into a society desperate for housing and most other resources. And these Jews arrived in Israel after the eagles landed exactly as they had left it in Solomon's time. The men, distinctive in their long, flowing robes adorned with tzitzit (fringes) at each corner, their twisted black *simmanim* (sidelocks) protruding from *kuftas* that covered the whole head, were certainly no sabras. The women, too, had not modified their dress from the fashions of First Temple times, and even the youngest of the girls kept their faces hidden beneath a colorful *gargush* (hood). Stepping off the plane in costumes right out of the Bible, the Yemenis had no knowledge of creature comforts familiar to the most hardened sabras. Cots with legs were foreign mysteries after centuries of spending the night on mats on the floor, so at first they used to sleep under the beds provided for them, marveling at the strange canopies. Mastery over the modern toilet eluded them, too, in the beginning. But the Jews of Yemen soon adapted to millennial technology and, more importantly, tasted newfound religious freedoms.

These riders of the Magic Carpet were not the first Yemenis to return to the Holy Land since the time of Solomon. Over the years, pioneering individuals had made the difficult journey, among them the famed Rabbi Shlomo Adani, in 1571. And a pioneering group of two hundred Zion-seekers had already come home in 1882, preceding the arrival of the first Russian Bilu pioneers in Jerusalem by several months, purely by coincidence. Included among the dedicated souls who made their way to Israel in the nineteenth century was a family from the mountaintop village of a-Tawila, four hours by car northwest of Sanaa in the al-Mahwit region. Yosef and his wife Bracha journeyed in 1899 with their sons Yhia, Said, and ten-year-old Hayim Tawili, my grandfather and namesake. The Tawil clan settled in Jerusalem on the slope of Mount Scopus, along with many other new immigrants from Yemen and Eastern Europe. Sorrow and messianic longing had merged to make Jews throughout the world see hope in Jerusalem. In the nineteenth century, Yemeni Jews had come by caravan and steamboat, passing through the Suez Canal and enjoying the hospitality of Alexandria's Jewish citizenry on the way. All this despite an Ottoman ban on Jewish departures from Yemen. But in 1949, the heroic journeys of past years would be forever overshadowed by the travels of their children, en masse, on eagles' wings.

As thousands of Jews swiftly departed Yemen in that twentieth-century exodus, the bittersweet truth became apparent: soon there would not be enough of them left to sustain a rich communal life. Already a shortage of ritual slaughterers had diminished the availability of kosher meat. Even in Sanaa, gathering ten men for prayer and Torah reading was proving an elusive goal. Yet some Jews remained in Yemen. In the rural areas of the north, where the imam's influence had ebbed considerably, persecution was not a way of life, and the hard-working Jews enjoyed the status of a chosen but accursed nation. They had earned the respect of both their Arab neighbors and the local sheikhs, who chose to ignore many of the regulations imposed by Yemen's rulers. In Hashid and Bilad al-Mashrik and Khulan Asham, in Saada and its vicinity, Jews could earn a decent living and participate in the court system. And with the gates of Yemen opened by the imam himself, it seemed likely that their right to leave the country, if necessary, was now virtually guaranteed. Besides, some believed, perhaps they should await the Messiah's arrival before departing for Israel. For those who failed to initially hop aboard the Magic Carpet, going to Israel constituted a possible religious infraction and, more significantly, a risk to their economic well-being. The Jews were seemingly protected from the edicts promulgated against them from afar.

Had those edicts been enforced, normal Jewish involvement in Yemeni society would have been precluded. The benevolence of Imam Ahmad, who in 1948 had wrested control over Yemen from the nationalists who had murdered his father, Imam Yhia, contrasted with the devastating proclamations of the latter's reign. In 1906, Yhia had made it a crime for a Jew to raise his voice in the presence of a Muslim or to touch a Muslim accidentally in passing. Especially acerbic was Yhia's reinstatement of the 1846 Latrine Law, saddling Jews with the burden of cleaning the country's the public latrines. But most oppressive was Yhia's revival of an ancient statute whereby every newborn child in the land was considered *fitra*, born into Islam, the natural faith, and was only later, by its parents or the influence of education, affiliated with Judaism or Christianity. In consequence of this law, Jewish children whose parents died reverted to being Muslims. To avoid such complications, Yemeni Jews would marry off orphaned children, even at the age of seven or eight, to guarantee them a family. These laws remained in effect during Ahmad's ascendancy, but they were not enforced in the northern countryside, and thus the Jews in this area were not affected by them.

Among those living in relative comfort in the south was Yhia ibn Daoud Suberi. Suberi was forty years old in 1949, and for a Jew he was considered a rich man. He owned some of the best arable land in the remote valley of Damt, below Sanaa, which he rented out to trustworthy Arabs. In rainy years, his income provided a comfortable life for his small family. Although Suberi was a widower, remarrying was not a pressing concern for him, since his two sons and his daughter were old enough to work. Along with dozens of other family patriarchs, Suberi vacillated when he learned about the exodus of his fellow Jews. He wanted to sell his land at the best price before he left Yemen to join his brethren in the young State of Israel.

Yielding to the pressure of the departing Jews, Suberi sent his three children ahead with a youth emigration movement. Promised by emissaries of the Jewish Agency that Sleiman (Shalom), Daoud (David), and Shameh (Shoshana) would receive careful guardianship, he hoped to join his young ones in the Holy Land as soon as possible. Meanwhile, they would live in a youth village and learn a profession that would contribute to the building of the state. Yhia, confident that Yemen's doors would remain open eternally, would wait out the emigration movement.

Once Operation Magic Carpet had dramatically emptied Yemen of most of its Jews, the torrent of exiting expatriates was reduced to a mere trickle. From 1951 to 1958, only a handful of the remaining four thousand Yemeni Jews found their way to Israel. Mustah Mustah, an entrepreneurial Arab trader, was behind the emigration of two thousand more in the waning days of the exodus. In 1959, the Jewish Agency offered the Saada-based merchant 100 rials for every Jew he was able to transport from the northern provinces to Aden as part of his monthly business travels. Mustah Mustah shrewdly pounced on the opportunity and initiated a meticulously organized operation in which Jews would meet him at an office in Saada and he would arrange for transportation to Aden. Mustah was an honest man; he would collect the Jews' money and valuables for safekeeping along the way and returned it faithfully upon arrival in Aden. There, they were met by Israeli aliyah officials who would fly them across the Gulf of Aden to neighboring Djibouti, where they would board a ship for a final jaunt up the Red Sea to the port of Eilat, then a pathetic shantytown surrounded by hostile Arab territory.

The fleeing Jews were a superstitious bunch. They attributed an automobile crash that interrupted one journey to Aden, for instance, to the fact that the passengers had disrespectfully stowed a Torah scroll named "Ezra" beneath the seat. By deliberately keeping these new immigrants away from major populated areas, the Israeli government hoped the mysterious Jews of Yemen would take a liking to pre-resort Eilat and not venture north to Tel Aviv or Jerusalem. Several hunger strikes by Yemeni Jews succeeded in reversing the policy, and they were brought north to settle in B'nei Ayish, Gedera, and Kiryat Ekron, near Rehovot.

Moshe Atzar was one of the hundreds rescued by Mustah. In 1961, his father, an ardent opponent of the exodus, had refused to give him permission to leave the country, forcing him to divorce his young bride, Miriam, who was about to leave for the Holy Land. It was then that Moshe decided to escape the authority of his father and Yemeni exile. Taking advantage of the opportunity afforded by Imam Ahmad, he would rejoin Miriam, remarry her, and begin a new life in Israel before the door was once more locked shut.

In the fall of 1961, during a state visit to the Red Sea port of Hodeida, Imam Ahmad was mortally wounded in an assassination attempt. A dangerous brew of socioeconomic and political tensions was nearing eruption, and the remnants of Yemen's Jewish population watched as the opposition movement gained power among merchants, intellectuals, and religious leaders angry at the system of tribal alliances and hostages through which the imam controlled the country. With the economy stagnant, emigration even of Muslims increasing, and alienation from the regime on the rise, the social crisis festered. Influenced by political and economic developments in Arab nationalist Egypt, the opposition found the courage to seize power. Imam Ahmad succumbed to his wounds in 1962.

And in the fall of that year, an anxious throng of four hundred emigration-minded Jews knocked down Mustah's doors with a more desperate escape in mind. The window of opportunity of the Magic Carpet era, the one they had expected would always allow escape to Israel, was closing before their eyes! Upon reaching Aden two weeks later, however, the Jews experienced a surprising change of mind, adamantly refusing to board the planes. The Israeli aliyah officials sent to greet them were dressed in short pants and did not wear kipot; they looked like Christians! To what sort of country were they relocating? Israel responded to their fears by flying in Mori Ya'avetz, a revered Yemeni spiritual leader who had already settled there. His emergency mission: convince the last Jews of Yemen to finally come home.

Luckily for them, Mori Ya'avetz succeeded. As their Eilat-bound vessel slowly made its way up the Red Sea on September 26, 1962, the delivered heard the latest news: Egyptian-backed rebels had stormed and captured Sanaa. Imam Ahmad was dead, the Hamad-a-Din family deposed. Their former country was now the Yemen Arab Republic. The doors of Jewish escape from Yemen, opened on the whim of a God-fearing imam, had been hermetically sealed.

When Yhia ibn Daoud Suberi learned about the revolution in the capital, he immediately grasped the folly of having tarried too long. He had missed the Magic Carpet flown by the Israeli government and had failed to participate in one of the subsequent escapes. His children, in effect, were orphans, for they were in Israel, and he was trapped in silent submission thousands of miles away. Along with two thousand other Jews, Yhia was now cut off from the rest of the world. Families that had wished to slowly ascend to Israel in stages were now separated by the new regime's regulations. Miles of desert and political indifference kept parents from children, husbands from wives, brothers from sisters. The return to Zion was incomplete.

Journalists and rabbis alike would compose dramatic histories of how the Jews of Yemen had been brought back to the Holy Land, film makers would concoct images of the clean sweep of Yemeni Jewry effected by the Israeli government. Schoolchildren would learn that the strange new settlers were all that was left from a glorious chapter in Jewish history. But unknown to most of the outside world, Jewish history's protracted chapter on Yemeni Jewry had not reached a conclusion.

Teacher with students. (Photo: Zion Ozeri, Mission VI)

Salem Jeredi and students. (Photo: Zion Ozeri, Mission VI)

Yosef Shetari, Hayim Faiz, ?, David Faiz. (Photo: Zion Ozeri, Mission VI)

Jewish Women of Saada

A meal in Naat, north of Raida, January 1990.

Part One

FIRST CONTACT:

NOVEMBER 1979–DECEMBER 1988

Chapter One

FROM JERUSALEM TO SANAA

November 29, 1979

Hurtling southward above desert sands beaten into submission by the sun's merciless rays, DuWayne Terrell peered through the tiny window of the airplane and was rewarded with his second glimpse of Sanaa, the ancient city with its towers of cut stone, fired clay bricks, and pristine white plaster. Clutching an entry visa and a United States passport, he hoped the customs officials would finally permit him to enter the capital of the Yemen Arab Republic. Three weeks earlier, on November 5, he had been turned away at Sanaa's airport and promptly sent back to Damascus, where he had struggled to produce the correct papers and suffered the shame and frustration of having his luggage, passport, and money stolen.

Now, his six-foot three-inch frame pressed into an unforgiving seat in the waning moments of another three-hour Sanaa-bound flight from Damascus, Terrell hoped for a more auspicious arrival. Armed with the right papers and emboldened by his harsh introduction to Middle East travel, he hungered not only for a smooth passage through customs but for assistance in accomplishing his self-appointed mission to the Yemen Arab Republic. He was a twenty-three-year-old man on a solo voyage to a nation nestled between conservative Saudi Arabia and pro-Soviet South Yemen, just across the narrow strait of Bab-el-Mandeb from Marxist-ruled Ethiopia. Terrell's calling was a bold one for a young native of Colorado Springs, Colorado, but it flowed naturally from experiences he had already known. Not many black men born on United States Air Force bases set out alone for Israel at the age of eighteen. But Terrell, raised as a devout Baptist, had done so in 1975, unwittingly commencing a journey that would allow him to explore mighty civilizations and take him on a whirlwind spiritual voyage.

Because of his religious upbringing, DuWayne Terrell had always wanted to see the Holy Land. In 1975, action succeeded desire, and when the teenage Terrell landed at Lod Airport, Israel was engaged in its harried annual preparations for the solemn fast of Yom Kippur, the Day of Atonement Sharing an airport taxi with a Yemeni Jewish family, Terrell arrived in Jerusalem just as the capital city was shutting down for the sacred rites. Two days later, exploring the minarets and arches and narrow stone alleyways that comprise the Old City, Terrell found himself standing in front of the Western Wall, the last vestige of the Second Temple, Judaism's holiest site. And there, praying at the wall before the eight-day holiday of Sukkot (Tabernacles), were his fellow passengers from the serpentine road to Jerusalem. An exchange of greetings and addresses, and once again Terrell and his new Yemeni friends parted company.

That address would remain with Terrell for two full years, as his visit to Israel steadily lengthened, tallied by his concerned parents back in Colorado Springs first in days, then in weeks, and ultimately in months and years. Terrell's spiritual search took him to countless communities all over Israel, precipitating edifying relationships with Jews who warmly welcomed the strange American into their homes. Terrell became infatuated with the land surrounded by so many enemy nations. The people of Israel were different; their perseverance beckoned him to stay longer.

So DuWayne Terrell prolonged his visit. One day, in need of hospitality in the coastal city of Netanya, he ferreted out the address he had recorded two years earlier and knocked on the door of Shalom Suberi, his sole Yemeni acquaintance. Invited to stay with the Suberis, Terrell began to learn about the Yemeni community in Israel. He lived in Yemeni homes in Netanya and Rehovot and in the exclusively Yemeni suburbs of B'nei Ayish, Gedera, and Kiryat Ekron. He befriended Yemeni children, ate meals with Yemeni families, and sang Yemeni songs, earnestly imbibing their exotic culture. Treating Terrell as a son, his Yemeni friends taught him Hebrew and introduced him to the Jewish religion. Terrell would never forget being drawn to the "warmth, simplicity, and sincerity" of the Yemenis. He wanted to investigate their mysterious origins, for they were unlike anyone else he had encountered during his travels.

Suberi told Terrell that Yemeni Jewry had only come to Israel thirty years earlier; Shalom himself had made the trip over barren desert with only his brother and sister, leaving their widowed father behind to sell his property. The Suberi children had been raised as orphans in numerous youth villages. Along with more than forty thousand other Yemeni Jews, the beneficiaries of Operation Magic Carpet, they had returned to the Promised Land after centuries of exile. Suberi's story, and the tales told by the other Yemenis the young Baptist encountered, inspired Terrell to learn more about Israel's Yemeni community. He read the prophecies about exiles returning on wings of eagles. He learned that the Jews of Yemen had staunchly preserved their traditions while in isolation, and were continuing to do so in Israel. Terrell studied the rich history, becoming familiar with Sanaa and Saada, Solomon and Ezra, sheikhs and imams. He learned that when the Jews finally departed after the imam's decree, the country of Yemen, left without artisans, had been devastated economically. And he learned of a scandal: the rueful treatment of the new immigrants when they arrived in Israel.

It was then that DuWayne Terrell made the most important decision of his life: he wanted to become a Jew—a Jew in the Yemeni tradition. Terrell's exposure to Yemeni Jews had kindled within him a desire to join the faith, and although he didn't know how to accomplish this, he promised himself that he would find a way. With his tourist visa about to expire, Terrell flew back to the United States, vowing to return to Israel. He did in 1979, immediately reappearing among his friends, the flyers of the Magic Carpet.

Terrell's intimacy with the Yemenis gave him an opportunity rarely granted to outsiders; looking through a window not often opened, he learned much about their lives and their spirit. As he grew closer to his adoptive community, he detected a perpetual tinge of sadness in the eyes of Jews he encountered, a melancholy born of some hidden pain. Even at times of celebration there was subtle mourning in a Yemeni home. And Terrell became aware that in every family, no matter how large, there were always one or two members absent, missing from the picture. An aunt, a cousin, a father. A sister or brother with whom there had been no contact in thirty years.

There are still Jews in Yemen? Yes, DuWayne, a remnant still exists there, the few unlucky souls who missed the Magic Carpet, the ones who thought the gates to Israel would remain open eternally. And in thirty years there has been no regular communication with them. Do the letters we send ever reach them? We don't know. No letters are ever received from Yemen, no phone calls either. With the establishment of the Yemen Arab Republic, the Jews of Yemen had been effectively cut off from the rest of the world. How were their relatives in Yemen? Were their aging fathers and mothers still alive? Were the few remaining Jews being persecuted? No one knew, and no Israeli could go to Yemen to find out, because Israel and Yemen were officially at war. With the exception of Shalom Mansura, the head of the Yemeni Organization in Rosh Ha'ayin, who was in touch with several Jews in Yemen, there were no contacts at all.

DuWayne Terrell, however, was a citizen of the United States; with a proper visa, he would be able to enter Yemen. How Terrell longed to see Yemeni Jews in their native surroundings. Perhaps visiting the natural setting for the beautiful culture he knew would help resolve his questions about converting. DuWayne Terrell would indeed be granted an unprecedented insight into the environment that had produced Yemeni Jewry, but he would also learn how dangerous the Middle East could be. As he would later write, from a dank cell in Sanaa's Central Prison, to the United States Embassy, "I wanted to get an internal look at the long since reclusive remnant of the Yemen, estranged by their demography and yet a source of pride to thousands of Israeli Yemeni Jews. It was an unrelenting request on my part which needed appeasing, and one which found me packing my bags in August of '79."

So it was that Terrell decided to make contact with the Jews who had not taking advantage of the Magic Carpet, remaining behind while their brothers were spirited away on eagles' wings. Armed with the presumed Sanaa address of Yhia ibn Daoud Suberi provided by Shalom in Netanya, Terrell planned to begin by calling on his only contact in the xenophobic country. Perhaps the elder Suberi would give him other names and addresses, or even formally introduce him to other Jews of Yemen to assuage their fears. If only Terrell could find him in a city of 400,000. But first concerns lay with entry to the country.

November 29 proved more fortuitous than November 5, and when Terrell successfully passed through Sanaa customs that Thursday, he immediately set our for Bab-al-Shaoub, the marketplace outside Sanaa's four-thousand-year-old walls, on his quest to locate Suberi. This was not an easy task for an English-speaking black man in an Arab marketplace, and Terrell's fruitless inquiries of the local merchants, none of whom seemed to recall Suberi, soon led to despair. On the verge of abandoning the search, Terrell was advised to scout out Bab-el-Yaman, a hot, crowded marketplace in the shadow of the Old City's turreted walls. Terrell did so the next day, and ambling among the white-robed Arab vendors in the market was met by a gaunt shadow of a man sporting a tattered, fringed robe, with a *kufta* and short, gray sidelocks concealing his weathered face.

The seventy-six-year-old Suberi escorted Terrell to the dilapidated shack he called home. The old man was but a shadow of the one who in 1950 had kissed his three children before sending them off to fly the Magic Carpet. Time and separation had transformed Suberi from a comfortable landowner into a virtual pauper. He was the last Jew in Sanaa, a city that once had been home to a community of eight thousand. Sanaa's last Jew lived among the wretched refuse of the capital city's most desperate class, in a rented shack above a filthy grain mill. He gingerly showed Terrell the yellowed letters he had received over the years from Shalom Mansura, his only connection to the outside world. And he thirstily drank in the information Terrell provided him—news about children long parted but never forgotten. Conversing with the old man in Hebrew, Terrell gave Suberi some precious letters from the son he had last seen thirty years earlier, letters from Shalom Mansura, too. After an hour or so, not wishing to burden the elderly man with an uninvited guest right before the Sabbath, Terrell excused himself and promised to return sometime soon.

After his visit with Suberi, Terrell left Sanaa and went to Jiblah, where he was eager to visit the Baptist Hospital. He spent several days there as an ordinary tourist, hiking the mountain terrain, attending church services, and singing premature Christmas carols in early December, 1979. It was at this point that Terrell made the fateful mistake of writing several letters to his friends in Israel, putting the letters in his Bible for safekeeping until they could be mailed, and putting the Bible in his backpack. Some weeks later, under interrogation in the basement of a police station, Terrell would have many hours to ponder his written musings.

On December 3, Terrell once again called on Yhia ibn Daoud Suberi in Bab-el-Yaman, asking the old man to serve as a guide. "Take me to the north country, where there are still village Jews, scattered, inaccessible, mysterious. Take me to Amlah and Sahin and Hidan and Khulan Asham, the places Jews went after they were thrown out of Saada in the 1960s." Two days later, the unlikely pair traveled two hours north to Raida, where they spent time some Jewish friends of Suberi's, chatting and loafing, enjoying a typical Yemeni meal like the ones Terrell had come to love in Israel. The next day, Suberi returned to Sanaa while Terrell continued northward, closer to the Saudi border, to the capital of the northern province, Saada.

Terrell spent the next two weeks were immersing himself in what was left of the Yemenite Jewish community. Staying with local sheikhs or Jewish families fascinated with his story, Terrell hopped from one obscure village virtually erased from the map to another, always finding someone who would welcome him into a large mud house overflowing with women and children.

Terrell located the settlements he so passionately sought by asking Arabs in the suqs of northern Yemen, "Where are the Jewish houses?" There would inevitably be a wee one nearby, and its inhabitants would invariably be surprised by the spectacle of a black man in sneakers and jeans bearing tidings from the Holy Land and offering to deliver messages in return. In Guraz, Terrell found himself in the home of Yhia Boni; Boni showed his unusual guest some missives sent by one Yehiel Hibshoosh of Boro Park, New York, in the 1960s and 1970s. These few scraps of paper were Boni's sole connection to Jews outside Yemen—truly a gossamer thread, yet one unattained by most of Boni's Yemeni co-religionists. The Jews of Hidan Asham eyed Terrell suspiciously when he arrived on a Saturday night. How could this strange man be a messenger from their loved ones in Israel if he traveled on the holy Sabbath?

It quickly became apparent to Terrell that Jewish tradition was still alive in Yemen. And he drank in with glee the information his friends in Israel had craved for decades. Do the Jews of Yemen want to join their brothers and sisters? Why can't a Jew obtain a passport or an exit visa? The answers Terrell received painted the picture of a community living in fear. During Magic Carpet, no passport was necessary to board a plane for the Holy Land; you simply had to be Jewish and have a desire to go home. After Magic Carpet, and more so after the 1962 establishment of the Republic, however, all citizens of the state, Jews included, needed passports and exit visas if they wanted to leave the country. But no Jew applied for a passport. To apply for a passport, you have to know what a passport is. And then, if you do, you have to be reasonably confident that you won't end up in prison for trying. In Yemen, in those days, Jews had been arrested for mailing letters to addresses outside the Republic, and even for attempting to purchase a stamp at the local post office. If such things could send you to prison, who would dare take a chance on applying for a passport?

Fear had overcome the Jews of Yemen immediately upon the revolution of September 26, 1962, Terrell learned. Following the deposing of the imamate and the declaration of the Yemen Arab Republic, a bloody civil war had consumed the nation through the end of the decade, the republicans backed by Nasser's Egypt, the royalists by Saudi Arabia. For the Egyptians, the coup presented an opportunity to weaken the Saudis as part of a drive to gain control of their oil fields; and thus, for the Saudis, getting the Egyptian troops out of the Arabian Peninsula was a top self-defense priority. With both states pouring in men, money, and equipment, Yemen would soon become Nasser's Vietnam.

By 1967, military victory was not in sight for either side, but the

Yemeni economy was in a shambles. With the eruption of the Six-Day War in June of that year, many Egyptian units had to be withdrawn to join the forces fighting against Israel. Nasser's losses in the war with Israel further undermined his ability to carry on the conflict in North Yemen. In October 1967 the last Egyptian troops pulled out. The fighting soon subsided, and at midnight on November 29, the People's Republic of South Yemen was proclaimed.

Throughout this decade of war and suffering, the Jews in the north, like their Arab neighbors, were often victimized by the conflict. While Jews were not forced to participate in the war as warriors, their villages along the Saudi border were bombed; at least two Jews were killed. The situation was truly paradoxical, because when the Republic was declared, the imamate's many discriminatory decrees were rescinded. No longer were Jewish males required to grow sidelocks, as specified by a seventeenth-century edict. And the *gizya* poll tax was canceled too, although Jews continued to grease the palms of local sheikhs. It was the only way to ensure a degree of protection, for they knew they couldn't expect much from the government in Sanaa. In an Arab country at war with Israel, state-sponsored hatred of the Jewish state had stirred up much animosity against the local Israelites.

Despite the sordid history that characterized their existence in Yemen after Magic Carpet, DuWayne Terrell found the local Jews living in an apparently relaxed atmosphere, enjoying cordial relations with their Muslim neighbors. The fifteen hundred Jews left behind ached to go to Israel. But the right to leave the country was not the only freedom of which they were deprived. They complained bitterly that they could not phone or write their relatives in Israel. At best, with a bit of luck, they would manage to persuade an occasional European visitor to northern Yemen to smuggle out some short messages and mail them from abroad.

Terrell marveled at the way his Yemeni hosts maintained their cultural heritage in its purest form in the face of formidable odds. Once again, the young man was stirred by their simple lifestyle and hospitality. He felt a strong desire to help them. But as Terrell was drawn closer into the community, he uncovered sad secrets never spoken of in public. He learned of the abductions, tragic episodes in which young women had been taken against their will and forced to marry and convert to Islam. He also witnessed the debilitating effects of the inability to communicate with the outside world. There were no longer enough Jews in Yemen to keep the ancient community alive. Teachers were necessary to pass the traditions on to the next generation, but the community was so small and poor that it could no longer produce the scholars it needed. The once rich treasury of Jewish erudition in Yemen was vanishing. In some cases, even the patriarchs of large clans barely knew any Hebrew.

As DuWayne Terrell explored the north country, he came to know the anxiety of everyday Jewish life in Yemen. A tremor. A minor earthquake. Armed soldiers, wary of Terrell's origins, pestering him with questions. While relaxing in a home in Hidan Asham one afternoon, Terrell was confronted by soldiers brandishing weapons and demanding to see his visa. "Do you know Hebrew?" they queried repeatedly. After the incident, Terrell's hosts pleaded with him to return to Sanaa: It is too dangerous up north. For our sake, leave the villages of the Jews.

From Hidan, Terrell returned to Sanaa and Suberi's lean-to, but he wanted a more permanent and comfortable residence. A quick visit to the United States Embassy gave Terrell the address of William Thomas, a sixty-year-old American businessman. Thomas, he was told, was a marketing mogul searching for oil in the desert of Yemen. He was in need of a reliable house sitter, and Terrell of a bed in which to sleep. Thus a partnership of circumstances was born between the two. Thomas went to Spain to join his wife, Kim, for Christmas. Terrell used the Thomas's Sanaa home as a base of operations.

By February 1980, Thomas had returned from Spain and Terrell's services were no longer necessary. Now the south country beckoned, and Terrell was determined to see Taiz, the city of domes, minarets, and labyrinthine bazaars, the site of Al-Aharafiya, a mosque from the days of Muhammad. Just outside Taiz lay the grave of Yemen's most revered Jewish figure, Mori Shalom Shabbazzi, the great kabbalist, scholar, and poet. Terrell traveled for hours past towering, jagged mountains, and past Shabez, the village where Shabbazzi was born in

1619. For years Terrell's friends in Israel had acquainted him with tales of Shabbazzi's greatness. Terrell knew that Shabbazzi had been a weaver by trade, that although his fame in Yemen came from his poetry, he had also been a leading kabbalist. Terrell had seen *Hemdat Yamim*, Shabbazzi's book of midrashim on the Torah. And he had heard of Shabbazzi's kabbalistic work, *Turab al-raml*, "The Sandy Soil," which taught its readers how to foresee their destiny by drawing figures in the sand with a stick. After *Turab al-raml*, Shabbazzi had become a household name, his work consulted by both Jewish and Muslim magicians, its author rumored to know and make use of a secret subterranean passage to Zion, a journey that could be completed instantaneously in a spiritual "leap." Shabbazzi's grave in Taiz consequently became sacred to both Jews and Muslims, the destination of an annual pilgrimage.

On February 4, 1980, a day he would not soon forget, DuWayne Terrell arrived in Taiz, anxious to approach the great Shalom Shabbazzi. By asking young Arab boys to direct him to the hero's grave, the Colorado man eventually located the burial site, opened a prayer book, and petitioned for guidance: Why have I been sent to this unfamiliar country to make contact with this reclusive people? How can I help them to escape? *What am I to do?*

From atop a rock-covered hill nearby, a sheikh watched the stranger kneeling before the grave of Shalom Shabbazzi. The man, obviously a foreigner, was wearing pants and muttering in a strange language. Something about him seemed amiss. The sheikh casually approached the dark-skinned stranger.

"What are you doing?" he demanded.

"I'm just praying at Shabbazzi's grave," came the reply in a halting Arabic.

The sheikh slowly backed away, unsatisfied with Terrell's simple response, and returned moments later with a policeman. Terrell watched nervously as the two men from Taiz rifled through his backpack and its contents spilled out onto the sand: clothes, travel documents, letters to be mailed to friends in Israel. Noticing the sheets of paper bearing an alien scrawl, the policeman scooped them up to examine them. It's Hebrew, he realized. These notes are meant for the Israelis. Fixing his gaze on Terrell, he decided that the stranger was too suspicious to be ignored

Before a word of protest could escape his lips, Terrell was arrested and hauled off to a police station somewhere in Taiz. A squalid cell, bars of iron locking him in securely. This was the beginning of a long ordeal of questioning and answering, of beatings and torture, and of writing both factual and nonfactual statements. DuWayne Terrell, the Colorado man was told by a sword-bearing warder, you are being charged with espionage. You are a spy for Israel. And so are all your friends here.

April 16, 1980
George Lane mulled over the facts nonchalantly. It seemed to be a routine case. Another missing American citizen, probably someone who accidentally forgot to tell his colleagues he was taking a leave of absence. He'll turn up and apologize for failing to report his plans to the embassy, then continue pursuing his economic aspirations here without batting an eyelash.

But protocol demanded that George Lane take action, for George Lane was ambassador of the United States of America to the Yemen Arab Republic, and had held that post for over two years. Who exactly is our vanished friend? One William Thomas, an American, aged around sixty years, probably in poor physical shape, employed in Sanaa by a Washington-based marketing concern. Searching for oil in Kuwait or Bahrain or something. Hasn't been heard from since March or early April. Lane instructed his embassy officials to make the conventional inquiries into Thomas's whereabouts.

The information Lane received from a source the next day, however, immediately changed the situation. Thomas may be under detention by National Security, the embassy had been told. The ambassador phoned Yemen's Deputy Foreign Minister and Chief of Protocol. He instructed his consul, John Vessey, to deliver a diplomatic note to the Yemeni government stating that Thomas's disappearance was a matter of official concern to the United States government and requesting that the Ministry of Foreign Affairs contact National Security to determine whether the American had, in fact, been detained. The ministry's reply, April 22, made it evident that vigorous diplomatic action was called for: Thomas was being held by National Security, and that was all George Lane could be told. Vessey visited the National Security Office, only to be informed that Thomas was being held with several Yemeni nationals on a security matter; no details could be divulged. Later on, Vessey met with the ministry's head of consular affairs, emphasizing his concern about Thomas and demanding to see him. But on May 3, Yemen's Ministry of Foreign Affairs informed the embassy that consular access could not be granted until a critical National Security investigation was complete. Lane would have to summon all his diplomatic contacts, rouse his skills, to save William Thomas from the wrath of National Security.

On May 6, Lane once again had Vessey deliver a note to the Ministry of Foreign Affairs: Thomas has been detained for at least one month without consular access. The communiqué elicited no response, and neither did the flurry of polite memoranda Lane forwarded in May. Finally, on June 19, consular access was granted to the American government and a consular officer visited Thomas at National Security headquarters in Sanaa. Thomas looked dejected and haggard. He asked the embassy to obtain some personal items and said he nothing of the charges against him.

June 24 saw George Lane plead the case of William Thomas at the highest level of the Yemeni government when he guardedly entered the lavish offices of His Excellency, Colonel Ali Abdullah Salih, the young, black-mustachioed President of the Republic. Salih told Lane that the embassy could have weekly access to Thomas, but he sternly noted the severity of the espionage charge; the mysterious investigation was continuing. And it continued throughout the summer with only sporadic contact between Thomas and the U.S. embassy. Now, however, messages could be delivered to him from Kim Thomas. William Thomas became anxious about receiving mail from his family. He urgently requested a new battery for his failing hearing aid. Unknown to Thomas, a silent, sullen neighbor just a few cells down in Sanaa's Central Prison did not have the luxury of communication. DuWayne Terrell, a fellow American citizen, had been shackled there for seven months. But how would U.S. officials know he was missing if he had never officially registered his presence at the American embassy upon arriving in Yemen?

George Lane was becoming impatient. The Yemenis were secretly trying an American citizen on a charge of spying, and he was powerless, unable to even ascertain the specific content of the accusations. And stories about espionage rings were now appearing in the Arab press. Lane glanced at an October 2 press story originating in Kuwait. It reported the involvement of *two* Americans in an Israeli–U.S. spy ring. According to the report, a secret trial had been held. Lane dutifully reported the details of the story to Washington. The latest information could only have been leaked by someone in National Security, and, if so, it was probably somewhat accurate. Who, then, was the enigmatic second American?

Lane's question would be answered on October 16. Washington cabled the embassy in Sanaa to tell its representatives in Yemen that "there is strong evidence that DuWayne Terrell has been living in Sanaa and he may be the 'other American' under arrest in Yemen. By locating Terrell's passport application from Jerusalem (Passport no. 23337078 issued January 30, 1979) the Department was able to contact his parents, Mr. and Mrs. Samuel Terrell of Colorado Springs, Colorado. Mr. and Mrs. Terrell state they have not heard from DuWayne for a 'long time,' which is unusual since he used to have more frequent contact with his parents. About a year ago he called them from Damascus reporting that he had lost his passport and airline ticket. His last letter was addressed from Sanaa. The parents are uncertain as to the date when the letter was received. Mr. and Mrs. Terrell, who have been greatly concerned about their son, tried to reach him by telephone October 15 but were not able to get through."

Four days later, on October 20, the United States embassy in Tel Aviv received a call from a kibbutznik far from the urban expanse of Israel's most modern and congested city. It was a young man who was concerned about his friend, an American citizen who had gone to Yemen a few months earlier and had not been heard from since. The kibbutznik had contacted his missing friend's parents in Colorado Springs, Colorado. Embassy officials took down the name of the missing American: DuWayne Terrell. The caller told them that the purpose of Terrell's trip was to become familiar with the Jewish community in Yemen. A confidential cable was sent to George Lane, the American ambassador in Sanaa, who would now have to deal with the probable detainment of a Mr. Terrell in addition to the Thomas case. The complexities of the situation were succinctly laid out in a cable from the State Department in Washington.

FM SECSTATE WASHDC
TO AMEMBASSY TEL AVIV PRIORITY
AMCONSUL JERUSALEM PRIORITY
INFO AMEMBASSY SANA PRIORITY
AMEMBASSY JIDDA PRIORITY
SUBJECT: ALLEGED ISRAELI ESPIONAGE RING IN THE YAR
REFS: A) SANA 6800; B) RIYADH 1682; C) TEL AVIV 19006

1. (SECRET – ENTIRE TEXT)

2. IN APRIL 1980, THE YAR [YEMEN ARAB REPUBLIC] NATIONAL SECURITY FORCES DETAINED AN AMERICAN CITIZEN, WILLIAM THOMAS, ON SUSPICION OF BEING PART OF AN ALLEGED ISRAELI ESPIONAGE EFFORT IN THE YAR. SEVERAL YEMENI CITIZENS ALSO ARRESTED. UNTIL RECENTLY, THERE HAS BEEN NO PUBLICITY ABOUT THIS CASE. HOWEVER, REPORTS HAVE RECENTLY APPEARED IN THE KUWAITI AND YAR PRESS. THERE HAVE ALSO BEEN REPORTS THAT THE YAR GOVERNMENT PLANS TO TELEVISE THE TRIAL OF THE ACCUSED YEMENI CITIZENS.

3. BOTH THE DEPARTMENT AND EMBASSY SANA HAVE BEEN VERY DISTURBED BY THE CONTINUED DETENTION OF WILLIAM THOMAS. WE HAVE MADE REPEATED EFFORTS TO OBTAIN CONSULAR ACCESS, BUT HAVE BEEN ONLY PARTIALLY SUCCESSFUL. WE HAVE NOT SEEN MR. THOMAS IN ABOUT 5 WEEKS. WE HAVE URGED THE YARG TO RELEASE MR. THOMAS.

4. THERE HAVE ALSO BEEN PERSISTENT REPORTS THAT A
SECOND "WESTERNER" HAS ALSO BEEN ARRESTED IN
CONNECTION WITH THE ESPIONAGE INVESTIGATION. WHILE
THE YARG HAS STATED THAT ONLY ONE USC HAS BEEN
DETAINED, IT APPEARS POSSIBLE THAT THE SECOND
INDIVIDUAL MAY BE DUWAYNE TERRELL, A USC WHO HAD
BEEN LIVING WITH THOMAS FOR SEVERAL MONTHS. EMBASSY
SANA IS CURRENTLY ATTEMPTING TO ASCERTAIN WHETHER
TERRELL IS, IN FACT, THE SECOND "WESTERNER." FROM
DISCUSSIONS WITH TERRELL'S PARENTS, WE UNDERSTAND
THAT HE IS AN EXTREMELY RELIGIOUS PERSON OF
CHRISTIAN FAITH WHO WENT TO JERUSALEM IN MAY 1978
TO LEARN HEBREW. TERRELL'S ADDRESS WAS THE BAPTIST
CONGREGATION, JERUSALEM HOUSE, P.O. BOX 20428,
TERRELL WAS ISSUED A U.S. PASSPORT 23337078 IN
JERUSALEM ON JANUARY 30, 1979.

5. FOR JERUSALEM AND TEL AVIV: REQUEST YOU PROVIDE
SANA WITH ANY INFORMATION YOU MAY HAVE ON
DUWAYNE TERRELL. BEYOND THAT CONTAINED IN REFTEL
C. PLEASE INFO DEPARTMENT.

And so, on October 25, 1980, almost eight months into DuWayne Terrell's lonely ordeal, the government of the United States made its first official inquiry about his whereabouts in a meticulously worded dispatch: "The Embassy of the United States of America presents its compliments to the Ministry of Foreign Affairs of the Yemen Arab Republic and has the honor to request the Ministry's assistance in locating an American citizen, Mr. DuWayne Terrell, who is believed to be missing in the Yemen Arab Republic." As the two-page note was being delivered to the government of the Yemen Arab Republic in Sanaa, Samuel Terrell received a telephone call from one of his son's friends in Israel: How is DuWayne? *Where* is DuWayne? Raya Dar, who claimed to be from Kibbutz Ma'abarot, had last heard that DuWayne was living with an elderly Jew in Sanaa. DuWayne could have become embroiled in controversy by associating with the

Jewish community in an Arab country.

If Terrell found trouble when he set out to meet the Jews of Yemen, the Jews of Yemen, for their part, certainly garnered a fair share of afflictions from consorting with him. Jailed for two months in Taiz, DuWayne Terrell had been compelled by his captors to write a seventy-page history of his travels in Yemen, which was immediately translated from English into Arabic. He spent hour after hour, day after day, detailing his four-year stay in Israel, where he had primarily worked with the Southern Baptists; his trips to Cyprus and Jordan and Syria and the Yemen Arab Republic; and his encounters with William Thomas, Yhia ibn Daoud Suberi, Mori Yaish al-Garni, and other Yemeni Jews.

Thirty days into Terrell's imprisonment, a brutal physical interrogation began. He wrote that he had go to Taiz as an agent of Israeli intelligence and had been trained during his stay in Israel. The interrogating officers dictated the incriminating statement after beating him into submission. At first Terrell had boldly refused to cooperate, but he had been summarily beaten with rods. Then, one still Taiz night, he had been awakened for a macabre confessional during which he would lose four toenails and faint five times. Dangling upside-down, ankles chained to the ceiling, Terrell was questioned and told that the electric wire under his head would be used to electrocute him. Using branches from trees, policemen beat the Colorado native on his feet and arms, inflicting permanent scars. And Terrell was also struck in the mouth with a rubber hose. By the end of his third subterranean session there was blood all over the room. DuWayne Terrell was a spy for the Jewish nation and would be treated as such until it was proved otherwise.

Terrell eventually complied with his captors when they promised that nothing would happen to the aging Yhia ibn Daoud Suberi. To protect Suberi, Terrell testified falsely against himself and the old man, and against his host William Thomas and Thomas's Kenyan friend, Farouk, and his Yemeni friend, Hassan. He stated that he, William Thomas, Farouk, and Hassan were all Israeli agents. Terrell also "admitted" he had taken photographs of military installations in Yemen and relayed the information back to Israel. He had even visited the military college in Rowdah to obtain drawings and information about the school.

In April, Terrell was transferred to Sanaa. Emboldened by the knowledge that there was an American embassy in the capital city, he told his captors that the Taiz police had forced him to lie against his friends. Meanwhile, William Thomas had been arrested, along with Mori Yaish, the chief rabbi of Yemen, Yehudah Halla, and Yhia ibn Daoud Suberi. Thomas's kindness to Terrell cost the sixty-year-old several beatings in May and June. Thomas, too, was hung upside down by his ankles but with his head under water in the pool at the old National Security Building. The water treatment, accompanied by beatings on the legs, occurred twice. On other occasions he was struck in the mouth or was made to stand in a leaning posture with his forehead against the wall after which his interrogators would pull out his feet from under him. Sometimes they hung him by an iron rod placed under his knees. All of the imprisoned men were fed on putrid rice and meat, which they ravenously consumed. Mori Yaish's children were allowed to bring him kosher food.

DuWayne Terrell had not been seen in nine months when the American consul, John Vessey, first met the young man and finally confirmed his arrest. And slowly things began to look better. On September 21 Terrell appeared before Muhammad Khamis, the chief prosecuting attorney. Khamis seemed to be aware that Terrell had testified falsely against himself and the others. He had Terrell once again recount his travels and experiences. Terrell's innocence was obvious, and Khamis privately acknowledged that the charges were rather dubious: "Your government has no need of you. They use satellites to monitor information," he said, noting as well that agents could operate out of the U.S. embassy under the protection of diplomatic immunity. But the case against Terrell continued despite Khamis's compunctions.

With November fast approaching, George Lane was feeling the pressure from Washington. Consular access to Thomas and Terrell had not been granted since September 6. So on October 30, the ambassador called on the Republic's newly appointed Prime Minister, Dr. Abdul Karim al-Iryani. Lane told him that the two arrests were casting a shadow on U.S.-Yemen relations, and that the situation would be exacerbated once American news organizations learned about it. This had become a real possibility, because U.S. Congressman Ken Kramer of Colorado had contacted the State Department on behalf of Samuel Terrell, DuWayne's father, who had reported his son missing. In July, the Terrells had sent their son an international money order for his birthday, but it had never been cashed. Kramer had written to Yhia M. al-Mutawakel, the Yemeni ambassador to the United States, and to Donald F. McHenry, the U.S. ambassador to the United Nations. Meanwhile, Kim Thomas was seeking the assistance of the Saudi ambassador to Spain. The story could go public any day, and then Iryani and his government would be working under the harsh, global spotlight of the American media. Lane stressed this to Deputy Foreign Minister Ibrahim al-Kibsi on November 13 and Minister of Interior Ali al-Uthrub on the 27th.

When Lane called on Vice President Abdul Aziz al-Ghani on December 10, he adopted a less benign approach. This is a very sensitive matter, Lane remarked, and no matter how the case is handled from now on, it is certain to hurt U.S.-Yemeni relations, especially if Yemen continues to keep the U.S. government in the dark on the legal status of case. On December 21, Lane met with Foreign Minister Ali al-Thawr to discuss the Thomas-Terrell case. Al-Thawr told Lane that the two were accused of spying for Israel, not the United States, and that judicial action had been suspended because the judge initially involved had been taken off the case. The head of National Security had been tasked with preparing a full report to President Salih. A contact later told Lane that al-Ghani was taking a special interest in the case and that he and Iryani were studying the situation. Lane confidently reported to Washington that "the most senior officials" of the Yemen government were now involved in the case and could be expected to be helpful.

The next American contact with Thomas and Terrell came on January 4, 1981 at the old National Security headquarters. As usual, an English-speaking security officer and a translator as well as a number of other officials were present, and they stayed throughout the fifteen-minute meeting. Both Thomas and Terrell appeared to be in good spirits and in reasonably good physical condition. Terrell immediately exclaimed, "We have a lot to tell you!" He then informed a consular officer that they and seven Yemenis had been tried on December 23 before the National Security Court. Each of them had appeared separately before a panel consisting of a military officer, a Islamic religious judge, a prosecutor in civilian attire, and the head of National Security himself. They were not told their rights or given defense attorneys, and were not informed of the verdict after the trial. But Terrell was optimistic, since there had not been a shred of evidence against him.

Lane was determined to extricate the United States and Yemen from this minor entanglement that foreboded such large consequences. On January 11, he once again ventured to Salih's office and asked him when the matter would be resolved. The President vaguely replied, "It'll be settled soon," refusing to be specific. Lane would not hear from Salih for some time, for on January 16, Muhammad Khamis, the Minister of Local Administration, was ambushed and assassinated while driving from Sanaa to the Red Sea port of Hodeida, and over the next few weeks Salih was preoccupied by the problems this entailed.

The death of Khamis was the turning point for Thomas and Terrell. When Lane called on Prime Minister Iryani on January 18, the Yemeni official opened the conversation by announcing that he had good news. President Salih, he explained, had decided to release Thomas and Terrell as a gesture of appreciation for the support President Jimmy Carter had given him, and therefore the release would take place before Carter left office on January 20. Lane excitedly cabled the State Department with a summary of Iryani's remarks: "Salih knew that Carter had done his best to serve the U.S. and the cause of peace during his time in office. He knew that President Carter was the kind of man who would be concerned over the fate of Thomas and Terrell, as he was over the hostages in Iran, and Salih therefore wanted this news passed to President Carter before he left office. At the same time, Salih instructed him to tell me that Y.A.R. was sincerely interested in developing closer relations with the United States. Salih asked that his best wishes be passed to President-elect Reagan, along with his hope that the beginning of a new administration in Washington would open a new era of cooperation."

DuWayne Terrell stepped into the warm light of day on February 8, 1981, after spending one full year shackled in the Yemen Arab Republic. He was officially expelled from the country, but the U.S. embassy had arranged tickets and reservations for a Yemeni Airways flight to Rome on the evening of February 9 for him and William Thomas. After debriefing American officials about his experiences, and once again offering a chronology of his detainment, an exhausted Terrell boarded a plane in Sanaa that would carry him away from the sun-beaten country of wadis and valleys, culminating the ugly episode that had begun on November 29, 1979.

Before boarding the plane, Terrell put some thoughts on his captivity down on paper: "I came to Yemen as a tourist, with a love for this country and people, carried Hebrew writing with me which, I suppose, I should not have carried, was arrested and kindled the suspicions of a nation, was interrogated, beaten and cast into prison. . . . I have undergone a traumatic experience that I will never forget, and one which I hope will help to fortify my belief in God and in the importance of doing good and serving one's fellow man."

The world first learned of the Thomas-Terrell case nine days later, when the *New York Times* reported their story on its February 17, 1981 front page. These events in 1980 kindled the first sparks, the initial thrust, the sowing of seeds that would blossom into a movement to free the repressed and nearly forgotten Jews of Yemen. Terrell would provide that movement's leaders with critical background information, insights into the inner workings of the Yemeni government. And most crucially, he would furnish them with elusive hard facts about the Jews of Yemen, painting an accurate picture of their day-to-day persistence.

July 31, 1981

DuWayne Terrell was back in Colorado Springs, but his new friends were not forgotten. The United States embassy in Sanaa received an urgent letter from him, requesting that they help obtain a passport for one Yhia ibn Daoud Suberi so that he could be reunited with his family in Israel. Sanaa replied that they could not locate Suberi and that the proper vehicle for communicating with him was international mail. On the subject of assistance in obtaining a passport, they advised Terrell that no action could be taken until Suberi actually decided that he wished to leave Yemen; at that point they would consider what they could usefully accomplish. Besides, the United States embassy was not in a good position to intercede with the Yemen Arab Republic on behalf of a Yemeni citizen, particularly if he intended to travel to the enemy nation of Israel.

So Terrell wrote to Dr. Iryani, asking the Prime Minister to give a passport to Yhia ibn Daoud Suberi, who had been held in a Sanaa jail for a year and a half before being released. Terrell learned that Mori Yaish al-Garni had also been set free, thanks to the intervention of friendly sheikhs of the northern Hashid Confederation, who took full responsibility for the rabbi. But there was no sense of closure for DuWayne Terrell. He vowed never to rest until the anguish of long-separated families was extinguished. Terrell's ordeal gave him new vigor to search for a way to rescue the Jews of Yemen. There had to be a way to win their freedom.

DuWayne Terrell.

Wedding of David ben Avraham (DuWayne Terrell), with Yhia ibn Daoud Suberi to the right, 1995.

Chapter Two

FAMILIES TORN APART

September 10, 1985

Daoud Hamami alighted from his plane at Sanaa International Airport and cautiously made his way to the arrivals hall, where he presented a Swiss passport and a Yemen Arab Republic entry visa to the leery customs official. The twenty-eight-year-old looked European enough with his milky-white skin and shock of light brown hair; one of the few tourists who occasionally turned up in the nation at the tip of the Arabian peninsula, thought the officer. Daoud (also spelled Dawoud) Hamami had indeed been born in Paris and was a citizen of Switzerland, as his papers indicated, but most people knew him as Pierre Goloubinoff, except in Israel, where as David Golon he was a resident of the city of Rehovot. As all this might indicate, French, Hebrew, English, and Arabic rolled off his tongue with identical ease.

In academic circles, as Pierre Goloubinoff, Hamami was a biologist from the University of Lausanne in Switzerland, with degrees in plant physiology, microbiology, and biochemistry. In 1985, he was a graduate student in the plant genetics department of the Weizmann Institute of Science. And for those who knew him as David Golon, he was a 1975 graduate of the Hebrew Gymnasium high school in Rehavia, Jerusalem.

Believers in genetic determinism would be wise to take note of a certain romantic encounter long ago between a Jewish maiden from Vienna and a prince from the German province of Thuringia, for in that episode lay the scandalous roots of Daoud Hamami's lineage . . .

The late 1830s were a time of transition for the Jews of Central Europe, who were beginning to dream of shattering the shackles of medieval bondage. This was particularly true in the territorial entity known as Germany, a mosaic of tiny fiefdoms, independent merchant cities, and sovereign states of greater or lesser size. The rulers of the centuries-old duchy of Schwarzburg-Sondershausen were related to all the crowned families of Europe, including the kings of Denmark, Holland, and the Saxe-Coburgs of England. In 1835 Duke Gunther Friedrich Karl II von Schwarzburg-Sondershausen was a young widower who had just inherited the throne from his deceased father, and he was being entertained by a troupe of Viennese ballet dancers performing in the castle of Schwarzburg. The lovely prima ballerina captured his attention, and he approached her after the final curtain came down.

The ballerina in question turned out to be a Jewish girl named Hava Stein, the daughter of a wealthy Austrian cattle dealer. Her paternal ancestors had come to Vienna from Spain via northern Italy three centuries earlier, Germanizing their Sephardic family name, Even, to Stein. Hava Stein strayed, and became the star of a ballet company touring the Austro-Hungarian Empire and Germany, refreshing shadowy castles and their bored owners. Young Gunther fell in love with Hava Stein, and things soon got out of hand when she became pregnant. Gunther longed to marry his Jewish mistress, but in 1836 the scion of a nine-century-old ducal dynasty could not marry a Jewish woman. Even if she had converted to Christianity, Hava Stein could never have become the consort of a scion of Schwarzburg-Sondershausen.

A compromise was sought and found. The very pregnant Hava Stein would indeed convert, but she would marry an old widower, Count Nicolsky, a good friend of the Schwarzburg-Sondershausens whose lesser status made the union possible. The baby girl born soon after their nuptials carried the surname Nicolsky, but Hava and her daughter never lived with the count. Instead they lived at Sondershausen, and Hava continued to be Gunther's mistress for the next seventeen years. Eventually he wed a Schwarzburg-Rudolstadt princess, but since none of his legitimate children gave him grandchildren, the only descendants of the illustrious Schwarzburg-Sondershausen dynasty were the offspring of Hava's daughter, whose given name, unfortunately, is no longer known.

Hava's daughter grew into a beautiful maiden, speaking several languages, including Yiddish, and fully aware of her mother's background. When she was seventeen, a Russian delegation visited Schwarzberg in order to discuss the German Customs Union, or Zollverein, and negotiate a trade agreement between her father and the tsar. The head of the delegation, a general, was seconded by a young Polish nobleman, a colonel named Alexander Wassilkovsky, whose family had been hereditary members of the Polish Diet since the sixteenth century. While the general and the duke talked finance, the colonel and Hava's daughter danced. They were married the same year. The new Countess Wassilkovsky moved to Retechino in Russian Poland, and proceeded to bear seventeen children to her husband. Seraphina Wassilkovsky, their tenth child, was born in Vilna in the early 1880s.

Seraphina was raised by her mother and father to be the a perfect wife for a promising young nobleman. The nobleman in question was Sergei Petrovitch Goloubinow, freshly graduated from the School of Oriental Languages in St. Petersburg. Sergei's grandfather, a Ukrainian captain of plebeian origins, had led a battalion of Cossacks into twenty-two battles against Napoleon, winning a title of hereditary nobility for himself and his descendants. Seraphina Wassilkovsky married Sergei Petrovitch Goloubinow just as he was commencing his career in the Foreign Service with an appointment by the tsar as translator for the semi-independent emir of Bokhara. The couple's first son, Vsevolod Sergeivitch Goloubinow, was born at the Russian consulate in Bokhara in August 1903.

Life in Turkistan and Persia was difficult, and Seraphina Goloubinow succumbed to typhoid fever in 1911. She was buried in Urmia, Persia, leaving behind a husband and three children. Vsevolod was raised intermittently in Persia, in Russia, and on the estate of his grandmother, Countess Wassilkovsky. By the time he came of age, the Bolshevik Revolution was wreaking havoc in Russia. The surviving members of the Goloubinow family took refuge in France. After graduating from the School of Chemistry in Nancy as a mining engineer, Vsevolod went to Africa to work in the gold and diamond mines. In 1948, he was interviewed by an adventurous French journalist named Simone Changeux on assignment in Africa. Soon afterward they were married, the only witnesses several natives and a gloomy priest who forbade any rejoicing after the ceremony because it had united a good Catholic woman with a member of the schismatic Russian Orthodox Church who refused to convert for the occasion.

Vsevolod and Simone returned to Paris, where, as "Anne and Serge Golon," they co-authored a best-selling series of historical novels set in the seventeenth century and featuring a heroine named Angelique. Their third child, Pierre Goloubinoff, was born in Paris in 1957 but was raised in Israel. How this came about is a tale in itself.

Already a successful novelist in France at the age of seventeen, Pierre's mother, Anne Golon, was a highly sensitive young woman. When the horrors of the Holocaust came to be known at the end of World War II, many people were genuinely horrified, but in most cases the shock wore off after a month or so. Young Anne Golon, however, never forgot, and the pain never subsided. The trial of Adolf Eichmann in 1963, followed by the Six-Day War in 1967, induced her to trade the quiet mountains of Switzerland for the tempestuous young nation of Israel. That same year she and Serge emigrated to Jerusalem and made it their home. The decision of a non-Jewish family to "escape the hardships" of Switzerland and "take refuge" in Israel soon came to the attention of Israel's intellgience services. It took the Shin-Bet nearly two years to decide that the Golubinoffs were not KGB agents and write them off as harmless lunatics.

Pierre Goloubinoff, as mentioned, grew up in Israel and attended college in Switzerland, then returned to the land of his youth to pursue a graduate degree at Rehovot's prestigious Weizmann Institute. But what's a young bachelor to do in the city of Rehovot? If he is sensitive to history and ethnicity, he will be unable to ignore the many Yemenite Jews walking the city's modern streets. If he is sensitive to feminine comeliness, he will be powerless before the exotic, dark-skinned daughters of Jews formerly from Yemen. In Pierre's case, both factors converged to spark a keen interest in the Jews of Yemeni origin who lived Rehovot and its suburbs. The inquisitive young scientist began to ask questions about his neighbors.

A casual observer of Israel's Yemeni Jews will investigate their food and dress, and perhaps their characteristic forms of song and scholarship. But Goloubinoff probed further, wishing to deepen his understanding of Yemeni Jewish culture. Visiting their homes and participating in their celebrations, Goloubinoff stumbled upon a nugget he adjudged a significant journalistic scoop. There were still Jews in Yemen, Jews completely isolated from the outside world. Twenty-three years had passed since the revolution; and in all this time, virtually no news from them had pierced its borders. Goloubinoff was both fascinated and disturbed. In the markets and offices and apartment houses of Rehovot lived people who looked normal enough—driving cars, paying taxes, speaking Hebrew like all other Israelis—but were burdened with the pain of having a brother, a sister, a mother, from whom they hadn't heard a single word, or received a single letter, in twenty-three long years. They didn't even know whether their family members in Yemen were alive or dead.

Cohi, a Yemeni girl whom Goloubinoff found quite to his liking, introduced him to some of her co-workers and neighbors. She soon became Pierre's wife-to-be, and he was soon immersed in the kindness and hospitality of the Yemeni community. Like DuWayne Terrell before him, Pierre Goloubinoff was invited into their homes for Shabbat and attended the weddings of their multitudinous children. On those occasions, Goloubinoff would watch as the mother of the bride erupted in tears—not joyous ones born of a daughter's marriage, but woeful ones that filled the eyes because of the grandmother who should have been here, and the uncles, and the cousins, and all the others left behind in Yemen. Even at the most ecstatic moments Israel's Yemeni Jews could not be fully happy. The sorrow Goloubinoff discovered motivated him to find out what had happened to the long-lost family members. He decided to go to Yemen, pledging to do so out of his own pocket.

But first Pierre Goloubinoff had to master the names and stories of those for whom his friends yearned. He met Moshe Atzar, a co-worker of Cohi, a man who was almost an orphan in Israel because he had left Yemen against his father's will in 1962 to join his treasured

Miriam. Moshe's mother, brother, three sisters, and father, whom he now thought dead, had never flown the Magic Carpet to the Holy Land. Moshe's face bled pure frustration. People he loved very much were most probably alive, but he could not communicate with them because of the senseless politics of the Middle East. But for his jaunt into the Republic of Yemen, Goloubinoff had become Daoud Hamami, a name that would allow him to fade into the crowd—and espy Yemen's Jewish community.

Goloubinoff, blessed with an exceptional memory, studied genealogy, the names of sisters and brothers, fathers and mothers, hard facts and minutiae that would convince the Jews of Raida and Saada to accept him as an emissary from their kin. Goloubinoff would gain their confidence by chronicling matters only their blood relations could have told him: that so-and-so, now a grown man, had a scar on his abdomen from when he was three years old and was burned by dye his mother was boiling for her basket-weaving business; that genies lurked in the foothills girding a certain village; that he knew the history explaining why a certain house had been given a certain name. Even though Goloubinoff looked nothing like a Yemeni, he would be accepted because he knew well-guarded secrets.

And Goloubinoff prepared for his mission by arranging to meet with a strange man, a swarthy convert named David Ben Avraham with long, black sidelocks. The taciturn Ben Avraham had visited the Yemen Arab Republic in 1979, and his experiences had been far from pleasant. As a youthful and naive adventurer, Ben Avraham had sought to make contact with the Jews of Yemen. He had also seen the inside of prisons in Taiz and Sanaa after being charged with espionage for carrying letters and notes in Hebrew. Upon his release and subsequent ouster from Yemen, Ben Avraham found his way back to Israel, into the arms of the Yemeni Jews there. Back then he had been a Baptist from Colorado named DuWayne Terrell, Goloubinoff learned. Now he was a dedicated adherent of Yemeni-style Judaism, having joined the faith in 1982 and adopted a new name. Goloubinoff shared Ben Avraham's passion for the Yemeni Jewish cause. And he would heed Ben Avraham's emphatic counsel: don't carry any written communication to or from the Jews of Yemen!

Goloubinoff also preceded his Yemeni sojourn with intense study of the writings of Amnon Kapeliuk, a well-known leftist journalist who boasted excellent connections with the Palestine Liberation Organization. Kapeliuk, an Israeli citizen, had visited Yemen twice, on a French passport, on assignment for the newspaper *Yediot Aharonot*, with official permission from the Republic to visit the country's Jews. But during his travels, Kapeliuk had been accompanied by a contingent of Yemeni security officers, the Mukhabarat, who scrutinized his every move. Yemeni policemen sat in on all of Kapeliuk's meetings with Jews, creating a strained atmosphere in which neither he nor the Yemenis could be comfortable and forthright. The people Kapeliuk interviewed had be careful what they said when answering the questions he posed. "Why would I want to go to Israel? I'm perfectly content here," they would respond. Kapeliuk empathized with their plight and supplied Goloubinoff with some basic information on the location of certain Jewish villages. The separated families, however, provided Goloubinoff with the most accurate details about the whereabouts of their loved ones.

Goloubinoff learned that the Yemeni government often exploited the alleged contentment of its Jewish populace for propagandistic purposes. In 1980, for instance, a Paris-based Arab weekly had reported that the Jews of Yemen were free to fulfill all the commandments of the Torah and had no desire to settle in Israel. Rather, they balked at the Zionist intimidators who urged them to uproot their peaceful existence in Yemen, and instead taught their children to love the Yemeni government. The article had concluded with a quotation from President Ali Abdullah Salih: "I do not prevent the Jews from leaving, but they do not want to leave. They are living in good circumstances. They are a people of the book, and I love their scrupulousness." His statement had inevitably found its way into the Israeli press.

As Pierre Goloubinoff prepared himself for his one-man crusade to seek and help the remnants of Yemeni Jewry, he became more and more dismayed at the indifference to their plight in Israel. He estimated that only ten of the one hundred and twenty members of the Knesset, Israel's national legislature, were even aware that there were still Jews in Yemen. Even many members of the Yemeni community in Israel knew almost nothing about the Jews in their former homeland, although the rumor mill feverishly ground out layers of supposition. Every once in a while a European tourist who visited Yemen would return with some crude photographs of Jews : :lling their wares in the markets of Saada, images which would find their way into the pages of major Israeli newspapers. But outside Israel, the existence of Jews in Yemen was virtually unknown, except to a few officials; the American diplomatic representatives in Sanaa, for instance, had instructions to keep an eye on the Jews living in the north country.

Goloubinoff grew angry at the Israeli government. Where had it been since the 1962 revolution, when the doors allowing Jews to escape from Yemen had been sealed? The separated families had petitioned the country's political leaders for assistance in the matter. They had attempted to publicize the predicament of their brothers and sisters, but all such efforts were officially discouraged. Staging press conferences to bash the Yemeni and Israeli governments and rally support for the cause, they were warned, would only hamper negotiations going on behind the scenes. Over the years, Israeli officials had indeed been sympathetic to the plight of Yemeni Jewry and had unsuccessfully sought to break through the impasse. But in Goloubinoff's view, Israel had not tried hard enough. When its behind-the-scenes efforts failed to produce results, it should have tried something else. Unfortunately, there was a high rate of turnover at the Yemen desk of the Mossad, Israel's intelligence service. The position was filled with a new incumbent every three years because it was regarded merely as a springboard into the higher echelons of the Mossad or the Foreign Ministry, and not as important in itself. No one remained on the Yemen desk long enough to learn much about the situation or come up with some new ideas. And finally, the world's major Jewish organizations, as was so often the case, faithfully respected the recommendations of Israeli security and therefore never vigorously or openly campaigned for the release of Yemen's remaining Jews.

In June 1985, Pierre Goloubinoff found himself in Switzerland for a boyhood friend's wedding. There, he applied for a tourist visa to the Yemen Arab Republic. And while his colleagues at the Weizmann Institute were enjoying their vacations over the High Holidays and the festival of Sukkot, Goloubinoff flew to Yemen by way of Athens on his Swiss passport, hoping to see the families of his friends if they were still alive—and if they were still Jews. He saw himself as on a primarily fact-finding mission. How many Jews remained in Yemen? Where did they live? Were their days pleasant or suffused with bitterness?

For his jaunt into the Republic of Yemen, Goloubinoff had become Daoud Hamami, a name that would allow him to fade into the crowd and espy Yemen's Jewish community. Extreme discretion was his watchword. Yemeni officials had a nasty habit of arresting, and in the best case expelling, any foreigner discovered conversing with a Jew. The foreign transgressor would be unceremoniously ushered through the international departure terminal of Sanaa's airport for the first flight out; prison, however, would be the fate of the Jew. As he had read in *Yediot Aharonot* only a few days before, two Yemeni Jewish jewelers had just been arrested after meeting with two Italian Jewish tourists who had promised to send them a Talmud. So Goloubinoff would be very cautious as he made his way through the bustling suq of Saada, scouring the stands with their burlap sacks of colorful spices for Jews, eyeing the bearded, robed sellers of silver articles and other crafts. Aside from names and characteristic dress, he had no other clues.

In late September, a lone European tourist could be seen roaming the marketplace in Saada, carefully studying the vendors hawking their wares. Suddenly, two young men were staring back at Goloubinoff, their dark, piercing eyes counting the bones of his body. Sitting cross-legged on the dusty ground, they began gesturing strangely, their fists twisting back and forth parallel to their ears. Suddenly, Goloubinoff realized what the two men were quietly communicating: "Do you have sidelocks? Are you a Jew?" He realized that he had finally made contact with some Yemeni Jews, but he knew that it would be out of the question to address them in

Hebrew in a public place. Goloubinoff slowly nodded and continued on his way toward the city gates. The two young men whose interest he had piqued followed him as he darted in and out of tiny darkened shops; when Goloubinoff exited Saada, they were still on his trail.

Walking along the barren dirt road toward the villages surrounding Saada, Goloubinoff heard the whine of an approaching car. Then, an ancient, battered jeep was passing him, churning up clouds of dust. Inside it were the two Jews from the suq.

"*Atah rotzeh la'alot imanu?*" they yelled out to Goloubinoff in Hebrew. "Do you want to come with us?"

"I'm afraid," Goloubinoff responded, the admonitions of David Ben Avraham reverberating in his heart as he trudged along.

"*Imshi,*" the Jews replied, "Continue." Goloubinoff did, ambling along while the jeep followed. They were in the Jewish cemetery of Saada. Suddenly, two strong arms flew out on the passenger side, pulling Goloubinoff into the vehicle, which immediately sped off. Goloubinoff introduced himself to his friendly captors as Daoud Hamami. He understood from everything that had happened so far that the two mysterious young men were taking a risk, perhaps greater than his own, but clearly he was on his way to the kind of meeting he had been hoping for. Over myriad cups of bitter coffee, lounging on cushions on the floors of their living rooms and dining rooms, Hamami would update the Yemeni Jews on events in the outside world. He would tell them about Shimon Peres, the Prime Minister of Israel, and Yitzhak Shamir, who would take over after him. He would tell about the bloody war in Lebanon. Was Jewish tradition alive and well in Israel? He knew he would be reluctant to describe the extent of Western assimilation in Israeli society. It was the afternoon before Yom Kippur, 1985.

Daoud Hamami, as we shall call Goloubinoff during his stay in Yemen, learned that the Jews of Saada had recently been expelled from the city and now lived in numerous tiny villages surrounding it. They were prohibited from doing business in the Saada suq; to make a living they would sell their jewelry and crafts to a cooperative Arab dealer and would sit with him in the marketplace. But to extract more portentous information, Hamami would have to gain the Jews' trust by passing their tests. "Who are you? What are you? Do you have any letters? Pictures?" they grilled him. Hamami replied that he had no letters but knew Moshe Atzar and Shalom Suberi and other names that rung bells of delirium.

In Yemen as in most Third World countries, the arrival of an exotic foreigner is cause for mass hysteria in the house, especially among the anxious young children. When Hamami entered Jewish homes, little feet and hands scampered over to touch the odd-looking visitor. Only once in ten years did an event like this occur. But after a while, the children grew bored of Hamami—his Hebrew was too hard to understand—and they trotted downstairs to play in the street with Arab friends.

"They're going to spread the news that I'm here. I'm not supposed to be here. I'm not supposed to be near a Jewish house," Hamami told his hosts. The older Jews in the room laughed and dismissed his fears. The children would not utter a single word about Hamami's visit; they may have been three and four years old, but they were well-trained. Hamami marveled at the children, who would play with their Arab neighbors and not say a word about something so world-shaking as the presence of a foreigner in the house. Still, it would not be wise to tarry too long. With nightfall approaching, minutes before Yom Kippur, the Jews drove Hamami back by jeep to the gates of Saada. It would have been too dangerous for him to sleep in a Jewish home overnight.

On Yom Kippur, the holiest day of the year, there were no Jews to be seen in Saada. But Hamami was able to find Jews during the holiday of Sukkot by asking where to buy silver. Once, a petite Arab girl walked him over to a shop where Hamami introduced himself to a teenage Jew and father of two, Moshe Sabari. Sabari was quite fearful of strangers, and it took much coaxing before he invited the strange tourist upstairs to converse. Hamami was attempting to gain Sabari's confidence by dropping the names of friends from Rehovot when the young man's mother entered the room. She immediately collapsed upon hearing the names of Moshe Atzar and his sister, Afyah.

"They're alive?" Sabari's mother exclaimed after recovering from the shock. Yes, your long-lost sister and brother, who escaped to

Israel and were never heard from again, are alive and well, Hamami repeated. But the mother of seven shed no tears of joy, for she did not remember her brother and sister well enough to even yearn for their presence. She had been too young when they left for the Promised Land, but she would arrange for Hamami to meet her mother and sisters.

Hamami was encouraged by these developments. He followed up by calling on the Jews of Wadi Amlah and Wadi Damaj. In Amlah, a valley east of Saada, his hosts slaughtered and roasted a kid in his honor. A large gathering of Amlah families talked enthusiastically of Zion and how they longed to be there. Hamami had initially hoped to inspire a desire to return in the Jews of Yemen, but he soon perceived that they, in their exile thousands of miles south of Jerusalem, could teach him more about Zionism than he them. The date was September 26, the anniversary of the revolution and the declaration of the Republic, the day the doors had closed on the Jews of Yemen in 1962. Hamami spent Simhat Torah, the concluding day of the Sukkot festival, sitting with some Yemeni Jews in their special indoor *sukkot*, decorated with fruits hanging from a temporary thatched roof. Filled with admiration for their fervor, he danced with them around their few severely faded Torah scrolls.

During the eight-day Sukkot holiday, Hamami was invited to attend the festival prayer services. The Jews of Yemen boasted no central synagogues; they convened instead in the large living rooms of their homes for prayer, sharing the few yellowed siddurim (prayer books). But wait! Some of the siddurim appeared to be brand-new, with perfect bindings and smooth, white pages! Unlike the battered old books, however, these clean new ones followed the liturgical tradition of the Ashkenazim, the Jews of Europe. Hamami opened one up and read the stamp inside:

NETUREI KARTA: BROOKLYN, NEW YORK

Hamami recognized the appellation as belonging to the "Guardians of the City," a radical fringe of the Satmar sect of Hasidim, notorious for its adamant opposition to the State of Israel and its embrace of the PLO and the Arab countries in the Middle East officially at war with Israel. Operating from New York and London, the Neturei Karta believed the secular State of Israel to be an abomination and prayed mightily for its destruction. Jews were only to return to Zion upon the advent of the Messiah, they maintained; by anticipating the messianic era, the Jews of Israel had committed a grievous sin and were doomed to failure. The fifty thousand Jews who had flown to the Holy Land during Operation Magic Carpet were surely transgressors in Neturei Karta's eyes, Hamami thought, whereas the ones who had remained were pure. But how had the Neturei Karta prayer books wind up in Yemen? Hamami envisioned a cluster of bearded men dressed all in black emerging from a plane in Sanaa. Why was Neturei Karta concerned with the Jews of Yemen?

Hamami's hosts told him that they had, in fact, had in fact been visited by strange-looking Hasidim from London and New York; a contingent had materialized periodically since 1979 bearing religious articles—Torah scrolls, siddurim, prayer shawls, phylacteries—in an effort to reach out to the long-lost Jews of Yemen. The mission of the men from Neturei Karta was certainly not to sway the Arab government to ease its communication or travel restrictions, for that would lead to emigration to Israel. They were only interested in intensifying Jewish religious observance and commitment in the Republic, a cause which they inadvertently sabotaged by demanding adherence to European customs and practices that were foreign to Jews of the Yemeni tradition. They told the Yemeni Jews, for instance, that eating rice on Passover, a long-standing Sephardic practice, was no longer permitted. The Neturei Karta men, seeing themselves as the only authentic Jews, made many attempts to tamper with Yemeni ritual. Nonetheless, the service they performed was valuable; they were a precious connection to Jews outside Yemen, relieving the pain of pure isolation.

Hamami had been smuggled into the Amlah region without a permit, but he was determined to meet the aging mother of his friend, Moshe Atzar. She was sick, his friends told him; actually, she was dying. Undaunted, Hamami entered a mud-walled house and was escorted into a room where an old woman lay peacefully on a mat on the floor. Hamami watched as her attendant leaned over and whispered a few words in her ear. The Atzar matriarch struggled valiantly to mumble something to the visitor, and Hamami knelt down at her side. "How many children do they have? How do they live?" she asked about her son and daughter, and he answered as best he could. Then she forced herself into a sitting position so that he could take a picture of the entire clan with its matriarch. When Hamami left, the old woman was exhausted. Two days later she passed away.

Hamami was astounded when he learned of the death of Moshe Atzar's mother. It was nothing less than providential that after twenty-three years, the one week when he was in Yemen should coincide with her passing. When he returned to Israel with the sobering news, Moshe and his sister would be able to observe the full seven-day mourning period of *shivah*, something the separated families in Israel were no longer able to do because they never learned of the deaths of their dear ones in Yemen in time to perform the rites as prescribed by Jewish law. At best a letter months afterward would bring the news. The recipients would sit *shivah* for an hour, in accordance with tradition, and spend the rest of their lives grieving because they had not been at their parents' sides in the time of anguish and suffering.

As he reflected on all this, Hamami decided to venture to the southern part of the Republic, to Taiz. There he would find the grave of the great Shalom Shabbazzi, the poet and kabbalist whose works were cherished by every Yemeni he had encountered. True, David Ben Avraham's woes had commenced while he was visiting the hero's tomb, but Hamami carried nothing incriminating on his person. So he journeyed south, past Raida, past Sanaa, until he stood atop al-Kahira, a mountain overlooking Taiz. He whipped out a camera to photograph the breathtaking vista. From afar, an armed soldier watched as the pale-skinned man in Western garb clicked away with his camera. He strutted over to investigate.

"This is a restricted army zone. No photography!" Lowering his camera, Hamami turned in the direction of the voice and saw a Yemeni soldier glowering at him. "Now you have your work cut out," he whispered to the spirit of Shalom Shabbazzi as the soldier debated his course of action.

"Come with me to the station," commanded the soldier, gun pointed.

"Leave me alone," Hamami responded.

"This is a restricted army zone," the soldier repeated, growing impatient with the European.

"What army zone? Can you show me a sign or something?"

"Come with me!"

"Leave me alone with your idiocies!"

"Give me the camera."

"No, the camera is expensive."

"Give me the film."

"How can I do that? The roll is filled with pictures of my trip!" Hamami replied. "What do you think, I photographed atom bombs?"

Suddenly, the soldier smiled and began to chuckle, relaxing his grip on his weapon, convinced that the foreigner was merely a harmless European tourist. *I am indeed more fortunate than DuWayne Terrell,* Hamami thought as he snapped a picture of the smiling soldier and the two parted ways. *But perhaps an iota of chutzpah is a powerful asset, too.*

When Goloubinoff returned from Yemen in October, he was nearly arrested for traveling to a country at war with Israel. He supplied Israel's Foreign Ministry with crucial information, including authentic letters he had decided to smuggle out at the last minute. Never before had the government documented names, places, dates, births, and deaths, all illustrated with Goloubinoff's photographs. More importantly for Goloubinoff, his amateur photographs and slides would function as a measure of solace for the separated families of Israel, providing the Yemenis in Netanya and Rehovot and B'nei Ayish with priceless news about those they had left behind. Goloubinoff organized evenings at local homes during which he would present his slide show and his findings. He was always moved by the reaction of his audiences to the images of their loved ones so far away. One night, he watched the face of Yhia Yarimi as an image of his mother, Zohorah, was projected onto a bare wall in B'nei Ayish. Yhia stood and stared at her with a gaping mouth. For one full minute, the room was dead silent; finally, Yhia was able to vocalize his emotions.

"She's so old!" he cried out bitterly. Goloubinoff understood his friend's despair. Yhia's mental image of his mother was from thirty years before, when she had been young and pretty, with no wrinkles marring her face. And now he saw the same visage morphed into the old woman on the wall. Yhia was in a state of shock. He didn't cry, because all the tears had been shed long ago; he didn't rejoice, for the same reason. He was simply reflecting on the painful passage of time, on the many moments together he and she had missed over those years, golden seconds which could never be recouped. It was not an occasion for jubilation.

In the home of Saada Zareb, who had arrived in the Holy Land in the early 1960s, Goloubinoff delivered what he deemed a message of hope: "Your mother is still alive." But the reaction was not one of elation, just confusion.

"How can that be!" Saada exclaimed. "I sat *shivah* for her fifteen years ago!" Victimized by the closing of Yemen's doors, deprived of information by Neturei Karta, she had thought her mother was dead.

As they left the Zareb residence, General David Maimon said to Goloubinoff: "I've been a general, I've been in charge of prisons, I've seen many things in my life. But I never thought I would see a woman born in Yemen, who came to Israel like me, saying she sat *shivah* for her mother, who is very much alive, fifteen years ago. What a tragedy."

Goloubinoff concurred, and was inspired to return to Yemen. With his neutral Swiss passport, he became a courier of information to and from that country. He would make the trip three more times in the next two years. During the fast of Ramadan in 1986, he would lose five pounds.

And each time the plant geneticist returned to Israel, he would have plenty of invaluable information both for the families and for the Mossad. To the families Goloubinoff would speak willingly, to Israeli intelligence reluctantly. Agents with the code names Amos, Yehudah, and Aryeh would call him in his laboratory at the Weizmann Institute. They would pick him and drive him to an apartment or restaurant in Tel Aviv for one-sided debriefings, Goloubinoff supplying the information, the Mossad listening attentively.

Heeding a colleague's advice, Goloubinoff never gave up his independence by taking money from the Mossad; at most he would accept a cappuccino at Cafe Apropos in Tel Aviv. The agent he usually spoke to, Aryeh, was a pleasant, polite man, humble enough to admit ignorance of the situation in Yemen. During the final weeks of his Ph.D. thesis at Weizmann, before he was to depart for the Du Pont Experimental Station in Wilmington, Delaware, Goloubinoff spent several hours with Aryeh, familiarizing him with names, dates, and places of importance. During one of their sessions, Aryeh spoke candidly: "Our official position is that we're in charge and doing everything we can. But believe me, Pierre, there is no hope. We will never get them out. Now that you are going to the States you can do something. Do it."

September 17, 1988
Secretaries busily scurried about, and incessant peals of the telephone rang a jangling symphony at the Phoenix offices of Arnold & Wolf, Attorneys at Law. William J. Wolf, a graying, bespectacled man, sat in his office at the helm of the bustling operation, perusing a copy of the *Jerusalem Post International Edition*. Bill, as the towering lawyer's friends knew him, earned his bread by toiling in the legal profession, but he also channeled his energies into a self-styled brand of Jewish activism which found him resting on his laurels this particular afternoon. Wolf's efforts on behalf of Soviet Jewry, trapped behind the Iron Curtain, had resulted in the abrogation of the Declaration of Cooperation between the American Bar Association and the Association of Soviet Lawyers. Wolf had embroiled himself in a more controversial matter when he assisted in the defense of John Demjanjuk, an Ohio auto worker accused of being the infamous Nazi concentration camp guard known as Ivan the Terrible.

But today, a Jewish concern that had never garnered much media attention caught the eye of Bill Wolf. "Yemenite Jews Said Facing Danger of Extermination," read the headline in the *Jerusalem Post*. The article quoted David Shuker, chairman of the Public Committee for Yemeni Jewry in Israel. Shuker waxed sorrowful about the arrival in North Yemen of two thousand terrorists from Lebanon, their presence in the country being ample cause for the Jews to the onset of a wave of robberies, rapes, and abductions. Shuker also claimed that many Yemenite Jews had been forced to convert to Islam, "If we remain silent," he wanted, "there will be a Holocaust just like there was in Europe. The accusing finger will point at Israel." Wolf hadn't known there were still Jews in Yemen. Like almost everyone else, he assumed that they had all been brought out by Magic Carpet. Who was David Shuker, he wondered, and what were his sources? Wolf decided to find out more and then to do what he could to help Shuker's cause.

A former neighbor of Wolf's in Phoenix, Dvora Rosenberg, had moved back to her native Israel, where she now resided in Kfar Sabba, north of Tel Aviv. Wolf phoned and asked her to help him locate David Shuker somewhere in Israel. Rosenberg complied, and on October 12, when Wolf arrived in Israel to meet with Shuker and other members of the Yemeni community in B'nei Ayish, she acted as an his interpreter. On learning the whole sad story of how the Jews in Yemen were not allowed to leave the country, and how they and their relatives in Israel had been out of touch for thirty years, Wolf promised to take up their cause.

Returning to Phoenix on October 21, Bill Wolf decided to begin by publicizing the situation. He authored a letter describing the condition of the forgotten Yemeni Jews and sent it to the editor of every Jewish newspaper in the United States and Canada, many of whom decided to print it. Readers of Wolf's message were invited to respond to him in Phoenix, whereupon he would mail them written documentation to substantiate his account of the problem, as well as instructions on contacting and influencing their senators and representatives. Determined to launch a national movement in the United States to rescue the Jews of Yemen, he founded the American Council to Save Yemenite Jewry.

The mailbox at the offices of Arnold & Wolf was soon filled with responses from across North America. Interviews with Wolf appeared in the columns of the *Boston Jewish Advocate,* the *Canadian*

Jewish News, the *Philadelphia Exponent*, the *San Diego Jewish Times*, and the *Sentinel* of Chicago. And the people whom Wolf touched began to contact their representatives in Washington. One of the Congressmen they got to was Mel Levine of California's 27th District. In a letter to some of his Jewish constituents, he replied that "the State Department and the Israeli Embassy have told me that they are aware of the assertions in the article and are conducting an investigation. However, considering the circumstances surrounding the flow of information, it has been very difficult for either of these agencies to confirm the allegations. In my own contacts with various agencies that monitor Yemenite Jewry, I too have been unable to confirm the article."

By December, Wolf began think that picketing the North Yemen embassy and the United Nations would be a good way to expose the human rights abuses against the Yemeni Jews. To his way of thinking, the most effective strategy for helping Jews in other countries was to mount a massive publicity campaign and involve the United States government, as had been the case with Soviet Jewry. The United States maintained relations with North Yemen; it could pressure the Yemeni government economically and politically. Wolf would ask his Senator, Dennis DeConcini, to speak with Secretary of State James Baker about it.

But first the Yemen Arab Republic would have to admit that its policies were discriminatory. Mohsin al-Aini, the Yemen Arab Republic's ambassador to the United States, vehemently denied the allegations made by David Shuker and Bill Wolf. "The Yemen Arab Republic has about a few hundreds of Jews in the country, who enjoy full citizenship and religious freedom, protection of the police and security forces," he responded to those who sent him letters of protest. "They are free to leave the country, and free to return at will. However, there is no truth to the rumor that Yemenite Jews are suffering certain hardships not experienced by other Yemenites, nor is there discrimination against any ethnic or religious minority. They are never forced to convert to Islam." The Yemen Arab Republic was stonewalling.

Richard Shifter, Hayim Tawil, Pierre Goloubinoff,
Laurie Johnson, David Ransom, Bill Wolf.

Hayim Faiz with Pierre Goloubinoff, 1995.

Chapter Three

"YOU MUST GO TO AMERICA!"

November 29, 1988

Pacing the length of a nearly deserted lounge in London's Heathrow Airport, David Shuker nervously awaited his flight to New York. He had never set foot in the United States; he could not speak a word of English; and he felt the weight of the world on his shoulders, for his daunting task was to save the forlorn Jews of Yemen by rallying support for them across the Atlantic Ocean. Sent to America by his fellow Yemeni Israelis, Shuker deemed his solo mission nearly impossible, but such were the burdens of public service. During an interminable El Al stopover in Britain, he pondered the progress he had failed to see since founding the Public Committee for Yemeni Jewry.

David Shuker had been born in the rapidly changing Yemen of the 1940s. His family had fled the Najran region intact and flown the Magic Carpet in 1950, settling in the Holy Land with thousands of other Jews from Yemen. Shuker's tender age at the time of his migration had enabled him to quickly acclimate to life in the equally youthful State of Israel; he had studied at a Jerusalem yeshiva and served in the army. His life of civic dedication had commenced soon afterwards, persisted through his 1964 marriage to his sweetheart, Naomi, and was coming to a climax in 1988 with his fight for the release of Yemen's silent prisoners. In 1980, Shuker had been elected chairman of the town council of B'nei Ayish, a village outside Rehovot comprising 220 families, 150 of them of Yemeni origin. Many of his neighbors wept day and night over family members they had left behind in the Yemen Arab Republic, never to be heard from again. Most of the separated families had come in 1961 and 1962, expecting loved ones to follow in their footsteps after selling off homes and businesses at the right price. But once the Republic was declared, it was too late.

Tidbits of discouraging information would occasionally filter out of Yemen through tourists, and Shuker, as village leader, would scrutinize the desperate Hebrew scrawls rife with biblical references. The verse "In the morning thou shalt say, 'Would it were even!' and at even thou shalt say, Would it were morning!'", from the conclusion of the terrifying account in the twenty-seventh chapter of the Book of Deuteronomy of the afflictions that would befall the people of Israel for infidelity to the Lord, characterized the pleas of one letter writer. There were requests for siddurim, Torah scrolls, and phylacteries, and for help in getting out of the country. Heart-rending excerpts of notes smuggled out of Yemen were occasionally printed in periodicals along with the eyewitness testimony of an American named DuWayne Terrell. And Shuker would read copies of messages mailed prayerfully to Yemen by his fellow Israelis: "We are healthy and strong and lack nothing but the sight of your precious faces. I plead with you to come to Israel and be with me. I weep daily from missing you. I have no one here."

As a result of Israel's 1982 invasion of Lebanon, thousands of PLO fighters formerly based there had to leave, and many of them found a haven in North Yemen. Rumors abounded that they had taken over Yemeni synagogues as mosques and were forced Jews to become Muslims. A Red Cross representative had delivered to the United States a cassette recording of an eighty-year-old man named Yhia ibn Daoud Suberi. Nearly blind, the Yemeni Jew was pining for the sight of his children and grandchildren in Israel. Stories like this one were what had driven Shuker to try to rescue his brothers and sisters from the desert land to the south., but surprisingly, his efforts met with resistance from some of his fellow Jews.

David Shuker decided to set up an official committee in B'nei Ayish to coordinate attempts to pressure the Israeli government to act. Shlomo Grafi, a friend of Shuker's, aided him, urging other towns and villages to join, asserting there was strength in numbers. Shuker posted proclamations and distributed fliers in the streets, beseeching Jews to get involved. An active member of the World

Union of Jewish Students, a convert named David Ben Avraham who had once traveled to Yemen, weighed in with his commitment of support. But Shuker first had to contend with those who disparaged him for making so much noise. He had to prove that the situation in Yemen really was intolerable and that its Jews really wanted to come to Israel. The documents and letters he had assembled would have to be corroborated by testimony from actual visitors to the Republic.

Years before Shuker's journey across the Atlantic, his office had initiated a massive letter-writing campaign to publicize the plight of the Jews of Yemen at the highest levels of the Israeli body politic. Shuker authored memoranda to Tovah Herzl in the Diaspora Section of the Foreign Ministry, to Knesset member Zevulun Hammer, and to Abba Eban, the former Foreign Minister, and met with several ranking officials. His meeting with Eban was disheartening. A former Foreign Minister of Israel, of all people, exclaimed incredulously, "Are there *still* Jews in Yemen?" Shuker also staked out the offices of the major Zionist agencies, only to be adamantly and definitively told, "There are no more Jews in Yemen." Nevertheless, by steadfastly providing accurate information to selected members of the Israeli press, he began to gain credibility.

Despite denials by the Israeli government, David Shuker convened a meeting in B'nei Ayish on November 9, 1984. The Public Committee for Yemeni Jewry was born, Shuker its chairman. The Committee's other members represented communities populated with Jews of Yemenite origin: Tzion Zahavi from Yavneh, Shalom Cohen from Gedera, and Yitzhak Katabi from Kiryat Ekron. Shuker's friend, Shlomo Grafi, joined the crusade, as did a man from B'nei Ayish whose parents and siblings were still trapped in Yemen, Moshe Atzar. Rabbi Ovadiah Ya'avetz of Kiryat Ekron also lent his name to the Committee's membership list—his father had been the chief rabbi of Saada. A chronology of Shuker's struggle for publicity was printed in the respected journal *Aphikim*.

With the arrival of 1985, Shuker was determined to go to the top. Prime Minister Shimon Peres, Foreign Minister Yitzhak Shamir, and Shlomo Hillel, Chairman of the Knesset received polite letters on the crude stationery of the Public Committee for Yemeni Jewry. The Committee demanded that the Israeli government achieve open mail communication, reunification of families, and aliyah of all remaining Yemeni Jews. Other epistles were regularly sent to cabinet officials and Knesset members. Minister for Absorption Yaakov Tzur responded to the Committee that "the government of Israel is doing everything it can for the Jews of Yemen, but I am not liberty to divulge exactly what it is doing. . . . Anything that must be done will be done."

As June approached, Shuker adopted a more personal approach, inviting several Knesset members to visit B'nei Ayish. Once ensconced in the warm setting of the village, they would hear first-hand from the separated families and view documentation of Yemeni Jewry's plight. Rabbi Meir Kahane of the Kach party—the Jewish Defense League of Israel—responded enthusiastically to Shuker's invitation and affirmed his support for the cause. Knesset member Haika Grossman also came to B'nei Ayish, later writing to Shuker: "I talked directly to Prime Minister Peres about your problem and my wonderful visit to the moshav. Peres promised that one of his men would stand by your side and keep in close contact, monitoring the situation closely so as not to do more damage than good. According to Peres, the older Yemeni Jews do not want to leave but the younger ones do. They desire open communication, but that is very difficult."

David Shuker grew more optimistic. He had successfully made Yemeni Jewry a topic of conversation among the country's most powerful figures. And in July, Meir Kahane submitted a formal request to Knesset Chairman Shlomo Hillel: he wanted the case of the Jews of Yemen to be put on the Knesset docket. Kahane, a notoriously vociferous speaker who had earned the reputation of an extremist, took it for granted that the government had the power to extricate Yemen's Jews; he wished to impress upon his fellow Knesset members the proper way to absorb them once they arrived. Standing at the Knesset podium, Kahane stated, "Who does not feel the pain of our brothers and sisters in Syria and Yemen? Whose heart does not break upon hearing what is happening there?" Kahane chided an earlier generation of Israelis for stripping the Yemeni Jews alighting from the Magic Carpet of their beliefs and customs, denigrating their traditional lifestyle, in a misguided paternalistic effort to "westernize" them: "I speak of the complete spiritual genocide of Yemeni Jewry." The leader of the Kach party digressed to dwell on the Israeli government's actions of decades before.

"I would like to cite one example, just one, of this horrible matter, from testimony given to me by the rabbi of Ponovitch, Rav Kahanamen. He relates that he once overheard the children who attend his school reciting, in the Grace After Meals, 'May the merciful one avenge us, may the merciful one punish Zipporah.' Rav Kahanamen didn't know what the root of these statements was and thought it might be a Yemeni custom. Afterwards he found out that it referred to a notorious Zipporah, a youth leader who had shaved off the peyot of these children, their pride, and forced upon them a lifestyle of desecrating the Sabbath," Kahane related. His speech was quickly spiraling into yet another Knesset free-for-all on matters of the heart.

"We heard here that for the Jews of Yemen, the only thing they have remaining is the siddur," Kahane continued. "I worry that when they come to Israel that will be taken from them as well. Therefore I state that without a guarantee that each and every child and all Jews of Yemen . . ."

"It is better to be a Jew without peyot here than a Jew with peyot there!" interjected Meir Cohen-Avidov of the Likud party.

"I'm not so sure, sir," Kahane continued, unfazed, "if some Yemeni disc jockey [in Israel] is better than a boy sitting in Sanaa learning Torah from his father or grandfather. This disc jockey, he is not what we dreamed of. Therefore I say that I am a Zionist just like everyone else here. I, too, made aliyah. But I am not prepared to see more of what I saw in the prison in Ramla. I sat there and saw Jews from Yemen who were murderers. How many Jewish murderers did there used to be in Yemen? How many rapists and robbers? How many? Who even heard of such a thing? There is no doubt that I am in favor of all the actions, but on the stipulation that when they get here, at the airport there be a delegation of rabbis who will ensure that all Yemenis who emigrate here will be absorbed into a religious setting. And if not, I'm not sure if it is worthwhile to bring Yemeni Jewry here."

David Shuker soon learned that discussions in the Knesset would never translate into action on behalf of the Jews of Yemen. Even increased awareness of their plight among Knesset members could accomplish little. The Public Committee for Yemeni Jewry would have to search elsewhere for assistance. In August 1985, the Committee published a manifesto which included the most current information on the status of Yemeni Jewry. It said, among other things, that "the exact figure of Jews living in the Yemen Arab Republic is unknown. According to a recent PLO statement, North Yemen plays host to a Jewish population numbering 4600, while South Yemen and Bahrain are also known to have a scattered, indigenous Jewish population. There are 33 major Jewish concentrations in North Yemen, most located in the districts north and northeast of Sanaa." The list would be made available on request by one David Ben Avraham. The manifesto added that there were at least 615 families in Israel which had direct blood connections with Jews in North Yemen. These families had in recent months staged peaceful demonstrations and participated in forums on behalf of their estranged kin.

The Committee's manifesto proffered a description of the daily life of Yemeni Jewry, broaching the sensitive but pressing subject of assimilation: "Although Jews have lived in Arabia for thousands of years, what could be the major cause of Yemeni Jewry's diminution as a people is assimilation." Several cases of marriages between Jewish women and Muslim men had been documented. Jewish males outnumbered Jewish females in Yemen by a great margin, thereby "posing a very serious problem to a community strictly bound by ethnic and religious purity." The living conditions of the Jews of Yemen were not viewed as desperate: "Jews enjoy religious freedom for the most part and are free to travel between cities. They own private vehicles and even operate taxis. They are private home-owners as well as land-owners, and are usually occupied with their trade at the family's workshop joined to their home. Religious books and artifacts are primarily received from the ultra-orthodox Neturei Karta of New York, owing to this group's good rapport with Yemeni officials, primarily for their anti-Zionist stand. However, demagogic literature serving to defame Israel may prove counter-productive, in the long run, to the welfare of Jews wishing to leave Yemen. The Jews of Yemen remain under the local protection of sheikhs and are required to pay an annual Islamic poll tax of one hundred rials, the equivalent of about $20."

On the topic of oppression, the manifesto noted that "in 1980 the government of the Yemen Arab Republic arrested four local Jews on suspicion of espionage for Israel. Periodic arrests of Jews have been common practice since 1975. The country's security system is paranoid about anti-government sentiments." Repatriation efforts were also mentioned: "The Association for the Advancement of Culture in Israel, under the directorship of Mr. Ovadiah Ben-Shalom, and David Shuker's committee have been stalwarts in efforts designed to bring out Yemen's Jewry." A plan had been submitted in private meetings with Chaim Herzog, Israel's President; Arie Dulzin, Executive Chairman of the Jewish Agency; Moshe Gilboa, director of the Diaspora Department of the Foreign Ministry; Hayim Aharon, director of the Department of Immigration and Absorption of the Jewish Agency; Akiva Levinsky, Treasurer of the Jewish Agency," and others.

The Public Committee for Yemeni Jewry's manifesto concluded by listing the names of Yemeni officials who were directly responsible for the safety of the country's Jews or could exercise some influence on the government's consideration of emigration en masse. Among them were Ibrahim al-Hadrani, a recorder at Yemen's Foreign Ministry; Ahmed Omari, mayor of Sanaa; Hamoud Bedar, local governor of Saada; Prime Minister Abdul Aziz al-Ghani; Abdallah Shalamish, deputy director of National Security; and Al-Kathi Ghalib Abdullah Rajeh, the Islamic judge of Sanaa.

On August 18, Shuker received a letter from the Jewish Defense League of Israel. The Kach party promised to pressure American politicians who might be able to persuade the U.S. government to offer financial aid to Yemen. This, in turn, might induce the Yemenis to relinquish their iron grip on the Jews of Yemen. Meanwhile, the Brooklyn-based *Jewish Press* ran a story about Meir Kahane's party enlisting in the cause of the endangered Yemeni Jews. A Brooklyn man named Robert M. Goldstein, the head of Matan Petroleum Corporation, read the story and fired off a letter to Kahane stating that he was "willing to put together a petroleum production program in Yemen, and after repaying the loans and deducting expenses, to give to the Yemeni government say 95% of what would normally be profits to the production company; or to drill elsewhere, perhaps in the U.S., and give the Yemeni government say 75% of the profits for development projects in their country, if they will allow the exit of all their Jews." Goldstein admitted that this was just the bare outline of a plan, but for Shuker his letter meant that news of Yemeni Jewry's plight was being disseminated, albeit at a snail's pace.

As 1985 faded into 1986, the families David Shuker represented grew more despondent. When Moshe Atzar wrote to Prime Minister Peres, his tone became increasingly brusque: "We turn to you. In the name of the families who have relatives and parents in Yemen, we have information that their situation is very difficult. They are burdened by police scrutiny, and it is difficult for them to make a living. We turn to you in these trying times in this method because we do not wish to go to the newspapers lest it make things worse for our dear ones there. We are concerned for their personal safety." Hinda Zindani of B'nei Ayish joined the ranks of the letter-writers. Her plea to Peres read: "Since I came from Yemen in 1961 I have not had any contact with my parents and my family, the branch left over there. My worry for their plight is great, and I cannot find respite for my soul any hour of the day or night. I know the great hardships of the Jews left in Yemen, and I know the Israeli government is doing what it can. Nevertheless, I ask you to meet with me personally."

By December 1986, David Shuker had abandoned all hope of Israeli intervention. For too many years his committee had been advised to proceed silently and refrain from public demonstrations. The Israeli government had monitored Shuker's every movement, tapping the phone line in his house. Shimon Peres was no longer Prime Minister, for Yitzhak Shamir had replaced him in a bizarre parliamentary compromise necessitated by the inability of either to obtain a majority in the Knesset, and he had become Foreign

Minister. In this capacity Peres received a nasty memo from the Public Committee for Yemeni Jewry, reminding him that "we have sat down with you a number of times and with Yitzhak Shamir, and in my humble opinion we have completely wasted our time with you. We see no ray of light in the darkness in the welfare of our brothers, parents, and relatives, the remnant. It is high time we stop the silence and go out into the streets and squares and raise hell about your laziness and see who can help. Therefore, we request of you that you make it more urgent in your eyes to deal with the plight of Yemeni Jewry. I know the Jews of Yemen are close to your heart."

No longer expecting anything from the Israeli government, Shuker turned to diplomats from other nations. Perhaps there was a way to communicate with the Yemeni government directly, without Israel as the middleman. Shuker telephoned a certain number in Cairo three times, vainly pleading with the secretary to the Yemeni ambassador to Egypt for an appointment—or at least for some words on the phone with him. Request denied. Undaunted, Shuker opted to head south for a meeting with the ambassador anyway, even though Yitzhak Shamir had cautioned him that an arrest would ensue. When Shuker arrived in Cairo and begged admittance to the embassy of the Yemen Arab Republic, he was denied a meeting with the ambassador. After all, he didn't have an appointment.

As the new Prime Minister of Israel, Yitzhak Shamir would now bear the brunt of the animosity of Israel's disgruntled Yemeni community. Moshe Atzar composed a personal entreaty to him on December 10, 1986, saying, "We have waited seventeen months for action since first meeting with you. There are among us those who never expect to see their fathers alive again. I found out about the death of my mother in Wadi Amlah in miraculous fashion, nevertheless I never merited seeing my mother and father since I left Yemen in 1962. I hope to greet in the Land the faces of my brother Shalom and my three sisters. I bring up my personal situation so you will view the situation more urgently, Mr. Prime Minister. In past months, we have gotten word that the situation is getting continually worse. Their sources of sustenance are dwindling with the advent of new technology in Yemeni society. Machines are replacing Jews as sources of leather and jewelry and other crafts. The strength of the rial has fallen 10 percent since 1962. Thus, the market for jewelry and other luxury items has fallen. Most Jews who started off in Yemen as well off are no longer so wealthy."

In January 1987 Shamir received a petition signed by families in Rehovot, B'nei Ayish, Rishon Letzion, Kiryat Ekron, and Gedera who had relatives trapped in the Yemen Arab Republic. His aides responded to the petitioners with assurances that the Israeli government was doing "everything we can." Shuker was incensed. He angrily wrote to Gidon Tadmur in the Diaspora Department of the Foreign Ministry that "for years we have pleaded our case. But apparently the blood of our relatives is not red enough to merit your effort and attention. We think we will have no choice but to raise our voices in public to the world community as to the welfare of Yemeni Jewry."

Shuker believed he had found a friend in Gidon Tadmur, who responded to his wrathful letter with genuine concern. Members of the Public Committee for Yemeni Jewry convened in Tadmur's Foreign Ministry office on December 22, 1987 for a strategy session. It was resolved that the Diaspora Department would strive to achieve family reunification with renewed vigor, presenting the plight of Yemeni Jewry before the United Nations in Geneva and before the boards of important Jewish organizations. Meanwhile, the Committee would proclaim its message from the podiums of synagogues across the world. Shuker frequently updated Tadmur by sending him copies of letters smuggled out of Yemen along with translations and elucidation's. On May 23, 1988, Shuker had an urgent request of Tadmur: Secretary of State George Schultz will arrive in Jerusalem in June, and the Committee wants a private meeting with him to discuss the deteriorating situation in Yemen. Please arrange for private meetings with Shamir and Peres. But Tadmur came up empty-handed.

The ninth day of the Jewish month of Av is the saddest day on the Jewish calendar, a 24-hour-period of mourning that commemorates the destruction of Solomon's Temple by the Babylonian king Nebuchadnezzar and of the Second Temple by the Romans, as well as a series of other tragic events in Jewish history. David Shuker understood that the Ninth of Av was an appropriate time to commemorate the ongoing modern-day tragedy of the Jews of Yemen. He organized an ambitious and well-publicized prayer service for Yemeni Jewry to be held in the shadows of the Kotel—the sole extant retaining wall of the magnificent Second Temple—on the night of July 23, 1988, the Ninth of Av. While Jews from all over the world sat on the cold, stone plaza before the Western Wall and chanted lamentations, relatives and supporters of the Jews trapped in Yemen gathered to pray for their brothers and sisters trapped in the desert thousands of miles to the south. Kaddish, the mourner's doxology, was recited for two Jews murdered in Yemen in 1986, a memorial candle was kindled in their memory, and chapters from the Book of Psalms were recited. The ceremony tugged at the heartstrings of Shuker and the members of the Public Committee for Yemeni Jewry. They vowed to forge ahead with their struggle.

But where to turn? All of Shuker's outlets for relief in Israel had been exhausted long ago, his sources of counsel all but dried up. But in this moment of need, a man whom Shuker had never met provided him with advice from afar on his next step. It was embodied in a recently smuggled message from Yhia ibn Daoud Sabari, the brother-in-law of Moshe Atzar. Sabari's wife had been abducted by a local Muslim sheikh. The troubled man's fiery words were neatly penned in narrow columns that made his note look like a Torah scroll, but they painted a fearful picture of Jewish life in the Yemen Arab Republic.

I am asking from you in all the words of the world that this letter will be taken to the attention of the government of the Jewish state or to any human being in the world willing or able to help us. It is very important that the world realize that we are grieving much and that we are persecuted every day, every hour of our life. And as the Torah says, "New sorrows push away the old ones." I am asking you to bring this message to the representation of America because America has an embassy in Sanaa and they have the power to prevent the persecutions that are hanging above our heads or even to take us out of Yemen. Every week new persecutions are burdened on us. They consider the dogs better than us since they started to listen to the radio and to see the television about the Arab repression in Israel. They say that they will retaliate on us for everything that is done to their brothers there. We do not have anything to rely on except the Holy One and you, our brothers. Please send this letter also to America, you our brothers that have the ability to implore their government in our name and tell them about the sorrows and the humiliations in which we live in Yemen. If you ask who died among us and who already became a Muslim since you left, I shall say that the question is irrelevant because we are all as if we were already dead. We are in delivery pains. Either we will die very soon or we will go to our country. But one thing is certain. We shall not sit humiliated any more among the Arabs. Since my legal attempts to regain my wife, I cannot go any more to visit my brother there out of fear that the local sheikhs will slaughter me. Brother, they are now overwhelming us physically. I am looking for a protector for my daughter because I fear that the Muslims will try to kidnap her as well. Finally, I implore to go and say a blessing in Jerusalem for all of us.

When Sabari's two sisters, Dhabia and Hawida, read his missive, they bolted to Shuker with tears streaming down their cheeks. "David," they cried, "you must go to America! It's our only hope." At first, Shuker disregarded the pleadings of his friends. Not only could the Committee not afford to sponsor such a trip, but Shuker could barely speak the English language. "Don't worry about that," the families had always responded. "God will help you." The plight of the Yemenite Jews, they felt, stirred up an emotional element that would shatter any language barrier; Shuker could still be an eloquent spokesman. During one such conversation, Pierre Goloubinoff was in Shuker's house. He tried to dissuade Shuker from crossing the Atlantic. His mission would be futile if he couldn't utter a word of English, Goloubinoff warned.

But David Shuker was determined to go to the United States. If he could not secure freedom of travel for Yemen's Jews, perhaps he could at least arrange brief family reunifications in a neutral third country not ensnared in the Arab-Israeli conflict. Shuker unsuccessfully sought American donors for a plane ticket. The American Jewish Committee denied his request for funds in a letter dated August 8, 1988.

> Thank you for turning to us. We here value our long-time association and are flattered that you turned to us for help. I have explored your interest on both sides of the ocean and find that while we are deeply committed to the welfare and condition of the Jews of Yemen, as we have been in the past, we are not set up to pay for transportation costs for your representatives to come to the U.S. for the stated purpose of winning support and funds for your enterprise. I beg you to understand that this is not a reflection of low priority or, worse, indifference to the plight of Yemenite Jews. What I should like to point out, however, is that different Jewish organizations have different functions and responsibilities and your particular concern about the Jews of Yemen belongs more appropriately to quiet efforts initiated by the Israel government as well as rescue and relief organizations, such as the Joint Distribution Committee.

By October, Shuker had not been able to locate a benefactor for his mission. And then, from out of the blue, he was visited by a lawyer from Phoenix, Arizona, named Bill Wolf. As was recounted earlier, Wolf had read an article about Shuker's work in the *Jerusalem Post* and had gone Israel to meet the man at the helm of the Public Committee for Yemeni Jewry. Impressed by Wolf's dedication to the cause, Shuker saw the divine hand at work when Wolf pledged his utmost cooperation, volunteering to be Committee's advocate in the United States. Immediately on his return to Phoenix, Wolf authored a letter about Shuker and sent it to every paper on a list he received from the *Greater Phoenix Jewish News*. And then he founded a one-man organization called the American Council to Save Yemenite Jewry.

These developments made Shuker more comfortable about his proposed journey to America. Thanks to Wolf, his name had begun to be publicized there. Moreover, one of the Committee's founding members, Shlomo Grafi, had recently moved to New York, so there would be someone to chauffeur him around that massive metropolis. When Avraham Melamed, a lawyer and one-time Knesset member for the Mafdal party, threw his significant financial support behind him, Shuker knew that he could no longer delay the inevitable. He purchased a ticket on El Al for November 29, armed himself with a document of consent from Rav Ovadiah Yaakov Ya'avetz of Kiryat Ekron, and even grew a beard in anticipation of a potentially raucous confrontation with the Satmar Hasidim, who had refused to help him work for the freedom of the Jews of Yemen.

And now Shuker was standing by himself in a Heathrow Airport lounge, profoundly aware of his mission to stanch the abundant tears of his friends. Images of his decade of unrewarded work raced feverishly through his mind. The petitions, the meetings, the pleas and the deaf ears on which they had fallen. Shuker could not sit sedately and map out a strategy, as is often done by the business people making the London–New York run, for he was venturing blindly into a strange country whose language he could not speak and whose political barons he knew not. His only fragment of a plan was to meet with Yosef Bacher of Neturei Karta, who had sent his Hasidim to scour Yemen's north country for Jews. Bill Wolf had invited Shuker to spend a Shabbat as his guest in Phoenix. Otherwise, Shuker had one month in which to inspire a movement that would free the Jews of Yemen; this in a country already supersaturated with lobbies and advocacy groups and Jewish organizations. Shuker feared that he would be invisible—just one more among the thousands of emissaries of Israeli charities landing annually at John F. Kennedy International Airport, vying for the spotlight and the cash. He prayed that he would at least be able to set the wheels of liberation in motion. But for now, he could do nothing but pace as he awaited his boarding call. The date was November 29, 1988, precisely nine years after the plane carrying DuWayne Terrell had touched down in Sanaa, spawning a crusade to save the Jews of Yemen.

A boarding call, and seven hours later the 747 carrying David Shuker descended into a blustery New York autumn afternoon. Shlomo Grafi was waiting patiently in the International Arrivals Building for his former neighbor, and the two embraced heartily when Shuker appeared. Then Grafi drove Shuker to his home on Ocean Parkway in Brooklyn for some sustenance and slumber. The next morning, Grafi escorted his friend around Manhattan. The sun shone brightly, but the chill in the air was unbearable for an Israeli accustomed to a more temperate climate. Shuker spent his first day in New York marveling at its magnificent edifices and the never-ending stream of cars and trucks clogging its highways and avenues, bridges and tunnels. But no game plan emerged from Shuker's first day of activity. That night, a telephone call was placed to Shlomo Grafi's home. The voice on the other end politely asked to speak with David Shuker. "Who knows I'm here?" Shuker thought as he was handed the receiver.

A man named Moshe Barr-Nea happened to know Shuker was in New York. "I've heard about you, I've heard about your work," Barr-Nea told the Israeli. "And I am at your service." Moshe Barr-Nea was approaching his sixties, but quite energetically. He offered to be Shuker's guide in the United States. "If your mission is to be a success, you'll need someone experienced to help you navigate the Jewish organization ocean that is New York." Barr-Nea would make the proper introductions and prepare English-language material on the Jews of Yemen. He would take Shuker from neighborhood to neighborhood and from one newspaper interview to another. And Barr-Nea would provide the names of people to whom Shuker could turn for assistance. Shuker replaced the receiver and paused to reflect on the conversation. "This is the hand of God at work," he told his friend Shlomo.

On December 4, David Shuker queued up on an unending line of men that wrapped itself around an entire city block in Crown Heights, Brooklyn. He stood in the bitter cold for three hours before finally passing through the entrance of the building at 770 Eastern Parkway. Then he was whisked into a room where the Grand Rebbe of Lubavitch regally sat, flanked on either side by an attendant and bodyguard. In accordance with a long-standing custom intended to make it possible for every visitor to have the means to make a donation to charity, and thereby earn the merit of this all-important mitzvah, the Lubavitcher Rebbe silently handed Shuker two dollar bills and blessed him. When Shuker asked to speak with the Rebbe about the Jewish remnant trapped in Yemen, the attendants, wishing to keep the line moving, pushed him aside. Suddenly the Rebbe began waving his hand as if calling his Israeli visitor back. The attendants brought Shuker over to the Rebbe's chair, and he leaned over and whispered into the Rebbe's ear for a full minute, describing the devastating physical and spiritual predicament of the Jews of Yemen. The Rebbe listened attentively and handed Shuker with two more crisp dollar bills, uttering a concise prayer as well: "*Bracha v'hotzlacha liyhudei Teiman.*" "Blessings and good fortune for the Jews of Yemen."

December 6 saw David Shuker and Shlomo Grafi seated in the New York offices of the American Jewish Congress, where they submitted an overview of Yemeni Jewry's plight. Shuker's encounter with the AJC officials was a rude awakening for him. They had no idea that there were still Jews in the Yemen Arab Republic; worse, they seemed unsympathetic to his request for help. How come the eighty thousand Yemeni Jews in Israel aren't making any noise, staging massive protest rallies, as we did for the Jews of Russia or Ethiopia? Why are you coming to us and not to organizations in Israel? Shuker's reply, through Grafi, was honest enough: We *did* try to get help in Israel, we've tried for forty years, but to no avail. The AJC officials promised to do what they could to help with Shuker's three requests: unrestricted mail correspondence and telephone calls, the right to send food, clothing, and religious articles, and permission for Yemeni boys to come to the United States for religious training.

Next came a meeting on December 15 with Abraham Bayer, the influential director of the Foreign Affairs Office of the National Jewish Community Relations Council. Shuker told Bayer that the members of his organization in Israel was so distraught that they were ready to sell their belongings to buy tickets to America so that they could demonstrate at United Nations Plaza, on the steps of the Capitol, and in streets outside uncooperative Jewish organizations. Bayer was taken aback by Shuker's intensity but seemed quite distressed about the Jews of Yemen. He vowed to exhort the myriad organizations under his organization's umbrella to take an interest in the situation. In addition, he arranged meetings for Shuker with some of New York's top political figures.

An America West jet ferried David Shuker from the frigid to the balmy on Friday, December 16. Upon landing in Phoenix that

morning following a five-hour flight, Shuker immediately felt more
at home. Palm trees and cacti lined the immaculate streets of the
Arizona city; rays of sun glistened off the shiny buildings, but this
time it was actually warm. The attorney William J. Wolf greeted
Shuker in the terminal at Sky Harbor International, and the two
lunched Israeli-style at the kosher deli Wolf owned in uptown
Phoenix. Eager to make his new friend's brief stay as productive as
possible, Wolf drove him to a prearranged interview with the *Greater
Phoenix Jewish News*. Then he took Shuker to his home, where he
met Wolf's wife and two young daughters and was given a room in
which to bed. As the day waned and the Sabbath approached,
another guest arrived. It was Pierre Goloubinoff, who had
conveniently just moved with his wife, Cohi, to Wilmington,
Delaware, where he worked at the experimental station of Du Pont
de Nemours and Company. Goloubinoff would be Shuker's
translator during his dialogue with the Phoenix Jewish community.

On Saturday morning, Shuker, Goloubinoff, and Wolf walked a
mile to the Beth El Synagogue. When they arrived, Shuker's mouth
dropped open. As an Israeli, he knew very little about Conservative
Judaism. Now he in for one shock after another: worshipers pulling
up to the synagogue in automobiles on the holy Sabbath, men and
women sitting together in the pews, the cantor using a microphone,
women called up to the Torah. But Shuker knew his mission was to
save lives; he remained in the sanctuary and waited his turn at the
podium. It came after the Torah-reading, when Shuker addressed the
assembly of five hundred worshipers in Hebrew while Goloubinoff,
standing beside him, translated into English. So in Phoenix, on
December 17, 1988, the members of Beth El learned of the reclusive
remnant of Jewish existence in Yemen, the glorious era of Magic
Carpet, and the distressing situation that had ensued. After services,
Shuker was surrounded by people eager to ask questions. Another
lecture was scheduled for Sunday evening at the Jewish Federation
offices, where Goloubinoff delivered a richly detailed eyewitness
account of Yemeni Jewry. Shuker asked everyone in attendance to
write letters of protest to Senators and Congressmen; the community
pledged its unconditional support for his activities. Pierre

Goloubinoff flew back to Delaware and Cohi, gratified to have provided some assistance, and David Shuker flew back to New York, wondering where his travels would take him next. For the moment, it was the home of Shlomo Grafi on Ocean Parkway.

Shuker spent the next few days communicating his message to various elements of Jewish New York's tapestry. On December 21 he addressed senior citizens in the Bronx and met with Mordehai Yedid, the vice-consul, at the Israel consulate in Manhattan. Yedid stressed that the Israeli government was quietly making a major effort on behalf of the Jews of Yemen; Shuker countered by reading him the letter from Yhia Sabari. Shuker was interviewed by the *New York Jewish Week* and the Jewish Telegraphic Agency. He met the vice president of the Hebrew Immigrant Aid Society, who promised to help pay the cost of bringing Jews from the Yemen Arab Republic to the United States and then immediately to Israel. But HIAS could only do this once Yemen's Jews were set free; it had little power to sway politicians to secure that freedom.

Shuker also found someone in Washington, D.C., to rally support for his cause among the capital's Jews. George Lichtblau was a retired U.S. Foreign Service officer who had visited the Yemen Arab Republic in 1984 while investigating the condition of migrant workers in the oil-producing countries of the Persian Gulf. North Yemen was on his itinerary because it was where many of the itinerant oilfield laborers came from, and he brought with him a shipment of prayer books and religious articles for the local Jews from New York's Satmar Hasidim. The State Department, at the behest of the Satmar Rebbe, had authorized his doing this because if sent by ordinary mail the articles might have been confiscated. The embassy of the Yemen Arab Republic gave its approval only after receiving assurances that the materials were strictly religious in nature and contained no "Zionist propaganda."

But official government permission failed to relieve Lichtblau's nervousness as he journey to the villages surrounding Saada. He knew that when Noel Grove, a *National Geographic* staff writer, had visited Yemen in 1979, his vehicle had been attacked by three young men who pilfered his luggage, precious camera bags, food, and bedding. And hidden in Grove's bedding had been a cache of Jewish books intended for Jews living in Ghuraz. "I had promised during my first tour of Yemen to bring them books," Grove wrote in *National Geographic*. "I had not the heart to tell the villagers that their holy books, after a journey halfway around the world, had been lost only twenty-five miles from their home."

Lichtblau gladly related his findings to David Shuker. Most of the Yemeni Jews, he said, were managing reasonably well as small traders, artisans, or even laborers. Since a large proportion of Yemeni men worked in Saudi Arabia and other oil-producing states, the Jews had no trouble finding jobs. In fact, the labor shortage had driven up wages and prices, and the money sent home by the migrant workers contributed to the country's relatively high standard of living. Remote villages had electricity produced by local generators. Many families now owned automobiles and television sets. On his return from Yemen, Lichtblau added, he had written an account of his visit for the *Jewish Monthly* and sent letters to other publications. And he had contacted a man who had knew the Jews of Yemen firsthand: David Ben Avraham from Moshav Azriel. Lichtblau promised Shuker his cooperation.

David Shuker's next Sabbath in America was spent on the Upper West Side of Manhattan. As the masses of last-minute Christmas shoppers scurried by outside in the rain, Shuker stood inside the Lincoln Square Synagogue before fifty men and women, telling tall tales that happened to be true. Shuker spoke of Yemeni Jewry's glorious history, of Shalom Shabbazzi, the magic of Magic Carpet, and the tragic current situation.

After leaving Lincoln Square, Shuker went up West End Avenue to meet one of the great masters of Jewish song, Reb Shlomo Carlebach. A balding and white-bearded Reb Shlomo was sitting among his Hasidim in the Carlebach Shul, enjoying a lyrical Sabbath hymn, when Shuker entered. Shuker told the room that he was an emissary from a desperate community in Israel whose closest relatives were trapped in Yemen; that his decade-long struggle had produced no fruit in Israel, so he had come to America as a last resort; that he had seen the hand of God during his travels here and had rallied some support for his cause. "I didn't know there were still Jews in Yemen," Carlebach exclaimed. "Now we must work to free them." Reb Shlomo kissed Shuker on the forehead and blessed him for his efforts on behalf of the Jewish people. Shuker was not permitted to leave the small synagogue until he had sung a famous Yemeni Sabbath hymn, *Dror Yikra*. Soon, the entire room was crooning along with David Shuker and Shlomo Carlebach, and Shuker knew that the same haunting melody was being hummed in the mud-walled houses of remote desert villages thousands of miles away.

Forty representatives of the World Union of Jewish Students gathered in New York on Monday, December 26, to learn about the plight of the Jews of Yemen from David Shuker and Pierre Goloubinoff, who had driven up from Delaware with his wife, who was outfitted in traditional Yemeni garb. Shuker urged the audience to write to their representatives in Washington; as Jews they were bound to all Jews scattered throughout the world. Afterwards, Goloubinoff placed an excited phone call to Israel. "I didn't believe Shuker would be successful here," he told Moshe Atzar, "but I was one hundred percent wrong!" Goloubinoff gave Atzar a brief account of Shuker's activities. The hundreds of families anxiously awaiting his return would learn that the man they had begged to abandon his job, wife, and four young children was working wonders in the land whose streets are paved with gold.

Part Two

CRACKS BENEATH THE DOOR:

DECEMBER 1988–MAY 1990

Chapter Four

MEETING AT STERN COLLEGE

December 28, 1988
The organization that would deliver the remaining Jews of Yemen from their captivity was born in the final hours of 1988 in a drab conference room on an upper floor of the building that houses Yeshiva University's Stern College for Women. Outside, on the teeming sidewalks of Lexington Avenue and 34th Street, Manhattan's daytime inhabitants hurried home from work, huddled in heavy coats, blissfully unaware of the history being made in the nondescript edifice where young women brave a double curriculum of religious and secular studies. Inside the overheated building, David Shuker had no idea that he was launching a movement that would eventually succeed where governments had for decades failed. Shuker was soon to return to Israel, and he was speaking at the establishment of an organization whose lofty goals paralleled those of his own group. But this organization was being set up to function on American soil. It would eventually be known as ICROJOY, the International Coalition for the Revival of the Jews of Yemen. And it would trigger my involvement in the rescue of the Jewish remnant trapped in the northern villages of Yemen.

Those remote enclaves atop craggy, sun-baked hilltops lay three generations removed from my consciousness in the final weeks of 1988. Yosef Tawil, my father, a man of enormous strength who had been orphaned at the age of two, had married Esther, a fellow Yemeni whose family had arrived in the reviving Holy Land in 1899. Together, they had raised two sons and two daughters in the foothills of East Jerusalem. When that part of the ancient city came under Jordanian control after the 1948 War of Independence, the family's

87

life had continued in New Jerusalem, the capital's western sector, which the next generation of Tawils learned to call home. My formal schooling there had inculcated within me a love for the peoples and cultures of the past, an appetite for knowledge which was responsible for my arrival in America in the 1960s. Judaic Studies at Philadelphia's Dropsey College, then a Ph.D. from Columbia University, with a major in Assyriology and a minor in Northwest Semitic. With the magical title "Dr. Tawil" came teaching positions at New York's City College, the Jewish Theological Seminary, and Yeshiva University. With a little luck came my romance with Dalia and our marriage in 1968. On August 5, 1969, our son Arik was brought into the world. That same day we established residence in the Washington Heights section of Manhattan; I have lived there ever since.

The activities of "Dr. Tawil" had thus been strictly confined to the cloistered halls of academia. As a professor of Hebrew Studies at Yeshiva, I enjoyed my forays into comparative Semitic philology, a field most would deem dry. My younger days at Dropsey and Columbia had inspired a passion for poring over ancient documents and then writing of my discoveries for all sorts of arcane journals. My later days were divided between the library and the classroom at the Washington Heights campus of Yeshiva, and the neighborhood had been my home for over nineteen years those final weeks of 1988. Any visitor to the Judaica section of the Yeshiva University library would immediately have noted the table I had commandeered; half-hidden behind the mountains of tomes distinguishing it, one would find a short, white-haired man scribbling illegible notations on a pad, dozens of texts spread out before him. Such was the image and niche I had carved for myself. And as the Fall 1988 semester waned, the tension among the young men filling the library for study was palpable. Finals season was upon us.

It was in that sterile setting that I received a telephone call in my tiny office at Yeshiva from someone named Moshe Barr-Nea. A man from Israel by the name of David Shuker was in New York, Barr-Nea said, and his mission was to save the isolated Jewish remnant in Yemen. Shuker represented the families in Israel that had been denied contact with their relatives for over twenty-seven years, Barr-

Nea continued, and he desperately needed my assistance. As one of the few New York academics of Yemeni origin, I had apparently earned a name for myself. But were there still Jews in Yemen? I too had been under the impression that Magic Carpet had airlifted every last Jew from the land of my great-grandparents.

Yes, there were still Jews in Yemen, David Shuker revealed bitterly when we met for the first time in an East Side coffee house later that week. Shuker, accompanied by Barr-Nea and Shlomo Grafi, described in painstaking detail the plight of the Jews of Yemen. After decades of Israeli inaction, Shuker said, he was turning to the United States government for help. But someone was needed to spearhead the colossal effort that would be necessary, and, so he claimed, I was the man for the job. I was overwhelmed: first by the news, then by Shuker's entreaty. So I hesitated, asserting that my days of teaching and writing were already quite full, if not burdensome. Taking on such a task would force me to sacrifice precious time. When I embark on a project, I throw myself into it, I told Shuker, and because this was a matter of great significance, I could not give him an answer right away.

But upon subsequent contemplation, I knew that Shuker had found a sympathetic ear. He came across as very warm-hearted, and his sincerity was crystal-clear. I pondered the sorrow I would have felt if I had been denied any contact with my parents for my entire adult life. My wife, Dalia, had also been unaware that Yemeni Jewry still existed, but she supported my adoption of their cause. We decided to answer David Shuker in the affirmative even though we hadn't the slightest idea of how to go about saving the Jews of Yemen. I met with Shuker again, and together we arranged to bring ICROJOY into the world at Stern College on December 28.

It was a young organization, lacking, among many other assets, a budget. Publicity was accomplished mostly through word of mouth. Telephone calls were placed, and Barr-Nea used a copier at the New York offices of Betar, the youth movement associated with Israel's Likud party, to print up fliers announcing a gathering of citizens intent on saving Yemeni Jewry. Yeshiva University's Rabbi M. Mitchell Serels, supervisor of the school's Sephardic and Yemeni

Studies programs, used his clout to free up a conference room. A correspondent from the Jewish Telegraphic Agency was invited. And Shuker, Barr-Nea, Grafi, and I all prepared short presentations, eagerly anticipating a respectable turnout.

By 5:00 p.m., night had already fallen and the few New Yorkers who had learned of our gathering began to fill the room. It was a meticulously orchestrated event. While Barr-Nea passed around petitions for the audience to sign, I delivered a brief overview of the protracted and glorious history of the Jews of Yemen, urging everyone in the room to join in our effort. Shuker followed with an emotional account of Yemeni Jewry's daily hardships and struggles, accenting his statement with the words of Yhia Sabari, the man whose letter had so grieved his relatives in Israel. Photographs of the Jews near Saada were passed out to the fifty participants. And after Barr-Nea talked of American Jewry's obligations, I was nominated as chairman of the new organization whose goals were spelled out in a declaration drafted that very night in Stern College.

Tevet 21, 5749
December 28, 1988

WHEREAS, the plight of the last remnant of Jews stranded in North Yemen demands the alerting of the American people and the mobilization of all Jewish communities and organizations;

WHEREAS, recent and desperate calls for help received from North Yemen confirm earlier reports and fears that the condition of Yemenite Jewry is deteriorating rapidly,

WHEREAS, the suffering of these persecuted Jews is unbearable and the sorrows of divided families grow more intolerable,

THEREFORE, we, the undersigned, hereby establish the

NATIONAL COALITION FOR THE RESCUE OF THE JEWS OF YEMEN

in New York City, the 20th of Tevet, 5749, December 28, 1988.

OUR AIMS:

1. To inform the United States Congress, American and world opinion, the media, Human Rights institutions of the United Nations and the civilized world of the plight of the Jews of North Yemen.
2. To demand the release of Jewish women raped and kidnapped.
3. To stop the enforced conversion of Jews to Islam and allow the "Marranos" to return to their Jewish faith.
4. To demand that the Government of North Yemen allow religious freedom, the opening of yeshivot and the sending of holy books and religious articles.
5. To demand that the Government of North Yemen allow the sending of relief to the starving and hungry.
6. To demand that the North Yemen authorities preserve sacred Jewish places, ancient synagogues, cemeteries and especially the graves of revered rabbis, teachers and leaders.
7. To demand that the Government of North Yemen allow the free exchange of letters and telephone calls between families divided for decades.
8. To demand visits between members of these families.
9. To demand the reunification of these families.
10. To demand that Jewish students be allowed to leave for study abroad; to allow students from abroad to come for study of the rich heritage of Yemenite Jewry.
11. To demand that the Government of North Yemen stop the oppression of these Jews by PLO terrorists evacuated from Lebanon.
12. To alert Jewish communities, organizations and congregations, to mobilize them for the RESCUE OF THE JEWS OF NORTH YEMEN!

The undersigned:

Sir Moshe Barr-Nea, initiator

Shlomo Grafi
Rabbi Mitchell Serels, Yeshiva University, Institute of Yemenite Studies
Prof. Hayim Tawil, Ph.D.
David Shuker, Chairman, Public Committee for Yemenite Jewry, Israel

Weeks later, the organization would become "international" and would fight for the "revival," not the "rescue," of the Jews of Yemen. The semantic advice on these points was given by government officials once our group began making a name for itself.

Among the fifty members of the audience in the conference room on December 28 was Lester Smerka. The bearded scrap metal dealer had learned of the meeting from his wife, Dalia, secretary at Betar's New York office, where our fliers were being run off. Smerka had come to Stern College intrigued by the existence of a beleaguered remnant of the Jewish people; he brought with him years of experience as a volunteer for Amnesty International, a major worldwide body dedicated to ending human rights violations. Smerka belonged to an Amnesty International "working group" which was assigned the cases of individuals around the world and devised and implemented strategies to right the wrong being perpetrated. Usually, a petition or letter-writing campaign achieved positive results, and Smerka felt that his expertise would be an asset to the young, resource-strapped organization whose birth he had witnessed.

Smerka and I had known each other in Washington Heights for twenty years. Our children had played together in the streets of the neighborhood at the northernmost tip of Manhattan. Now, Smerka would become my right-hand man in my newfound role of rescuer. He was a hard worker, and his counsel was accepted wholeheartedly. It was Smerka who convinced the founding members of ICROJOY to approach their problem through the perspective of human rights violations, namely the dearth of communication between the families in Israel and the families in Yemen, the cruel travel restrictions, and the abduction of women. Smerka became ICROJOY's director of correspondence, eventually filling reams of paper with letters to the most unlikely of addresses. He wrote to the general manager of the Document Control Division at U.S. Postal Service Headquarters inquiring about mail service to Yemen; to the director of Peace Corps Yemen about teaching English to the Jews; to the ambassadors of European countries doing business with Yemen. Smerka would write about the abduction of women: the daughter of Daoud Katabi and the daughter of Yakub Faiz and the daughter of Yosef Khubani, all of whom had been forcibly converted to Islam in order to wed Arabs.

Sitting silently near Lester Smerka in the second row of the Stern College conference room was a thirty-five-year-old woman who immediately caught my attention. She held a yellowed copy of *Yediot Aharonot* and kept waving her hand throughout the question-and-answer session. Perhaps it was her persistence that prompted me to ignore her. But after the program came to a close, she approached me undeterred, and uttered the words that would focus ICROJOY's efforts in its youngest days and give it its earliest victories: "My uncle and cousin were murdered in 1986, and I'd like to know what you're going to do about it."

Sarah Dahari Halla was an American citizen who lived in the Bronx, I soon learned. She came from one of the largest clans in Raida, a mountaintop village north of Sanaa; Avraham Yitzhak Halla and Yhia Yehudah Halla, her uncle and cousin, had been murdered by Arabs in 1986 according to a story she had found in *Yediot Aharonot* and now displayed to ICROJOY's members. Sarah, herself born in Athar, had flown the Magic Carpet at four years of age to the Holy Land, where her nuclear family settled in Rosh Ha'ayin. But the Hallas left behind uncles, aunts, and cousins in the Yemen Arab Republic. Sarah was the first Halla to reach the shores of America. She, too, had not heard from her relatives in three decades. At that time I wasn't even able to locate Raida on a map, but I knew enough to realize that Sarah Dahari Halla would be a valuable asset. ICROJOY had found an American citizen who could claim a direct family relationship with Jews trapped in Yemen. Perhaps she would be reason enough for the U.S. government to get involved in the plight of Yemeni Jewry.

But as the conference room in Stern COllege emptied, the

horrifying truth entered my mind. I had agreed to become the chairman of an organization intent on freeing a people whose location and condition I did not yet fully grasp. This was a job for the Jewish organizations whose time and money were earmarked for Jews the world over. How could I spearhead such an effort with neither a mastery of the details nor a firm emotional attachment to the cause? Would I be able to continue publishing, or would my scholarly reputation perish along with time for Dalia, Arik, and twelve-year-old Taphat?

These questions weighed heavily on my conscience as the world ushered in 1989 and Yemeni Jewry entered its twenty-seventh year of isolation, and they dominated my mood when I received a telephone call from Delaware: My name is Pierre Goloubinoff, I work at DuPont, I've heard of your appointment to the chairmanship of ICROJOY, I would love to meet you and help you. Goloubinoff claimed he had been in Yemen and could provide me with the details I lacked. So Goloubinoff and his wife drove up to New York from their Delaware home. They spent the entire night at my apartment, impressing upon me a sobering assertion: any delay in freeing the Jews of Yemen would cause them to disappear. Goloubinoff stressed that the Jews he had met were spiritually fragmented from living among thirteen million Muslims. Preserving their religion, in the era after Magic Carpet had drained Yemen of most of its Jews, was proving difficult to say the least. Pierre and Cohi presented pictures and slides, most of which shocked me and broke my heart.

"You know nothing about present-day Yemen!" Goloubinoff exclaimed.

True, I knew about the distant past, the ancient educational system, the geography and topography, the legendary Jewish communities, the scholars and mighty leaders, soil that had produced generations of Zion-seekers. But Magic Carpet had changed all that. The world of the remaining few was crumbling around them.

"You bet your broken penny I know nothing about Yemen," came my reply. Of course I was immersed in Yemeni culture, but I was ignorant of the most practical and relevant facts. So Goloubinoff filled me in. The two of us—two university scholars—conversed through the early morning hours, Goloubinoff imploring me to fight vigorously for Yemen's Jews. Overnight we became steadfast friends as Goloubinoff described how the shortage of religious articles would soon spell disintegration for the Jews of Yemen. There were no teachers left in the country, and economic pressures were eroding the father-son tradition by which customs and beliefs were handed down. A rich new life with Yemeni brethren would be possible in Israel, if only we could get them there. Sleep eluded me that night. Time was running out.

Soon after Goloubinoff returned home, the valuable information he provided was supplemented by even more recent eyewitness testimony from two different sources. The first, a couple from Washington, contacted me with the news that they had just returned on December 20 from a fifteen-day exploration of the scattered Jewish communities of northern Yemen. Barbara and Doug Gephen had visited Yemen on United States passports, and their story was added to ICROJOY's meager files:

On arriving in Saada, the Gephens headed for the marketplace, hoping to find some Jews. They looked here and there for men with peyot selling silver jewelry, and they soon found what they were seeking. There were several Jews seated at three tables in the middle of the Saada suq, and the Gephens cautiously approached them. Western tourism was virtually nonexistent in Yemen, so their presence drew enough attention to hamper attempts at private conversation. As wealthy Westerners the Gephens were indeed a spectacle, and the Jews, in consequence, were apprehensive about discussing anything other than their merchandise. Only one man nervously responded to the Gephens' questions. How many Jews are there in Yemen? "One thousand," the man answered. Do they want to leave? He made a gesture with his hand that the Gephens interpreted to mean "right away." Moments later, the Yemeni whispered in English, "Police!" and quietly drew their attention to a military post located not far from where the Jewish vendors were hawking their wares. Barbara and Doug realized that conversation in public could not continue.

Only later, in the privacy of their mud-walled, sun-beaten houses, did the Jews of Yemen open up to Barbara and Doug. The Gephens stayed in the home of a bright, amiable twenty-two-year-old. The young man had been married at fourteen and was the father of two; two other children had been claimed by the high infant mortality rate in the Yemen Arab Republic. "Our house is your house," the Gephens' hosts often chanted. Apparently it was many others' as well, for it was teeming with grandmothers and grandfathers, uncles and aunts, nephews and nieces, and an assortment of more distant relatives all blessed with large families. Posters of President Salih adorned the walls. "To show that I am a good Yemeni," explained the young man. The Jews slaughtered their own meat and made their own wine and matzah for Passover. And they were quite perplexed by a certain Jewish ritual Barbara and Doug described to them: the bar mitzvah.

Once, when they returned to the Saada market after having visited a Jewish home, an elderly Jew lumbered by, and without even making eye contact, muttered "Shalom." When the Gephens turned around, he had all but disappeared among the narrow and congested alleyways. "It almost didn't matter," wrote Barbara Gephen. "The connection was made and perhaps that was all that was needed or possible."

The Gephens reported that the Yemeni government had become more watchful of the Jewish community in the past five years, relocating their Saada stalls to an area closer to the military post. The Jews were permitted to study Hebrew and speak it among themselves, but were forbidden to do so with foreigners. Of course, they were prohibited from sending any letters abroad. Moreover, the Yemeni government was using Neturei Karta's anti-Israel stance to justify its opposition to aliyah. The Gephens estimated that a full twenty percent of the Jewish populace was trying to assimilate by changing names and cutting off *peyot*.

ICROJOY's second source of current information was a continent-hopping Manhattanite who had made Yemen a stop on one of his travel adventures. Isaac Pollak was a sprightly antiques collector with an eye for Jewish artifacts. In 1988, he and a friend were scouring Ethiopia for relics of its Jewish past. In Addis Ababa, the capital, he met a ninety-year-old woman who ran a small hotel and also happened to know where one could find Jews across the Red Sea, in the Yemen Arab Republic. So from Ethiopia Pollak ventured eastward, crossing the straits of Bab-el-Mandeb and landing in Sanaa in his quest to find Yemeni Jewry. Upon returning to New York, Pollak gave us an account of his experiences there.

Pollak said that there were traces of a once-flourishing Jewish culture everywhere in Yemen. He had seen many houses, now occupied by Arabs, that were decorated with Stars of David or had scarred doorposts from which mezuzahs had obviously been gouged. Before Magic Carpet, these had been Jewish homes. Pollak's first sighting of a Yemeni Jew came one morning when a motorcyclist whizzed by, trailing a billowing cloud of dust. The motorcyclist's long, black *peyot* were flying in the wind, and a large *kufta* covered his head. Tzitzit hung from the four corners of his robe-like garment. Pollak's first direct contact with Yemeni Jewry occurred in the Sanaa marketplace. Six Jewish men were lurking cautiously in a silver shop, toting chickens. They were incommunicative at first, until Pollak realized that to converse with them he would have to squat down as if patronizing the stall and whisper his queries. Meanwhile, the Jews would stand behind their wares, their eyes nervously darting back and forth. They mumbled that their most critical needs were phylacteries and Bibles and anything written in the mother tongue. Pollak was chided for using the word "Israel" in conversation and was taught to employ the expression "The Exotic Land" in its place.

Before long the New Yorker found himself immersed in their world. The prayer shawl and phylacteries Pollak had brought with him for his own daily prayers did not return to New York. The Jews he met were in desperate need of all sorts of ritual objects and holy texts. When Pollak displayed a wallet-sized photograph of his son, Ovadiah, the room erupted in laughter. Unfortunately, the Ramaz School pupil was wearing the small, knit yarmulke popular among modern Orthodox children; the Yemeni Jews did not believe Ovadiah was Jewish because the kipah did not cover his entire head. Pollak was moved by their sincerity and authenticity, and he wrote in his journal on October 21, 1988 that

they have nothing. They have no Torah scroll that they desperately want, no tefillin, no seforim, they are simple and I find them beautiful. Their eyes dart about to see who is here and who is watching and listening. They get rocks thrown at them, and their peyot pulled. When a Muslim looks at them, they look away. An incident we actually saw is that one of these Yemeni Jews was walking down the street . . . and there was a Muslim walking toward him. And the Jew gives way, and the way the Muslim of Yemen went by was in an insolent fashion. It was his right to walk down the center. And it was the Jew's obligation to walk around him or cross the street.

As I slowly digested the information provided by Pierre Goloubinoff, and the eyewitness accounts of Barbara and Doug Gephen and Isaac Pollak, the crime being perpetrated against the Jews of Yemen grew more heinous in my eyes. The situation was indeed desperate. I had resolve on my side, but what next? My sole connection with the seat of government in Washington, D.C., had been as a tourist. My experience lay in taking Dalia, Arik, and Taphat to see the White House during visiting hours, not in negotiating with officials at the State Department. And ICROJOY had already discovered that there was little chance that the major American Jewish organizations would back us. In early December, we had sought the advice and support of the lobbying virtuosos in those organizations with their much-vaunted Washington connections. David Shuker, Shlomo Grafi, Moshe Barr-Nea, and I had sat in the Park Avenue South offices of the National Jewish Community Relations Advisory Council (NACRAC) with representatives of the American Jewish Congress, the Joint Distribution Committee, the Conference of Presidents of Major Jewish Organizations, and the Anti-Defamation League, all of whom seemed to be quite laid back about Yemenite Jewry. They had done nothing for thirty years and had no intention of radically changing their apathetic policy.

This had served as my rude introduction to the world of the American Jewish organizations. I had been elected to speak for Shuker on this particular occasion, and I told those gathered that the time had come to save the Jews of Yemen. Families in Israel and the Yemen Arab Republic were living in extreme distress, I said, and I called upon the country's Jewish organizations to help us to help the helpless. But Shuker, Grafi, Barr-Nea, and I were then asked questions we found largely insulting. How many Jews are there in Yemen? We estimated the number to be between one and two thousand, but our cross-examiners' involvement seemed to hinge on there being a more dramatic number. I responded that if even one Jew was trapped in Yemen, he deserved his freedom.

Abraham Bayer was at the helm of NACRAC in December 1988. At the meeting's conclusion he admitted that the Jewish organizations represented in the room could foster support in Washington for our cause. But first we were asked to write letters to Yemen in anticipation of the Jews there writing back. It would be a futile exercise, I exclaimed. Twenty-seven years had passed with scant correspondence. Come back in three or four months with responses from Yemen, we were nevertheless told.

"I don't understand your attitude," I remarked. We are here to help to save the Jews of Yemen. This is *your* responsibility. This is exactly what you did for the Russian Jews. You also have to do it for the Jews of Yemen, even though there are so few of them. You turned the world upside-down for the freedom of one Jew, Natan Sharansky. What about the precious children in Yemen? *You must be getting paid so much to do something!* David Shuker, sitting behind me, could not understand a word of English, but the sense of my outburst did not escape him. I had surprised even myself. But upon reflection much later I came to understand the anemic response to our pleas. Israeli intelligence had quieted the Jewish organizations in the United States precisely as it had done to the separated families of Israel.

"We don't like being patronized," I told the organizational representatives. We were a scrawny human rights group, but we had our pride, and we had emerged discouraged from the NACRAC meeting. A subsequent encounter with two delightful women from the Joint Distribution Committee had proved equally disappointing. At the JDC, Lester Smerka and I were treated respectfully and sympathetically, but inaction marred the congeniality.

By the time ICROJOY was born at Stern College later in the month, its members knew they would be on their own. America's Jewish organizations had not offered to help. And since ICROJOY was made up of ordinary citizens, it embarked on a policy I labeled "Mr. Smith Goes to Washington." Several Smiths, to be precise. We would somehow make contact with sympathetic members of Congress and government officials. We would bombard them with reams of paper containing thousands of signatures. Then, hopefully, we would meet them face-to-face. But in the earliest days of 1989, as an El Al 747 carrying an exhausted David Shuker touched down at Ben-Gurion International, ICROJOY had no list of accomplishments. It existed only on a piece of paper locked away in a darkened apartment in Washington Heights.

January 23, 1989

A daily plenary session in the heart of Jerusalem. As Aryeh Gamliel, representing the Shomrei Torah party, approached the Knesset podium, a sheaf of papers in his hand, the few members of the Israeli parliament present at the early morning hour assumed poses of relaxed attention. Gamliel began his remarks. Once again, the Jews of Yemen were on the Knesset's agenda.

> Mr. Chairman, honorable Knesset, I have read a statement that was made by senior officials of the Yemeni government who were speaking about the situation of Yemeni Jewry. Dr. Abdul Karim al-Iryani, the Yemeni Foreign Minister, says in an interview with an Egyptian newspaper that "the Jews live in security, peace, and tranquillity, their lines of work have not changed, and they benefit from all their citizens' rights, economic and social." He also explains that the "stance of Yemen on this issue"—not allowing Yemeni Jewry to leave Yemen—"stems from resolutions of the Arab League which ban the return of all Jews in Yemen, Egypt, Iraq and all other nations to Palestine or any other place in the world." And he says they stand with the resolution of the Arab League regarding this matter.

The Egyptian ambassador, Ahmed al-Shajeini, also speaks similar words, that the Jews dwell in security and tranquillity.

It is natural for them to say such things. Natural that they cover up everything that is happening over there. But we know that the condition of Yemeni Jewry is very difficult. They find themselves in a terrible predicament. And I find it obligatory to bring before the government and the Knesset a letter that arrived not long ago, which was mentioned in the statement of Knesset member Ovadiah Eli. I wish to read you the heart-breaking letter of a Yemeni Jew, without names and identifying details.

The letter says: "Dear precious brothers in the Land of Israel, with the help of God we will see you soon. Our brothers, your letter arrived and we rejoiced mightily because you are living. We, among whom the curses in the Torah have been fulfilled, our sons and daughters have been given over to another nation, and we long to live like Jews. They steal our daughters away, our sons they convert. We beg that this letter be swiftly transmitted to the government of Israel, so they see that we are in pain, and lowly and disgraced. And even in the Torah it is written: later hardships will make you forget the earlier ones. Please turn to the government of the United States. We know that the United States has the power to help, and can pressure Yemen to free us, and allow us to live like human beings. We have no savior but the Holy One, blessed be He. You there in the Land of Israel live in tranquillity, and all our cries are not heard by you, even though we put matters of life and death on your heads. Cry our cries to the government of Israel. Tell them of our pain and disgrace. With my right hand I have uttered an oath obliging you to work for us. We who have signed this letter find it hard to believe how the government of Israel is unable to turn to countries like Britain and the United States. All we want to do is live like human beings. And we ask: where is the government of Israel at this time? Where are the Jews in other countries? Are they waiting until there are no more Jews left in Yemen? Are they waiting for the Messiah? Thousands of myriads of peace be upon you, precious brothers. With God's help, soon, in Jerusalem."

Gamliel looked up at his colleagues and paused. "I wish to deal with this topic before a full session of the Knesset."

January 24, 1989
An organization that hopes to make history must have a mien of respectability and an air of professionalism. To win Washington's

confidence, ICROJOY needed an image that would radiate both ardor and aplomb. We began acquiring the necessary bells and whistles shortly after the Stern College meeting, and our metamorphosis came on the heels of an innocuous letter from the New York offices of Morrison Cohen & Singer, attorneys at law. Peter D. Weinstein, a lawyer with this firm, was moved by the plight of the Jews of Yemen and wondered if his legal expertise could be of assistance.

His assistance would, in fact, prove indispensable during the first six months of ICROJOY's existence. Accompanied by Saadia Shapiro, the legal advisor recruited for ICROJOY by Shlomo Grafi, I traveled beneath Manhattan by subway to meet Peter Weinstein. He recommended that ICROJOY enhance its image by becoming a nonprofit corporation with tax-exempt status. Weinstein, aided by Shapiro, would facilitate its transformation into ICROJOY, Inc. The change would be an elaborate affair, requiring ICROJOY to enlist "name" members for a board of trustees, register with the Charities Bureau of the New York State Attorney General's Office, and satisfy certain statutory membership provisions before receiving a Certificate of Incorporation. The corporation would ultimately have no members. I would be its president, Lester Smerka the vice-president, Shlomo Grafi the secretary, and Saadia Shapiro the treasurer.

Next, ICROJOY needed a home. Operating out of my apartment would only destroy its credibility, imparting the appearance of a neophyte's haphazard operation. ICROJOY deserved its own office, its own telephone line, and its own conference room, and we found both in a Lower Manhattan building near City Hall. I had been renting space at 150 Nassau Street in which I ran a modest, one-man financial-aid consulting firm, a decent source of income back when I had been between positions at the Jewish Theological Seminary and Yeshiva University. But once I became a full-time professor at Yeshiva I had begun to neglect the business. So 150 Nassau Street became the address of ICROJOY. Stationery and business cards were ordered, along with receipts for donations. ICROJOY even adopted a logo, borrowed from a Yemeni federation in Netanya. The logo depicted two shofars heralding freedom while two Jews danced in the shadow of a Tree of Life. A student of mine from Yeshiva, Boaz

Mori, began circulating petitions on Yeshiva's Washington Heights campus, as did Cohi Goloubinoff in Philadelphia.

Now ICROJOY only lacked an honorary board of trustees with which to attain a degree of prestige. The young organization would be successful if it could approach Washington with an appropriate degree of humanitarian authority and sincerity. I turned to an old colleague of mine from the 1970s, Elie Wiesel. Almost twenty years earlier, when I was teaching Hebrew at the City College of New York, Elie Wiesel had lectured there on history and philosophy. We had remained friendly through my stint as Professor of Bible at the Jewish Theological Seminary, which Wiesel frequented. By 1989, Wiesel had been crowned a Nobel laureate, and his name was a symbol to the world of the uniquely Jewish ability to triumph amidst great suffering. I went to Wiesel's East Side apartment with his harrowing personal history as a Holocaust survivor in mind, and after explaining the plight of the Jews of Yemen I importuned him to head the board of ICROJOY.

Woven into the fabric of Jewish tradition by the prophet Zechariah is the image of the Messiah humbly arriving in Jerusalem perched on a white donkey. "Rejoice greatly, O daughter of Zion, shout, O daughter of Jerusalem. Behold, thy king cometh unto thee, He is triumphant, and victorious," Scripture says. Recurring dreams of Zechariah's vision had pervaded Elie Wiesel's nights as he wasted away in the embers of Auschwitz, he told me. And along with that image came the legend that the Messiah's point of departure would be Yemen. The legend had generated great eschatological fervor among Yemeni Jewry over the centuries and had, as well, inspired Wiesel's special interest in the Jews of Yemen, whose authenticity and simplicity much impressed him. He gladly joined the board of ICROJOY.

Many other names would eventually be added to ICROJOY's swelling masthead. Professor Hayim Soloveitchik, my wife's cousin, was one of them. Several Senators would also lend their prestige to ICROJOY: Alfonse D'Amato and Daniel Patrick Moynihan of New York. Dennis DeConcini of Arizona, Robert Graham of Florida. The list further included Representative Benjamin Gilman of the House Foreign Affairs Committee, Mel Levine, a Jewish

Congressman from California. James Scheuer representing the Bronx, and Stephen Solarz representing Brooklyn.

The executive board of ICROJOY, Inc., would come to include William J. Wolf, Esq., as "Western States Director." Wolf had dismantled his American Council to Save Yemenite Jewry when ICROJOY was born. Bernard Englard, my personal accountant, also graced the masthead with his name, as did Legal Counsel Saadia M. Shapiro, Esq. ICROJOY's executive secretary was Tova Najjar Weisberger, a delightful young woman whom I had met at a Columbia University symposium. She had learned of ICROJOY from a newspaper article and offered us her secretarial services.

On paper, ICROJOY indeed became a formidable force. But in truth, it was a financially strapped group that could barely afford the rent for its office at 150 Nassau Street. And by the end of February 1989, no groundbreaking conquests lay beneath its veneer.

February 26, 1989

Lester Smerka's tiny Volkswagen was rapidly approaching retirement as it wheezed and sputtered down I-95. Four hours after leaving New York, Lester, Shlomo Grafi, and I were finally entering Maryland, and the soreness in our legs had been replaced by a combination of optimism and trepidation in our hearts. We were embarking on ICROJOY's inaugural expedition to Washington with no room for plane fare in the budget. Tomorrow we were to meet an aide to Senator DeConcini in the morning, and Laurie Johnson, the officer on the Yemen desk in the State Department's Office of Arabian Peninsula Affairs in the afternoon. Bill Wolf was flying in from Arizona to join us, and Pierre Goloubinoff would be driving down from Delaware. Perhaps the wheels of liberation would soon begin to turn.

As cars of more recent vintage accelerated to pass us in the Maryland countryside, we reviewed ICROJOY's negotiating strategy. It was an approach we would later deem immensely productive. First, shunning hyperbole, we would never provide inaccurate information. We would be precise. There were approximately fifteen hundred Jews in Yemen, not four thousand or ten thousand. We understood their economic and social status in Yemen. When discussing the abduction of women, we could only confirm five such cases. For each episode, we had a date and the names of an abductor and a victim. Government officials would not be fooled by irresponsible allegations of mass kidnappings; five abductions would be enough to make a case.

Secondly, we would set aside our personal religious or Zionist predilections. True, in our heart of hearts, we all wanted to see the Yemenis in the Holy Land; resettlement in the Diaspora would not be redemption in the spiritual idiom of Yemeni Jewry. But these were issues of the heart, and more universal human rights issues had to be our focal point. Washington was not interested in King Solomon and Imam Ahmad, in Zechariah's prophecies and Shabbazzi's poetry. A strictly "human rights" perspective could only call for freedom to emigrate from Yemen to someplace else—whether Israel or Antarctica could not be a concern. We were an American organization, and our goal was to reunite separated families. We could not state that we wanted to bring Yemeni Jewry to Israel, and we could not have direct contacts with the Yemeni families there, the Sabaris and the Atzars and the Zindanis. As we well understood, the very name "Israel" was politically charged in the Arab world, and the Yemen Arab Republic, however much it might wish to cooperate on the emigration issue, was officially a staunch supporter of the PLO.

Finally, we were keenly aware of the amount of pressure the United States could put on the Yemen Arab Republic. As one of the Middle East's more moderate and relatively stable nations, Yemen had been consistently rewarded with American dollars. In 1987, the United States had given Yemen over $34 million in aid, and from 1946 to 1985 it had given $300 million in economic and military loans and grants. Development credits from the World Bank to Yemen totaled $533 million, and the United States wielded great influence over the International Development Association and the International Bank for Reconstruction and Development, which funded the World Bank. There was certainly plenty of leverage if we could persuade the government to use it.

ICROJOY was going to Washington prepared. It had contacted the few public servants it felt were sensitive to human rights issues, especially those who had previously fought for Soviet Jewry. It had studied the hierarchy in the State Department and knew who was responsible for managing U.S. relations with the Yemen Arab Republic. And ICROJOY was willing to spend quality time with the assistants to the aides to these officials in its effort to attract the attention of the leaders of millions of people. Credibility and competence—not an enormous budget—would be paramount, we hoped. The Volkswagen pulled precariously off I-95 and headed for a Holiday Inn outside Washington.

February 27, 1989

Clothed in suits and ties, the five-member ICROJOY delegation hit the pavements of the District of Columbia, ready for the first day of the organization's official activities. Bill Wolf the Arizonan had arranged a visit to the offices of Senator DeConcini, co-chairman of the Commission on Security and Cooperation in Europe, but ICROJOY never met the Senator this particular morning. Instead we were greeted by Mike Amitay, his young aide on Jewish issues, and Jane Fisher, another staffer. They were attentive as we explained the plight of beleaguered Yemeni Jewry. Pierre Goloubinoff delivered eyewitness testimony from his three visits to Yemen, and Lester Smerka and I both spoke.

Not knowing whether we had succeeded in impressing the urgency of the situation upon them, we proceeded to the State Department's Near Eastern Bureau. In its office of Arabian Peninsula Affairs, we sought the officer on the Yemen desk, Laurie Johnson. An appointment with her had been surprisingly easy to solidify. I had simply called her on the telephone and introduced myself as "Professor Hayim Tawil." The title "professor" seemed to be a magical word that opened doors and garnered me much respect, something it had not accomplished in thirty years in the classroom. Johnson, friendly and outgoing over the phone, consented to receive our delegation on the 27th of February. We were greeted that morning in the by a tall, sophisticated brunette somewhere in her thirties; we found that in person Johnson was also convivial and respectful.

"You and I are going to make history," I told her. "We're going to get the Jews of Yemen out." ICROJOY repeated its presentation, and Goloubinoff produced his map of Yemen's scattered Jewish settlements. But ICROJOY's briefing was superfluous; Johnson demonstrated that she, along with the entire Near Eastern Bureau, was already quite familiar with the plight of Yemeni Jewry. Now, however, having learned about the existence of icrojoy, the State Department might begin to see some signs of concern on the part of American Jewry.

The same held for Stanley Roth, the aide to Brooklyn Representative Stephen Solarz, and Los Angeles Representative Mel Levine, whom we visited next. We certainly were the first American Jews to broach the topic of Yemeni Jewry in Washington, for throughout the 1980s the World Union of Jewish Students, the American Jewish Committee, the Anti-Defamation League, and B'nai B'rith had voiced their apprehensions to the government. As a result, the United States embassy in Sanaa had been told to keep an eye on the Jews in Raida and Saada. But that was the extent of the action taken.

February 27 drew to a close in the Rayburn Building, where members of Washington's congressional elite wage biennial battles for office space. One such piece of prime real estate was the plush office of Michael Van Dusen. A trim, tanned man whose distinguished gray hair complemented his dignified mannerisms, Van Dusen had served for a decade as staff director of the House Subcommittee on Europe and the Middle East, chaired by his boss, Congressman Lee Hamilton, Democrat of Indiana. An appointment with Van Dusen had been arranged through a few phone calls to Hamilton's office. Van Dusen was one of the many Washington insiders who would prove crucial to ICROJOY's cause.

America's relationship with the Yemen Arab Republic, we soon learned, vexed Van Dusen. As the most populous state in the Arabian Peninsula, boasting strong ties with Saddam Hussein's Iraq and protectorates in the Horn of Yemen, Yemen was of great interest to the United States. In the early 1980s, American companies had commenced drilling for oil there. Yemen's tenuous relationship with its nearest neighbor, the gigantic Saudi Arabian oil machine, was complicated by the horde of Yemeni migrant workers streaming north across the unmarked desert border. America's cautious stance toward the Yemen Arab Republic, Van Dusen explained, had to be seen in the context of the Cold War. To the south lay fiercely communist South Yemen, and any change of power in the north would put the Republic's new leaders in control of the Bab-el-Mandeb, the Red Sea's southern outlet; the unhampered flow of ships through the Suez Canal was at stake in the stability of the lower Arabian Peninsula.

Before 1962, when the Hamad-a-Din family was in power, the United States had not sought no formal relations with Yemen. But the fall of the imamate, the revolution, the civil war, the bitter Egyptian and Saudi involvement, and the tribal component had changed all that. There was too much at stake in Yemen for the United States to ignore it. In 1989, Michael Van Dusen wanted to improve the relationship with the Arab state. In the past, America had done this by strengthening the needy country's military, providing it with aircraft and equipment, and training Yemeni army officers. Taiwanese technicians were retained by the United States to operate and maintain some of the more advanced equipment. On the economic and agricultural front, the United States had shipped tons of rice, developed acres of barren land, installed an effective Peace Corps program. Now ICROJOY was giving Van Dusen another area in which to establish dialogue with Yemen. It was a sore point, entailing human rights violations. There is a small, abandoned community of Jews living in very rural areas . . .

Van Dusen's decade as staff director had endowed him with proficiency in the Middle East's intricate politics. He had learned that a nation of ample breadth and brawn can tolerate a certain amount of criticism from the United States. But when dealing with the more diminutive states of the Arab world, America must proceed cautiously before publicly censuring a national policy. Van Dusen knew well the layer of pride blanketing the Arab world; he knew that reproaches often ruffle the feathers of these heirs to ancient civilizations. Van Dusen preferred the slow route of quiet, private diplomacy. The almighty United States was a relatively new kid on the block, and Yemen would be much more receptive to delicate persuasion than to press conferences in the Rose Garden, resolutions at the United Nations, and harangues on the Senate floor. Michael Van Dusen was receptive to the ICROJOY delegation, and his expertise would make a dramatic contribution to the organization's rescue of Yemeni Jewry.

Pierre Goloubinoff, Lester Smerka, Shlomo Grafi, Bill Wolf, and I nearly collapsed as ICROJOY's first day in Washington came to a close. Within an eight-hour span, we had navigated the dreadful District of Columbia traffic—in taxi cabs driven by olive-skinned Middle Easterners—five times, had delivered our detailed presentation five times, and had forgotten to include time for meals and other necessities. We were all pleased by what we had accomplished, but Goloubinoff, a Swiss citizen, emerged from February 27 with a special sense of excitement. The Western European countries in which he had lived were certainly democracies, but in Switzerland and France ordinary citizens feel quite distant from the government. Everyman—uninvolved in politics, not a member of a political party, and with no politicians among his friends—can rarely make a difference on the other side of the Atlantic, so Goloubinoff had been quite skeptical about the approach ICROJOY had adopted.

But as Goloubinoff reflected on our meetings with Laurie Johnson and Michael Van Dusen and Stanley Roth and Mike Amitay and Mel Levine, he began to see that there was something extraordinary about the American version of democracy: it was a system that seemed to work. Ordinary citizens had rallied around a cause and approached Washington. And Washington's response had been cautiously positive; officials there were actually willing to enter into a working relationship with five ordinary people intent on saving some Jews in a foreign land. Our campaign had slowly gathered a critical mass, and now we stood on the bottom-most rung of Washington's political ladder—under the most auspicious of circumstances. For the most part, ICROJOY was echoing information Washington already knew, but it was advancing the right plea at the right time. In ICROJOY the Department of State had found honest and trustworthy individuals, people who were not competing for profit or fame, with whom to remedy the plight of Yemeni Jewry.

Isaac Pollak buying ancient Yemeni mezuzah, 1987.

ICROJOY delegation at Bab al-Yemen, September 1989.

ICROJOY's first encounter with the Jews of Yemen, September 1989.

Yosef Levy in Ga–al–Yahud, September 1989.

ICROJOY delegation with Charles Dunbar and Georgia Debelle, September 1989.

ICROJOY delegation with Abdul Karim al-Iryani, September 1989.

ICROJOY delegation at at-Tawila, September 1989.

Mike Van Dusen chairing discussion of US-Yemeni relations including situation of Jews of Yemen on the occasion of President Ali Abdullah Salih's visit in January 1990.

Lester Smerka, Yosef Levy, Stephen J. Solarz, Hayim Tawil, outside Ma'amoun Hotel, Saada, August, 1990.

Stephen J. Solarz dining with the Hamoud Bedar, governor of Saada.

Moshe Sabari and Israel Sabari listening to speech by Stephen J. Solarz.

Tova Weisberger with Yehudah Halla and members of his family, September 1990.

Amram Halla and wife, January 1990

House of Amram Halla, January 1990.

Sarah Dahari Halla with members of her family, September, 1989.

Moshe Dahari Halla in Old Sanaa, January, 1990.

Yosef Levy with new Sefer Torah in Saada, January 1990.

Father of Yhia ibn Daoud Sabari kissing hand of brother of Moshe Atzar.

Daoud Faiz receiving prayer shawls from ICROJOY delegation, September 1989.

Yhia Nahari, January 1990.

Yosef Levy and Hayim Tawil with Sheikh Asurabi (wearing jambiyah), Saada, August, 1990.

Hayim Tawil and Yosef Levy with contract for land to build a school and mikveh. To the left wearing the jambiyah is the Sheikh of Beit Harash.

Chapter Five

MR. SMITH GOES TO WASHINGTON

April 4, 1989

Sarah Dahari Halla had stood defiantly in the conference room at Stern College in December, demanding that ICROJOY obtain the release of her closest kin from Raida, the arid valley north of Sanaa. The bubbly woman's name and story had been forgotten during the first months of ICROJOY's activities and its first trip to Washington. But today, Lester Smerka and I sat across from the pert Yemeni in an apartment on Bolton Street in the Bronx as she recounted tales of the Halla family, its partial escape on the Magic Carpet, the murder of two of its members in 1986, and the entrapment of the others through 1989. ICROJOY knew Sarah as one of the few United States citizens who could claim a direct blood relationship with Jews in Yemen, and the only one who had pledged her services to the organization. In the summer of 1989, those services would prove invaluable as an ICROJOY delegation stood outside a mud-walled Jewish home in Raida. But in the early spring thaw, Sarah Dahari Halla merely acceded to a seemingly innocuous request: she allowed Smerka to author a letter on her behalf.

The short message, typed on ICROJOY stationery and addressed to Secretary of State James Baker, stated:

> I am a citizen of the United States, living in New York's 8th Congressional District represented by Congressman James Scheuer. In 1986, the State Department reported the murder of two Jewish men in the Yemen Arab Republic. I am related to both of them. Please find out what has happened to the rest of my family. I would also like to know how I can: 1) open a steady flow of letters to and from them. 2) send them money, clothes, or

religious articles. 3) Also invite them to visit me in New York as soon as possible. Once they have permission to leave Yemen I will purchase their round-trip tickets from Yemen to New York and back to Yemen. All this must be arranged with guarantees of the absence of government or private reprisals.

Halla enclosed a letter intended for her relatives, addressed "to my uncle Yagov Halla el-Dahari, and to my uncle Amram Halla el-Dahari, and to my aunt Hamida the wife of Yagov Halla el-Dahari, and to the children of my uncle Salem Ben-Yehudah Halla el-Dahari," and to many others. In two day's time, ICROJOY was heading south to Washington again. There, we delivered the letters to the State Department as Sarah's personal plea for assistance, accompanied by notes to Baker from dozens of Congressmen echoing the concerns of the Halla family. We little imagined that the words of Sarah Dahari Halla would find their way from the Department of State to the embassy of the Yemen Arab Republic on New Hampshire Avenue, then, via diplomatic pouch, to a government ministry in the heart of Sanaa.

April 6, 1989

The magnificent works of art adorning the wood-paneled walls belied the unassuming features of the man sitting calmly behind the mahogany desk. The members of ICROJOY's second delegation to Washington fidgeted in their seats. They had navigated the never-ending hallways of the State Department, passed through a series of double-doors, seen the long conference table and the couches and the artifacts, and now they were face to face with Ambassador Richard Schifter, one of Washington's most effective human rights advocates. Schifter's grandfatherly appearance camouflaged his mastery of the art of negotiating; he looked downright out-of-place in this ornate room. But the Assistant Secretary of State for Human Rights had earned the office. Years of mediation had taught Schifter both his fortes and his limits. The human rights specialist would always take one step backward in order to bounce two steps forward, and he considered table-pounding an unproductive technique.

Richard Schifter could transmit his country's most urgent desires in a quiet but productive manner. His greatest coup had been the release of the millions of Jews trapped behind the Iron Curtain, for whom he had discretely negotiated. Schifter had even attended a seder at the American embassy in Moscow, sitting among bewildered refusniks having their first taste of the strange Passover foods that embody both bondage and freedom. The Moscow seder, presided over by a yarmulke-wearing Secretary of State George Schultz, was all the more moving because it had climaxed years of disastrous attempts to win the freedom of Soviet Jewry. Patience featured prominently in Schifter's personality, and the personal ties he forged with high-ranking Soviet officials eventually closed that dark chapter.

A singular event had brought Richard Schifter to a career in diplomacy. Jean Kirkpatrick, American ambassador to the United Nations, had implored her good friend to represent his country at the United Nations Human Rights Commission. But Schifter's preoccupation with human rights was more subtly the product of his having grown up Jewish in Nazi Germany. Schifter's parents had not survived the Holocaust.

So Schifter channeled his efforts into righting modern-day wrongs, and he found himself in an America concerned with violations of human rights. In 1948, the United Nations General Assembly adopted the Universal Declaration of Human Rights. One of its provisions was the right to leave one's country, a freedom perpetually denied by one country or another. Above all other nations, the United States dedicated itself to the effective application of human rights principles throughout the world. Sometimes that took the form of issuing "warnings" or expressing "concerns," other times it meant seeking relief for specific individuals or families.

Richard Schifter felt that the American government was more responsive than any other democracy to the intercession of individuals—even at the risk of jeopardizing a foreign policy or relationship. The United States even had human rights officers in its hundreds of embassies throughout the world; their sole job, to identify human rights problems and report them to Washington. And the United States is the only country which drafts annual reports detailing the state of human rights in every nation on earth, probably because it is the only nation that can get away with it. Schifter found it a grating experience when the reports were published and America sat in judgment of its allies and antagonists. The most recent Human Rights Report on the Yemen Arab Republic, issued on April 6, 1989, painted an unflattering picture of the country.

> Civil liberties remained significantly restricted, and the government continued to exercise a large measure of control over political life. . . . Automobiles are routinely stopped and searched and the identification of the occupants demanded at intersection checkpoints throughout the country, especially at night. . . . Restrictions exist on free speech but are largely confined to the urban areas because of the government's limited control in the countryside. Some Yemenis believe that they may experience difficulty if they are overheard criticizing the government by national security agents. The Information Ministry owns and operates the radio and television stations, as well as the major newspapers. The government removes articles from Yemeni publications which its censors deem inappropriate. Several foreign publications, including English-language newspapers and magazines, are available in the cities, but those containing material deemed offensive are withheld from distribution. In the past, the government has suspended publishing licenses for extended periods to punish independent publishers. Self-censorship is also practiced at Sanaa University, whose professors and senior administrators must receive NSO [National Security Office] clearance before being hired. Most professors, including the many expatriates, do not complain about government interference in their courses or curriculum development. Student organizations independent of the government are not permitted.

On the subject of the country's Jewish population, the report stated that almost all of the once substantial Yemeni Jewish population has emigrated to Israel, but a small number—1,000 or fewer—remains, mostly in rural areas in the north of the country. There are no synagogues, but Jews are permitted to practice their religion, including religious instruction, in private homes. Jews usually live in relative harmony with their Muslim neighbors. There have been unconfirmed reports that the country's small Jewish population is subject to discrimination.

The virtual obsession of the United States with human rights violations in other countries began during the administration of President Jimmy Carter. Richard Schifter's task was to make Carter's policy initiative an essential part of State Department operations and thinking. As Assistant Secretary of State for Human Rights, he imposed a fusion of human rights concerns with foreign policy. The United States certainly had the power to make other countries respect human rights; according to Jimmy Carter, history demanded that it do so. In articulating this vision during his farewell address on January 14, 1981, Carter uttered some of the most powerful words of his Presidency:

> The struggle for human rights overrides all differences of color or nation or language. Those who hunger for freedom, who thirst for human dignity and who suffer for the sake of justice—they are the patriots of this cause. I believe with all my heart that America must always stand for these basic human rights. At home and abroad. That is both our history and our destiny. America did not invent human rights. In a very real sense, it's the other way around. Human rights invented America. Ours was the first nation in the history of the world to be founded explicitly on such an idea. Our social and political progress has been based on one fundamental principal: The value and importance of the individual. The fundamental force that unites us is not kinship or place of origin or religious preference. The love of liberty is a common blood that flows in our American veins.
>
> The battle for human rights at home and abroad is far from over. We should never be surprised nor discouraged because the impact of our efforts has had and will always have varied results. Rather, we should take pride that the ideals which gave birth to our nation still inspire the hopes of oppressed people around the world. We have no cause for self-righteousness or complacency, but we have every reason to persevere both within our own country and beyond our borders. If we are to serve as a beacon for human rights, we must continue to perfect here at home the rights and the values which we espouse around the world. Remember these words: We hold these truths to be self-evident, that all men are created equal, that they are endowed by their creator with certain inalienable rights, that among these are life, liberty, and the pursuit of happiness. This vision still grips the

imagination of the world.

The Human Rights Bureau Carter created works alongside the regional bureaus in the Department of State. If both offices conclude that a nation's violations warrant American pressure, the item is added to the "agenda" in relation to that country, and the State Department's routine instructions direct the U.S. ambassador to broach the subject with local officials.

Officials of the Human Rights Bureau also routinely meet with delegations of private citizens concerned about human rights violations in one place or another. So the scene in Richard Schifter's office in early April of 1989 was not unusual. He had agreed to meet with ICROJOY because it was concerned with the human rights of the Jews of Yemen, particularly the denial of their right to leave. The members of ICROJOY knew that beleaguered Jews were a cause very close to Schifter's heart. They knew that success with Schifter hinged on the presentation of facts that were accurate and relevant, not on the delivery of mailbags overflowing with ambiguous letters of protest. In the end, Schifter would convince his State superiors to treat the case of Yemeni Jewry quite differently than that of Soviet Jewry. He understood that it was only with the Soviet Union that the United States could apply direct pressure on a human rights issue, because the Soviet Union was already an adversary, and therefore the additional strain on relations would not be crucial. But different circumstances permitted and required different tactics. The case of Yemeni Jewry would dictate much more delicate maneuvering, because the United States was loath to offend the Yemeni government. And this was a government, in Schifter's mind, that would feel the wrath of the PLO if it allowed its Jews to emigrate, for Israel would surely be their ultimate destination.

But the members of ICROJOY did not know that the PLO's fears about the migration of Yemeni Jewry would indeed be realized as they talked to Richard Schifter in his massive office. When the members of the delegation strode purposefully into the room, they were greeted by a man who immediately demanded that they stop sending him petitions from Yeshiva University students. It would be more practical, he said, to talk for an one hour or so.

Schifter proved to be almost awkwardly shy, but his presence was powerful. At one point during the session he was interrupted by a telephone call from the ambassador in Moscow and returned beaming from the conversation. A dissident locked up in a Soviet prison has been freed after years of quiet diplomacy. The story would never make the papers, of course, for in Schifter's world silence was truly golden.

Even before ICROJOY's presentation was completed, it was evident that Schifter had already formed an opinion about the group. He knew the organization to be both serious and unaffiliated, which was not true of some of the other Jewish groups which he had met. Among them were the Yemenite Jewish Federation and the American Sephardic Federation, competing for the lucrative title of "Savior of the Jewish People." And Neturei Karta in Brooklyn was claiming a monopoly on dialogue with Yemeni Jewry. Schifter's State Department colleagues warned him that the Yemeni government was being approached by organization after organization suddenly obsessed with Yemeni Jewry. Certainly the Jews there would stand a better chance if the effort to save them was united, but which Jewish group would the United States authorize to treat with the Yemen Arab Republic? The decision had fallen into Schifter's lap.

We soon learned that Schifter was willing to work with ICROJOY, but only if it took a vow of silence, removing itself and its activities from the public eye. Since December, however, ICROJOY had not been a model of patient restraint. In March, among other things, it had organized an evening about the plight of Yemeni Jewry at community center in Teaneck, New Jersey. More significantly, I had convinced the organizers of a concert featuring Israeli singer Shoshana Damari to let me open the show by telling the tale of ICROJOY to the packed house in Manhattan's Town Hall. ICROJOY's activities would indeed require some tempering if the Department of State was to accept it as a governmental interlocutor. Secrecy would be paramount, and information would only be disclosed on a need-to-know basis. As ICROJOY chairman, I would be perceived as both cocky and paranoid, but my organization's activities required tight control if they were to be successful.

Our exercises in diplomacy would eventually be regulated by another man who was sitting in Richard Schifter's office on April 6 along with Laurie Johnson, Lester Smerka, Pierre Goloubinoff, Bill Wolf, Shlomo Grafi, and myself. David Ransom, a tall, trim statesman who could easily have melted into the sea of dark-suited men saturating Washington's sidewalks, quietly absorbed the scene unfolding before him. Ransom was the boss of Johnson, the Yemen desk officer, and he brought to the table a treasure trove of wealth and experience in dealing with the Yemen Arab Republic. As the chief Arabian Peninsula Affairs officer in the Near Eastern Bureau, Ransom was the negotiator and policy formulator for all U.S. activities vis-à-vis Yemen. A much younger David Ransom's first post in the Foreign Service had been Yemen, back in 1966. Fierce civil war fighting had forced the United States to leave abruptly in 1967, but not before Ransom became aware of the existence of the remnant community of Jews in the northern part of Yemen, surrounded by millions of Muslims.

In 1975, Ransom had returned to the Yemen Arab Republic as the deputy chief of mission to the American ambassador, whereupon he renewed his contacts with the Jews. Never one who enjoyed being cooped up in the office, baking in Sanaa, Ransom often wandered the remotest parts of the country, taking a four-wheel-drive vehicle through the rural and quite roadless terrain. During these junkets, Ransom would sometimes explore the rugged mountains and dried-out wadis that comprise much of Yemen's northern region. During one such tour near the city of Saada, where a man with Ransom's strange, light complexion had never before been seen, a robed civilian had come bolting out of his house, arms flailing and mouth shrieking, attempting to get Ransom's attention. There seemed to be some sort of emergency.

"*Khutub! Khutub!*" the man exclaimed repeatedly when Ransom pulled over. That meant "books," he realized, but the man's gestures did not make any sense. So Ransom began to reply in Arabic, "What do you want? What do you mean?" before the answer suddenly came to him. The man was a Jew: a Jew looking for books that had been promised to him by a certain group of foreigners. The precious religious texts had yet to be delivered. Ransom learned that the Jewish villagers lacked the most basic religious articles; they were alone and isolated and had been so for decades.

Upon his return to Sanaa, an irritated Ransom had approached Yemen's Foreign Minister, telling the official that he could not continue to deny the Jews the basics of their religious experience: "If they lack books, it's your fault. You wouldn't deny an Arab citizen a Koran, even if he were in jail. Yet these people, who are some of your citizens in the Republic, cannot get hold of the Torah." And the Foreign Minister had actually concurred. But Ransom knew that any policy of the Yemen Arab Republic regarding its few Jews had to be viewed in the broader context of Middle Eastern politics. With the way it treated its Jewish population the litmus test of its allegiance to the Arab cause. Yemen's hands were tied.

Ransom's two previous tours of duty in the Yemen Arab Republic had made him a popular figure in Sanaa, and Mrs. Ransom, a public affairs officer in charge of English-language classes and exchange programs, had played a major part. The two of them had built a home which was perpetually filled with military officers and diplomats and businessmen and educators. The Ransoms had created a lively salon in the swank suburbs of Sanaa; they were in the business of bridging a great cultural divide. Thus Ransom knew Yemeni society quite intimately.

David Ransom's diplomatic life had been spent overseeing U.S. forays into Middle Eastern politics. He felt that the task of diplomacy was to bridge differences, particularly cultural differences, which he regarded as more divisive than political ones. Speaking Arabic was one way to bridge the chasm, because it said, in effect, "I know who you are, and I like who you are." Arabic validated the identity of the Yemenis and simultaneously offset the image of the United States as a behemoth, acting without regard for the interests and concerns of others. The bullying quality of American foreign policy loomed large in the mind of David Ransom, and he strove constantly to alter that image.

Ransom analyzed the Yemeni government's position pragmatically. First, the Yemen Arab Republic breathed political dilemma. It was situated between the most radical left-wing government in the Arab world, the People's Democratic Republic of Southern Yemen, and the most conservative and Muslim government in the Arab world, the Kingdom of Saudi Arabia. On the issue of Yemeni Jewry, the proud nation could assume it would be denounced by both neighbors. But Yemen needed American companies to develop its oil, it looked to the United States for weapons, and it craved foodstuffs from the fruited plain. And Ransom considered the Arabs honorable men who would do anything for someone they deemed honorable, diplomats who would set aside abstract issues to resuscitate a friendship or alliance.

A warm relationship with Yemen was high on David Ransom's political agenda. American companies were inaugurating oil production in Yemen, and commerce had to proceed smoothly. More importantly, America had to play peacekeeper in a region where the dying Soviet Union was still infiltrating as an arms supplier and a political antagonist. The key to saving the Jews of Yemen was to avoid making them a confrontational issue, instead viewing them as a problem that could be painlessly solved in the context of a broadening relationship. Since the Yemenis were honorable men in Ransom's eyes, he would be able to show them the error of their ways. The Americans would tell the Yemenis, much to the latter's embarrassment, that they had a more restrictive policy than many of their Arab allies. The Jews of Morocco and Tunisia and Egypt all had the right to leave.

As an Arab League state, Yemen was out of step, behind the times. The nation's primary decision-maker was its President, Ali Abdullah Salih, a former air force officer. He was served by a cadre of Yemenis mostly educated in the West, a cabinet possessing extraordinary talent and breadth of mind. The Yemen Arab Republic was no Mickey Mouse operation, and Ransom that the urbanity of its leaders would surely prevail. Rescuing the Jews through traditional diplomatic channels—rather than a clandestine helicopter invasion—stood as a distinct possibility.

Ransom longed to stabilize relations with Yemen. Concessions had already been granted to the Hunt Oil Company and the Exxon

Corporation to tap Yemen's minor oil fields. Now the United States would seek a solution to the Jewish problem. Members of Congress, swayed by ICROJOY, had put Yemeni Jewry high on their agendas, but Ransom, Schifter, and Michael Van Dusen doubted that Congress alone could win freedom of emigration. In what is termed Track I Diplomacy, the American government charges its contacts and ambassador with ameliorating a situation, often dispatching Congressmen to a foreign country to communicate directly. Here, when tackling a Middle East obstacle, the experts surmised that Track II Diplomacy would be crucial. In Track II, private citizens play the role taken by elected officials in Track I, primarily because private citizens have greater freedom to meet people and travel, especially in times and places where it might be politically suicidal for elected officials to do so. The Yemen Arab Republic in 1989 was one such time and place.

Thus, in Richard Schifter's office on April 6, we began to feel that our ambitious dreams for ICROJOY were nearing fruition. Our other activities while in Washington included meetings with a legislative assistant to Congressman James Scheuer, with the staff director in the office of Congressman Gus Yatron, chairman of the Subcommittee on Human Rights and International Organizations, and with Connecticut Senator Joseph Lieberman. But in Richard Schifter and David Ransom, we believed, ICROJOY had made significant inroads into the Washington power structure. Honesty and integrity were proving to be the best policy. Scores of effusive thank-you letters would be mailed from 150 Nassau Street as soon as we got back to New York. Pierre Goloubinoff would spend another two hours with Laurie Johnson at the Yemen desk, telling her the names of Yemeni Jews and where they lived.

From their homes in New York, Arizona, and Delaware, the members of the ICROJOY delegation could never precisely estimate the extent of their influence in the nation's capital. But they were all gratified to know of a memorandum issued by the Congressional Human Rights Caucus on April 18, 1989, announcing a Special Order to "recognize the thousands of Jews around the world who remain oppressed and denied their basic religious rights and human dignity. Make no mistake, Jewish persecution continues." And listed among the persecuting countries was Yemen, where "approximately 4,000 Jews are victims of targeted killings, unlawful arrests, detention without trial, mail censorship, travel constraints, and restrictions on emigration."

As U.S. ambassador to the Yemen Arab Republic, Charles Dunbar reluctantly became the official with personal responsibility for the Jews of Yemen. Thanks to ICROJOY's putting pressure on the State Department back home, the rugged, middle-aged man at the helm of America's Southern Arabian outpost now had to dive head-first into the "Jewish problem." Dunbar was a relative newcomer to Yemen's delicate political situation, having only greeted the dusty Sanaa skyline in 1988. During nomination and confirmation for the post, Dunbar had learned of the isolated Jewish community's woeful endurance. But at first, Washington had ordered its agent in Sanaa to merely keep tabs on the Jews; their situation, he was told, required light supervision, not vigorous, hands-on management. Dunbar, like his predecessors, understood that to Washington the Jews were a long-term issue. Increased mistreatment would raise eyebrow stateside, but for the time being, no action was planned.

By April 1989, a newfound zeal was dislodging the policy of apathy. For some reason, several of Dunbar's good friends were suddenly preoccupied with the Jews of Yemen. An old chum named David Ransom, country director for Arabian Peninsula Affairs, was sounding increasingly anxious, and so was an up-and-coming diplomat named Laurie Johnson. A colleague in the Bureau of Human Rights, Richard Schifter, was also weighing in with his concerns. Then there was this organization called *icro*-something . . .

During his few months in Sanaa, Charles Dunbar had assimilated much information about the Jews and their millions of Muslim neighbors. The Jews were not victimized by daily, systematic discrimination, but their apprehensions were multiplying as the Yemen Arab Republic cultivated its citizens' animosity toward Israel. Hostility can be bred quite effectively by state-controlled radio and television programming. Although the Jews and Muslims of Yemen were alike socioeconomically—and a certain amount of symbiosis had survived the millennia—legal distinctions between them abounded. Jews did not serve in the army. They could not bear arms in a country where every male sports an ancient *jambiya* and its modern-day equivalent, the submachine gun. Most significantly, they could not obtain passports and consequently were not free to travel. And the Jews were denied the right to communicate with the outside world.

Early into his three-year appointment, Dunbar identified the principal Muslim players in the daily lives of the country's Jews. The sheikhs who controlled the villages surrounding Saada were a curious band of robed and bearded men with a refreshing awareness that their task was to preserve peace and champion the rights of everyone living under them. Dunbar knew of several sheikhs who would definitely provide protection for Jews in danger. Dunbar enjoyed a cordial relationship with one sheikh in particular who also happened to be Yemen's Deputy Prime Minister for Interior Affairs. Sheikh Mujahad Abushwareb often expressed concern for the welfare of Yemeni Jewry.

Then there was the Mukhabarat, the local "security" force infesting the northern part of the country. The Mukhabarat tended to not be very understanding. Long ago it had realized that the Jews were different, and therefore it watched them and the people with whom they made contact. Sometimes interrogations and incarcerations followed such encounters. As one of the most highly visible foreigners in the Yemen Arab Republic, Charles Dunbar could never set out for Saada to see Jews. The risks—both to his personal safety and to the Jews—were too high. But perhaps others more loosely associated with America could venture northward.

Finally, there was the Yemeni government itself, which had no relationship of any kind with Israel. Like the other Arab nations, it was officially at war with the Jewish state. Like the other Arab nations, it objected to Israel's Law of Return, which grants all Jews the right to settle in Israel and become citizens. It did not want to strengthen Israel in any way, even by adding several hundred tired and feeble Jews to the country's swelling populace. By allowing Jews to emigrate, Yemen would helping Israel. The ban on emigration was a matter of principle.

As a sliver of the moon reflected its pale light off the white marble of Washington, April 6 came to a close. In Sanaa, the first warm rays of the sun were stirring the city's inhabitants to life, and shrill calls to morning prayer emanated from loudspeakers atop minarets. Charles Dunbar slept soundly in the comfortable apartment provided by his government. Near Yemen's northern border, the Jews were slowly rising from their mats on the floor, and the faint clatter of morning activity filled the houses of families called Sabari and Suberi and Zindani. Two thousand miles to the north, dawn was breaking over a nation preparing for Passover, the celebration of freedom. Alarm clocks rang in nondescript apartment houses along the Mediterranean coastal plain, rousing David Shuker, Moshe Atzar, Shalom Suberi, and Hinda Zindani from slumber. Along America's eastern seaboard, Pierre Goloubinoff, Sarah Dahari Halla, Lester Smerka, Richard Schifter, David Ransom, Laurie Johnson, and Michael Van Dusen had already turned in for the night. The players in an extraordinary human rights struggle fortified themselves before another day.

May 23, 1989
Ties were not loosened over crisply pressed shirts in Richard Schifter's office, but stiff formalities and scripted presentations had long ago ceased. Instead, with the tension broken, the eight people present exchanged light banter during ICROJOY's third visit to the powerful chamber from which the Human Rights Bureau was run. White-haired Richard Schifter was there, of course, along with David Ransom and Laurie Johnson, who chatted with me, Pierre Goloubinoff, Lester Smerka, and Shlomo Grafi. Tova Weisberger, our attractive, young executive secretary, dutifully recorded the scene in her notebook, adding an air of professionalism to the five-month-old ICROJOY. Schifter's eyes seemed excited, and the diplomat wore a slight grin every time he looked my way. Something was afoot.

And after several minutes of dialogue, Schifter broke the news.

"Professor, we think you will be able to go to Yemen sometime very soon."

When the words sunk in, I gripped Goloubinoff's hand to steady my own shaking. ICROJOY had never expected a trip to the Yemen Arab Republic. What were we to do there? How would that win freedom for the Jews? Would a Tawil actually be returning to the magical land abandoned by the Tawili family in 1889? Schifter interrupted my thoughts with a phrase which immediately thrust me out of my reverie: "Professor, you have a meeting at one o'clock with Ambassador Mohsin al-Aini." With the ambassador? With the ambassador. Today? Today.

Actually, it was in twenty minutes, Schifter continued. Luckily, the State Department is only blocks from the Watergate Building, where the Yemen Republic's embassy is housed. ICROJOY should begin designating a five-member delegation, Schifter said, for a possible trip at the summer's end. They would be protected by the American and Yemeni governments, and would meet the Jews of Yemen, delivering religious supplies and moral support. But technicalities would come later; my most immediate task was to get to the Watergate. I would wear my yarmulke, and although the others balked I would take only Tova, in her long skirt, to sit and silently take notes. Descending from Schifter's office, I shared an elevator with David Ransom, who cornered me and said: "Professor Tawil, we would like you to lead the delegation to Yemen." But how can a Jew lead a delegation to such a country, I protested.

"You're an American citizen. Your passport just says you were born in Jerusalem."

"How do you know?"

"We know."

Mohsin al-Alaini was a gentleman, not a newcomer to diplomacy. As the Thomas Jefferson of the Yemen Arab Republic, he had authored the country's constitution at its postrevolutionary birth in 1962, and now occupied its most crucial foreign post, ambassador to the mighty United States. Before Washington, al-Aini had represented the Yemen Arab Republic in Moscow, London, Paris, and the United Nations. But Mohsin al-Aini's small country relied heavily upon the world's richest nation, so only a little goading had been necessary to clear room in his schedule for a Jew from New York. As that Jew from New York, I nervously entered the embassy with Tova and was immediately ushered into a stunning office, decorated with rich oriental rugs and museum-quality wall hangings. The ambassador, a short, dark man with curly hair, greeted us warmly. Did we want something to eat? No, thank you, we only eat kosher. How about coffee, or cold water? Tova and I finally acquiesced to coffee served in glasses, which were brought in by an attendant on silver platters, and the ambassador seemed to respect our bizarre request. We began speaking to the ambassador about an even odder plea.

"I understand that you would like to travel to Yemen," al-Aini stated.

"Yes," I replied. "We would very much like to see our brethren, to see how they feel, what they need, and maybe to bring some religious supplies. We know there is religious freedom and you respect the Jews there. If we can just bring some supplies . . ."

"Absolutely. Why not?" al-Aini exclaimed when I had finished my explanation. I had been respectful toward Yemen, expressing a love for its culture and its art. I was a Yemeni who simply wanted to explore his roots, not to generate an international scandal. But what sorts of things would I be bringing the Jews of Yemen? The Yemeni government wanted to examine them first. What kind of books would I be delivering? Only prayer books, nothing to incite a revolution—or a desire for emigration. When would I like to come? September, if that is all right with your government.

Suddenly, the ambassador lifted the telephone off his desk and called Sanaa, and soon he was having a fast-paced conversation in Arabic, which I understood, with Foreign Minister Abdul Karim al-Iryani. Yes, it shouldn't be a problem, al-Aini declared at the conclusion of the conversation. "You will be the guest of the Yemeni government," which will grant visas to five American citizens. Dr. Iryani will await your arrival in Sanaa. Oh, and Professor Tawil, lots of luck on your trip.

In under a half-hour, a crack of light had begun to appear beneath a door that had been hermetically sealed since 1962. The Yemeni government was allowing contact between its Jews and their brothers in other countries. ICROJOY would be able to go to Yemen without fear of detention or imprisonment. The day's events had been remarkable for both their gravity and their swiftness. My meeting with al-Aini concluded with a conversation about the scholarly research that allowed me to call myself a professor of Semitics. Together, we discussed ancient Assyria, and the Phoenicians, and the influence of Eastern Semitic on Northwestern Semitic.

Tova and I exited elated into the blinding afternoon sun and humid May air, and quickly jumped into a cab. The other members of ICROJOY were waiting eagerly. "What happened?" Shlomo Grafi cried, then turned pale when he heard about al-Aini and Iryani and the Watergate and the five visas. ICROJOY was going to Yemen, but Grafi, as an Israeli citizen, would not be able to participate. Pierre Goloubinoff was also subdued; his Swiss citizenship would prevent him from taking part in the next ICROJOY adventure. Meanwhile, I was already beginning to formulate a strategy. We would be meeting the Foreign Minister himself, a man who truly believed the Jews to be an integral part of Yemen, their emigration from Israel a horrible mistake. So we would have to arm ourselves with the tales of sorrow produced by years of separation. The men running the Yemen Arab Republic were human beings, and there can be no argument against tears.

June 28, 1989

At first Sarah Dahari Halla thought it was her hated alarm clock that was signaling the arrival of Wednesday morning in the Bronx. But the small bedside timepiece would not respond to her repeated raps, and besides, it was only 6:00 a.m. It must be the telephone, Sarah concluded, lifting the receiver to utter a half-dead "Hello?"

Moments later, Sarah Dahari Halla was bolting out of bed, wide-eyed, very much awake, beset by a flurry of emotions. On the other end was a voice she had never heard before, but somehow it rang close in her heart, and it belonged to her uncle, Salem Halla. He was calling from Yemen. The branch of the family that had been cut off from the world since 1962 was making its first contact with one of the Hallas who had ridden the Magic Carpet. Salem only had ten minutes, so uncle conversed hastily with niece in Arabic, telling her everything was fine, all was well with the Hallas from Raida, the country was treating them well. "We lack nothing and we are happy." Sarah overwhelmed Salem with a flood of tearful questions: "Do you remember my grandmother? Do you remember my father?" Ten hours of conversation would not have been enough to bridge thirty years of heartbreaking silence, but suddenly a click and a dial tone replaced the voice of Salem Halla el-Dahari.

Sarah replaced the receiver and sat deliriously on her bed until her heart rate returned to normal. Then she began to ponder the dialogue with her uncle. Apparently her letter to James Baker had worked wonders, but several details of the conversation began to gnaw at her. When she had asked her uncle what the weekly Torah portion was, he had replied, "Parshat Lech Lecha," which wasn't due to be read for several months. He had given her a telephone number in Sanaa for return calls, but the Hallas lived in Raida. He had spoken in a purely Arabic tongue, but Yemeni Jews communicate in Judeo-Arabic, which is seventy-five percent Hebrew. Perhaps her uncle had been forced to use Arabic so that someone, presumably a government official, could listen in on what he was saying. At one point, Salem had indeed uttered something to a man standing at his side somewhere in Yemen.

Parshat Lech Lecha, thought Sarah, the portion of the Book of Genesis in which God commands Abraham to leave his place of birth, uproot himself from the pagans in his midst, and go to Canaan, the future Land of Israel. Could Salem have been sending her a message that all was truly not well in Yemen, that it was not love of the Republic that was keeping the Hallas in Arabia, between stars and sand? Sarah would later confirm that it was not an impostor who had called the Bronx on June 28, and she would speak to Salem again—in Sanaa, because he did not have a telephone in Raida. The two conversations would be analyzed in a series of phone calls between New York and Washington. Was Salem being forthright about his desire to remain in Yemen? Could anything of what he had said be deemed accurate? At that stage, only one thing could be certain: ICROJOY had made its first contact with the Jews of Yemen

Chapter Six

JOURNEY BACK IN TIME

September 5, 1989
Fourteen tremendous cardboard cartons lined the hallways of an already severely congested apartment on Bennett Avenue in Washington Heights. Contained in them were all sorts of things that had not reached the Jews of Yemen in four decades: religious articles, sacred texts, prayer books, all meticulously packed by my wife Dalia. Still other cartons were brimming with disposable plates, forks, and knives, aluminum foil, baked goods, toilet paper, boxes of spaghetti, containers of sardines, jars of peanut butter, bags of potato chips and raisins, and a great number of cans. Seated around the dining room table amidst maps and files and rings of smoke, nervously scrawling pages of notes, were the five participants in a landmark event: ICROJOY's first trip to the Yemen Arab Republic, and the first officially sanctioned delegation of Jews to enter the country since 1962, not counting Neturei Karta's PLO-sponsored encroachments.

Richard Schifter's plan had come to fruition. Tomorrow, the people, their supplies, and the precious cargo would all be on a Lufthansa jet bound for Frankfurt and then Sanaa. ICROJOY would be meeting the Yemeni Foreign Minister, Dr. Abdul Karim al-Iryani, and the hundreds of Jews trapped in his country. I had personally returned to the Yemeni embassy on New Hampshire Avenue to collect our five United States passports, now bearing the intricate stamps of Yemeni visas. It was to be a secret mission; even the Jewish organizations that had denied ICROJOY assistance could not be told. In July, Lester Smerka and I had enjoyed a chuckle at the offices of the American Sephardic Federation while its officers declared that ICROJOY would flounder without its input and control. This evening, we were receiving an intensive briefing from Pierre Goloubinoff, who stood blithely at the head of the table wearing an unprofessorial red shirt and goatee, and relating the geographical and socioeconomic lessons of his 1985–87 journeys. We were told of the steppes and the mountains and the valleys carving toward the Red Sea, the malarial coastal plain, the hot cities and remote villages, Hashid, Wadi Amlah, Sahin, dozens of names and places.

Around me at the table sat the other four Arabian travelers, two men and two women whom I had hand-picked to accompany me. They were quiet, unassuming people not likely to attract undue attention or raise a ruckus in the Yemeni desert. To my left was a smiling Sarah Dahari Halla, born in Raida and brought to Israel at the age of four. Now she would be returning to Raida and to her numerous aunts, uncles, and cousins who had not flown the Magic Carpet. ICROJOY hoped her few memories and recollections would win us the acceptance of the Raida community. Lester Smerka and Shlomo Grafi listened carefully to everything Goloubinoff said, although the Yemen Arab Republic visas ICROJOY had obtained did not bear their names. Across from Smerka sat the other female member of the delegation, dark-haired Tova Weisberger, ICROJOY's twenty-three-year-old executive secretary, American-born but of Yemeni origin. Tova's passport did bear a visa, and she would be part of the delegation.

The two men who would be on their way to Sanaa tomorrow sat to my right. First was one of my students at Yeshiva University, gentle nineteen-year-old Boaz Mori. American-born Mori would be handling the video-camera work as ICROJOY combed the cities and villages of Yemen, documenting the trip for later review by the State Department. He would be communicating with the young Yemeni men of his age, most of whom were married with children. Richard Schifter had discovered ICROJOY largely through Boaz's petitioning efforts; now those efforts were being rewarded. Boaz Mori, too, longed to see the land of his grandparents.

My friend Yosef Levy, a short, olive-skinned man with jet black hair and penetrating brown eyes, sat quietly next to Boaz. Yemen was not only the land of Yosef Levy's grandparents, it was his own birthplace. Born in 1938 into the most prominent family in Sanaa, Yosef Levy lived with memories of a youth spent in the dusty alleyways of the capital city, whose prosperous Jewish neighborhood abounded in children and Torah-learning and joy. At the turn of the century, his famous grandfather, Yhia Yitzhak HaLevi, had served as the Chief Rabbi of Yemen, a brilliant man who had been the Jews' interlocutor with the imamate; he was nationally recognized as one of the so-called Two Yhias of Yemen. The other Yhia? Imam Yhia himself. Yosef Levy was thus heir to a legacy of service to Yemeni Jewry. By 1949, Sanaa had been emptied of its substantial Jewish populace and an eleven-year-old Levy had ridden the Magic Carpet to the Holy Land.

In Israel life went on, though more harshly than in Yemen. Yosef Levy matured, became a teacher, moved to America, where he discover a small but content Yemeni community in Brooklyn, and married in the 1960s. In Israel his vocational opportunities had been stymied by the cultural biases of the national educational system, but in Brooklyn he devoted himself to teaching the Yemeni heritage to a new generation of youngsters. Many of his neighbors were concerned about relatives and childhood acquaintances still trapped in the country of their youth. So in 1975, Levy had mailed packages of holy books to the northern villages of the Yemen Arab Republic. But there had been no response from the Jews there.

As the years passed, Levy never remotely imagined that he might one day visit the house of his birth. He had not considered it a possibility when he was my student at the Jewish Theological Seminary in the 1970s. Certainly the thought had not yet crossed his mind at the time of our most recent encounter, at a symposium on Sephardic literature in March. My phone call to him several weeks earlier had changed all that.

"Yosef," I had told him, "you and I are going to Yemen." Levy was flabbergasted, but I explained that ICROJOY needed someone who understood the Jews of Yemen, someone who in addition to knowing Judeo-Arabic could speak the emotional language of the people we would be meeting. Ancient refrains and melodies still rang in Yosef's ears. He would be able to pray with Yemen's Jews, to eat and converse with them comfortably. With a hint of a smile perpetually emanating from his round face, Yosef came off as a warm person of sweet gentility, someone whom the Yemenis would find it difficult not to befriend.

Luckily, Levy's initial reluctance soon gave way to accession, then to guarded enthusiasm. And a personal meeting at 150 Nassau Street with Janice, Yosef Levy's wife, finally secured permission for him to go. After all, our mission was an unprecedented and risky one. Yosef knew it as he sat in my living room in early September taking notes, Sarah Dahari Halla knew it as she puffed nervously on a cigarette, Boaz Mori and Tova Weisberger knew it as they paid stiff attention to Pierre Goloubinoff's briefing, and I shared their anxiety as I put pen to the notepads spread out before me.

Before long the pages of those notepads were filled with words and diagrams. Nestled in the mountains, Sanaa was the most important, the largest, and possibly the oldest city in Yemen. With population of one million people, Sanaa had been the country's capital for two thousand years; many of its buildings were over eight hundred years old. And the skyline? A magical tableau of domed mosques and patterned brick minarets rising above vineyards and shops where glass was stained and baskets woven.

Sanaa was described as a massive figure-eight. Its eastern sector comprised the walled Old City, with towering mountains to the east accessible via Bab-el-Yaman, the ancient gates where the road from Dammar enters. The Turkish-built New City was in the western sector, bisected by Abdul Nasser Street and ending in Ga-el-Yahud, the three-hundred-year-old Jewish neighborhood, now inhabited by Arabs. Near the Square of Freedom commemorating the 1962 revolution, opposite the Central Bank of Yemen, we would find the Taj Sheba Hotel, built atop graves in Bab-a-Sabah, where the imams had made their homes. Permits were required to leave Sanaa Province; roadblocks and guardposts peppered the Sanaa-Saada highway in order to prevent smuggling from Saudi Arabia into the Yemen Arab Republic.

The Yemeni populace was ethnically Arab, primarily descended from the many ancient south Arabian peoples. Arabic was the nation's official language, Sunni Islam its predominant religion. But in the northernmost reaches, the Zaydis, embracing a branch of Shi'ism, prevailed. Among them, we would find the Jews.

Although ICROJOY's cargo was legal, approved by the Yemeni ambassador himself, it would still be subjected to a rigorous inspection—and possible confiscation—once the delegation arrived in Sanaa. So from each of the hundred texts of the Torah and the hundred High Holiday prayer books, Lester Smerka had clipped out the page that read "Printed in Israel." From the regular prayer books, Smerka had wisely removed the "Prayer for the Soldiers of the State of Israel." Then, into the boxes went volumes of the works of the great Shalom Shabbazzi, whose grave in Taiz we hoped to visit. Into our suitcases went prayer shawls for the heads of the communities, hundreds of garments with tzitzit (fringes) for the children, and $7,000 worth of tefillin (phylacteries) for the young men. These items were buried among dozens of donated women's dresses and robes. In the end, each suitcase contained religious supplies valued at thousands of dollars, cargo which would be even more valuable in terms of spiritual impact.

But religious supplies don't grow on trees. Airfare for five and the cost of two weeks worth of hotel rooms, food, ground transportation, and security had certainly not been waived for ICROJOY by Yemen's nascent tourist industry. And the Jewish organizations we approached were loath to give us any financial support. Fortunately, the influence of a divine hand—in the form of a timely $40,000 loan that my wife secured from a Manhattan investment banking magnate—got ICROJOY off the ground both figuratively and literally. The magnate in question was Michael Steinhardt, a prominent philanthropist and collector of Judaica. Into ICROJOY's dwindling bank account the $40,000 had gone, and by September it had all but disappeared as the apartment filled with boxes and my desk became piled high with airplane tickets and documents from Universal Travel & Tourism.

We had been endowed with ample financial support, but getting hold of the huge quantity of religious articles crammed into our swollen suitcases had proven to be a superhuman task in itself. Even the dozens of Jewish booksellers in a city like New York cannot produce hundreds of books and ritual objects on a few week's notice. Dalia struggled valiantly to buy up a significant portion of New York's tefillin supply without being able to tell the sellers why the phylacteries were needed. We spun tales and concocted stories in order to obtain copies of the great Shalom Shabbazzi's works. Then Dalia traveled to Crown Heights in Brooklyn to meet with the Lubavitcher Rebbe, who gave ICROJOY his fervent blessing along with dozens of free shofars and mezuzot for the needy Jews of Yemen. That August, the delivery men on Bennett Avenue had noted a puzzling and dramatic increase in the number of packages addressed to me.

In my apartment on September 5, Pierre Goloubinoff's task was to prepare us for what we would find upon entering a Jewish home in the northern country. According to Goloubinoff, success hinged on the delegation's ability to win the trust of the Jews it met. Our difficult task was to befriend a community that would immediately doubt our authenticity. The anxious Jews of Yemen, isolated for so long, would accuse us of being agents of the Republic.

Hours north of Yemen, in offices where only code names are uttered, another organization was eagerly awaiting the ICROJOY mission's send-off and return. The Israeli Mossad is responsible for the physical well-being of the Jews of the Diaspora. It is the world's smallest intelligence agency, and reputedly the most savage. Founded in 1951 on the orders of David Ben-Gurion, the first Prime Minister of the new Jewish state, the Israeli Institute for Intelligence and Special Operations, known worldwide as the Mossad, Hebrew for "institute," has a tiny staff but a catalogue of coups that far overshadow its occasional blunders. It has at its disposal an Israeli population boasting innumerable talents, languages, and geographical origins, and has been known to attempt infiltrations, penetrations, and assassinations in high-risk Arab countries, although most of its operations abroad take place in relatively low-risk Europe and North America.

For Yemeni Jewry, the doors of emigration had been sealed since September 26, 1962, and little is known about Mossad activities in Yemen from that date on. The Mossad was certainly aware of the

Jews remaining in Yemen, for it had debriefed Pierre Goloubinoff at great length If there had been any attempts to rescue Yemeni Jews, those operations had certainly not been successful. In any case, as the name ICROJOY gained recognition in Washington, the Mossad seemed to come awake, suddenly seeking to be involved in the rescue effort, and ICROJOY hesitantly had to comply. My fatigue on the night before the mission to Yemen was partially the result of the bizarre relationship between ICROJOY and the Mossad, a partnership initiated by the latter.

Only Lester Smerka and my wife knew that I had just returned from a clandestine four days in Tel Aviv. My association with the Mossad had begun in August, with an urgent telephone call from a man in the Israeli embassy in Washington. It was "very important" that I come immediately to discuss my upcoming trip; the embassy would pay my plane fare. A briefing in Washington soon became a clandestine trip to Israel in the final week of August 1989. Upon landing in Tel Aviv, I was met by an official near the iron bust of David Ben-Gurion that greets arriving passengers.

We circumvented customs and drove at death-defying speed through the sprawling city straight to the Dan Accadia Hotel, where I was given a fine suite at Mossad expense. There, I spent hour after hour talking to two men who identified themselves only as "Gadi" and "Amos." These were obviously pseudonyms. With brown skin and a shock of black hair, Amos was a Yemeni Jew, but Yemeni mothers rarely name their sons Amos. I sat with Gadi, a tall, handsome man, and his shorter, stockier partner, as we looked down at the crowds on the sweltering palm-treed boardwalk stories below, talking about ICROJOY and the Jews of Yemen. I was told to observe the Jews, find out about their welfare, take copious notes for Mossad consumption, and never do anything suspicious. Apparently, the Mossad deemed going to the Yemen Arab Republic dangerous, and thirsted for information. I viewed these overtures from the Mossad as attempts to hitch its wagon to our star.

Feeling that a refusal to cooperate with the Mossad would cause problems we didn't need, I reluctantly agreed for the sake of the Jews of Yemen. With plentiful connections in the State Department, the

Israelis could easily have jeopardized our mission by painting a negative picture of ICROJOY. One phone call would have ruined it all. It was impossible to refuse the Mossad without risking the destruction of all the relationships we had forged in Washington. I chose not to inform Washington of my quiet little excursion to Tel Aviv. Instead, Dalia became my personal geyser of excuses, spouting forth my whereabouts—"He's on vacation in Cocoa Beach, in Florida"—to friends, neighbors, and government officials. Even my own father in Israel did not know that I was only minutes away from him, in Tel Aviv. "I haven't heard from your husband in a while," a puzzled Laurie Johnson told Dalia one week before we were scheduled to depart.

September 6, 1989

The Lufthansa jet making the Frankfurt-Sanaa run carried its usual assortment of passengers as it broke Yemeni airspace. In its cabin, Arabs in suits and keffiyehs sat among wealthy German businessmen and weary Texas oil executives. The incessant whine of mammoth engines drowned out murmurs in several mother tongues. In its belly, fourteen tremendous cardboard boxes that had journeyed from New York a day earlier shifted softly with the turbulence of the descent. Within a half-hour, the ink-black atmosphere had given way to the soft glow of the lights illuminating the Yemeni capital, and as the aircraft taxied down the runway five passengers peered through its windows with particular urgency, unable to discern anything in the distance. As the plane rolled to a stop in the silent night, they exchanged nervous glances. Years earlier, a Southern Baptist from Colorado had landed on the same runway; so had an eccentric plant geneticist from Switzerland. Their stories had planted a seed in the minds of the creators of a crusade whose moment of truth had suddenly arrived. It was 11:30 p.m. in the ancient city of Sanaa, and the first five Jews to ever enter the twenty-seven-year-old Yemen Arab Republic with explicit permission to visit its Jews were on the ground. ICROJOY's dreams were beginning to come true.

I looked across the aisle at Yosef Levy, sporting his habitual white shirt and gray slacks, a childlike grin brightening his countenance, and immediately imagined a scrawny eleven-year-old darting in and out of colorful Sanaa alleyways in 1949. Yosef was in a daze, hardly able to believe where he was. Lines of worry clouded the expression of Sarah Dahari Halla, whose memories of Raida were fleeting at best as she pondered the prospect of returning to her birthplace. Boaz Mori and Tova Weisberger had regained consciousness after hours of travel, their curiosity aroused. And my own thoughts had turned to a golden hilltop village called a-Tawila, to robed men and veiled women from the faded black-and-white photographs that had decorated the homes of my youth.

But first ICROJOY had to handle a more pressing concern: Sanaa airport security. As each suitcase was meticulously inspected by regally robed security agents, our passports were taken for study by officials, and we were each subjected to a rigorous interrogation: Where are you from? Where were you born? Where in Yemen will you be traveling? What exactly will you be doing in those places? How long will you be staying in the country? I was positive that the answers to these questions had already been provided during lengthy conversations between Sanaa and Washington, but we waited three hours nonetheless. There was little trust between us and the security officers, and nine blank video cassettes were retained with promises that they would be returned the following day.

Our departure from Kennedy International Airport had proven emotionally draining enough. Fervent hugs and kisses with spouses and children were exchanged in a chaotic departures building as five Lufthansa employees struggled with our cumbersome belongings, marveling at the amount of food and clothing each suitcase contained. Once we reached Frankfurt, we stopped speaking Hebrew, communicating only in English. My American-style suede yarmulke had been replaced with a large, brightly embroidered Yemeni one. There was no more time for planning or reconsidering. In the blink of an eye, we had landed in Sanaa.

While the members of the ICROJOY delegation underwent interrogation, the fourteen cartons that had accompanied us, we discovered, were removed from the jet and transferred to a government ministry for a rigorous inspection. Meanwhile, a cordial representative of Universal Travel & Tourism had entered the terminal to welcome us. At 3:00 in the morning, with passports returned, our gear distributed between two minibuses, we finally pulled away from Sanaa International Airport and drove through the silent streets of the capital city. Our destination: the Sheraton Hotel on its more modern outskirts.

The most unusual aspect of Yemeni life is its obsession with qat. Afternoon in Yemen inaugurates a national exercise in lethargy, during which virtually every man and boy retires to his abode to chew qat, a mild stimulant made from the leaves of the short, green qat bushes which proliferate in the country's verdant valleys. Qat, like coffee in many nations, is a social narcotic. As Yemen's long, equatorial day ebbs, the commotion of the marketplace is replaced by the more tranquil, if not comical, scene of men gathering with bunches of round leaves protruding from their mouths and round bulges filling their cheeks. It is an age-old rite that even Shalom Shabbazzi wrote of in a seventeenth-century poem entitled "Qat and Coffee."

Qat is the drug of choice among the Yemeni elite. And ICROJOY would soon be thrust face-to-face with the leaders of the remarkable Yemen Arab Republic. We awoke on September 7 to find Abdul Aziz, our courteous travel agent, waiting in the dimly lit Sheraton lobby. Aziz was a tall, dark Ethiopian severely addicted to cigarettes and qat. But he was also a workaholic, and he arrived at the Sheraton with an announcement that bespoke the magnitude of the barriers broken by ICROJOY: that morning we were to meet with Dr. Abdul Karim al-Iryani, the Deputy Prime Minister and Foreign Secretary.

Like most of the highly intelligent, urbane officials of modern-day Arab governments, Dr. Iryani had been educated in the West. Along with his Ph.D. in biogenetics from Yale, though, came a family history of service to the Republic deeply entrenched in his persona. Most prominently, Iryani's uncle had been as the young nation's President, and his brother had risen to become one of the most respected linguistics scholars in the Middle East. The office of the Deputy Prime Minister is housed in a modern building opposite Ga-el-Yahud. We pulled up in front of it and were immediately escorted upstairs into a waiting area decorated with kaleidoscopic Yemeni rugs and a magnificent portrait of Ali Abdullah Salih. Iryani seemed to be more accessible than his American counterparts; all sorts of private citizens were freely milling about, anticipating their conversations with the Foreign Secretary.

ICROJOY's turn came shortly. Soon we were seated before Dr. Iryani, a surprisingly short man who greeted Sarah, Tova, Boaz, Yosef, and myself enthusiastically. Iryani wore a dark European suit and tie, and his dark face was clean-shaven, constantly flashing a white-toothed grins. The tension was quickly broken when I introduced Yosef to the Foreign Secretary, who appeared honored and humbled to meet the grandson of the great Yhia Yitzhak HaLevi. Of course Iryani had heard of the famous family known as "Beit Yitzhak"! Yosef was stunned, and fell silent as I began to discuss my own field with the Foreign Secretary. Iryani shared my preoccupation with comparative Semitics and archaeology, and for over a half-hour the conversation was confined to academics. Arab etiquette that demanded we save business for last.

Only during the final ten minutes of the meeting did the Jews of Yemen become a topic. I requested the installation of two telephones for their use, one each in Saada and Raida. Then I asked for the installation of two post office boxes in the same cities. We made a "humanitarian request" that Yhia ibn Daoud Suberi, age eighty-six, be allowed to leave the Yemen Arab Republic for medical treatment abroad. We also asked about the possibility of opening a bank account to pay the salaries of six teachers; and about the employment, either by ICROJOY or the Republic of Yemen, of teachers of basic English and mathematics for the Jewish community. I inquired about maintaining the grave of Shalom Shabbazzi, and temporarily bringing two exchange students to the United States for intense Jewish education and training. We did not expect the Yemenis to take immediate action on any of these points; we simply wanted to establish a relationship of mutual trust and respect with them. Iryani proved to be a genuinely likable person, and it was hard to believe that he supported his government's senseless stance on the Jewish people. The modern leaders of the Yemen Arab Republic had no inherent dislike for Jews; they simply seemed to be kowtowing before their mighty Arab neighbors.

Yosef Levy agreed with my impressions when we emerged into the street. In Ga-el-Yahud, the old Jewish quarter of bleached stone houses in beige and white, Yosef immersed himself in the brilliant past. He remembered the Jewish homes now inhabited by Arabs, but the memories were not mournful. The Jews of Sanaa had not been wiped out; their children and grandchildren were now walking the streets of Tel Aviv and Jerusalem. Nostalgia fueled Yosef's tears as he stumbled upon the small house that had been his family's home, and even discovered a yellowed scroll bearing his father's signature. Upon further inspection, Levy determined that the document was the one with which Ga-el-Yahud had been acquired from the imam in 1905 as an area for Jewish settlement.

Exploring the quarter's busy marketplaces, Yosef and I located the pitiful last Jew in Sanaa. Yehudah Tzadok was a seventy-four-year-old panhandler living like an animal in a ramshackle hut among the decrepit of Sanaa. Arab children needled him mercilessly as he wandered narrow alleyways in search of palm-reading customers. Tzadok was the prototypical Jew who had not taken the Magic Carpet; life without the company of fellow Jews had become a nightmare of poverty and loneliness. Rosh Hashanah was fast approaching, so Yosef and I gave Tzadok a shofar to blow, and he did so elatedly. The company of two concerned Jews provided Yehudah Tzadok with much more comfort than the money we gave him. As the only Jew in a city of hundreds of thousands, he lamented his lack of funds and companionship. Unfortunately, ICROJOY could only temporarily relieve these needs. Yehudah Tzadok would later die in Yemen. He never saw the Holy Land.

September 8, 1989
Friday morning. Balmy air wafted beneath a brilliant sun the ICROJOY caravan—minivans, not camels, since it was the twentieth century—weaved its way over rock and brush, through the volcanic landscape of the road to Raida. Our driver had spread a filthy blanket across the dashboard to prevent the instrument panel from overheating, and Arab pop music crackled from the radio. In the

distance, ancient mud-walled fortress towns and emerald valleys were also being warmed that late summer day, but I felt eerily chilly inside the rumbling van. We were slowly approaching the north country. Soon we would be pulling into villages inhabited by Jews. Would they accept our advances, invite us into their homes, trust our organization? Would we be rejected, mistaken for government agents? The utility of months of round-the-clock preparation—and years of political struggle—was about to be determined.

My anxiety had not subsided by the time Raida came into view. Sparse patches of shrubbery dotted the rocky terrain upon which the village of the Jews had been built. Its sun-beaten dirt streets were empty as we ground to a halt in front of a cluster of rectangular two-story and three-story houses. Low stone walls divided plots of stubby land. Here and there a rusted bicycle lay on its side in what would be a front lawn, a lone chicken pecked at the parched earth. Sarah and Tova, without an inch of skin exposed, stepped gingerly out of the van. Boaz alighted with his videocamera humming, Yosef and I followed, and we found ourselves before the terraced abode of a Raida Jew. The delighted shrieks of children could be discerned in the distance, as well as the high-pitched wail of an infant. But oddly, there was not a person in sight.

Five Americans in their strange dress, accompanied by armed Arab guards, do not go unnoticed, though. Suddenly, a tiny head peeked out from behind a crumbling wall. It belonged to a young boy, around eight years old, with locks of curly black hair cascading from above his ears, wearing a beautiful navy-blue robe and an ornate kipah. His curious friends soon scampered over to gaze at the spectacle, boys in robes and girls in exquisite hoods and dresses. "Where is your father? Where is your mother? Where does the Halla family live?" we inquired in the Judeo-Arabic dialect of the Yemeni Jews. Sarah Dahari Halla and Yosef Levy repeatedly declared their identities. But the children refused to divulge any information, not knowing or believing who we were. They had been trained to be wary of strangers, even those claiming to be brethren. Fifteen minutes later, our adamant assertions had achieved no progress. Frustration began to set in.

Then an old man hobbled out of the house to behold all the hubbub. Gaunt and hunched over, with his dirty white beard concealing the top of an arresting floor-length robe of azure blue, he was the boy's grandfather, and it was with him that we would have to establish our bona fides. But how could I prove I was Jewish to a Jew who had inherited the most authentic and least tainted version of the religion? My yarmulke meant nothing to the man; any intelligent intelligence agent would know to obtain and wear one if he wanted to infiltrate the community. Sarah and Tova wore nothing distinctively Jewish, and our boxes of Hebrew books spoke nothing about us. What identifying mark did we possess that would produce no doubts, carry with it no traces of disguise? I combed my pockets for a religious article of some kind but found nothing. But I could feel something between the pocket and my leg underneath it. My tzitzit! The fringes hanging from the four-cornered garments worn by Jewish men! I quickly loosened my sweat-soaked shirt to allow the distinctive white strings to fall out. The old man smiled and nodded in recognition and acceptance. We were Jews who had come to help.

Other Jews began to pour out of the house to greet us, cheering and swarming the minivans, the men in their robes and keffiyehs, with sidelocks down to their shoulders. Women descended in their flowery, embroidered dresses, jewelry jangling and looking like my grandmother in faded photographs. As they beat on tinny tambourines to welcome us, a verse from the Book of Exodus penetrated my mind: "And Miriam, the prophetess, the sister of Aaron, took a timbrel in her hand; and all the women went out after her with timbrels and with dances."

We had entered biblical times once more. The Jews hoisted me on their shoulders and upstairs we went to the *mafraj* of the Halla family, with great fanfare. Seated on cushions on the stone floor, adults and children gathered around us excitedly to hear our story, and we their tales. The dozens of residents of Suq-el-Jadid, Raida's Jewish enclave, filled the room, eager to see the gifts we had brought. As I opened one of the ICROJOY cartons, men, women, and children began to beg for the prayer books and the volumes of Shabbazzi poetry. Young boys beamed as they displayed the new prayer shawls that replaced their frayed and tattered ones.

Meanwhile, an aging man and woman began weeping on the shoulder of their great-niece, Sarah. The Dahari Hallas were still grieving over the murder of their two sons in 1986, and they spoke in fear of reprisals from the Arab who had committed the dastardly deed. We learned that the two young brothers, although construction workers, had moonlighted as amulet-writers. Their untimely demise had come when one of their Arab clients cried foul over an amulet that had supposedly brought harm instead of protection. And the Halla family was reeling from a more current tragedy: Moshe Dahari Halla, Sarah's first cousin, son of one of the murder victims, had recently been crippled in a hit-and-run accident. Subsequently, an ill-fated operation in a Sanaa Hospital had left the young father of one impotent. Moshe was not in Raida, however. The Yemenis had flown him and his brother Hayim to Amman, the capital of Jordan, for more surgery.

Familiar names abounded in Raida. Baking in one of the houses in Suq-el-Jadid, we found a sickly, ancient man from Sanaa for whom the town's residents were magnanimously caring. He was eighty-six years old, and the length of those years had worn away the use of both his dulled eyes. A few strands of gray hair protruded from a brown face that was shriveled along with the man's mouth, which muttered verses from Scripture to pass the day. Beneath a billowing white robe, two brown, bony legs rested on a grungy mat. Crouching on the floor, I took his aged hands in my own and asked his name. "Yhia. Yhia Suberi." It was Yhia ibn Daoud Suberi! The man who had kissed his sons and daughter goodbye four decades earlier, and had never heard from them since. But I was able to bridge that painful gap. Cradling Suberi in my arms like a baby, I told him that Shalom and David and Shoshana were alive and well in the Land of Israel, that he was a grandfather many times over, that soon he would join them in the Holy Land. The old man began to weep, then burst into joyful song. He kissed my hand and forehead repeatedly, then placed both his wrinkled hands on my head and blessed me. Hope had come alive for the Jews of Yemen.

Many of them had electricity and gas lamps in their homes, they owned automobiles and motorcycles, but their simple lives were marked by dread, and by isolation from their brothers and sisters. Our fears regarding the state of Yemeni Jewry had been confirmed. The dearth of religious articles was eclipsed by the absence of properly trained teachers of Torah. Spiritual deterioration was beginning to set in. Wherever our travels in Yemen took us, the Jews would receive our presents with an unbridled joy that I envied. Their legendary devotion to Torah study was intact—and mind-boggling. Simply by sharing faded texts, young boys had acquired the ability to read Hebrew and Aramaic effortlessly from any direction, including upside-down. Now these bright-eyed children gathered earnestly around Sarah. She was their connection to Jewry outside Yemen, and she played the part beautifully, engaging in animated conversations with the people of her birthplace.

Yosef Levy was given the deference to which both his esteemed surname and his gentle personality entitled him, although his modern appearance was initially cause for confusion: how could he be a Jew if he had no beard or sidelocks? Wherever we went, Levy was tested by the Jews we met, and he would always pass with flying colors by leading prayer services, reading the Torah, and singing the songs of his youth. In the synagogue in Saada, Levy found the few prayer books he had sent in 1975, but he realized that most Yemeni Jews had learned to pray without the benefit of textual aids. Prayers and Torah were taught by heart, passed down from father to son in an oral tradition that dated back centuries. But there were subtle changes in Yemeni Jewish behavior that troubled Yosef Levy. In his grandfather's time, strict observance of Shabbat had been the magnificent hallmark of Yemeni Jewry, so much so that the entire Friday was spent in feverish preparation for and anticipation of the Day of Rest. Now, the Jews worked right until sunset on Friday. To Levy this laxity in preparing for the Sabbath constituted a *yeridah*, a fall from grace.

Yosef Levy was even more disturbed by other metamorphoses in the Yemeni Jewish character. Growing up in Sanaa, Yosef had known his fellow Jews as bastions of modesty, quiet men and women who acted humbly and with great reserve and gentility. Yosef's mouth fell open in shock, though, when he first saw a Yemeni Jewish man raising his voice in anger. Slowly, the influence of non-Jewish neighbors had effected a change in the tiny Jewish community. In Levy's youth, illiteracy had been unknown among Yemen's Jews, but no longer. Some could not read; many others could not answer simple questions about Judaism. Now, there were no teachers of Torah in Yemen; there was no leadership structure. The knives of the ritual slaughterers were in order, the Shabbat raisin wine was properly made, but spiritual deterioration was quite evident. The men had learned to pray without tefillin, and some even refused the tefillin ICROJOY attempted to distribute, preferring prayer books instead. Their *mikvaot* (ritual bathhouses) were few and far between, and the ones that did exist tended to be putrid. And the Jews were consuming qat in massive quantities, spending large sums of money to chew the leaves, which they believed have marvelous properties ranging from the aphrodisiac to a cure for diabetes. In afternoons the Jews, like their Arab neighbors, would lounge about with qat filling their cheeks, in order to fantasize and obsess. Where was the purity of yesteryear?

Levy's observations helped us grasp the gravity of the situation. As we toured the northern countryside, attending in festive weddings and circumcisions as honored guests, falling in love with the primitive lifestyle of the Jews of Yemen, we perceived the ravages of isolation. We felt the despair of the communities in Asahen and Ghuraz, bereft of a Torah scroll. We felt the tense relations between Jews and Arabs as pistol-bearing security guards followed our every move, even sitting with us in synagogue. Outside Taiz, we stood at the grave of Shalom Shabbazzi and recalled the man who had fortified the faith of Yemeni Jewry. In Saada, we witnessed the intense scrutiny given the Jewish shopkeepers of Suq Yom al-Had by the local police. We beheld the throngs of Jews calling for our attention and financial assistance from the courtyard of Saada's Ma'amoun Hotel. We experienced the destitution of Yehudah Tzadok, the last Jew in Sanaa, and shed tears as precious young boys in Raida and Wadi Amlah and Hidan Asham and Sahin read passionately from the books we had brought for them. We even dined on paper plates in the home of Ambassador Charles Dunbar.

The days were long, emotional, and thoroughly exhausting.

Shortly before we returned to New York, I was stopped in the streets of Saada by a robed Jewish man and his young son. They had learned of ICROJOY's arrival in the Yemen Arab Republic and were searching desperately for the religious articles we had brought. Our delegation had not visited their village, and they had obviously traveled for hours to find us. Father and son were both crestfallen when I explained to them that we simply had nothing left; the fourteen tremendous cartons were quite empty. I had no choice but to reach under my shirt, remove my tzitzit, and hand them over to the boy, whose large brown eyes sparkled with excitement. My tzitzit could easily be replaced in New York; perhaps on his small body, they would sustain a family until its freedom could be won.

Chapter Seven

"OPERATION ESTHER"

September 17, 1989

The sun rose at 5:00 a.m. to bake Saada, and in their Spartan rooms in the Ma'amoun Hotel, the members of the ICROJOY delegation were preparing for another grueling day. Soon we were to head back to Sanaa and board a plane for New York, leaving behind the simple, beautiful Jews of Yemen. I headed downstairs for some coffee and fresh air.

They were waiting for us in the lobby, brandishing AK-47s. Two Yemeni security agents immediately recognized me as I stepped into the Ma'amoun courtyard, and the sight of their weapons made morning coffee quite unnecessary. The two men demanded to search all the delegation's suitcases, and for the next hour we argued with them, urging that they contact their headquarters, and insisting that our Arab guides could attest to the innocence of the delegation: that we had photographed nothing militarily sensitive, that there was no cause for such an inspection. But I realized that the orders for this early morning surprise had probably come from the Yemeni National Security Office. The Mukhabarat men were presumably following orders, and our guides would be unable and unwilling to help.

The agents knew we were American citizens, and I was quite confident they would do us no harm. Nevertheless, their bluster frightened us. I asked permission to call Charlie Dunbar or Dr. Iryani in Sanaa. Absolutely not. I refused to allow the security agents near the suitcases, instead proposing a compromise: we would hand over whatever the members of the delegation were carrying on their persons. This turned out to comprise two audiotapes, one 35 mm. roll of film, 150 Polaroid snapshots, and three of Boaz's video cassettes, much of the material we had used to chronicle our journey.

As I held the security agents at bay with argumentation, we quickly loaded the luggage into our two vans. Before pulling away to avoid any more trouble, I demanded and received the telephone number of one of the agents, vowing to call when the delegation reached Raida. When we arrived Raida over three hours later, I immediately dialed the number in order to threaten swift and harsh reprisals by the U.S. government. No ringing at the other end. The number was fictitious. My next call was placed to the embassy of the United States in Sanaa. After I had apprised Georgia DeBelle, the U.S. chargé d'affaires, of the situation, we returned to the Dahari Halla residence to eat for the last time with the aunts, uncles, and cousins of Sarah Dahari Halla. There we were finally introduced to the injured Moshe Dahari Halla and his brother Hayim. The two had just returned from two months of mysterious government-sponsored medical care in Amman. Moshe claimed that his leg injuries had been healed in the Jordanian hospital but he still suffered from impotence. The quirky twenty-year-old spoke of his intense desire to go to the United States for treatment. He would even be willing to leave his wife and young daughter, "America," for several weeks.

The Yemen Arab Republic's sudden burst of concern for an injured Jew surprised me. Why had the Yemeni government gone out of its way to provide for a member of a populace it refused to set free? I would later discover that Moshe and Hayim had in fact been used to perpetuate a fraudulent claim on the part of the Arab state. In Amman, the brothers had been interviewed by a Jordanian TV while Jordanian police looked on. The brothers' dark and exotic faces had subsequently appeared on a Jordanian television program which was picked up in Israel. While this gave Israeli viewers irrefutable proof that there were still Jews trapped in Yemen, what Moshe and Hayim said to the interviewers made the Yemeni government's Jewish policy appear generous and humane. As reported in dozens of newspapers around the world, the program claimed that the North Yemeni ambassador to Jordan had greeted them at the Amman airport.

The ambassador, who also appeared with the two brothers on television, said that this was a humanitarian act on the part of the President, who wanted to emphasize that there is no discrimination in Yemen.

Replying to questions on the situation in North Yemen, the brothers said: "We don't feel there is any discrimination. We learn together with the Arabs in public school. In our area there are about 150–200 Jews. There are those among us who learn in the synagogues and the older ones go to public school. But until this day we don't know how to read or write. We both work as locksmiths."

When asked if Jews are permitted to travel abroad, Moshe replied: "Jews don't like to travel abroad but I think whoever wanted to could do so. The fact is that I requested to be treated outside North Yemen and the President granted my request and even suggested that I go to Jordan."

Parting from the wonderful Dahari Halla family proved especially difficult. A bond of mutual love and respect had formed between the five of us and the residents of Raida. We promised to return, bringing more books, more tzitzit, more news from the outside world. We vowed to alleviate their financial straits and labor for their release.

Two weeks had flown by in a heartbeat; ICROJOY now had the responsibility of detailing the plight of Yemeni Jewry to the Department of State. To that end, we took steps to preserve all the meticulously gathered information remaining from the Saada confiscation. So on September 18, before leaving the Sanaa Sheraton for the airport, we put the videotapes, rolls of film, and handwritten notes where the male airport officials would surely not search: beneath the clothes of Sarah and Tova. But security at Sanaa International Airport was ready for us. As the delegation passed through metal detectors before boarding the Lufthansa flight, Sarah and Tova were ushered brusquely into a side room where a female agent frisked them, immediately discovering and confiscating nine video cassettes, eight rolls of film, two audio cassettes, and pages of notes I had recorded during our travels. No embassy officials were present; airport security seemed to know exactly what it was looking for. It was a second, humiliating loss, and our vociferous protests were fruitless. I decided to make a scene in the airport, threatening to call Dr. Iryani in the middle of the night if *icrojoy*'s materials were not returned, delaying the flight for twenty minutes by refusing to board in the film's absence. But to no avail.

The Lufthansa jet cleared Yemeni airspace, and our sweetest of journeys ended on quite a bitter note. From Amman I called Georgia DeBelle to report the latest incident, and from Frankfurt the same was conveyed to Laurie Johnson in Washington. We spent many hours in the air pondering the breath-taking foreign land we had just explored. Our brothers and sisters lived simple, wholesome lives in deprivation, bereft of religious necessities and teachers and of communication with their fellow Jews. Yet the rulers of the Republic were not the ruthless tyrants I had judged them to be. Discrimination was not on the books in Yemen, though it appeared to be the tacit law of the land in the north country. ICROJOY had initiated crucial dialogue with the government; barriers of distrust were slowly coming down. We had proven our proficiency as amateur diplomats, so touching down at Kennedy Airport did not symbolize the termination of ICROJOY's activities. Rather, it intensified our commitment to the task at hand.

The clouds of secrecy in which the mission was shrouded began to dissipate soon after we embraced our families in the International Arrivals Terminal. A bouquet of flowers from David Ransom and Laurie Johnson awaited my return to Washington Heights. "You had a difficult trip with a lot of success," read the card. But within one week, I was back in Tel Aviv, compelled to talk to the Mossad. I had not the faintest desire to deal with the Israelis, but they insisted, and I feared the consequences of refusing. Bereft of photographs and notes with which to describe my travels to Gadi and Amos in the Dan Accadia, I reviewed my experiences from memory.

At one point during the debriefing, I was driven to the office of the Prime Minister in Jerusalem, an hour away along the country's principal paved artery into the Judean Hills. There, Yossi ben Aharon, Yitzhak Shamir's chief of staff, ushered me into his office for a half-hour conversation. Around us sat General Avigdor Kahalani, a

Yemeni, and several grim-looking military advisors who declined to identify themselves. I spoke candidly: The Yemen Arab Republic takes care of its Jews. The nation's one discriminatory policy, though, is that of denying them emigration, an obstacle that can be erased through careful, quiet negotiation and by cultivating trust—not through threats or clandestine operations.

Perhaps my recommendations were considered, perhaps they were cast aside at once as the babblings of an amateur. Either way, I was back in a Mossad vehicle for an immediate return to Tel Aviv, then a more lengthy return to New York. Over the next two years, I would have many a conversation with men from Israeli intelligence. Shlomo Gal, a senior Mossad officer, would on one occasion tell me that he could not understand why Israel had never done anything to secure the release of the Jews of Yemen.

Three important weeks of the semester had already evaporated by the time I set foot again in Yeshiva University. But my mind was elsewhere, and it would remain fixed on that elsewhere for several more years. Soon many others would learn about my little diversion and excursion. ICROJOY, through Yeshiva University's public relations office, issued a carefully worded statement to the Jewish Telegraphic Agency, emphasizing how "grateful" the Jews were "to the government of the Yemen Arab Republic." From the JTA offices in New York, bulletins were dispatched to hundreds of subscribers, and ICROJOY's name and story materialized in the pages of the *Canadian Jewish News* of Toronto, the *Jewish World* of New York, the *American Jewish World* of Minneapolis, and the *B'nai B'rith Messenger* of Los Angeles. Readers of Miami's *Jewish Floridian* and Nashville's *Jewish Observer* learned that "for the first time in nearly four decades, American Jews of Yemeni descent were able to visit the country of their ancestry, the Yemen Arab Republic." The *Jewish Ledger* of Rochester, the *Missouri Jewish Post & Opinion* of St. Louis, and the *Algemeiner Journal* of New York declared that "Yemeni Jewry is believed to be the most ancient Jewish community in the world. It is said to be able to trace the establishment of the Jewish community in Yemen back to the time of the Queen of Sheba." The *Baltimore Jewish Times*, the London *Jewish Chronicle*, and the *Greater Phoenix*

Jewish News stated that Yemen's Jews, "although isolated from mainstream Jewry for centuries . . . succeeded in preserving Jewish knowledge and culture."

As I set out to compose a day-by-day analysis of our visit for the State Department, I realized that ICROJOY was slowly beginning to accomplish its goal. Hundreds of Yemeni Jews might soon be joining their brothers and sisters in Israel; it would be a truly landmark event in Jewish history for freedom of emigration to be granted. ICROJOY's project deserved a name, an identity of its own. So before mailing my fourteen-page report to Washington, I attached a simple cover sheet that invoked the memory of my mother, Esther, an honorable and devoted Jewess in the Yemeni tradition. ICROJOY's crusade suddenly became known as "Operation Esther." Underneath the title, I inserted a sentence from Scripture that conjured up images of an ancient, faithful people experiencing redemption. It was a verse from the Book of Esther:

"The Jews had light and happiness and joy and honor."

October 4, 1989
United Nations Plaza, a matrix of offices and conference rooms where sensitive international polices are molded, glistens on Manhattan's East Side. Among the many nations lightly treading the art of diplomacy there this particular morning was the Yemen Arab Republic. Its well-preened Deputy Prime Minister and Foreign Minister, Dr. Iryani, sat with Ahmed Hassan, his loyal secretary, and Yemeni U.N. ambassador al-Ashtal, across from Tova Weisberger and myself as we congenially addressed concerns born of ICROJOY's mission to Yemen, Operation Esther. First on the agenda was retrieval of the materials confiscated from us in Saada and at Sanaa's airport, and indeed Iryani opened the discussion with the apologetic disclosure that our Polaroid photographs had been sent to the Yemeni embassy in Washington. They would be mailed directly to me upon their arrival in the nation's capital. The return of nine video cassettes, four or five audiotapes, eleven rolls of film, and written materials, however, had been delayed by Yemen's preoccupation

with Revolution Day, September 26. I handed Hassan a short catalogue of ICROJOY's missing property.

But more than a review of our informational losses, the meeting at the Yemen mission would be remembered as an occasion when Iryani lent us his ear. I talked about the causes and devastating ramifications of the Jewish *mohar,* the dowries of Jewish girls, which often amounted to $30,000. Despite the noncompliance of Yemeni Muslims with the federal ceiling on the Muslim *mohar* price, I suggested that the government enact a law to limit the *mohar* to a price Jews could afford. I attributed the Saada community's disunity to the lack of a Torah scroll, possession of which would bring the community together for prayer. Iryani volunteered to send a Torah scroll through the Yemeni embassy. I requested permission for Moshe Dahari Halla to come to the United States for medical treatment. Iryani responded that Moshe was scheduled to return to Amman for another operation in six months, and if that failed, the young Jew would be able to come to America. Did we know of Moshe and his brother's interview for Jordanian television? The Deputy Prime Minister hoped it had dispelled rumors of PLO aggression against Yemeni Jewry. I inquired about the possibility of support for Jewish teachers. Iryani said that ICROJOY could open an account in a Yemeni bank with branches in Raida and Amran, from which teachers would be able to draw salaries. Furthermore, triweekly English and Arabic lessons could be arranged. Finally, Iryani pledged that steps would be taken to preserve the deteriorating grave of Shalom Shabbazzi.

A more thorny issue was that of Jews visiting the Republic. Dr. Iryani stated that any American citizen without an Israeli visa on his passport could obtain a Yemeni tourist visa. But, fearful of an influx of Jewish visitors who saw themselves as "ambassadors" to the Jews of Yemen, he preferred that all religious and cultural contacts be arranged exclusively through me, and that no group besides ICROJOY would be allowed into Jewish homes. The sole exception: Neturei Karta, due to its long-standing relationship with the Yemeni government and the PLO. Visas would continue to be issued to Neturei Karta emissaries, despite the possibility that they exploited the Yemeni Jews in some ways.

I was pleasantly surprised to learn that the Deputy Prime Minister had been thinking about Yhia ibn Daoud Suberi. Iryani knew that Suberi had once been a rich man but had become impoverished in 1972, unsuccessfully attempting to reclaim his land in the courts. Suberi had once frequented the government ministries in Sanaa, we were told, had been granted some money, and had even seen President Ali Abdullah Salih on several occasions.

I did not know it at the time, but ICROJOY's conversation with Iryani at the United Nations would provide the soil for the November journey to the Yemen Arab Republic of Yehiel Hibshoosh. A somewhat eccentric eighty-year-old with a U.S. passport, Hibshoosh was the first person to take advantage of the Foreign Minister's concessions. Not counting the members of ICROJOY, he was the first foreign private citizen to visit the Jews of Yemen with the Yemeni government's explicit sanction.

Born in Sanaa in 1910, Hibshoosh had fled to the Holy Land in the 1930s, and had resided in Brooklyn for many years, writing books of Jewish interest. In November 1989, white-haired Hibshoosh returned to Sanaa and toured the northern countryside to see the isolated Jews for himself. Taking hundreds of photographs, the aging but vigorous author subsequently reported to the Israeli news media that there were fifteen hundred Jews in Yemen, and while in no immediate danger, their condition was nevertheless poor. This, of course, was true, but Hibshoosh also succeeded in endangering the lives of the Jews he visited, afflicting them with run-ins with the Mukhabarat. By traveling in restricted areas or along back roads without permits, the eighty-year-old invoked the wrath of Yemen's security apparatus.

In Sanaa, Hibshoosh managed to obtain an audience with Dr. Iryani and elicited promises of progress from him, assurances that found their way into the Israeli press. Just two months later, a 200-page instant book appeared in Israeli bookstores. Entitled *The Remnant in Yemen,* it was published by the "Hibshoosh Family Press." In it, Yehiel Hibshoosh detailed his experiences in Raida and Saada and the northern villages. He told how he had "saved" the Jews just by visiting them. Color photographs of the families I had come to know spoke volumes. A people straight out of the Bible persisted in Yemen.

October 25, 1989
Two genres of mail originating at 150 Nassau Street were traveling to addresses across the country. The first was of the form-letter variety, typed on ICROJOY stationery. Dozens of them were being sent to the figures named on ICROJOY's masthead, the Congressmen and private citizens who had joined our crusade in its earliest days. Among them were Senators Alfonse D'Amato and Daniel Patrick Moynihan and Representatives Benjamin Gilman and Stephen Solarz, all of whom were told:

> It is our pleasure to advise you that there have been significant developments in our efforts to help the Jews of Yemen. The State Department and the Yemeni government, both aware of your support for our cause, have negotiated a trip to Yemen which took place last month. I and four other American Jews of Yemeni descent spent two weeks in Yemen, visiting with the Jewish people and distributing religious books and articles. For the benefit of continued cooperation with the Yemeni government we have changed the name of our organization to the International Coalition for the Revival of the Jews of Yemen. Thanks to your support we have merited a successful beginning. Your support is vital for continued success.

The second letter was typed on plain paper and addressed to Ambassador Richard Schifter. It was from Sarah Dahari Halla, 2185 Bolton Street, Bronx, New York, and it said:

> Thank you for making my recent trip to Yemen a reality. It was like a dream to finally be reunited with my family. While in Yemen, I discovered a problem suffered by a family member which I would like to bring to your attention. One of my cousins, Moshe Dahari Halla, is a young man of 22 years, married, with one child. Last year he was a random subject of an interview by a French news team inquiring about the condition of the Jews of Yemen. When he finished the interview, he got on his bike to go home. A few minutes later he was struck by a hit-and-run driver. He sustained

severe internal injuries. He underwent six or seven operations in Sanaa, and was then sent to Amman, Jordan for further medical treatment. It seems that the government of the YAR has bent over backwards to help him, as they have picked up the cost of his treatments.

Unfortunately, as a result of those treatments, he has become impotent. According to the information we were able to gather from the English-language medical transcripts, he apparently suffered nerve damage. We understand that this condition can be reversed with proper and prompt medical treatment. I am therefore requesting that you urgently prevail upon the government of the YAR to send him to the United States for the treatment which is available at several first-rate institutions. On the basis of this being an obvious humanitarian affair, I urge you to have Moshe brought to the USA prior to the state visit of President Ali Abdullah Salih. Kindly let me know the status of this matter, either directly or through Dr. Tawil.

As governments on both sides of the ocean gained confidence in ICROJOY, the organization had gained confidence in itself. With our delicate amalgam of patience and persistence, we were poised to make major breakthroughs. One body that seemed to recognize this was the Joint Distribution Committee. A telephone call to me had led to a meeting with Michael Schneider, the JDC's executive director, and that October meeting had been followed by a momentous announcement: the JDC would assume financial responsibility for all of ICROJOY's ventures. The time for rescuing Yemeni Jewry was now; it was the JDC's last chance to latch onto success in that area. There would be more missions to Yemen, until every last Jew had been safely accompanied to Israel. Michael Steinhardt would be recompensed for his $40,000 contribution. The JDC, one of the Jewish organizations that had originally spurned our efforts, was now welcoming ICROJOY under its wings. We were happy to oblige. I began making calls to Universal Travel & Tourism.

November 6, 1989
Hours of oratory had come to a grateful conclusion in the Knesset, and its members were finally preparing to settle on the wording of an official declaration. Twenty-seven years after the doors of

redemption had closed on the Jews of Yemen, Israel's parliament was spending a day discussing their plight. Eliezer Mizrahi of the Agudat Yisrael party had inaugurated it, telling the chamber,

It is as yet unknown why all the Jews did not come to Israel during Magic Carpet. Some seem to think that those who remained lived in remote places and did not have enough time to reach the assembly sites, or were not healthy enough to make the long, arduous journey. Conflicting reports arrive regarding the state of Yemeni Jewry. Different statistics talk of 1,000 to 10,000 Jews. But the disheartening conclusion of academicians, journalists, and men of vision alike is clear. The state of Yemeni Jewry is poor. The fact is that the Jews left behind in Yemen are unable to leave Yemen, unable to unite with their families in Israel and the world, they lack mail communication with relatives in Israel and the world and almost forty years have passed without change. . . . I call upon the government to do all it can to speedily bring the exiled Jews of Yemen up to Israel, whether with the help of the United States or by any other means, and the sooner the better.

Shulamit Aloni of the leftist Meretz party had followed, and after exchanging barbs with Mizrahi, who was the representative of a religious party was her Knesset nemesis, she related a conversation with an elderly Yemeni man, once a rider of the Magic Carpet:

We asked him this question: How did your fantasy of flight differ from reality? The man began to count and say: "It's written that we would come on eagles' wings, and we came on eagles' wings. It's written that all would come, including the blind and the lame, the pregnant and the nursing together, and they came. It's written that the desert would sprout, and it has. It's written that they would come from the north, south, east, and west, and that happened." He continued to cite verses from the Book of Joel: that once again the elderly would relax and children would play in the streets of Jerusalem, and that has happened. And as he spoke of verses, he suddenly raised his voice and exclaimed: "And through all this, not all have come here." And he begged me not to forget those who remained.

The Shomrei Torah party's statement had come next, on the heals of Shulamit Aloni's. Its spokesman, Yosef Azran, said:

We have merited, with great and constant effort, the destruction of the iron curtain cloaking Eastern Europe and Russia, and the prophecy that "we will be like dreamers" has been fulfilled in our days. Furthermore, if such is God's desire, the words of the prophet Isaiah will soon come true: "Lift up thine eyes round about, and see: they all are gathered together, and come to thee; thy sons come from far, and thy daughters are born on the side." With the help of God, we will merit an ingathering of exiles from all nations of the Diaspora, and a redeemer shall come to Zion.

Next came Yitzhak Levi of the National Religious Party.

When Russian Jewry was trapped, representatives of the public turned to the government. And they said, you must do something for the Jews of Russia. And the government said every time: quiet, quiet, quiet—we are working, we can't publicize it, we can't talk about it, silence must prevail. Precious time passed until the public could remain quiet no longer. A grass-roots movement of demonstrations and publicity began, causing a commotion in the country, a commotion internationally. I think history proves that commotion is ultimately more effective. I turn to the government that has told us for twenty years: don't talk, be quiet. . . . The question is, will we act this way forever? The question is, how many years or decades must we live with their tiresome answer: you cannot speak about it, you cannot publicize it, you cannot know about it, we are working? I do not doubt that the government is working, but perhaps other public intermediaries should get involved.

Shmuel Halpert of Agudat Yisrael had then commented:

The Jews of Yemen are a wondrous group. They have preserved the flame of Torah since the time of the First Temple. Yemeni Jewry has produced righteous personalities, rabbis and leaders, aside from the poets and songwriters whose tunes are embedded in the Jewish people. However, to our great pain, much of what had been preserved for two thousand years was damaged when the exile of Yemen came to Israel during operation "On Eagles' Wings." Who among us does not remember the pictures and images of Yemeni children with their peyot shorn off on kibbutzim and in other absorption centers? Who cannot recall the anguish of entire families forced to lead secular lives that wreaked havoc with their unique family structure and uprooted their wondrous inheritance of generations? As we judge the case of Yemeni Jewry today, there is no doubt that we must strive without letup for the two thousand that remain there, and it is upon the government of Israel to do all it can to transport them to Israel—in a manner that respects their heritage, in order that those images from "On Eagle's Wings" not return to haunt us again.

And the words of other Knesset members, echoing or qualifying these sentiments, filled forty pages of transcripts by the time the declaration came to a vote. Submitted by Rehavam Ze'evi of the Moledet party, the declaration was in four parts.

1. The Knesset sends a heart-felt blessing of brotherhood to the remnants of Yemeni Jewry who never managed to go up to Israel during Operation Magic Carpet.
2. The Knesset recognizes with fear and trepidation the situation of Yemeni Jewry regarding persecution by the authorities there.
3. The Knesset calls upon the government of Israel to do everything possible in order to expedite the release of Yemeni Jewry and bring them up to Zion for reunification with members of their families, tribes, and nation as they return to their one and only birthplace in the Land of Israel.
4. The Knesset calls upon the government to prepare for absorption of the imminent aliyah and to preserve their traditions, their Torah, and their way of life.

Sips of water, then Vote no. 4 of November 6, 1989: 16 for, 0 against, 0 abstentions.

January 2, 1990

"It's ICROJOY's second mission, and we're working twice as hard!"

Lester Smerka had donned work gloves and was carting carton after carton from my apartment as he addressed the videocamera filming his every move. This time there were twenty-one tremendous cardboard boxes snarling traffic in Apartment 24B. Within them were packed five hundred ordinary prayer books, two hundred High Holiday prayer books, and codes of Jewish law for children and rabbis alike. And then there were the two jewels nestled deep inside two of the containers: Torah scrolls for needy communities in the Yemen Arab Republic. ICROJOY's own supplies were precious, too. The boxes also held an eleven-day supply of hot cocoa, coffee, tea, salami, soups, sauces, tuna fish, cheeses, mayonnaise, peanut butter, jelly, oil, honey, iced tea, mustard, apple sauce, and cakes. We had crammed chocolates, wafers, potato chips, and presliced, vacuum-packed meats into the cartons as well, cushioning them with prayer shawls on each side. Keeping kosher can tax the wallet and complicate travel. Lufthansa Cargo would once again be required to engineer logistical feats; the Department of State was once again dispatching five unofficial emissaries to the Yemen Arab Republic.

The participants in Operation Esther Mission II differed slightly from those in ICROJOY's initial excursion. Yosef Levy, Sarah Dahari Halla, and I yearned to return to our roots, and would indeed be doing so tomorrow. But joining us would be two newcomers to Yemen: First was Varda Hubara, Dalia Smerka's middle-aged cousin of Yemeni extraction. Varda, principal of the day school at Manhattan's Park Avenue Synagogue, would be the second female participant, facilitating ICROJOY's acceptance into the tight-knit circles of Yemeni Jewry. Varda's fluency in the unique Judeo-Arabic dialect was critical. The second neophyte on Mission II was rhapsodic Lester Smerka, my neighbor from Washington Heights, a powerful man who had labored endlessly on behalf of the Jews he would soon be visiting. He would replace Boaz as videocamera operator.

From Sanaa's airport, we once again sped through the darkened boulevards of a slumbering Sanaa, leaving our luggage behind for inspection. The only stirrings were those of the uniformed soldiers stationed at each intersection to intercept weapons smugglers. But ICROJOY arrived untouched at the Hadda Hotel; Universal Travel & Tourism mysteriously claimed that the more spacious Sheraton had no vacancies that first night. Hadda, our hotel's namesake and location, is a swank suburb of the capital city where many of the country's influentials make their homes.

Our first order of business upon rising several hours later on January 4 was to transfer our supplies and belongings to the Sheraton, and as ICROJOY suitcases began to fill the Hadda's lobby for the brief trip across town, Sarah and Lester observed a familiar-looking man dialing a room number at the lobby's house phone. He was young and seemed to be Jewish, and as his dark face turned Sarah immediately recognized it as belonging to her cousin. It was Moshe Dahari Halla of Raida! He had passed the night in Sanaa after meeting the previous day with Dr. Iryani. We learned that Moshe came often to the capital city in order to speak with the Deputy Prime Minister and Foreign Minister. And Iryani had always granted him an audience; together they had contemplated Moshe's possible return to Amman for more corrective surgery and projected future visits of the five Jews from America. Upon realizing that the ICROJOY delegation was due to arrive the very next day, Moshe had decided to remain in Sanaa overnight to greet us.

After meeting with Moshe, Dr. Iryani had flown to South Yemen, where he was needed for critical deliberations about the future of the southern Arabian Peninsula. We would not see him during this trip; he would continually be shuttling back and forth between Sanaa and Aden, for a political metamorphosis was under way. The two Yemens were striving to become one once again.

Although by the mid-1980s the governments of the two Yemens had professed dedication to the eventual reunification of the country, few political observers had envisioned its occurrence in the near future, if ever. South Yemen, the People's Democratic Republic of Yemen, was more intimately aligned with the Soviet Union than any other Arab state, and the structure of its government and the Yemen Socialist party—the only political party—resembled the Soviet model. Thousands of expatriates from the Soviet Union, East Germany, and Cuba were serving in South Yemeni government ministries and enterprises. The authoritarian regime of the Yemen Arab Republic also relied heavily on the Soviet Union as a source of military equipment and training, but it retained close, albeit frequently strained, ties with the strictly anti-Communist monarchy in Saudi Arabia. PLO men filled the government's ranks as well. A spark of optimism had bolstered the North Yemeni economy in 1984, when the Hunt Oil Company announced that it had located commercially exploitable oil fields about 70 kilometers from Mahrib, the ancient capital of the Queen of Sheba; in the economically backward south, however, the outlook was bleak.

In the 1970s and 1980s, relations between the two Yemens had been characterized by armed showdowns but also by copious proclamations of Yemeni brotherhood. In 1979-82, the South Yemeni regime in Aden had supported an attempt by the leftist National Democratic Front to overthrow the government in Sanaa to the north. The venture had floundered for both military and political reasons, and in the mid-1980s the governments of both states had affirmed the goal of eventual Yemeni unity. In 1982, a joint constitutional commission approved a draft constitution for the projected "Yemeni Republic." The document designated Sanaa as the capital of the new state, Aden as its economic hub, Islam as its state religion, and Islamic precepts as the cornerstone of its ideology. The combined population would rival that of Saudi Arabia and presumably would make the new state a major player on the Arabian Peninsula. Now those dreams were coming to fruition. Dr. Iryani and his South Yemeni counterparts had set out to create the Republic of Yemen, a union that would ultimately prove extraordinarily fragile.

As a result, however, Iryani would be quite unavailable during ICROJOY's second journey to the Yemen Arab Republic. Coalescing two anxious governments, two excitable armies, and two wayward civil service establishments is no easy task. Meanwhile, the five members of the ICROJOY delegation spent their first full day in Yemen in the lobby of the Sanaa Sheraton, awaiting the delivery of their twenty-one cartons before proceeding to the north country. In a conference call, I discussed the delay with Georgia DeBelle, chargé d'affaires at the United States embassy, and Charles Dunbar, the ambassador.

Meanwhile, in discussions with Lester, Yosef, Sarah, and Varda, I reviewed each person's responsibilities. As ICROJOY's treasurer, Lester was charged with overseeing the group's financial arrangements, including the bakshish, the numerous gratuities necessary for doing business in the Republic. Yosef, our religious and cultural advisor, was instructed to secure Yemeni Jewry's authorization of ICROJOY's representation of its interests abroad. In addition, Yosef would study the social and cultural transformations the community experienced since the mass emigrations of 1949–50, and he would deliver words of Torah after communal meals or meetings—religious lessons without which no gathering is deemed complete. Varda was asked to explore the life of the Yemeni Jewish woman, and Sarah already understood the purpose of her presence in Yemen. As a blood relative of the Jews of Raida, she was once again to bond with her wonderful family and comfort them.

After the brief session, Lester and Yosef retired to the Sheraton's dimly lit coffee shop to wait some more. Before long a bellboy approached them bearing startling information.

"Your cartons have arrived," he said, "and they have been placed in a storage room in the basement."

Something was certainly amiss, Yosef immediately thought. Last time, ICROJOY's material had been delivered directly to our rooms at the hotel. Why would it be locked up in storage? Descending after the bellboy into the bowels of the Sheraton, Lester, Yosef, and I indeed discovered that the young man had been mistaken. There were no cardboard boxes filling the storage room's shelves, only a paltry stack of dusty books lying in one corner. But the books, with their red bindings, looked strangely familiar. Lester selected a volume and dusted it off, and identified it as one of the hundreds of prayer books he had prepared for shipping four months earlier in Washington Heights. It was an ICROJOY book that had been distributed to the Jews of Yemen in September! He opened his find to the inside cover, heard its new binding crackle, and read the stamp that had been recently imprinted:

NETUREI KARTA: BROOKLYN, NEW YORK

This served as our rude introduction to the activities of the Satmar Hasidim in Yemen, and I was furious. Somehow the sparse items ICROJOY had been able to bring into the country were being removed from the homes of the Jews and collected in the Sheraton by Neturei Karta. We soon learned that Yosef Bacher, the group's director in Yemen, often used the Sanaa Sheraton as his own base of operations. As far as he was concerned, ICROJOY was encroaching on Neturei Karta's territory. I vowed to investigate exactly what had transpired during the four months between Missions I and II.

After retrieving the twenty-five volumes and locking them in my hotel room, I returned to the Sheraton lobby and discovered that Ambassador Dunbar and Georgia DeBelle had arrived for dinner. We sat with the two officials for two hours discussing, in hushed tones, ICROJOY's primary concerns and objectives for Mission II: arranging for a post office box and a telephone by means of which the Jews of Yemen could communicate with the outside world; orchestrating the release of Yhia ibn Daoud Suberi, who had not seen his three children in forty years; hiring two local teachers for the Jewish community; and persuading the government to allow two Jewish students to travel to the United States for several weeks of rabbinical training. DeBelle took notes on a pad resting on her lap, beneath the table. Every five minutes, a waiter slowly walked by for no apparent reason. Soon, Thursday, January 4, had come to a close.

Friday morning, the Muslim weekly *Yawm-al-Gumah,* or day of gathering (for prayer). ICROJOY's valuable cargo finally arrived, and we immediately headed north to Raida and the family of Sarah Dahari Halla, young Moshe still tagging along. Lunch took place after an ecstatic welcome in the Halla home, a house with accommodations for animals on the ground floor and crude stone steps taking us to the living quarters upstairs. With reinforcing rods still protruding from the concrete in various places and at every angle, the Halla residence had been left intentionally in an unfinished state, because Yemeni law exempts unfinished homes from tax assessments. Lunch confirmed the delegation's suspicions concerning Neturei Karta: the Jews of Raida complained bitterly that Yosef Bacher had forced them to part with the gifts ICROJOY had distributed in September. I reviewed the candidates for a teaching position in Raida with the community's elders, and we designated Yhia Yitzhak Nahari, a learned, venerable patriarch to formally train the Jewish children there. With the Sabbath fast approaching, ICROJOY bid farewell to the Jews of Raida and drove north to Saada. We pulled in front of the Ma'amoun Hotel as the last sliver of a golden sun sank beneath the mountains to the west, and we greeted the Sabbath with the Jews of Saada.

Richard Schifter   Abdul Karim al-Iryani

Hayim Tawil and Annette Strauss, 1990.

Chapter Eight

January 7, 1990
The Tenth of Tevet is a fast day that punctuates the Jewish calendar in the dead of winter. It commemorates the beginning of the siege of Jerusalem by Nebuchadnezzar, the king of Babylon, an event that signaled the beginning of the end of the First Commonwealth. It is the first day in a sequence of lamentation that culminates seven months later with the more intense restrictions of the Ninth of Av, the day on which the First Temple was destroyed in 586 B.C.E., and the Second Temple in 70 C.E. ICROJOY chose the Tenth of Tevet as the day on which it would present its two Torah scrolls to the Jewish communities of Saada and Asahen, to Jews whose forthcoming redemption we hoped this occasion would portend.

In Saada and in Asahen, despite the lethargy induced by fasting, there were outbursts of feverish singing and dancing as the priceless Torah scrolls were revealed and then proffered to the two grateful communities for kissing and touching and reading. Once again I envied their appetite for Torah. These were Jews truly experiencing light and happiness and joy and honor. Most of them had not seen a Torah scroll in years, and that deprivation further enthused the celebrations. Tears flowed freely from the eyes of the elders as young boys took turns proudly reciting the words of Abraham, Isaac, Jacob, and Moses. Several men had to be prevented from kissing our feet, a gesture of great gratitude. We concluded each ceremony with the signing of a document attesting to the receipt of the Torah scroll, and containing a vital promise: that the Jews of Saada and Asahen would make their newfound treasures available to any Jew who came to pray.

The next several days were of the eighteen-hour variety, spent distributing books to the Jews of Sagin and Bilad Arhab and Raida and Na'at and Hidan Asham and Ghuraz and, of course, Saada. We selected Sleiman Faiz of Saada as the second teacher; he would also own the telephone and post office box we hoped the Republic would install. Rarely, if ever, in Yemeni history had a Jew brazenly applied for banking or postal services, but Lester, Yosef, and I took a crash course in Yemeni bureaucracy by passing hours in Saada's post office and bank, while Sarah and Varda probed the Jewish women for information. They reported a sobering infant mortality rate and revealed that Jewish women—fearful of using Saada's hospital—were giving birth at home, with no doctor in attendance.

In Saada, we met once with Abed, the son of Sheikh Asurabi of Saada, inviting the flattered young man—in the name of the United States Department of State—to participate in an American program for foreign entrepreneurs. Next we visited the villa of the sheikh himself, a palatial edifice ringed by fragrant orchards and vineyards. The sheikh, initially wary of our hiring of teachers and our tentative plan to erect a small school building in his domain, seemed placated by two gestures: our presentation of a wristwatch in gratitude for his protection of his Jewish population, and an invitation—also in the name of the State Department—to participate in an exclusive program for foreign dignitaries. All our meetings with the sheikh occurred in the presence of his personal driver.

In Raida, I was approached menacingly by three Kalishnikov machine guns affixed to three Arabs demanding an audience with "the American who promises to buy land." Our Yemeni security guard tried to calm them, but the men only loosened their vise-like grips when I reluctantly parted with three packages of American cigarettes. Land disputes are Yemen's most common cause of murder, and I certainly did not want to become another statistic. It was at that moment that I realized how much personal danger was inherent in Operation Esther. Later, even one of the security guards engendered tension. As Jews squeezed into Yhia Yitzhak Nahari's crowded living room for *ma'ariv*, the evening prayer, the confused and agitated guard shoved one of them. I admonished the Arab for treating Jews disrespectfully in our presence.

In Sanaa, we realized that the personnel of the U.S. embassy were also burning the candle at both ends. Ambassador Dunbar, Georgia DeBelle, Brad Hanson, the embassy's political officer, and Jeffrey Baron, its economic officer, were in constant contact with the Office of the Foreign Minister. Since Dr. Iryani was genuinely unavailable, they had resorted to communicating with Ahmed Hassan, his secretary and right-hand man. The embassy staff, working across the street from the Soviet military residence, gladly accepted our letters and documents for secure transfer to the United States via diplomatic pouch. And Dunbar was distressed over a bulletin that had just come over the wire from Washington: the Department of Agriculture had denied the Yemen Arab Republic a $15 million grant through an economic assistance program called PL-480. The news would certainly reverberate throughout the higher echelons of the Yemeni government and was sure to hamper the ambassador's negotiating efforts. Meanwhile, Georgia DeBelle was working day and night on the paperwork required for opening a post office box and a bank account.

Pleased to find the embassy staff so supportive and devoted, we decided to ask three young Jews from Saada to come down to Sanaa and meet Charles Dunbar and Georgia DeBelle, Brad Hanson and Jeffrey Baron. These diplomats had rarely, if ever, encountered any of the Jews for whom they were laboring so diligently. In addition, we invited the sheikh's son, Abed, and the sheikh's personal driver to meet the embassy foursome. Agricultural development of the northern region was one topic of deliberation, along with Abed's future participation in the State Department's entrepreneur program. Privately, DeBelle repeatedly underscored the importance of cultivating—monetarily, if need be—the backing of the sheikh's driver.

January 13, ICROJOY's second-to-last day in the Yemen Arab Republic, was a Sabbath, so we had to refrain from using the telephone, our critical link with Charles Dunbar and his colleagues. Respectful of our religious observances, Dunbar, DeBelle, or Hanson drove to the Sanaa Sheraton a total of five times in order to relay information concerning the climax of Mission II: a meeting with Dr. Iryani scheduled for 9:15 the next morning. And indeed, at precisely 9:15 a.m., while one of our surly security guards waited outside,

Yosef Levy and I were ushered graciously into the Foreign Minister's office and invited to sit across from a tired-looking Iryani and Ahmed Hassan. Polite banter, then directly and frankly to the point: My deepest apologies for being unavailable—reunification with South Yemen is imminent, as you know. The post office box, the telephone, and the bank account have been approved. I will secure explicit instructions from the Ministry of Communications.

But what of the old man, Suberi? Does he not merit reprieve? There was no need to lapse into the eighty-seven-year-old's tale of woe. Iryani knew it well. He knew Suberi as the *mu'allem*, the teacher.

"But how can I be guaranteed that the old man will not go to Israel?" Suberi's mere presence in the Holy Land seemed to be a threat. An absurd vision of the feeble old man leading Zionist battalions across the desert entered my mind.

"What," I asked, "are you afraid that the old man will become Israel's chief of staff?"

A broad smile filled Iryani's small face, easing the tension if but for a moment. No, he conceded, Suberi would not rise through the ranks and one day order Yemen's destruction.

And what of allowing two students to return to America with ICROJOY for several weeks? We assured Iryani that they would not wind up on the next flight to Tel Aviv.

"Your problem," the Foreign Minister replied, "is something called the Law of Return." All Jews are guaranteed immediate absorption into Israeli society. Granted the opportunity to go to Israel, a Jew will go. By freeing Jews, I populate the State of Israel.

"You, too, have a problem," I told Dr. Iryani. "How long can ICROJOY continue to restrain the Jewish lobby? Impatient organizations in America want Congress to punish Yemen for its discriminatory laws. Your country has already been denied PL-480 aid."

He smiled again. In two week's time, he and his President would be traveling to Washington for trade talks, audiences with Congressmen, and conversations with George Bush. I wished Dr. Iryani a successful visit, and he promised to call me when he arrived in the United States. At 10:45, Yosef and I were back on the street, with twelve hours left in Yemen. By 1:00 p.m., we had opened a bank account for our teachers, Sleiman Faiz and Yhia Yitzhak Nahari. They would be able to withdraw their monthly salaries in Saada and Amran, respectively. We bid hearty farewells to the embassy staff at a reception in Ambassador Dunbar's home. While ICROJOY dined on disposable plates, finishing off what remained from its cartons of supplies, Dunbar bemoaned the lack of progress. To comfort him I recited the penultimate verse of the Book of Ecclesiastes: "The end of the matter, all having been heard: fear God and keep His commandments; for this the whole man." You are doing your job, fulfilling your responsibilities. The rest lies not in your hands.

Still another verse from Scripture rang true for me when I returned to the world of New York and Yeshiva University the next day. As I sat down to draft a report entitled "Operation Esther: Mission II," it occurred to me once again that ICROJOY's every move was being carefully guided, its members carefully guarded. ICROJOY was acting in the right places, at the right times, bridging gaps which unwieldy governments and politically entrenched private organizations could not. After decades of failure, breakthroughs were slowly and secretly coming, but this time from an upstart group, another place. Beneath the title on the cover page went the following verse from the Book of Esther:

> "For if thou altogether holdest thy peace at this time, then will relief and deliverance arise to the Jews from another place."

January 22, 1990
Saddam Hussein's private jet, its landing gear already deployed, turned sharply into its predetermined approach and rapidly descended toward an empty runway. The Iraqi air force pilot brought it down with ease, and brought it to an uneventful stop with equal ease. Almost immediately, a cortege of shiny black vehicles, all with tinted windows, exploded from a hangar and raced toward the aircraft. Soon, portable stairs appeared at the jet's side, uniting its cabin door with the pavement fifteen feet below. With stairs in place,

the cabin door swung open and two men wearing dark suits materialized from within, flanking the exit. Then, a tanned, trim man with thick black hair and an equally thick black mustache emerged into the frigid air. He looked to be in his forties as he surveyed the scene before him. It was Colonel Ali Abdullah Salih's first trip to the mighty United States, and the Yemen Arab Republic's first state visit to American soil.

The Yemen Arab Republic is a poor country, and its President does not have an aircraft of his own. So for the transatlantic journey, Ali Abdullah Salih had borrowed the plane of an old friend. Saddam Hussein and he had attended the Air Force Academy together in Baghdad. Young men in their teens and twenties tend to be quite impressionable; friendships from those years often survive the years. Most of Yemen's senior military officers were educated in Iraq, and all of Yemen's political leaders are culled from the military. Thus the two nations, one just north of the Arabian Peninsula, the other straddling its southern tip, enjoy intimate relations. Considering the sudden invasion of Kuwait that would take place a mere six months later, not to mention that massive retaliation by the United States and its coalition allies soon afterwards, Salih's arrival that day would be the century's highwater mark in U.S.-Yemeni relations. Allegiances often evaporate in times of war.

Occasional political insurrections also link the two Arab League nations of Iraq and Yemen. Salih had been President since July 1978, his two immediate predecessors having been assassinated within eight months of each other. In 1990, he was serving his third five-year term, setting government policy, appointing technocrats to administer his government, and relying on his military and security forces to preserve his regime. Internal security was maintained by the National Security Office, whose agents had broad discretion, especially when national security matters were believed to be involved, to detain citizens for questioning, search their homes, and monitor their activities, telephone conversations, and correspondence. President Salih's surprisingly long tenure in office had witnessed constitutional modifications, armed forces upgrades, and civil service improvements. He ruled over a needy nation of over ten million with an undeveloped physical and social infrastructure. Where to turn for economic assistance if not the United States?

But unbeknownst to the colonel, trade and commerce would not have a monopoly on his time in Washington, New York, and Dallas. True a White House rendezvous with George Bush lay ahead, as did a luncheon with captains of the oil industry at the Willard Hotel hosted by the Vice President. Capitol Hill was on his itinerary, too, and there Salih would find a legislative branch obsessed with the fifteen hundred Jews living under his protection. ICROJOY knew that Salih was coming and had prepared diligently for his state visit, paving the way for a congressional barrage.

In his home on our last night in Sanaa, Ambassador Dunbar had pulled me aside for a private conversation. Hayim, I would like you to do something for me. For the first time in Yemeni history, a Yemeni head of state is going to the United States. Salih has been personally invited by Bush. As Vice President, Bush visited Yemen several times. And the oil industry lies close to the Texan's heart. Also, Yemen is strategically crucial regarding relations with the Saudis. I think it would be nice if you could do something for Salih in the U.S. Maybe if you could get him $15 million worth of PL-480 aid, if it's possible. You know, the Food for Peace program. *How?* You'd be surprised how far your influence reaches in Congress. Talk to them all. Ben Gilman, Lee Hamilton, Stephen Solarz . . .

So ICROJOY had worked the phones, obtaining funds for Yemen. Solarz wrote to Richard T. Crowder, Under Secretary of Agriculture for International Affairs and Commodity Programs, about the $15 million feed-grain program: "I hope favorable consideration of this modest yet desperately needed program can be expeditiously given." David Ransom won me a tentative audience with Salih scheduled during his stay at the Waldorf-Astoria in New York. And the Jews of Yemen became topics of discussion wherever Salih traveled in the United States. Before his interlocutors would discuss economic aid packages, Salih would be probed about the Jews—in the halls of Congress, at oil industry receptions, even in a private meeting with George Bush. Foreign Minister Iryani and Ambassador Alaini sat with their President as his eyes were opened to the human rights concerns of the American government. In expertly choreographed confrontations, Ali Abdullah Salih was handled delicately. First, oil alliances would be reviewed, then suddenly human rights. What about the Jews? We're concerned about the Jews. The Jews, the Jews, the Jews. Salih would be assailed from all sides.

While visiting the White House, Salih heard a crowd of demonstrators just outside condemning him and his government. If they are not removed by your police, Salih stated, I will not go through with this visit. The U.S. response: There are also demonstrators in front of the White House right now protesting President Bush and his administration. We are not going to remove them, and we're certainly not going to remove anyone else. This is the way our society works. You are our friend, we are not trying to embarrass you. All we want is your cooperation on human rights issues.

This was certainly not Salih's introduction to the plight of Yemeni Jewry. Back in 1984, there had been confidential discussions between Sanaa and Washington about an evacuation conducted by the International Red Cross, complete with United Nations observers. The United States wanted Salih to write a communiqué ordering Yemen's Jews assembled, under government protection, in a place where they could board waiting ships. But the political climate in the Arab world had never been right.

Next, Hamilton, Gilman, Levine, and Solarz converged on Capitol Hill to meet with President Salih, Foreign Minister Iryani, and members of the Yemeni parliament. Opening and welcoming remarks were offered by Hamilton, followed by a statement by Gilman: We hope to have more opportunities to meet, we hope to visit North Yemen in the future, we must work together to soften the policies of South Yemen.

Talk of Yemeni reunification, then a comment from Representative Gilman: There is another issue. We want to address the problem of the Jewish community.

"I appreciate your concern," Salih responded, "but there is no serious issue to be raised here. It's not a serious issue. I assure you they have full and equal rights according to the constitution. We have no problems with this. Of course, we welcome any Yemeni citizen of the Jewish faith if they do not possess an Israeli passport. We'd like to ask you to give equal attention to Palestinian rights."

Gilman's rejoinder was short and to the point: "We don't have authority over the Palestinians. But we raise issues. We hope that equal attention will be given around the world. In that vein, please allow Jews to travel freely abroad."

"We have no difference in treatment between Muslims and Jews. Even Yemeni Jews who left in 1949–50, if they want to come back, they can."

The floor went to Mel Levine. The California Congressman joined Gilman in emphasizing the importance of the Jewish community and what the President had already brought about: "We know there is progress, and we are grateful, as we try to be responsive to human rights around the world. We hope for continued progress, in particular regarding the two exchange students and the old man, although you do not have to respond to this if you do not want to."

Salih did not want to, preferring instead to nod his head and utter a meek "Thank you."

The discussion moved on to a variety of subjects: relations between North Yemen and Texas, Soviet influence in the Arabian Peninsula, Yemeni nationals residing in the United States. Finally, the Congressmen presented Salih with a letter whose text had been conveyed by ICROJOY through Michael Van Dusen.

One Hundred First Congress
Congress of the United States
Committee on Foreign Affairs
House of Representatives
Washington, DC 20515

January 22, 1990
His Excellency Ali Abdullah Salih
President of the Yemen Arab Republic

Dear Mr. President:

We would like to express our deep appreciation for the gracious and courteous humanitarian assistance that you, Foreign Minister Iryani and your government have extended to Dr. Hayim Tawil and his colleagues during their two recent visits to the Yemen Arab Republic.

The open distribution of religious articles brought by Dr. Tawil to the Jewish community in Yemen reflects well on our two countries' shared commitment to freedom of religious expression. We hope that this cooperation can continue and can be expanded. Your help and support in enabling this cooperation is deeply appreciated.

In this regard, we wish to enlist your support: to allow Yhia ibn Daoud Suberi to travel to the United States and see family members; to expand student exchanges to include members of the Yemen Arab Republic's Jewish community; and to enable the Jewish community to obtain better medical care and greater access to postal and telephone communications.

We view these as important humanitarian issues and believe we can work together to improve conditions for this community within the context of our improving bilateral relations. Yemen is an important country in the Middle East and for the United States. Your visit is a signal of this and we are confident that our ties can continue to expand to our mutual benefit.

We appreciate the opportunity to meet with you and wish you and members of your delegation a pleasant and successful visit to the United States.

With best wishes,

Sincerely yours,

Lee H. Hamilton
Chairman
Subcommittee on Europe
and the Middle East

Benjamin A. Gilman
Ranking Minority Member
Subcommittee on Europe
and the Middle East

Stephen J. Solarz
Chairman
Subcommittee on Asian
and Pacific Affairs

Mel Levine
Member of Congress

At a subsequent meeting with ICROJOY, Richard Schifter and other State Department officials concurred that it was imperative for the Yemeni government to manifest real progress in three areas by March 20: freedom for Yhia ibn Daoud Suberi; the installation of post office boxes in Saada and Raida and the establishment of telephone communications to the outside world for the Jews in North Yemen; and the inclusion in student exchange programs of Jewish, not just Arab, Yemenis. As conveyed to the Yemeni ambassador, America's foreign policy craftsmen all shared this resolve.

As the President of the Yemen Arab Republic became increasingly aware of America's concerns, Jewish organizations awoke to his presence in the country. Depending on their predilections, his state visit was either an opportunity to curry favor with the Yemeni leader or a time to assert their relevance in the fight to free the Jews of Yemen. Neturei Karta, in particular, wished to claim a monopoly on associations with the Arab nation. So on January 24 Salih was greeted by a full-page advertisement opposite the federal page of the *Washington Post* welcoming him to the United States. Beneath Arabic greetings and a handsome portrait of a regal-looking Ali Abdullah Salih, the Satmar sect lavished praise on Yemen's ruler.

On behalf of the large numbers of Orthodox Jews, members of our organizations, and synagogues, we extend our most heartfelt welcome to His Excellency

President Ali Abdullah Saleh

of the Yemen Arab Republic and to the accompanying delegation, on his visit to our shores.

We want to express our gratitude and appreciation to president Saleh for his virtuous, just, and benevolent treatment of all citizens of the Yemen Arab Republic. We specifically want to thank him for the continuous prosperity and religious freedom that the Jewish citizens are enjoying in the Yemen Arab Republic.

We wish the president success in all his endeavors on behalf of his countrymen, and may the almighty G-D bless his efforts with success.

Neturei Karta of the U.S.A.
G.P.O.B. 2143
Brooklyn, NY 11202

Two days later, when Salih arrived in New York, there was another advertisement in the pages of the *New York Post*.

THE AMERICAN YEMENITE JEWISH COMMUNITY

IS PROUD TO WELCOME HIS EXCELLENCY

ALI ABDALLAH SALAH

PRESIDENT OF YEMEN ARAB REPUBLIC

AND

THE DEPUTY PRIME MINISTER OF YEMEN AND MINISTER

OF FOREIGN AFFAIRS

DR. ABD EL CRIM ALARIANI

TO NEW YORK CITY

WE PRAY THAT HIS EXCELLENCY

WILL SUCCEED IN ALL OF HIS

JUST AND NOBLE ENDEAVORS.

Elisha Najjar, President   Dr. Israel Grama, Chairman

Yemenite Jewish Federation   Committee for the Jews of Yemen of
                                                          America

The Yemenite Jewish Federation of America is affiliated with the American Sephardic Federation, which had been made aware of the Yemeni remnant as early as 1974. Lester Smerka and I had petitioned for assistance in the ASF's Park Avenue offices during the summer of 1989, only to be derided for quietly working hand-in-hand with the State Department. You should go public, they said, to the steps of the United Nations, to the mass media; behind-the-scenes diplomacy will get you nowhere. Furthermore, you should come under the umbrella of the ASF. We had adamantly refused, and several months of inaction later, the ASF wanted to participate in the struggle. Now that Ali Abdullah Salih had come all the way to their shores, it was high time to have an audience with him and simply settle the matter.

But Ali Abdullah Salih would not meet with any Jewish group, including ICROJOY, during his short stay in the United States. As the Yemeni presidential entourage entered the lobby of the Waldorf-Astoria on Friday afternoon, January 26, a phalanx of Yemeni ASF members suddenly appeared, staging a boisterous protest before the Yemeni leader, demanding a meeting with him to discuss the release of Yemeni Jewry, demanding Salih's response. The President was humiliated and outraged. The demonstration did not advance the cause of Yemeni Jewry. Salih's staff complained to Washington, and I got a disappointing phone call from David Ransom right before the onset of Shabbat: Ali Abdullah Salih would be unable to see me. Too many Jewish groups were vying for slots of his time; he did not wish to cause an uproar by meeting with ICROJOY and no other organization.

With our rendezvous abruptly canceled, I began to focus on a valuable suggestion David Ransom had offered. President Salih was due in Dallas in several days. The city of Dallas and the Hunt Oil Company were going to host a reception in his honor. It would be a good idea, Ransom said, to talk to Annette Strauss, the mayor of Dallas, and get her to mention the Jews of Yemen to the President. Strauss was well-known in Washington; her husband, Robert, had chaired the Democratic National Committee during the Carter administration, later serving as U.S. ambassador to the Soviet Union. The executive and legislative branches of the federal government had already had their say. It would be important for Salih to hear concerns for Yemeni Jewry echoed by some of the crucial trade partners who comprised his country's lifeline. But mayors are busy people. Why would Annette Strauss spare twenty minutes for an unknown professor from New York?

I sought the counsel of another busy person. Dr. Norman Lamm, the president of Yeshiva University, is a brilliant man who saturates even the most mundane matters of administration with an extraordinary brand of scholarly learning. Dr. Lamm set aside a half-hour for me. "The President of Yemen is here," I told him as we met in his offices at Amsterdam Avenue and 185th Street. Salih will be meeting oil magnates in Dallas, I explained Annette Strauss is hosting a reception for him. I need to see her before Salih arrives in Dallas. It is vital that I meet with her.

Dr. Lamm picked up the phone and a dialed a number in Dallas. "I need you to arrange an appointment with Mayor Strauss," he said to the party on the other end. The next day, I was on a Dallas-bound plane with a duffel bag of photographs and letters and documents. The Texas rabbi Lamm had conversed with obviously had well-placed contacts in the mayor's office. Annette Strauss had agreed to give me a half-hour of her time.

From the airport I took a cab straight to City Hall, where Strauss greeted me warmly and listened attentively: The Jews of Yemen, I told her, have been isolated from their loved ones for forty years because of Yemen's discriminatory policies. Here are photographs, here is testimony, these are their stories. Please tell Ali Abdullah Salih you are aware of their plight. Please mention the Jews to the President of Yemen. Strauss leafed through the material and nodded. Yes, she would inject human rights into her conversation with Salih. She would express ICROJOY's gratitude to the Yemeni government, and our hope for progress in the humanitarian areas of medical assistance, educational opportunities, and family reunification. The Jews—and oil—would be topics of conversation in Dallas. It was a microscopic step, but when you are delicately negotiating a people's release, minutiae often merge, building momentum, generating results.

Part Three

OPENING THE GATES OF FREEDOM:

MAY 1990 – MARCH 1992

Chapter Nine

"WHOEVER SAVES ONE LIFE"

May 22, 1990
It was a solemn ceremony that commenced at precisely 12:00 noon. Ali Abdullah Salih, the President of the former Yemen Arab Republic, slowly and purposefully hoisted a crisp new tricolor into the azure sky above Aden. The flag bore vertical bands of red, white, and black, a cousin to the banners of other Arab League states. Below, in the crystalline waters of Aden's harbor, warships fired salutes, and blasts from the horns of civilian vessels pierced the warm air enveloping the sprawling port city. At that exact moment, the People's Democratic Republic of Yemen, the Arab world's only avowedly Marxist state disappeared; simultaneously, the parliament of the Yemen Arab Republic dissolved. With unity declared, North and South had merged into the Republic of Yemen.

The Republic of Yemen was built on aspirations of newfound weight in Arab councils, on the dream of consolidated muscle in population, oil reserves, agricultural potential, and cultural heritage. And the weight of these optimistic expectations fell squarely on the shoulders of the slim man in the finely tailored suit. Forty-eight-year-old Ali Abdullah Salih had been chosen to head the Republic's five-man presidential council; his Vice President was Ali Salem al-Baidh, former head of the South Yemeni Socialist party. Salih retained his former cabinet, however.

Hours to the north, past Taiz and Sanaa, at the terminus of the country's snakelike main highway, the Jews could not know the ramifications of unification. Besides, apolitical sheikhs far removed from parliament still dominated their isolated villages. In New York and Washington, ICROJOY and the State Department could only

183

speculate as well. The fate of the Jews of Yemen still lay in Salih and Iryani's hands, but we had seen little progress since the pair had flown back to their country aboard Saddam Hussein's private jet.

As Israel ushered in 1990, a new coalition of concern for Yemen's Jews had taken root. Prime Minister Yitzhak Shamir had invited a triumvirate consisting of General Avigdor Kahalani, General David Maimon, and Rabbi Ratzon Arusi to his office for a strategy session on the Jews of Yemen. The three had officially become the sole line of communication between Yemeni Jews in Israel and the government officials charged with freeing their loved ones—to the chagrin of some of the Israeli blood relations. *Maariv* construed the move as an intensification of government efforts to release the Jews, quoting the Prime Minister's promise that "we will not rest or silence ourselves when Jewish communities are in danger or denied the right to travel freely and reunite with their brothers in Israel."

In April, Arik Hadad, the mayor of Kiryat Ekron, traversed mountain and desert to visit the Jews in the exotic land to the south, returning with over six hundred photographs and a three-hour movie of his journey. Those images and Hadad's words would ultimately be printed in numerous Israeli publications. Hadad, of Moroccan descent, used his French passport to gain access to the Jews of Yemen, and exploited his encounters with them to ensure his reelection. In Israel, David Shuker decried Hadad's claims that in the course of one visit he had "rescued" the Jews of Yemen. Yemeni officials would later tell me of their outrage about the public display; they craved privacy and behind-the-scenes negotiation.

And since Salih's visit to America, a voice—transmitted on powerful radio waves emanating from the capital city of the Jews—was being picked up on receivers in the Arabian Peninsula: "This is Kol Yisrael in Jerusalem for the remnants of the exile of Yemen. Our precious and beloved brothers and sisters, greetings to you, and many blessings from Jerusalem, the holy city." Israel's national radio news program had inaugurated biweekly, 25-minute broadcasts to the Jews of Yemen, easing their years of isolation with news bulletins, songs, and simply the static-filled sound of a radio program especially for them. The many Yemenite Jews who tuned in were now able to experience Israel's Memorial Day and Independence Day; they could listen to familiar prayers and tunes over the airwaves, and learn new ones. Charlie Dunbar later told me about the Yemeni government's annoyance over the Kol Yisrael broadcasts. The Israeli government, said Sanaa, was jeopardizing ICROJOY's quite efforts.

Freedom to emigrate still seemed distant; there had been little progress on that front. ICROJOY had convened on April 18 to set a bold agenda for the upcoming months.

ICROJOY

International Coalition for the Revival of the Jews of Yemen
A Society for Jewish Yemenis and Americans

Agenda

I – IMMEDIATE GOALS

1. To establish two (2) synagogues, one (1) each in Raida and Saada, to be administered under the auspices of the government of the Republic of Yemen (ROY).

2. To construct two (2) mikvaot (ritual baths), one (1) each in Raida and Saada.

3. To sponsor three (3) students, one each from Raida, Saada, and Asahen.

4. To sponsor one (1) rabbi and one (1) teacher from abroad who will serve in Yemen.

5. To arrange for mail delivery to Yemen Jewry with the participation of the ROY government, independent of the official postal service.

6. To secure ROY government permission for ICROJOY to travel to Amlah and Hidan Asham in order to inquire into the needs of the Jewish communities in those two areas.

7. To encourage the ROY government to conduct a census of the Jewish community in Yemen.

8. To secure the release of money held in Yemen's Central Bank belonging to Yhia ibn Daoud Suberi; to use this money, which

cannot be exported in dollars, for Jewish community needs within the country, and to reimburse Suberi in dollars abroad.

II – FUTURE GOALS

1. Family reunification for one specific family of approximately 30-35 people.
2. To secure from the ROY government for Yemen Jewry the same, internationally recognized freedom of travel enjoyed by Yemeni Arabs.

Whether the nascent Republic of Yemen would respond favorably to ICROJOY's agenda remained to be seen. Salih's new country would certainly be confronted with routine pressure from the West. A mere two days into the nation's existence, Mohsin al-Aini, the brand-new Yemeni ambassador to the United States, received a letter from Congressmen Lee Hamilton, Stephen Solarz, Benjamin Gilman, and Mel Levine deploring the lack of progress since their last communication of January 22. This time, however, recent policy changes initiated by ICROJOY had made it possible for more foreigners to enter the country and get a glimpse of its Jews.

Private citizens were becoming a hindrance to our efforts. *Yisrael Shelanu* of May 25 reported on the activities of Tzemah Kadi, a Brooklyn man who, after years of fruitless petitioning, had obtained a Yemeni visa due to ICROJOY's energies. Kadi aspired to be the messiah of Yemeni Jewry. We had unfortunately crossed paths with him during Mission II in January. Now word of his endeavors in Yemen had found its way into the mainstream press. In an article for which I refused to be interviewed, David Argaman wrote:

To Kadi's anguish, there in the Sheraton Hotel was another delegation from America, under the leadership of Professor Hayim Tawil of Yeshiva University, the purpose of whose visit was identical to Kadi's: to assist the local Jews. But a man like Tzemah Kadi does not raise his hands in surrender just centimeters from his goal. Before actually visiting the Jews, he first turned to deal with his unexpected rivals who had sprung up on the scene.

In Brooklyn, thousands of kilometers from the events, he related with undisguised pleasure how he stood honorably in the face of the "enemy." "When I got to the hotel, Hayim Tawil's group was there, a Jew whom I don't know as Yemeni at all, who suddenly decided that he wants to help the Jews there. Every time they planned to go out, I would sit—advised of their plans in advance by the driver—in the hotel lobby, and they would retreat because they didn't want me to see them leaving. You should have seen what they looked like. Only at the end, just before they left the country, did they manage to distribute to the Jews the books they had brought. . . .

. . . Aware of his rival waiting for him in faraway America in the person of Professor Hayim Tawil, Kadi decided to perform a sophisticated maneuver. In all the Jewish settlements he produced a document saying, "Tzemah Kadi will be our president for religious and economic matters, as he is the most knowledgeable of our affairs, and we permit him to speak in our name on internal and external matters." Signing in each case were the heads of the local community and the local sheikhs of the region. Thus, Tzemah Kadi became president of the Jews of Yemen.

ICROJOY hoped that it had forged a concrete relationship of friendship and trust with the residents of Saada and Raida and the other isolated villages, one that could not be impeded by well-intentioned but overzealous good Samaritans. We were looking forward to a speedy return to those magical villages, for Operation Esther was to continue in the new political era, with a new banner flying above the Gulf of Aden. Little did we know that our arrival in the Republic of Yemen would coincide with events that quickly spiraled into out-and-out war in the Middle East.

August 2, 1990
Saddam Hussein's legions plowed into tiny, oil-rich Kuwait swiftly and efficiently, gobbling up the land in a twenty-four-hour attack that sent governments throughout the world into a frenzy. Loath to repeat the folly of Neville Chamberlain, the British Prime Minister whose name will always be associated with the short-sighted policy of appeasing Hitler, the Western world sent its foreign policy crafters

and military strategists into grueling, coffee-sustained action, assessing alternatives, devising deadlines and timelines and troop movements. Unwittingly cast into the quandary would be the Republic of Yemen, which greeted the ICROJOY delegation as we disembarked in Sanaa on August 2 at 2:30 that Thursday morning. Operation Esther: Mission III was under way, but in several hours the attention of the world would be fixed on the unanticipated aggression to the north.

There were four of us this time: myself, Yosef Levy, Lester Smerka, and Moshe Sharabi, a Brooklyn acquaintance of ours who had recently traveled to Yemen on an ICROJOY-nourished tourist visa. In March 1990, Sharabi and his cousin had stood in Taiz above the grave of the great Shalom Shabbazzi, capturing pans of the unmarked area on his videocamera, images which were later shown to ICROJOY. In Taiz, Sharabi had met a man named Abdullah who confirmed the precise location of Shabbazzi's final resting place. Abdullah, it turned out, was a contractor who had erected a new school building very close to the grave site. Sharabi had also encountered Miriam Abdu, the self-appointed caretaker of Shabbazzi's tomb, a Jewish convert to Islam. Abdu confirmed Abdullah's testimony regarding the subterranean tomb's authenticity. Shabbazzi lay about six feet below the surface and a hundred yards away from a "holy" spring.

Sharabi's compelling account of the contractor and caretaker induced ICROJOY to forward $300 to Abdullah, along with a polite request that he shield the site from any damage or danger. In July, I had telephoned the governor of the Taiz region to discuss ways to protect the grave, but he claimed that the responsibility lay with the mayor of the city. Then, on July 28, I had received a disturbing call from Abdullah, ICROJOY's new "friend." He told me that the grave was in danger of being destroyed by excavations connected with the expansion of the school adjacent to the site. I immediately sent telegrams to the mayor of Taiz and Foreign Minister Iryani, pleading the case of the endangered tomb. I had heard nothing since. Now Moshe Sharabi and Lester Smerka would be traveling to Taiz to reinspect Shalom Shabbazzi's grave site. We hoped it would not be too late.

Aside from our personal luggage we carried three hundred mezuzot for the doorposts of Jewish homes and three Torah scrolls, one from New York and two flown in from Paris and collected during our stopover in Frankfurt. Two Torahs were for the many Jews of Hidan Asham, and the other one was for Ghuraz's Jews. Laurie Johnson had warned us that things would be different in the aftermath of reunification. Soldiers from the now-defunct People's Democratic Republic were stationed at the airport and throughout northern Yemen; in the Saada region particularly there was tension between the South Yemeni troops and the local sheikhs, and we should expect complications at the airport. Johnson was correct. After being greeted warmly by Abdul Aziz of Universal Travel & Tourism, the ICROJOY delegation proceeded to customs, where officers immediately confiscated our Torah scrolls, mezuzot, blank videotapes, audiotapes, and film. Next came my personal set of tefillin and Yosef Levy's, the soldiers barely refraining from prying open the shiny black leather boxes to examine the small pieces of parchment inscribed with biblical verses.

I protested vigorously to Abdul Aziz. We had never experienced such intrusions before, I declared. We would not leave the airport without our phylacteries, which were necessary for our morning prayers. Abdul Aziz entered a private room with the officer in charge. Ten minutes later they emerged and Aziz handed me my tefillin; somehow, he had managed to persuade the officer to release them. And shortly before 4:00 a.m. the ICROJOY delegation left for the Sanaa Sheraton, the last group from the Frankfurt flight to exit the airport into the warm night air. At 6:00, a car pulled up in front of the Sheraton to whisk Moshe and Lester away for the drive south to Taiz. Yosef and I remained behind, for we had many tasks to complete. All this as columns of Iraqi troops began crossing the Kuwaiti border two thousand miles to the north.

Yosef and I had to be in Sanaa that day in order to confer with officials at the U.S. embassy and help them prepare for the Sunday arrival of Representative Stephen Solarz and his entourage. The Brooklyn Congressman was indeed coming. Solarz had already stopped by the ICROJOY offices at 115 Nassau Street, where I briefed him for nearly two hours. The visit of a U.S. Congressman to the Middle East, we would soon learn, could not have occurred at a more inopportune time.

The men and women whom American citizens send to Washington often become world-class travelers on Uncle Sam's lightly regulated tab. Congress exercises much command over foreign policy as a result of its power to appropriate funds for foreign aid and to regulate arms sales. So the visit of a member of Congress to a needy Third World nation will usually win him a meeting with the country's leaders. Senators and Representatives often use such opportunities to advance favored causes, humans rights among them. An emissary of Washington visiting the Republic of Yemen would expect to call on Ali Abdullah Salih. Visits to the offices of the Deputy Prime Minister, the Foreign Minister, and other cabinet members would also be in order.

Ten years earlier, Stephen Solarz had actually gone to Yemen in an effort to see its Jews first-hand. On Capitol Hill, the Congressman from Brooklyn represented one of the most heavily Jewish districts in the country; his position on the Foreign Affairs Committee had enabled him to visit beleaguered communities in Syria, Iran, and the Soviet Union. But when Solarz arrived in Sanaa in 1980 and asked permission to visit the north country, the request had been flatly denied. The Yemeni government never offered an explanation, but Solarz theorized that a visit by an American Congressman to the Jews of Yemen might have led to problems with radical rejectionist elements in the Arab world, the PLO in particular.

In 1990, Solarz decided to try again. But this time he was familiar with the work of a small, New York–based organization of modest means. ICROJOY offered the Congressman its assistance, arranged for him to meet the Jews of Yemen, and provided him with interpreting services. Solarz would be the first U.S. Congressman to visit the Jews of Yemen, and many security arrangements and logistical preparations had to precede his arrival.

By 10:00 in the morning, Yosef and I were standing in the spacious offices of the Yemen Reconstruction Bank, waiting to check on the status of ICROJOY's teachers' account, expecting to find it nearly depleted. But to our surprise, $1,900 remained for Yhia Yitzhak Nahari of Raida and Sleiman Faiz of Saada. For some reason, the two teachers had failed to withdraw their salaries from the account for several months. We soon learned that after two months of regular withdrawals, the local bank branches had refused to give any more money to Nahari or Faiz.

That afternoon, Moshe Sharabi called me from Taiz with more disturbing news. Our worst fears. The grave of the great Shalom Shabbazzi has been destroyed. An Arab school building sits atop the kabbalist, poet, and seer, atop the man with the underground tunnel to Zion. On the spot where a black man from Colorado was arrested. Near the hilltop where a Swiss botanist avoided arrest.

When Sharabi and Smerka arrived in Taiz, they discovered that construction of the school's new wing was proceeding so expeditiously that anything that might have existed beneath the foundation had surely disappeared. Arabs converged on the two ICROJOY men as they videotaped the construction site, testifying that they were indeed standing on the famous grave. Miriam Abdu recognized Sharabi from his March visit and led him and Smerka to the holy spring of Shabbazzi, where they filled a jerrycan of water as a memento. The waters near the Shabbazzi grave possess therapeutic powers, according to Yemeni Jewish legend.

A genuinely apologetic Abdullah told Moshe and Lester that he had been powerless to do anything. There had been no way to avert the destruction of the grave site. Nonetheless, with the help of some local children, Abdullah had recovered four human skeletons which they had subsequently interred on an adjacent hillside. Moshe Sharabi despondently summarized the situation, for he was deeply troubled to have witnessed the desecration of the remains of a hero of Yemeni Jewry, the great scholar and poet who had nurtured generations of Yemenis with the elegance of his written word. Sharabi and Smerka, unable to do anything more, headed back to Sanaa.

Another man seeking to suppress the hysteria on August 2 was Ambassador Dunbar, and quite understandably so. All of America's Middle Eastern embassies had been thrown into various stages of alert due to Iraq's hours-old invasion of Kuwait. And Dunbar also had to orchestrate the visit of a U.S. Congressman to the region. We met up with Charles Dunbar at the home of the embassy's new deputy chief of mission, Bruce Strathearn, who had just arrived in Sanaa two weeks earlier with his wife and their two young sons. The Strathearns were an itinerant diplomatic family whose most recent stop had been the embassy in Sri Lanka. Strathearn replaced Georgia DeBelle, so we began updating him on the Jews of Yemen and their precarious situation. When Dunbar arrived at the Strathearns, the conversation turned to the Solarz visit. We suggested several venues for the Congressman's face-to-face encounter with the Jews of Yemen. I also urged the ambassador to push for the temporary release of Moshe Dahari Halla and the permanent release of Yhia ibn Daoud Suberi. It was time for the Republic of Yemen to act upon its charitable words and show us some results.

August 3, 1990
ICROJOY's Torah scrolls, mezuzot, and film survived a thorough customs inspection and arrived at the Sanaa Sheraton by early Friday morning. We were ready to depart at once for Raida, but there were two Jews loitering in the lobby while the hotel staff looked on warily. Sleiman Nahari, from Na'at, had come to welcome us, and the son of Raida's Yhia Yitzhak Nahari was also in town. Sleiman complained of stomach pains and did not look well; he distilled arrack for sale to Arabs, and was known to have a drinking problem himself. Nahari reported that his wife, pregnant during Mission II, had given birth to a healthy son. We gave Sleiman information about his wife's branch of the family in Israel, but not before receiving an update of our own: Sarah Dahari Halla's great-aunt had passed away, and Hayim Dahari Halla, Moshe's brother, had married Sleiman's daughter three months earlier, for a dowry of 300,000 rials, approximately $20,000.

As we conferred with our two visitors in the dimly lit lobby, a well-dressed man in his forties approached us and identified himself as "Rajah" from the Ministry of Tourism. Rajah, coming off as courteous and reserved, claimed to be head of tourism for the north country and announced he would accompany ICROJOY on its journeys. Although he initially conversed with us only in Arabic, he soon revealed an excellent command of the English language. I spent many hours with Rajah as we navigated the serpentine highways of the Republic of Yemen, and I would later report the following to the Department of State:

> Rajah's immediate superior is Mujahid Abushwareb, head of all the Mukhabarat. Rajah is thus likely head of domestic security for the northern part of the country.
>
> His father was a high-ranking army officer killed in Aden in 1955 in a skirmish with British forces. The family is from the traditionally wealthy, landed elite. His own son, now in the army, is soon to marry. Rajah lives in the Sanaa area; he inherited much land from his father, whose business affairs his mother continues to manage.
>
> Rajah, though his mother's only child, has many half-brothers through his father's other wives. Sharp-witted, he has the reputation of a fearless fighter. He professes an affection for similarly courageous and intelligent people. He seems to know all Yemen's Jews by name, their problems, their occupations, their homes.
>
> Rajah professes a great interest in Jews and sees them as part of Yemen's history and culture. . . . Rajah professed great love for the songs of Yemen's Jews, especially those of the Sanaa community. He claimed to own a commercially-available videotape of an Israeli Yemeni dance troop, but since the quality was poor, he hoped to secure another copy.
>
> Rajah spoke strongly against the northern sheiks, predicting that within a decade their power would be gone. He described the north, between Raida and Saada, as the most dangerous part of the country, prey to tribal brigands (who do, however, honor Arab tradition by not preying on tourists and foreigners). He spoke vigorously against the Saudi seizure of the Najran. He supports Iraq against Kuwait, claiming that Iraq had given Yemen $100 million (half in cash) to build a convention center near the Sanaa Sheraton.

The ICROJOY van pulled away from the Sanaa Sheraton, with Rajah, Sleiman Faiz, and the son of Yhia Yitzhak Nahari aboard, and headed north toward Raida and the first of many Jewish villages. By the time we pulled up in front of the mud-walled Dahari Halla home in Suq-el-Jadid, the sun was rising over New York, and the United Nations building on Manhattan's East Side was rising from the dead. As the day grew older, the U.N. complex formed its own vortex, drawing diplomats, journalists, and commentators from near and far, brewing up a sweaty palmed crisis-intervention center for the consumption of Saddam Hussein in Baghdad and television audiences worldwide.

A coalition of concern was growing among the United States, Europe, and Saudi Arabia. Resolutions were being drafted and proposed. And the spotlight was soon to turn to the Republic of Yemen, a nation that had been cast into a quagmire of ghastly proportions with its friend's invasion of Kuwait. The members of the Arab League share one seat—and one vote—on the United Nations Security Council; the seat passes between individual Arab nations on a rotating basis. In August 1990, the Third World Republic of Yemen, longtime ally of Iraq, a country pining for agricultural and economic aid from the United States, sat in that uncomfortable position. Yemen would be required to vote on a harshly worded ultimatum proposed by the world's superpowers: an order for Saddam Hussein to immediately evacuate his forces or face the wrath of every oil-importer on the planet. The measure was sure to win approval, but the United States would not look favorably on any country tampering with its unanimity. Where would Ambassador al-Ashtal declare his nation's allegiances lay? What would Yemen do?

By the time he landed in the Republic of Yemen, Stephen J. Solarz, Congressman from Brooklyn, found himself in a country that had adopted a stance diametrically opposed to the United States. Yemen had shrugged off American pressure and was rhetorically supporting Iraq. Solarz's difficult mission as an American envoy would be to seek that same government's cooperation regarding its Jewish population. Moreover, the Congressman's next scheduled stopover after Sanaa was Baghdad, where Solarz was supposed to have a tête-à-tête with Saddam Hussein finalized weeks before. It was a poorly timed trip. Baghdad was immediately canceled, for Solarz realized it would be "inappropriate, to put it mildly, to meet with the Butcher of Baghdad in his capital as he was in the process of digesting his ill-gotten gains." And Solarz was somewhat averse to having his beaming visage splashed across the front page of the *New York Times*, beneath a caption reading, "U.S. Congressman Stephen Solarz shakes hands with Iraqi leader Saddam Hussein."

As secure phone lines and cables dutifully conveyed instructions between Washington and the Middle East, ICROJOY sat in the *mafraj* of the Dahari Halla home in Raida. We delivered two boxes of clothing and $50 sent by Sarah from New York, and had a very important conversation with Moshe Dahari Halla, the young man suffering from urological and neurological problems in the wake of the hit-and-run accident and surgery. Yosef and I captured on a small tape recorder the following promises from him: that he would appear on Sunday, August 5, as summoned, before Deputy Prime Minister Mujahid Abushwareb in Sanaa in order to receive a document allowing him to leave Yemen; that he would proceed immediately thereafter to the Sanaa Sheraton; that he would return immediately to Yemen after medical treatment in the United States; and that in the United States, he would not attempt to make contact with anyone or generate any publicity regarding his trip and medical treatment. When the conditions were repeated before the mysterious Rajah, who witnessed everything, he commented matter-of-factly, "Not to worry. If he doesn't come back his family will be arrested and his house confiscated." Rajah wrote out the conditions on a piece of paper, and Moshe Dahari Halla signed his name to the document.

During Operation Esther's previous missions we had habitually returned to Saada for Shabbat, generally pulling in late on Friday afternoon, with only minutes to spare before sundown. This time proved no exception. We enjoyed another beautiful seventh day of the week with the Jews of Saada, upon whom we tried to impress the importance of the impending visit from Congressman Solarz. The meeting on August 7, in the courtyard of the Ma'amoun Hotel, had been coordinated by none other than the local sheikh, the regional governor, and a representative of the federal government in Sanaa. We requested that Saada's Jews attend the "town hall"-style event in full force. Please invite Jews from around the region. And please dress and behave in a way commensurate with the importance of the

Congressman and the high-level Yemeni authorities who have arranged the meeting.

Saturday night was filled with emotion as we presented the three Torah scrolls to the deliriously grateful Jews of Ghuraz and Hidan Asham. Returning exhausted to the Ma'amoun at midnight, we received a telephone call from Abed, the son of Sheikh Asurabi of the Saada region, inviting the delegation to dine with him the next day in Sanaa. Luckily, we were scheduled to leave for the capital city in the morning, so I accepted the offer—that we would refuse to eat almost everything would become known later. At 2:00 Sunday afternoon, the ICROJOY van pulled into the circular driveway of the Sanaa Sheraton. Lester, Yosef, Moshe, and I piled out onto the sidewalk after the half-day trip from Saada, and found three Yemeni men dressed in traditional *galabiya* and *jambiya* patiently awaiting our arrival: Abed, Aref, the son of the sheikh of the Ghuraz region, and the latter's cousin. Back into our vehicles we went.

At the Abu Awas restaurant on Zubairi Street, the ICROJOY delegation and the three affluent young men were joined by Brad Hanson from the U.S. embassy. Conversation centered around Abed's father, who desired to come to America for orthopedic treatment of leg wounds sustained during one of Yemen's numerous conflicts. Three hours later, we were back on the street, and then back in a Sheraton lobby crawling with Iraqi pilots. That's when I spotted a dejected Moshe Dahari Halla weaving his way toward us through the clusters of military personnel. Abushwareb had not been in his office all day, Moshe reported; the young man could not obtain final clearance to leave the country because on August 5, we would later learn, Abushwareb and Foreign Minister Iryani were in Baghdad.

That night, Brad Hanson and Bruce Strathearn came to finalize plans for Stephen Solarz's visit to the north in two days' time. The Congressman was to arrive with Harrison Goldin, former New York City comptroller, and Mrs. Goldin, a fundraiser for Solarz. The Congressman would be staying in the well-fortified embassy compound. Since the Yemenis had placed at our disposal a helicopter seating only eight, we worked out the following plan: Strathearn, Stanley Roth, Solarz's legislative assistant, and I would leave to Saada by car at 5:00 Tuesday morning. Lester, Yosef, and Moshe Sharabi would return by themselves on Monday. And the helicopter would transport the Congressman and the rest of his entourage. From the Sheraton, the two consular officers sped to the airport to greet Solarz and update his staff. They exhorted the Congressman to choose his words in public carefully—he would be accompanied every step of the way by officials of the regime. And every word the Jews of Yemen told Stephen Solarz would be recorded and reported to the authorities. At this point it was revealed to poor Stephen Solarz that his luggage had been lost in transit.

Charles Dunbar joyfully related some wonderful news the following afternoon: Moshe Dahari Halla has been granted permission to leave the country by Ministers Abushwareb and Iryani! Halla already had a Yemeni passport from his sojourn in Jordan, thus simplifying the process significantly. I deemed the temporary release of this needful Yemeni Jew to be the most meaningful accomplishment in ICROJOY's twenty months of existence, a giant leap toward fulfillment of our ultimate goal. The Yemeni government was inadvertently acknowledging that if a Jew required life-enhancing assistance abroad, a visa could not be denied. Could not the same logic be applied to sickly old Yhia ibn Daoud Suberi, or to any Yemeni Jew tormented by decades of separation from his own flesh and blood?

Moshe Dahari Halla was our challenge to Yemen on a human rights medical case. For a young man in his twenties, Moshe had already experienced a lifetime of adversity. His father had been murdered in 1986, his leg nearly lost in 1988. He had endured weeks in hospitals in Sanaa and Amman, and now sought to reverse the consequences of medical procedures received there. But ICROJOY knew there were more personal grounds for Moshe's temporary release: Mujahid Abushwareb, the Deputy Prime Minister, was a sheikh of the Hashid tribe, which controlled Raida. The Jews of Raida, all of them skilled artisans, were famous for their ability to make excellent shotguns. And Moshe Dahari Halla's father had once made weapons for the father of Mujahid Abushwareb.

August 7, 1990

For a full hour, the helicopter glided noisily above tortuous terrain until the greens and grays of mountains and precipitous cliffs gave way to a bright desert landscape. Stephen J. Solarz was making the Sanaa–Saada trip the easy way. In his hands lay a copy of Maimonides' *Iggeret Teiman*, the Epistle to Yemen, whose eight-century-old text once allayed the fears of a generation reeling from messianic bewilderment, providing a salve that staved off the almost-certain Islamization of Yemeni Jewry. And Solarz would arrive in Saada to find a Jewish community looking and living as if it were still Maimonides' time.

At 9:15 a.m., the helicopter appeared over Saada, and the Jews raced out to surround the strange bird descending from the sky. Rarely, if ever, does a helicopter land in Saada, and never had one transported a distinguished guest to visit the Jews; the Arab populace was impressed. This was an historic moment. From a stubby field Solarz was escorted to the "town hall" meeting in the Ma'amoun Hotel, where he—bare-headed, in a light-blue polo shirt and beige slacks—confronted co-religionists wearing *kuftas* and *galabiyas*. Many were lounging in chairs for the first time in their lives, marveling at the "royalty" from America. When the Congressman entered, he shook hands gently with the strange-looking men who surrounded him. A smiling Yosef Levy followed and was immediately swamped by Jews attempting to kiss his hands, their way of expressing genuine affection. Not a woman was in sight as Solarz spoke and Levy expertly converted his comments and queries into the tongue of the Jews.

"Shalom Aleichem," the congressman began. "My name is Steve Solarz. I come from the United States of America. I represent a large community of Yemeni Jews who live in New York. The Jewish community in the United States is very interested in the welfare and well-being of the Jewish community in Yemen. You have not been forgotten. You are very much in the thoughts and the prayers of the United States. I tried to meet with you ten years ago in 1980. I came here. I went to Sanaa and requested permission to come to Saada. At that time the government was not willing to give me permission to come and meet with you. But ten years have passed and a lot has changed. When I was told by the Yemeni embassy in Washington that I would be able to come here, I decided to make a return trip. My friend Mr. Tawil has told me about the Jewish community in Yemen. He is a great friend of your community. He is a champion of your cause and he helped to arrange my visit here this morning. I rely on him for advice and assistance. He has my complete confidence.

"I have come here this morning to find out from you about the conditions are like for the Jews of Yemen. I want to know about any problems you may have. I want to know how the Jewish community in the United States can be most helpful to you. The United States government also has an interest in the Jewish community in Yemen."

Solarz continued throwing out questions to his audience: Do you have any synagogues in which to pray? Would you like us to send you some rabbis? If we established schools in Saada, would you send your children there, or would you continue to educate them at home? Why did you remain in Yemen after the establishment of Israel?

I had specifically warned him not to broach the subject of Israel, but Solarz erred, asking the forbidden question, "If you had a chance, would you prefer to remain in Yemen or would you prefer to go and live in Israel?"

"Yemen! Yemen! Yemen!" came the cries immediately. A candid response to the inquiry would not be forthcoming; the Ma'amoun was chock full of Arab security guards and dignitaries, among them the governor of Saada, a representative of President Salih, and several important sheikhs.

After the meeting, the Solarz entourage toured the city walls, sat on the floor in the modest Sabari home, and browsed the Jewish silvercrafting stalls in the Saada marketplace. Orange palaces of mud and stone, marketplaces bedecked with olives and grapes and qat, little girls in exquisite black hoods. Solarz attended a remarkable reception in a four-story, mud-brick house, flanked by communal elders who presented young boys reciting lengthy sections of the Torah from memory: words transmitted flawlessly from father to son to son. Later, Solarz watched as the Jews baked bread in their ancient brick ovens: "The best bread of my entire life."

The helicopter took off at 2:00 p.m. and turned south toward

Sanaa, the bizarre visit of the American Congressman relegated to the history books. More than a clash of cultures, the encounter between the Jews of Yemen and a Jew risen to an American zenith shattered a time continuum, bringing under one roof a people unchanged by the centuries and visitors immersed in a thoroughly modern world. But they were united under the banner of a singular destiny.

August 9, 1990
Moshe Dahari Halla entered the Sanaa Sheraton's lobby at 2:30 a.m. after bidding farewell to wife and child, aunts, uncles, and cousins in a small village called Raida. Where the young man was headed certainly qualified as a different planet, although he would not be seeing much of New York during his secret visit. In my hotel room were the obligatory articles for his journey to the United States: plane tickets purchased the day before at the Lufthansa office in Sanaa and a suit, shoes, shirts, socks, and underwear to replace his traditional Yemeni garb. Moshe was to attract as little attention as possible during his stay in America; we even assigned him a pseudonym, "Morris Canon." And a private room assigned to Mr. Morris Canon was being prepared at Columbia Presbyterian Medical Center in Manhattan. Dr. Michael Wechsler in the Squier Urological Division had been briefed by Dalia Smerka, and was scheduling the delicate surgery to take place immediately, as time was of the essence. Wechsler, deeply moved by the harrowing story of Moshe Dahari Halla and the efforts of ICROJOY, would perform the operation himself—and was refusing to accept even a penny of his usual hefty fee.

At 4:00 a.m., the ICROJOY delegation and the mysterious fifth man, sporting a shirt and pants for the first time in his life, departed for the airport. But with long, black peyot protruding from above his ears, a large *kufta* covering his head, and an olive-toned Middle Eastern complexion announcing his origins, Moshe Dahari Halla never exactly melted into the crowd. While awaiting our connecting flight in Frankfurt, I was approached by a journalist who asked intrusively, "Is he a Jew from Yemen?" The media already! We quickly led Halla to a quiet area of the lounge to shield him from prying eyes. With that task accomplished, I headed toward a bank of pay phones and dialed a certain number at the Israeli embassy in Washington.

"We already have one Jew out," I told Yaakov Amitai, an information officer there.

"What?!"

At Kennedy Airport, we hustled a confused Morris Canon through the labyrinthine arrivals terminal, coaxing him into a taxi cab, directing the driver to head straight for 168th Street in Manhattan. In our mad rush, we forgot the jerrycan of holy Shalom Shabbazzi water at the luggage carousel and would never see it again. Columbia Presbyterian was prepared for the new patient's arrival; he was quickly escorted to a room registered to Mr. Canon. We breathed a collective sigh of relief at the conclusion of our protracted August 9. Morris Canon, as his doctors and nurses soon learned, did not speak a word of English but possessed a bubbly personality that was infectious. We were confident that the key to Mr. Canon's recovery was some long-overdue exposure to quality American medical care. Mr. Canon would be confined in his hospital room for ten days, and I planned on taking the subway system's A-train to speedily shuttle between the hospital and my apartment sixteen blocks uptown. But before saying goodbye for the night, there was one more telephone call to make. I dialed a number in the Bronx.

"Sarah," I proudly told the party on the other end, "your cousin is in New York."

"What?!"

Yes, Sarah, you may come and see your cousin. He has made history.

My written account of Operation Esther: Mission III, August 2–9, 1990, underscored the significance of Moshe Dahari Halla's release. ICROJOY had embarked on a painstaking, step-by-step process that elevated the individual to great heights. Every soul merited a breath of freedom. So to the report's title page I appended a phrase borrowed from the Talmud:

"Whoever saves one life, it is as if he has saved the whole world."

Hayim Tawil, Bruce Strathearn and members of the Irgi family, August 1990.

Yosef Levy, Hayim Tawil, Jewish residents of Ghuraz (Saada) with new Torah scroll.

Chapter Ten

"WE'RE ALREADY IN THE SKY."

August 25, 1990

Mr. Morris Canon spent ten days in the Milstein Building at Columbia Presbyterian Medical Center. During that time, the doctors and nurses attending to his needs noted the dark-skinned man's foreign tongue, the long strands of jet-black hair that cascaded from above his ears, and the secrecy in which his presence was shrouded. Morris Canon's private room was frequented by only two well-wishers: a gray-haired man from Washington Heights and a younger woman from the Bronx whose olive-toned complexion matched the patient's. They protected the patient from any outside inquiries, and upon his release, impotence cured, shepherded him into a cab and transported him to the Bronx woman's apartment for three weeks of recuperating.

Only Dr. Michael Wechsler, Morris Canon's urologist, knew that the man upon whom he had operated was married and the father of one, that Moshe Dahari Halla lived thousands of miles away in a mud-walled house, that he was a player in a human drama slowly building to a crescendo. And while Moshe recovered, a village called Raida was monopolizing much of the conversation between Washington and Sanaa. Back in Raida, another man's lot was about to change. Yhia ibn Daoud Suberi, the near-blind, sickly eighty-seven-year-old, had kissed his Shalom, David, and tiny Shoshana goodbye in 1949. A shadow of the once-wealthy landowner from the valley of Damt, Suberi had passed the years in loneliness, witnessing the entrapment of his people, later watching in resignation the unproductive comings and goings of DuWayne Terrell and Daoud Hamami and even Hayim Tawil. But Suberi still craved the touch of children and grandchildren, thirsted for the land he would never be able to see.

-My tiny office in Yeshiva University's Furst Hall is not the most dramatic of settings, but that is where I got the call as the Fall 1990 semester was foisted upon us.

"Professor Tawil, are you standing or sitting?" It was Laurie Johnson from the State Department.

"What do you want me to do, sit or stand?" I asked, my curiosity piqued.

"I have very important news for you," she announced.

"Laurie, let me sit down."

"The Yemeni government has decided to let Yhia ibn Daoud Suberi come to the United States." But Hayim, you must promise us there will be no publicity, that the entire affair will be low key. The old man must stay quietly in New York for two months, and then he can go wherever his heart desires. And I assume his ultimate destination will be the State of Israel."

As Laurie Johnson's words sunk in, I envisioned Yhia ibn Daoud Suberi as I had come to know him from three trips to Yemen. The tiny, wilting body, the opaque, useless eyes, the chocolate skin and gray beard, the high-pitched, almost childlike voice that never seemed to cease, the utterances that confirmed his razor-sharp mind and keen wit. Yhia in his regal, white *galabiya*. Yhia with his brightly embroidered kufta. Yhia grasping his *regel hashlishit*, or "third leg," the walking stick wrapped in tattered cloth that never left his side. Yhia, the father of three whom Yemen had rendered childless. Not only was the Republic of Yemen acquiescing to family reunification for the *mu'allem*, it was tacitly acknowledging his eventual settlement in Israel, the sworn enemy. This was an achievement that dwarfed the case of Moshe Dahari Halla, who in a short time would find himself back in Raida.

ICROJOY's next task, Johnson continued, was to return Halla to Raida and retrieve Suberi from that ancient village. He can leave right away? Yes. Then you will go this September, right away. I began making calculations in my mind. Could my career afford another unexplained absence from Yeshiva? Was my participation in

Operation Esther: Mission IV even necessary? Both answers were no, to my dismay. I told Yosef Levy and Lester Smerka to begin preparing for another transatlantic journey. They would bring back Moshe Dahari Halla and launch Yhia ibn Daoud Suberi's long journey home.

September 13, 1990
The Persian Gulf crisis precipitated by Saddam Hussein had not ebbed by the time Yosef, Lester, and Moshe landed in Sanaa shortly after midnight. Lufthansa no longer landed in Amman; all its Sanaa-bound flights now had stopovers in Cairo. Its flight attendants and crews were now tarrying only three hours on Yemeni soil before returning to Cairo, instead of spending five days on the ground and then returning to Frankfurt. We fear that hostilities may erupt in Yemen, a member of the crew told the ICROJOY delegation. And the Republic's coalition with Iraq was prompting many others to stay away; Sanaa International Airport seemed quieter than usual, and the Sanaa Sheraton was almost completely vacant. The threat of war was taking its toll.

The U.S. ambassador to Yemen told Yosef and Lester that the bridges of cooperation, laboriously fashioned by the United States and the Yemenis in recent months, were crumbling before his eyes. Saudi Arabia, America's ally, was pondering the expulsion of the one million migrant Yemeni oil workers. Ali Abdullah Salih had only communicated personally with Charles Dunbar once since August 2. And even though its population had nearly doubled due to unification and Iraq was no longer supplying the usual financial subsidy, the Republic of Yemen was not seeking augmentation of U.S. aid. Yemen was lucky that every cent of its American aid had not been cut, Dunbar reflected bitterly. The two countries seemed to be collaborating on one issue alone: the Jews. If Congress decided to punish the Yemenis financially for their U.N. vote, Dunbar worried, progress on the Jewish issue, however slow it had been until now, would grind to a halt. ICROJOY must prevail on Congress to see some good in the Yemeni government in light of its generosity to Moshe Dahari Halla and Yhia ibn Daoud Suberi.

It was in this bizarre context that the Republic of Yemen had suddenly elected to release Suberi. Why now? The question lingered in my mind during the weeks preceding Mission IV, and Yosef and Lester posed it to Dunbar the next afternoon. After depositing Moshe Dahari Halla in a taxi that would take him back to Raida, the "delegation" had contacted the embassy staff and agreed to meet at Dunbar's home to discuss ICROJOY business. Even Charlie Dunbar, it turned out, did not have a good answer for ICROJOY. He could only note that two Somalis had also recently received visas at Deputy Prime Minister Abushwareb's behest. And Abushwareb had been in genuine contention for the presidency when Ali Abdullah Salih was chosen. Despite the increase in his diplomatic duties begotten by the Gulf crisis, Dunbar set aside an hour to dwell on the Jews of Yemen. Yosef Levy petitioned for the temporary release of two Jewish transfer students, and brought up the location of a school, either in Raida or Saada, and the problems of residence and security for a rabbi and coordinator amidst threat of war. The ambassador commented that Abushwareb had personally guaranteed the safety of a rabbi in Raida or Saada, and this should allay ICROJOY's concerns.

Permission may have been granted for Yhia ibn Daoud Suberi's long-overdue release, but Smerka and Levy's task was not simple. After arriving early Thursday morning, they needed to ascertain whether the old man from Raida had actually received a Yemeni passport, get it stamped with a U.S. visa, and ensure the safe arrival of both passenger and travel documents at Sanaa International Airport for a Sunday night flight. With Rosh Hashanah fast approaching, Sunday was the latest ICROJOY could afford to leave. Moshe Dahari Halla, in Sanaa on Friday, reported that the Jewish community in Raida were aware that their eldest member was leaving forever, although no one seemed to know who would be escorting him out of the country. And the Jews of Raida, elated to see Halla, told him that the old man had been given a passport.

Smerka and Levy wished to accomplish one thing more during their short stay in Yemen: tie up a loose end from Mission I by going back to see Yehudah Tzadok, the impoverished last Jew in Sanaa, ridiculed by children in the suq, humiliated by years of scrapping for sustenance. So on Friday morning, Lester, Yosef, and a guide set out for Ga-el-Yahud, the old Jewish quarter of the capital city. Tzadok's shack beneath the mill was locked, the pauper nowhere to be found, so Lester and Yosef proceeded to Bab-el-Yaman, the bustling Sanaa marketplace in the shadows of the city's imposing fortress-like walls. They returned to the Ga in late afternoon, before the onset of Shabbat, and found Yehudah Tzadok in his squalid abode. Yosef communicated with the sickly man in Arabic and Hebrew. "Tell us your story, Mori Yehudah, tell us your plight." He did.

Yehudah Tzadok, like Yhia ibn Daoud Suberi, had never anticipated the closing of the doors in 1962. The elderly, shrunken Jew had once owned several plots of land, property he refused to relinquish in the heady days of Magic Carpet. Tzadok watched his two brothers, Yosef Salah Yerimi and Yaakov Salah Yerimi, fly off to the Promised Land but did not follow them. "Perhaps they are still alive." During the days of the imam, there had been some sort of land dispute—particulars long forgotten—after which Tzadok was imprisoned for about seven years and repeatedly tortured. To obtain his release, he had converted to Islam, but never in spirit. The Sabbath day was still holy to him, and he observed the Jewish holidays to the best of his ability. He knew that the New Year would be ushered in next week. But the Raida Jews refused to accept Tzadok for his own protection: under Islamic law, one who recants his Muslim faith is subject to the death penalty. Ever since, Yehudah Tzadok, his land expropriated, had subsisted on the meager proceeds from begging and writing amulets for illiterate Arabs.

"Do you want to go to Israel?" Yes, but it is too dangerous to ask that.

"Where are the prayer book and tefillin I gave you last time?" Gone. Soldiers came and took everything.

Yosef Levy's eyes brimmed with tears as he bid farewell to Yehudah Tzadok, handing him 200 rials and walking away with a feeling of helplessness. Every Jew had a story, each soul merited his time and effort, but another aging Jew's release was on Yosef's agenda. Yemen is a landscape of personal tragedies; even its architecture evinces a Jewish past. When he was leaving Ga-el-Yahud, the Arab residents of the Jewish quarter asked him why all its houses are connected by secret exits and subterranean passageways. They are escape routes for pogroms, Yosef responded, the tunnels of life for a wary Jewish community. He and Lester then returned to the Sheraton for Shabbat.

September 15, 1990

Rajah, the Mukhabarat man who had accompanied ICROJOY throughout Mission III, arrived at the nearly deserted Sanaa Sheraton at 10:00 a.m. to discuss logistical arrangements for the release of Yhia ibn Daoud Suberi. "Suberi already has a passport," Smerka told Rajah, imploring him not to bring the old man to Sanaa until after the Sabbath. But Rajah doubted the existence of a passport; ICROJOY's sources must have been misinformed, he insisted. With their flight departing in thirty-six hours, Levy and Smerka did not want to risk a mix-up; the Republic's benevolence might not last beyond September 16. Telephone communication with the Jews of Raida was impossible. So Rajah took a cab to Raida at ICROJOY's expense to settle the matter.

At 2:00 p.m., a cab carrying Rajah and the fragile Yhia ibn Daoud Suberi pulled up in front of the Sheraton. Emitting a ghastly hacking cough, the old man looked more feeble than usual, but he greeted Yosef Levy enthusiastically. "There was no passport," Rajah explained, "but I will get him a new one. And if we find the other one, he will have two!"

A jittery Yosef and Lester were in no mood for jokes; their man had to leave the country on Sunday night. But Rajah did not seem worried. He had Suberi's pictures taken at a photographer's shop two blocks from the hotel and used them to prepare a passport. Meanwhile, the hotel nurse examined the old man, pronouncing his blood pressure normal and his overall health relatively sound, except for a case of bronchitis. She prescribed cough medicine and vitamins. Later in the evening, Ambassador Dunbar and Bruce Strathearn, the deputy chief of mission, arrived at the Sheraton unannounced to visit Suberi, the man whose freedom they had helped secure. The embassy staff would never call ICROJOY on the Sabbath.

Darkness descended on Sanaa, and Yhia ibn Daoud Suberi fell soundly asleep on the first mattress he had ever touched.

September 16, 1990
Sunday afternoon. The venerable Yhia ibn Daoud Suberi now sported Western clothing, though a bright blue *kufta* still covered his tiny head. Moshe Dahari Halla stood at Suberi's side, attending to his needs. Smerka and Levy had given the ancient one his first bathtub experience, and it seemed to have produced a rehabilitative effect. Suberi kept muttering long prayers from memory, his colorful walking stick clenched in his hand, as he waited to board the eagle that would belatedly whisk him away. But by 2:00 p.m., Rajah had not contacted ICROJOY with an update and the old man still did not have a passport. Time was running out.

At that point, Moshe Dahari Halla decided to tell Yosef and Lester that he knew the whereabouts of the first passport, the one that had disappeared. The two ICROJOY men were not amused by the revelation. "Where is it?" they demanded.

"Raida," came the answer. Yes, Sleiman Nahari of Raida has the passport, Moshe calmly explained. Suberi had lived with Nahari for the past two years, and there was a petty money dispute involving a delinquency of 1,000 or 1,500 rials. Nahari was holding the passport as collateral! Yosef told Moshe to call Raida and admonish Sleiman Nahari. The Republic of Yemen needs the passport in Sanaa right away; ICROJOY promises to settle the monetary feud. This is no time for such antics.

Sleiman Nahari knew quite well how desperately the Americans needed Suberi's passport. When he entered the lobby of the Sheraton at 7:30 p.m., he announced his demands to a disgusted Yosef Levy. But the ICROJOY representatives had no alternative. So Nahari walked away from the Sheraton with 1,000 rials and 250 more for cab fare back to Raida, while Yosef stood in the lobby holding Yhia ibn Daoud Suberi's passport in his trembling hands. The Lufthansa flight was departing in four hours, and the *mu'allem* still required a visa permitting entry into the United States.

Lester Smerka immediately placed a telephone call to Bruce

Strathearn at the embassy: We have a passport and it must be stamped! Tell Rajah to forget about the second passport. Within minutes, an embassy vehicle had appeared in the Sheraton's circular driveway. Consular Officer Deborah Elliott materialized and relieved ICROJOY of Suberi's passport. A half-hour later, she returned with the finished product: a few bits of paper that would release Yhia ibn Daoud Suberi from the Republic of Yemen and admit him into the United States of America. Yosef and Lester sighed deeply and gratefully. Their sightless passenger was oblivious to most of the day's machinations, but he was anxiously awaiting his ascent, his trip home.

Suberi received one last visitor before departing for the airport. Ambassador Charles Dunbar spent fifteen minutes with the remarkable old man who embodied the persistence of Yemeni Jewry. The ambassador had just emerged from a tense meeting with Abushwareb. The Deputy Prime Minister, feeling the strain of the Gulf crisis, had yelled at Dunbar for much of the "conversation"; Jewish matters were discussed only at the conclusion. Dunbar promised Levy and Smerka that two American security personnel would be present at the airport later in the evening. And then he bid farewell to the *mu'allem*.

When Suberi, flanked by Yosef Levy and Lester Smerka, finally hobbled into the nearly deserted departure terminal at Sanaa International Airport at 11:30 p.m., not an eye could be pried away from the spectacle. Electronic sliding doors parted before the old man whose doors of escape had opened. Porters and armed guards watched in silence as the man who had missed the Magic Carpet slowly made his away past the security doors and into the departure lounge. Lester Smerka lifted the old man off the ground and gently carried him up the stairs, onto the plane. Yhia ibn Daoud Suberi got the window seat and Yosef planted himself to the *mu'allem's* right. Takeoff.

"Yosef, when will we be leaving?" crackled Suberi in his harsh Judeo-Arabic dialect.

"We're already in the sky!" Levy responded, grasping Suberi's wrinkled hands tightly, watching tears stream down his cheeks.

"We're in the sky."

Two nations that were publicly trading salvos in an escalating war of words had quietly united to free the elderly passenger in the window seat, now fast asleep, his face bathed in the ethereal yellow glow of an in-flight sunrise. As Suberi slept, America's foreign policy crafters debated their next move. They were bridging cultural and political barriers; each inter-governmental communiqué had to be carefully considered, its language delicately formulated.

ACTION MEMORANDUM
SECRET (WITH SECRET/EXDIS ATTACHMENT)
TO: THE SECRETARY
THROUGH: P - ROBERT KIMMITT
FROM: NEA - JOHN H. KELLY

SUBJECT: Messages of Appreciation to Yemeni Foreign Minister and Deputy Prime Minister on Yemeni Jews.

ISSUE FOR DECISION
Whether to send messages of appreciation to the Yemeni Foreign Minister and Deputy Prime Minister for their assistance in two humanitarian cases involving Yemeni Jews.

ESSENTIAL FACTORS
Yemeni Foreign Minister Al-Iryani and Deputy Prime Minister Abu Shuwarib were instrumental in obtaining permission for two Jews to depart Yemen. The first came to New York for surgery and returned to Yemen, and the second, a very elderly man, was reunited with his family in New York after a separation of forty years. Both cases, and particularly the second, had been the focus of strong Congressional interest.

These messages will indicate to the recipients the importance we attach to the welfare of the Jewish community in Yemen, and our desire for continuing cooperation with the Yemeni government in trying to improve the conditions of that community. President Bush has sent a message of appreciation to Yemeni President Saleh on this issue. This was appropriate, since the decisions could not have been made without Saleh's approval. However, we think it is also important to acknowledge the key roles played by the Foreign Minister and Deputy Prime Minister.

RECOMMENDATION

That you approve the attached cables.

And so it was.

IMMEDIATE   SANAA
IMMEDIATE   TEL AVIV, JERUSALEM
EXDIS
E.O. 12356: DECL: OADR
TAGS: PREL, PHUM, YM, IS, US
SUBJECT: MESSAGE FROM THE SECRETARY TO DEPUTY PRIME MINISTER ABU SHAWARIB ON YEMENI JEWS.

1. SECRET ENTIRE TEXT.

2. PLEASE TRANSMIT THE FOLLOWING MESSAGE FROM SECRETARY BAKER TO DEPUTY PRIME MINISTER ABU SHAWARIB THANKING ABU SHAWARIB FOR HIS ASSISTANCE IN HELPING THE YEMENI JEWISH COMMUNITY. NO SIGNED ORIGINAL TO FOLLOW.

3. BEGIN TEXT.

DEAR SHAYKH MUJAHID:

I WOULD LIKE TO EXPRESS MY PERSONAL APPRECIATION FOR ALL YOUR ASSISTANCE WITH TWO HUMANITARIAN CASES WHICH WERE RAISED DURING PRESIDENT SALEH'S STATE VISIT TO WASHINGTON LAST JANUARY. AS YOU KNOW. MOSHE DAHARI-HALLA UNDERWENT A SUCCESSFUL OPERATION IN NEW YORK IN AUGUST AND IS NOW BACK WITH HIS FAMILY IN YEMEN. MUALLIM YAHYA TSABARI [i.e. Sabari] WAS REUNITED WITH HIS FAMILY IN NEW YORK IN MID-SEPTEMBER. I UNDERSTAND THAT WITHOUT YOUR

HELP THESE EVENTS WOULD NOT HAVE TAKEN PLACE.

I HOPE THAT THESE AUSPICIOUS EVENTS WILL SIGNAL THE BEGINNING OF AN EVEN CLOSER COOPERATIVE RELATIONSHIP BETWEEN OUR TWO COUNTRIES ON THIS AND OTHER IMMEDIATE ISSUES OF HUMANITARIAN CONCERN. OUR EMBASSY IN SANAA LOOKS FORWARD TO CONTINUING TO WORK WITH YOU ON SUCH MATTERS.

SINCERELY YOURS,

JAMES A. BAKER, III

END TEXT. YY

December 5, 1990
Yhia ibn Daoud Suberi lived on Bennett Avenue in Washington Heights for two months, and during that time barely a soul in the building was conscious of his presence. The Republic of Yemen had ordered a two-month "cooling off" period, and ICROJOY complied. Life in the 34th police precinct of New York City can be contrasted quite effortlessly with day-to-day existence in Raida. In Suberi's new world, stately apartment houses and skyscrapers of steel replaced mud-walled huts and the villas of sheikhs. My living room couch became the old man's bed, my family his own. Dalia valiantly nursed him back to health, Arik and Taphat played the role of playmates, affectionately naming him *"Am Yhia,"* Uncle Yhia. Dr. Rubin, our family physician, prescribed medicine for Suberi's bronchitis. Arik bathed the feeble man regularly, awoke three times nightly to take him to the bathroom, and filmed Suberi using the exercise bicycle, Suberi enjoying my rocking chair, Suberi donning tefillin, Suberi reciting morning prayers by heart, Suberi splaying his fingers over his face and intoning the Priestly Blessing, Suberi enjoying Yemeni

music, Sony headphones covering his ears and a smile of contentment creasing the furrows of his brown face. Suberi learned how to slap my children "five," and would constantly intone, "*Mori Hayim, zakhita,*" Master Hayim, you have gained merit.

During this period, no guests were permitted in the Tawil residence; we became the most antisocial family on the block. Hayim is paranoid, neighbors must have thought. But caring for an eighty-seven-year-old is as time-consuming as tending to an infant's needs. Dalia, on duty around the clock, quickly learned that Suberi was blessed with vigor and acuity despite his years. The days passed quickly with much to keep him occupied and chipper. There was the clandestine arrival of General Avigdor Kahalani, representing Ahai Li, the Israeli government's task force on Yemeni Jewry. There was the first telephone call from Shalom in Israel, and the emotional reunion in my apartment. And then there was the visit of two Suberi grandchildren to Bennett Avenue.

We learned from Shalom that two of the *mu'allem's* grandsons, Doron and Eyal, were in the leather business and were currently living in Soho in Lower Manhattan. So in an East Side restaurant one morning, I related the news: "Your grandfather is here in the United States."

"What?!"

Yes, he's here, he's staying in my apartment, but no one is to know. Don't tell anyone.

"When can we see him?"

Anytime you want. So Doron and Eyal, typically Israeli-looking men in their early twenties, appeared in 24B and embraced their tiny grandfather, a man from another planet. Suberi touched his grandchildren, shed tears of happiness, understood that his years of separation were history. Then the old man pressed his fingers to the top of Doron's bare head to bless him, and suddenly stopped, instead delivering a slap to his grandson's cheek.

"Where's the *kufta*?" Suberi, like a tyrant, demanded. Why is the head not covered? The family's three generations, raised in disparate cultures, indeed belonged to different worlds.

Shalom Suberi all but moved in, occupying much of his father's time. The two had a lot of catching up to do. Shalom's hospitality in the 1970s had inspired nineteen-year-old DuWayne Terrell's expedition to Yemen. The Southern Baptist's harrowing experiences had generated a movement in Israel, and that crusade had caught fire in the United States and sired ICROJOY. So the denizens of 24B during the fall of 1990 represented eleven years of struggle on behalf of the Jews of Yemen. Dalia had the most difficult time of all, catering to Shalom and his father's demands and preventing Shalom from absconding with his father to Israel and jeopardizing our progress. The two Suberis were never allowed to remain alone. Eventually, Dalia developed a painful ulcer from the stress and was forced to spend several days recuperating in Columbia-Presbyterian. During that time, Yhia called daily to comfort her.

At night, when I returned from my classroom and books, Suberi would recount his several lifetimes of experiences. The old man reiterated his claim that he had once been quite wealthy, and soon began to reveal more details. There is cash hidden in the Nahari house in Raida, he told us. There is $40,000 in my name in an American bank in Sanaa, deposited decades ago and suddenly recalled. Please retrieve my money for me. "Do you have an account number?" No. "A certificate, any evidence or proof?" No. Despite the dearth of information, I promised to find the old man's lost treasure during the next mission to Yemen. "Give me the power of attorney to act as your agent." We penned and signed an agreement.

Meanwhile, ICROJOY was sending thank-you letter after thank-you letter to the men and women in Washington and Sanaa who had made Suberi's release a reality: ambassadors, ministers, secretaries, consular officers, members of Congress, and legislative assistants on two continents and from two disparate cultures. David Ransom moved on to the Europe Bureau and began grooming himself for an eventual ambassadorship. Laurie Johnson stepped down from the State Department's Yemen desk, so we wished her much success on her return to school; she began training to become a consular officer in a prestigious foreign post. I hoped that Andrea Farsakh, who replaced her as Yemen desk officer, would prove to be as conscientious and helpful.

I also read of the escalating tension in the Middle East, watching from afar as Yemen's allegiance to Iraq continued to wreak havoc with its already enervated economy, further isolating it from other Arab League states. On October 21, Saudi Arabia suspended residence privileges for Yemenis, setting off a mass migration of at least 750,000, depriving the Yemeni economy of $350 million a month in remittances from the Saudi earnings of the expatriates, the country's largest source of income. As more Yemenis headed south, smuggling, housing costs, and unemployment skyrocketed.

On November 16, Yhia ibn Daoud Suberi's two-month term in America expired; it was time for him to go home. His Shalom, David, and Shoshana awaited him in the Holy Land, and an Israeli government eager for tangible results was desperate to see the old man on the Ben-Gurion tarmac: I was sure the Israeli news media would be congregating about the *mu'allem* in force. His Israeli transit visa already prepared, Suberi had grown weary of my four ells. Who would escort him on the plane and help him down the stairs in Tel Aviv? Israel offered to send a representative, but I wouldn't hear of it. The Israeli government had played no part in Suberi's release and did not deserve the honor of bringing him home. As chairman of ICROJOY, I knew we had to shun honor and the spotlight; any publicity for the organization and its activities might have damaged our relationship with the Republic of Yemen. So I placed a call to a certain guest scholar at the University of California-Berkeley, and asked him to help Suberi fly home.

Of course I'll do it, Pierre Goloubinoff responded. In ICROJOY's infancy, before coups and victories, Goloubinoff had devoted days of his precious time to encouraging us and briefing us. It was his impressive store of knowledge that helped persuade the State Department to deal exclusively with ICROJOY. It was his infatuation with the Jews of Yemen that provided the movement to free them with momentum and resolve.

Goloubinoff flew in from San Francisco on December 5, leaving a nine months-pregnant Cohi behind. Suberi donned my blue dress shirt, blue blazer, red tie, and overcoat. He cradled my head and blessed me, and together we walked out onto Bennett Avenue, the old man firmly grasping his "third leg." Dalia came too. Yoscf Levy, Lester Smerka, and the Suberi grandchildren joined us at Kennedy Airport, and Goloubinoff obtained a wheelchair to roll Suberi into the TWA jet. The ingathering of the Yemeni exiles was continuing in 1990. I kissed the old man goodbye and watched him board his eagle.

Maariv, the next day, reported on the *mu'allem's* arrival in the Holy Land, forty years late.

"It was very moving. Daoud Yhia came down from the plane, kissed the soil, we all wept. His three children, Shalom, Shoshana, and David were waiting for him, as well as one grandson. He blessed them and we all wept." This was related yesterday by Brig. Gen. Avigdor Kahalani, who was an eyewitness to the landing in Israel of Daoud Yhia Suberi, aged 87, the first immigrant from Yemen in the past 38 years, who arrived at Ben-Gurion Airport. Thus a 40-year separation between the aged father and his children, who had waged a stubborn fight all these years for his immigration, came to an end.

The home of the son Shalom in Netanya, where the old man was taken, was filled with emotional relatives, thirsting to hear every word the old man had to say. But he spoke very little, was moved to tears and ceaselessly recited the *Shehehiyanu* blessing. Of the colorful traditional garb, only the colorful *tarbush* was left. He uses a carved walking stick, decorated with scraps of colored fabric and held by a leather strap. His beautiful, heavily lined face is surrounded by a beard and earlocks. He hears through a deaf-aid and is supported by his sons when he walks.

Yhia Suberi left Yemen over two months ago. Since then he has been staying with his grandchildren in New York. Forty years ago Yhia parted from his sons Shalom and David and daughter Shoshana in Yemen, in the hope of meeting them again soon in the Holy Land. Suberi was an honored figure in the Jewish community and owned much property. He wanted to liquidate his businesses before emigrating. His hope was not fulfilled. The authorities confiscated the family property and, like the other members of the Jewish community, he found himself with his property taken away from him, living in poverty and degradation.

The son Shalom recounted: "Despite the hard reality, father zealously maintained his Judaism, and this is what kept him going. Even in the most difficult years he worked to restore their faith to the young people who had moved away from it because, and because of this activity he was arrested several times on suspicion of espionage." His last arrest was in 1980. Yhia was then arrested along with three of the community members and found guilty of spying—because of letters he had received from Israel through a young American who visited Yemen. He was sent to jail but released a year later following secret diplomatic and international intervention.

I would later learn that Shoshana, who had been raised on a kibbutz by Eastern European foster parents after flying the Magic Carpet as a one-year-old, could barely comprehend her newfound father's utterances; she did not understand the Judeo-Arabic dialect spoken by Yemeni Jewry. And only later would Pierre Goloubinoff inform me that upon landing in Tel Aviv he had been brusquely pushed aside by Mossad officials, who surrounded the old man and ceremoniously presented him to the Suberi children. David Shuker was at Ben-Gurion that evening; he, too, had the taint of ICROJOY on his fingertips, and was prevented from greeting Suberi. Neither Goloubinoff nor Shuker nor the acronym ICROJOY appeared on the evening news. As instructed, Suberi divulged no details when he was interviewed on the popular evening news program "Erev Hadash":

"Who took you out of Yemen?"

"I can't say. I can only say good men took me out."

In media reports and coffeehouses, Yhia ibn Daoud Suberi's release became a coup by the Israeli government.

Chapter Eleven

DECLARATIONS AND DEMANDS

December 8, 1990

Yhia ibn Daoud Suberi, teacher and father, darling of the Israeli media, savored his day in the sun, his newfound family deeply gratified by the attention and warmth enveloping the *mu'allem*. In Washington, Congressmen and foreign policy crafters quietly exulted in the victory they knew to be their own. But their counterparts in Sanaa, as Ambassador Dunbar would later assert, became increasingly agitated as publicity swirled about the lost Jews of Yemen. Dr. Iryani found the television coverage in Israel disturbing, a breach of his government's agreement with Washington and ICROJOY. Yemen's high ministers—especially members of the fundamentalist Islah party—were quite sensitive to the allegations leveled against them in the Israeli press. The *mu'allem's* release, unbeknownst to ICROJOY, only discouraged further progress instead of accelerating the process.

It would be more than six months before another Jew exited Yemen. ICROJOY's activities during the winter and spring of 1991 were confined to strategy sessions and lobbying in Washington. We met Andrea Farsakh, the new Yemen country director, and forged closer ties with Congressman Benjamin Gilman, the Rockland County Representative and influential Foreign Affairs Committee minority leader. Farsakh also heard from Abraham Bayer of the National Jewish Community Relations Advisory Council. Bayer desperately wanted his organization to be in the picture. The Persian Gulf crisis had become the Persian Gulf War, so the eyes of State Department officials and the entire legislative branch were rarely diverted from the Middle East. Yemen's economy was reeling from the absence of tourists and the return of almost a million migrant

219

workers from Saudi Arabia. Richard Schifter in Human Rights monitored the situation closely, attempting to determine the war's impact on Yemeni Jewry.

But different sources were presenting different accounts to the public. Accurate information lay buried beneath layers of politically motivated images of the life of Yemeni Jewry, portrayals of either tranquillity or torment. Among the former was a memorandum sent by Neturei Karta, sworn enemy of the effort to free Yemeni Jewry, to the Department of State.

While we applaud all U.S. government efforts on behalf of human rights the world over, we must register our dismay that the U.S. government extended its protective mantle over pro-Israeli-Zionist groups operating propaganda machines in a foreign nation, to the detriment of the concerned peoples. The U.S. has always striven to be even-handed, especially in the volatile Middle East and it must continue to maintain this approach.

The Israeli and American-Zionist intentions in Yemen are suspect. They are not now, or ever were in the past, intended to selflessly help the Jewish citizens of Yemen.

The ultimate goal of the Zionist government and all its affiliate organizations throughout the world, is to gather all the Jews of the world under their jurisdiction. To that end, they must fabricate situations of religious and ethnic persecution, oppression, and potential massacres within that region in order to get its Jewish inhabitants to voluntarily flee their communities, abandoning their possessions, family cohesion, and in particular their spiritual identity to a regime that is hostile to their way of life and whose stated goal is to rob them of their ethnic orientation in order to "absorb them into the Israeli mainstream." It is something that they would never accept of their own volition.

After stating these above-mentioned facts, we ask why the U.S. State Department used its good offices to obtain traveling privileges for Dr. Hayim Tawil and other Zionist agitators posing as tourists in Yemen. The ostensible purpose of Dr. Tawil's visit was to distribute Jewish prayer books among the Jews of Yemen, books that were distorted to include prayers for the Israeli Defense Forces. The true purpose of this visit was to present himself in the United States as benefactor and savior of the Yemenite Jews, enabling him to issue "press releases" for various "rescue committees" and emergency conferences. We do not see why the United States should be a party to such devious practices.

Furthermore, Ambassador Schifter, at a public gathering, stated that Hayim Tawil is an agent of the U.S. government.

Ambassador Schifter, who is responsible for implementing U.S. government policy on human rights, ought to serve the interests of the United States government and its constitutional guarantees for human rights and religious freedom and not serve the interests of groups or foreign governments.

It is against the interests of the Yemenite Jews and U.S.-Yemeni relations for the U.S. to even appear to be aiding Zionist propagandists operating in Yemen. Any assistance extended to Jews should be fastidiously kept to religious and material aid, in no way connected to nationalistic ideology.

Then came the grass-roots organizations in Israel that thrived on hyperbole. Their logic: exaggerate the plight of Yemeni Jewry, invoking forced conversion, rape, and plunder, to shock government and citizenry to take action. Instead of downplaying the persecution, as Neturei Karta did, they intensified its nature in press releases, rankling the Yemeni government and hampering ICROJOY's efforts.

"ORI TEIMAN"
THE ASSOCIATION FOR THE REMNANT OF YEMEN AND ARAB JEWRY

How many Jews live in Yemen?

There are some 10,000 Jews living today in Yemen. This figure is based on lists made by heads of families, which we have in our possession. There are some 400 divided families alone. Nearly all the men of the community are married to two or three wives and have 10-15 children. In Greater Yemen there are about 4000 Jews in the towns of Rida, Sa'dah, Amlach and the surrounding area. In the region of Haidan Asham, there are about 6000 Jews. This is confirmed by visiting journalists.

The Israel Government and the Established as a whole ignore the existence of Yemenite Jews. This is apparent in official documents which I have in my possession and which can be made available to anyone who wishes to see them. One of these documents, published by the Zionist Congress, says that there are no more Jews in the Yemen. In an Israeli government document signed by Minister Ronnie Milo, the estimated number of Jews is given as 800-1,000. In ignoring the real number of Jews in the Yemen, the Government of Israel is allowing the Yemen authorities to do whatever they want with the Jews there, and in practice to facilitate their physical annihilation.

Our demands of the Government and citizens of Israel and of world Jewry and the media are as follows:

We turn to you with a plea that you do not stop up your ears, close your eyes and silence your mouths, for Israel cannot be insensitive to what is happening in the Yemen, and cannot but be shocked to the core by the contents of these letters. And it does not matter whether a letter is sent by 10,000 Jews or 10 Jews only. It is your job to cry out and to rescue the Jews from their despair. This you are not doing. Therefore, you have no place in the Government of Israel and should be replaced by those better fitted to do this job.

IN PLAIN TERMS, A HOLOCAUST IS TAKING PLACE IN THE YEMEN—

THOUGH NOT A HOLOCAUST OF EUROPEAN JEWRY.

WE CALL UPON THE GOVERNMENT OF ISRAEL, THE MEDIA AND JEWS THROUGHOUT THE WORLD TO TAKE ACTION.

We managed to break through the Russian Iron Curtain.

The Yemen Curtain is easier to push aside.

Unfortunately there is another curtain which has to be torn down—the curtain of insensitivity of the Government of Israel.

Thank you for your attention.

Eliav Sela

Chairman

Eliav Sela's visions of genocide often found their way into the Israeli press, and from the pages of *Yediot Aharonot* and *Maariv* they arrived on the desks of State Department officials in Washington. The patently false accounts vexed temperamental Yemen. In one such report, which appeared in *Yediot* on February 19, 1991, Sela charged that after a pro-Iraq demonstration in Saada, a mob attacked Yemeni Jews and severely beat two elderly women, one of whom died as a result of her injuries. Naturally, Washington ordered Sanaa to investigate the veracity of Sela's statements. Ambassador Dunbar complied and cabled a message back to the State Department:

POLOFF DISCUSSED REF B WITH A SOURCE WHO HAS GOOD ACCESS TO INFORMATION ON YEMENI JEWS IN SAADA. THE SOURCE HAD NOT HEARD OF AN INCIDENT OF THE KIND DESCRIBED IN REF B AND SAID REPORTS OF MUSLIM/JEWISH CLASHES IN SAADA AND OF THE TWO JEWISH WOMEN BEING WOUNDED, POSSIBLY KILLED, WERE SIMPLY UNTRUE. SUCH AN INCIDENT, THE SOURCE ASSERTED, WOULD CERTAINLY HAVE COME TO HIS ATTENTION.

Further cables would reveal that the Jewish community was becoming politically active in the aftermath of Saddam Hussein's defeat:

The independent press has reported that Yemeni Jews have joined several of Yemen's nascent political parties and that the country's leading Islamist grouping has countered by advocating expulsion of the Jews to Israel. A well-placed source confirms that Jews were recruited into one of the parties and that the party's leader was castigated by a leading Islamist for taking the initiative. While it is unlikely that the ROY would allow the Jews to go to Israel, the apparent decision by the Yemeni Jewish community to raise its low political profile is of interest as is the willingness of at least one political party to put into practice the liberal principles it preaches.

Dunbar's reports from Sanaa detailed a harsh conservative backlash against the admission of Jews into the Constitutional Liberals party. But his days in the Yemeni capital were numbered; the termination of his tenure, known for months by Washington insiders, was made official in March. Dunbar returned to America that summer. His June departure, in fact, all but coincided with the arrival of another ICROJOY delegation in the Republic of Yemen. Preparations for Operation Esther: Mission V, whose visit to Yemen would prove to be the most critical three weeks in icrojoy's existence, began in earnest in April.

April 18, 1991

With Mission V on its agenda, ICROJOY again invaded the white palaces housing the public servants of the nation's capital. We met with Michael Van Dusen, staff director for Lee Hamilton, and Stanley Roth, aide to Stephen Solarz. In Richard Schifter's office, and later in the more modest niche belonging to Debbie Bodlander, Benjamin Gilman's aide for Jewish affairs, we outlined our goals for the fifth trip: lay the groundwork for synagogue construction in Raida and Saada, and obtain temporary travel visas for three Jewish students—the same way thousands of Muslims were coming to study in the United States. But win freedom of travel for the Jews of Yemen? Enable the first families in thirty years to begin pouring out of that country? Such notions were only entertained in my mind's theater of the absurd. We had to progress slowly, letting the Yemenis grant concessions at their own sluggish pace in a perverted quid pro quo of lives and American agricultural aid. Could American-Yemeni relations ever be resuscitated in the wake of the Persian Gulf War?

The answer to this question, in fact, lay in the hands of several influential men on both sides of the Atlantic. From the American mission at United Nations Plaza, over a secure scrambled phone, I spoke with Charles Dunbar in the Yemeni capital and we reviewed the meaningful names and policies: Dr. Iryani, the Foreign Minister, was the only cabinet member who showed any good will toward the Jews of Yemen. He wanted to get along with the United States. And he might be willing to permit three Jewish students and two Jewish tourists to visit America if the PL-480 program was renewed.

But would Washington's executive and legislative branches support the linkage of PL-480 and the Jews of Yemen? Yemen's passive support for Saddam Hussein had not been forgotten. George Bush and James Baker III still harbored deep animosity toward the Yemenis because of their friendship for the Iraqi dictator. For agricultural aid, for the student exchange programs, for the return of the Peace Corps, America would require much more. The release of at least one entire extended family of thirty-five or forty members. A private statement of agreement in principle to freedom of travel for the Jews of Yemen. As a good Republican eager to preserve the dignity of a Republican President, Benjamin Gilman objected to the meager gesture of one family's release. Democratic Congressmen were be more easily mollified; they would require less for the PL-480 renewal. And congressional approval would have to coincide with the nod from the Yemeni cabinet. Iryani must sell the plan to his ultra-conservative government, especially its royalists factions, and to President Ali Abdullah Salih. We had to create a consensus among all these players, Dunbar counseled, if we were to open the doors for the Jews of Yemen.

May 23, 1991

I landed in dusty, dazzling Sanaa for the last time as the capital city slept, bracing itself for another summer inferno. Operation Esther: Mission V was inaugurated with a wink from Yosef Levy, across the aisle in his white shirt and gray hat, as the Lufthansa jet alighted. Neither of us knew that our stay in the Republic of Yemen would last significantly more than the intended two weeks. Nor did we foresee the pivotal accomplishments that would accompany our extended sojourn: the opening of doors, the release of Jews, the reunification of families long separated—the stuff of dreams.

There were six of us this time representing the International Coalition for the Revival of the Jews of Yemen, an organization whose days were numbered, as I would soon learn. Yosef, Lester Smerka, and I were accompanied by two newcomers to the Arabian Peninsula and one native-born woman. Joel Kirschner peered out the tiny window into the black. An observer from the Joint Distribution Committee—Yemeni Jewry's financial backbone—Kirschner would take copious notes as ICROJOY traveled the length and breadth of Yemen. Another invited guest, the fifth member of the delegation, was to do the same for us. And Shoshana Tobi, who had flown the Magic Carpet as a child, was returning to her birthplace. Shoshana, a well-known Yemeni performer from the Inbal Dance Group, blessed with a robust voice, had emigrated from Israel to the United States, married, and set out on a career entertaining Yemeni expatriates with the song and dance of their homeland.

Kirschner, dispatched by the JDC's executive director, Michael Schneider, to scrutinize our activities, would return to New York with a report detailing the sorry state of Yemeni Jewry and praising ICROJOY's contributions. Kirschner noted, after his "very disturbing and difficult trip," that

> although it is estimated there are 1500–1600 Jews in the country, it is clearly a changing number. During the stay there were three weddings and many of the women are pregnant (average age of marriage for women is 14). The conditions regarding hygiene, and health care are deplorable, though probably no different than the general population. Most of the Jews buy qat (a narcotic), which is not a cheap item. The silversmiths (mostly Jews) in the Saada region have clearly been affected by the dramatic decline in tourism. The suq in Saada was empty and the Jewish shopkeepers opened the stores for us after which they were closed. There is plenty of produce available in the marketplace and the stores are stocked with all household needs. This country is a third-world country and the Jews are part of the third-world mentality, having money for qat while having no money for Similac.

Suddenly we were in the airport. Gone was the tense atmosphere that had once welcomed us to the Third World nation. On this, our fifth trip, the German Lufthansa manager, once antagonistic to ICROJOY because of our frequent tardiness, hugged me and wished us a successful visit. The airport security chief, a Mukhabarat man, kissed me on the cheeks, for I was already a well-known figure in Yemen. Passport control proved no problem, and our seventeen suitcases found their way into the three vans provided by Abdul Aziz and Universal Travel & Tourism. Unfortunately, two paintings purchased by Dalia for Sheikh Asurabi of Saada were riding a conveyor belt somewhere in Frankfurt's airport, lost forever. The delegation and the rest of its belongings exited Sanaa airport in the dead of night. Destination, once again: the Sanaa Sheraton.

Or so we thought. But the drivers did not head for the outskirts of the capital city and the Sheraton's friendly confines. Instead, we penetrated the city center, pulling up at 1:30 a.m. before the Taj Sheba, an elegant hotel, reputed to be the country's finest. The Taj sits opposite the Central Bank of Yemen on Ali Abdulmoghni Street, where roadways are paved and sidewalks frequently swept, where the cry *Allah Akhbar*, "God is Great," blares from minarets at 5:00 a.m. delivering an Arabian Peninsula wake-up call.

I quickly comprehended the ramifications of a stay at the Taj Sheba: we were now in the heart of the city, accessible and visible to all, especially the Mukhabarat. The United States embassy lay miles away, in the quieter suburbs. Eventually we determined the immediate reason for the sudden change in plans: money. In 1991, the American dollar equaled 12 rials in the bank, but 25 rials on the street; UT&T insisted on paying the Sanaa Sheraton in rials, not dollars, and that dispute had led to the booking of four spacious rooms for ICROJOY at the Taj Sheba. Yosef and I occupied one, Lester and ICROJOY's guest, another. Joel Kirschner and Shoshana Tobi had their own rooms. Lights were doused and the sounds of slumber soon filled our rooms. Wake-up was in four hours.

Mere seconds later, or so it seemed, the sun's brutal rays had already begun scorching the beige palaces of Sanaa. The delegation was to set off for Raida at 9:00 a.m., but then came a telephone call and a change of plans. The ambassador requested my presence in the embassy. So I stayed behind while the others headed north to purchase land for a synagogue and mikveh. Ahmed, the embassy driver, pulled his van into the heavily secured embassy compound and I entered Dunbar's private quarters, where he and Bruce Strathearn, the deputy chief of mission, greeted me cheerfully. Strathearn, an experienced diplomat fluent in Arabic, was a tall

Midwesterner who had married a diminutive Syrian Christian woman. Immediately the ambassador made his intentions clear. His three years were up, he explained, and he wanted to go home, but he was going to remain in Yemen while ICROJOY was there. Awaiting Dunbar in America were his son's college graduation and a respectable position under Richard Schifter in Human Rights.

During ICROJOY's absence, the ambassador had attended an enormous rally for the conservative religious party, Islah, the tribally based party of the north country, in a football stadium packed with fifty thousand cheering Muslims. From the diplomats' viewing gallery, Dunbar had spotted several Jews, distinctive in their peyot, and without the traditional *jambiya* at their sides. Exiting the stadium, Dunbar violated his policy of never being seen communicating with Yemeni Jews. He approached one of the Jews and asked, "What are you doing here?"

"*Jit mah Jirani*," came the reply. "I came with my neighbors." I came with my neighbors to participate in the rally of an Islamic-based political party. For Dunbar, underlying the humor and irony was a lesson: Jews *do* fraternize with their Muslim countrymen, and take on protective coloration by attending the rallies of their neighbors, showing that they stand on the correct side of the political spectrum.

Dunbar reiterated what he had said on the phone two weeks earlier. Our job, he stated, was to foster a spirit of cooperation between Americans and Yemenis. That was the key to freedom for the Jews. Neturei Karta, the anti-Zionist Satmar fringe group, had "coincidentally" arrived in Sanaa three days before us. Still active in Raida but substantially weaker in Saada and Hidan Asham, Neturei Karta would be a thorn in our side. But do not mention the group to Iryani, Dunbar insisted. The Yemeni Foreign Minister is under tremendous pressure from the Muslim right and cannot ignore the Satmar's presence. Do not ask him to. Instead, concentrate your efforts on Congress, be the intermediary between Washington and Iryani. Stay in Sanaa while the rest of the group travels north.

I did. But on Thursday afternoon, after hours of mysterious UT&T delays, Yosef, Lester, Shoshana, Joel, and the guest had yet to depart for Raida and Saada. They would not head north until Friday morning, May 24. By that time, Moshe Dahari Halla had appeared in the lobby of the Taj Sheba along with ten other Raida Jews. Congregating in their distinctive *galabiyas* and earlocks, the newcomers caused quite a stir among the elegant businessmen in three-piece suits softly traversing the Taj's grandeur. Yhia Yitzhak Nahari, the teacher we had hired, was one of our visitors. We soon learned that Nahari no longer worked for ICROJOY—he had forsaken us for Neturei Karta, which probably was paying him better. Another sobering tidbit: Neturei Karta had approached Dr. Iryani and given him some damaging reports on Israeli media coverage of Yhia ibn Daoud Suberi's release. The Satmars blamed the Foreign Minister for aiding and abetting the entry of Jews into the Holy Land.

On Friday morning, I returned to the embassy compound for a second meeting with Ambassador Dunbar, this time in his garden among blossoms and trees, adjoining the embassy swimming pool. A disappointed Dunbar related a seeming change of heart by Dr. Iryani. At a Thursday afternoon rendezvous, the Foreign Minister had seemed uninterested in ICROJOY's proposals despite his earlier enthusiasm for trading PL-480 and other program renewals for Jews. Apparently we were pressing for too many concessions at this stage. "This is really too much," Iryani had uttered repeatedly.

Nonetheless, I felt that our demands were reasonable and crucial: a statement in principle promulgating freedom of travel for the Jews, the temporary release of three students and two tourists, the construction of schools and synagogues and mikvehs in Raida and Saada, and the reunification of one complete family—if not in one shot than in segments. This and nothing less would satisfy Benjamin Gilman, I believed, though I understood Iryani's objections to the release of one large clan at once. Such a scene in the airport would be politically disastrous, evoking images of a mass exodus, exposing Yemen's willingness to play the American game, providing grist for the ever-churning mill of antagonistic elements within the government. But the four-pronged proposal, I asserted, would certainly stifle the dangerous cries for blood that were bound to emanate from American Jewish organizations. Those groups, hungry for tangible results but unwilling to work for them, were bound to raise a ruckus eventually, one that could jeopardize our sensitive and secret negotiations.

My final request was for assistance in reclaiming Yhia ibn Daoud Suberi's money. There were few clues with which to proceed, but the very sight of Yemen's Central Bank outside my window each morning, mocking me as I indulged in a smoke to calm my nerves, reminded me of my solemn promise to the *mu'allem*. Can the embassy use its connections in Sanaa's financial community to locate the old man's lost treasure? We'll see what we can do, came the reply.

Shabbat all alone in the Taj Sheba. I reviewed the weekly Torah portion and found time for introspection and relaxation; Dunbar and the embassy already knew not to call. At 7:00 p.m., after the seventh day's departure, Yosef Levy phoned from Saada. It was the first contact we had made since Friday morning, and the connection was an extremely poor one, garbled and static-filled. With much effort, I conveyed the following instruction: return on Monday with four prospective visa recipients, Massoud Zindani, Ida Zareb, Moshe Sabari, and Salem ben Yousef Atzar, but do not tell them why I want to see them. At this point in time, I did not wish to create a stir in the Jewish community, one that would fuel enmity and supposition. Unfortunately, those would come later.

At 8:30 p.m., a delegation of twenty Jews from Suq-el-Jadid in Raida arrived at the Taj Sheba and demanded an audience. So for the rest of the day I spent time with my brothers, lending a sympathetic ear to their various medical and financial problems. But our policy forbade donating funds to individuals; ICROJOY supported communal projects only, in order to prevent altercations and jealousy. Instead, I reimbursed my visitors for their round-trip carfare and bid them a good night.

May 26, 1991

Yemen's modern Foreign Ministry is located opposite Ga-el-Yahud, the ancient Jewish neighborhood of Sanaa. On Sunday morning, I found myself again in the office of Dr. Iryani, the Foreign Minister, discussing lexicology and Sabean inscriptions and the fascinating Himyaric dynasty. For a moment, I was a professor of Hebrew studies again. A full half-hour into the exchange, as was Iryani's wont, the Jews of Yemen became germane to him. Regarding their plight, the Foreign Minister articulated a liberal approach: Yemen is a democracy. Human rights are respected here. Ideally, Jews should be able to leave the country along with their fellow Arabs. But they must travel to a neutral nation; they may not go directly to Israel. Can I allow an entire family like the Zindanis to exit at one time? Absolutely not, that would just provide ammunition for my enemies. And it is unnecessary for your people to come here to process the Jews; we can handle that ourselves, and you can meet them in Frankfurt.

In principle, Iryani seemed sympathetic to our position, but he needed more convincing. ICROJOY had already persuaded Congress to renew the PL-480 program once before, I reminded him, when Ali Abdullah Salih visited America in January 1990. Stephen Solarz, the Brooklyn Democrat close to the Yemeni government, had become an influential man in Washington. He had supported America's involvement in the Persian Gulf and now had Bush's and Baker's respective ears; he would push for another PL-480 renewal. But it would take some work to convince Benjamin Gilman to do the same. The mere reunification of one family would not be enough. We wanted a secret declaration of freedom of travel along with a physical gesture confirming Yemen's charitable intentions: the immediate release of individual Jews and families. We needed something tangible to bring back to the United States in order to appease powerful Jewish organizations poised to go public. Now was the time to move.

Oh, one more thing, Dr. Iryani, I continued. You might be interested in a certain member of our delegation, a woman born in your country before the revolution. Her name is Shoshana Tobi, and she sings Jewish and Yemeni folk songs quite proficiently, melodies evoking your heritage. Would you be interested in hearing Shoshana perform? Here is a tape containing some of her songs. Please enjoy it.

And with that, I headed back to the Taj Sheba both encouraged and confused, unable to qualify the meeting as a success or failure. At that time, I did not know that my casual reference to Shoshana Tobi would contribute more to the warming of American-Yemeni relations than hours of increasingly idle chatter. Moshe Dahari Halla greeted me amicably at the Taj Sheba, and I was grateful for the company of a co-religionist after days alone in Sanaa. I envisioned Halla's family in the Holy Land with ICROJOY's help. "Are you willing to move from Yemen?" I asked Moshe. The color drained from his face, his expression went blank. Leave Yemen forever? Take my wife, our daughter, our newborn son? Moshe was overwhelmed and flustered and unable to give a definitive answer. Go back to Raida and ask your wife, I demanded. I must know as soon as possible.

The very fact that Halla's response was now being sought signified that ICROJOY had reached a crucial juncture in its brief existence. Dunbar confirmed this later in the afternoon when I arrived at the embassy to review the Iryani meeting. The ambassador would soon be composing a cable to Bush and Baker explicitly linking PL-480 renewal with family reunification and a secret declaration of principles. I urged him to accentuate the urgency of an agreement and the crossroads of history where we stood. An opportunity like ours—with Yemen hungry for wheat and the reestablishment of rapport—came along so rarely.

But as I discovered the next day, America understood quite well that opportunity was knocking. Ambassador Dunbar had talked with Richard Schifter in Washington over a secure telephone, and he related the latest kink to me the next morning: there is a new PL-480 problem; the United States is asking for more . . .

In the four decades of the State of Israel's existence, its people had survived three massive onslaughts from their Arab neighbors, enlarging the tiny nation's territory in the aftermath of each attack. The U.S.-brokered Camp David Accords in 1979 had brought détente to the tense Israeli-Egyptian relationship. In the early nineties, in the wake of Saddam Hussein's defeat, another attempt to bring permanent peace to the region was being inaugurated. This attempt would eventually take Israel's leaders and their Palestinian counterparts from Oslo to the South Lawn of the White House, but the precursor to this development was the Madrid Conference. In October 1991, the nations of the world were to gather in the Spanish capital to deliberate the prospects of a Middle East peace. It was an effort spearheaded, in part, by the United States. And the United States needed support from the Arab League nations, the Republic of Yemen among them. So America was playing hardball with Yemen. Renewal of PL-480, Dunbar had to tell the Yemenis, would come at a price: a Yemeni public statement of support for the young, controversial peace process. Otherwise, the concept of releasing Jews in return for agricultural aid could not even come to the table. Baker was still furious at the Yemenis, and he was demanding plenty.

I left the embassy compound discouraged; it seemed that ancillary concerns were diverting attention from the Jews of Yemen, the very locus of American involvement in the international dialogue. My loneliness in the Taj Sheba did not last long, for at 12:30 p.m. the ICROJOY delegation returned from Saada, and Yosef, Lester, Joel, and Shoshana tumbled out of the vans after a bumpy seven-hour ride. Along with them were Massoud Zindani, Ida Zareb, and Moshe Sabari, none of whom could fathom why I had summoned them to the Yemeni capital. So I brought them to my room, sat the three young men down on the bed, and delivered the news: You have been selected to travel to America with us. We hope you will be able to leave with us soon, although we cannot guarantee it. You will be making history.

Tears began to stream down Yosef Levy's cheeks as he watched the reaction of his Yemeni brothers. They were truly overwhelmed at first; elation only set in when the initial shock dissipated. Massoud Zindani had not laid eyes upon his sisters, Saada and Hinda, since childhood, since their departure, in 1962, for the Holy Land. And now—if Iryani gave us the nod—we would be taking him to New York, and Saada and Hinda would fly in from Israel to be reunited with him after decades of pained existence. Massoud remarked that it all seemed like a dream as we visited our photography shop of choice and purchased passport pictures for him, Ida, and Moshe. Back in the Taj Sheba, we filled out three Yemeni passport applications in Arabic. Abdul Rahman Mutaher, the friendly Mukhabarat man who watched our every move and was familiar with every component of the Jewish community, participated in the entire process; ICROJOY always held discussions and made decisions in his presence in order to foster trust and respect. The "three musketeers," as we dubbed the Saada trio, dined with us and slept with us in the luxury hotel, spending their first nights ever on real beds.

Bright and early the next morning, Tuesday, May 28, the delegation set out for Raida and Suq-el-Jadid. It would be my only escape from Sanaa during Mission V. We proudly surveyed the barren plot of land on which one day a synagogue and school would stand, and we visited the home of Moshe Dahari Halla, where Jews from Na'at and other surrounding villages had assembled to greet us. Moshe introduced his daughter, America, to the delegation, and then the five-month-old boy who owed his creation in part to ICROJOY. We will let you know soon about our decision, Moshe said.

Another Raida resident whom ICROJOY had never visited was Mori Yaish al-Garni, a rough character hardened by his imprisonment in 1979 following the DuWayne Terrell episode. With Abdul Rahman in tow, Yosef and I visited Mori Yaish's impressive home. The man showed us the remains of his Raida factory, which he claimed had recently been gutted in a suspicious blaze. I don't know who was responsible, Mori Yaish declared, but I lost six million rials due to the fire. Can you help me out?

No, Mori Yaish, we do not provide individuals with financial assistance. But I have a better proposal for you. Menahem, your fourteen-year-old son, is reputed to be a particularly gifted young man, interested in pursuing Jewish studies and mastering the techniques of ritual slaughter. Let us take him back to America. The coarse Yemeni could not give us a definitive response; America was halfway around the world, and he would have preferred his older son to go.

From the Yaish home, I traveled back to the Hallas in Suq-el-Jadid on the back of Binyamin Khubani's motorcycle, dust flying in my face as the vehicle flew perilously over the arid expanse, Binyamin's black peyot fluttering in the wind. Over a traditional lunch on the floor in the Halla's *mafraj*, we finalized plans for construction of the school and mikveh, then signed a contract with the Raida Jews before Raida's sheikh. Once again, we wanted to initiate our project with the blessings of the influential Arab governor of the region; ICROJOY delivered the thousands of dollars to the Jews specifically in his presence. Then they purchased the plot of land from the sheikh, and our work in Raida was done.

As I was about to enter the van for the drive back to the Yemeni capital, I was approached privately by a Jew with whom I was not acquainted. He obviously knew about ICROJOY's plans, for he quietly asked why he was not being considered for a trip to the United States. Then the young man lowered his voice and adopted a more sinister tone: "I can make a lot of trouble for you. I am working for Amos." Amos, the Mossad man from the Dan Accadia in Tel Aviv. Amos, to whom I had spent hours describing the condition of Yemeni Jewry. How did he know the mysterious "Amos"? Flustered by the threat, I ignored the man and climbed into the van. Regrettably, jealousy was beginning to poison a joyful process.

To jealousy was added pure animosity when we returned to Sanaa. Waiting for ICROJOY in the Taj Sheba were the irksome Habib brothers from Saada, Sleiman and Said. The Habibs were difficult and argumentative. Beside them stood Sleiman Faiz, the oldest son of Yhia Faiz from Hidan Asham. Their demand: You cannot allow Ida Zareb to go with you to the United States. And you cannot take his friend Binyamin Khubani. If you do, we will destroy your relationship with the Saada Jews. "If you take him, we will hire a *qabili* to kill you!" *Qabilis* are native Yemeni tribesmen. I reflected sadly that my first death threat in Yemen had come from a Jew. And why the invective against Ida Zareb, a gentle man who I had grown to like? Because of a horrible family feud, a virtual war between the Zareb-Khubani and Habib-Faiz clans of Saada. One so deeply embedded in their psyches that a Zareb had once shorn the peyot of Sleiman Faiz.

Abdul Rahman, the Yemeni intelligence officer, was present during our encounter with the meddlesome trio. Said Habib, he postulated, was a collaborator with the Mukhabarat, providing the Yemeni government with information about the Jewish community. This contention compelled us to view Habib's threat with caution. I yearned to be independent, but Yosef Levy, eager to avoid trouble, urged me to give in. Negotiating with the Yemeni and American governments, facing Neturei Karta and the Mossad and the

Mukhabarat, seemed easy compared to dealing with the Jews of Yemen. We eventually succeeded only with the patience of Job.

Chapter Twelve

STEPPING INTO HISTORY

May 31, 1991

A glorious Friday evening sunset. Shabbat was descending on Sanaa when a van pulled into the Taj Sheba driveway. Ambassador Dunbar alighted and entered the hotel. I'm on my way to Iryani in the Foreign Ministry, he said. I want to confirm the deal before I send my cable to Washington, to see if we have Salih's approval. But there's still one obstacle to remove: Schifter has advised me not to bother with the cable unless the Yemenis issue that declaration in support of the Middle East peace process. After telling me this, Dunbar returned to the van and headed for Ga-el-Yahud and the Foreign Ministry.

Shabbat in the Taj Sheba passed uneventfully, but the madness returned immediately upon its conclusion. There were more unpleasant encounters with the Habib brothers, and their harangues against Ida Zareb. And then came the visits from friends of Zareb, urging us to ignore the Habibs. Finally, there were passport applications to complete for the large Sabari family—in case freedom of travel were declared. I recorded a tally of the Sabari family into my notebook. It consisted of twenty-two people who could be divided into three distinct groups:

First Group
1. Yhia ibn Daoud Sabari – age: 50 (husband)
2. Hamama Sabari – age: 37 (wife)
3. Salem Sabari – age: 15 (son)
4. Balqis Sabari – age: 16 (daughter)
5. Yehudah Sabari – age: 13 (son)

6. Ezri Sabari – age: 9 (son)
7. Yhia Sabari – age: 5 (son)
8. Ezra Sabari – age: 4 (son)
9. Said Sabari – age: 3 (son)

Second Group: Two Married Sons

A 1. Moshe Yhia Sabari – age: 22 (husband)
   2. Bardaqusha Sabari – age: 19 (wife)
   3. Saida Sabari – age: 3 (daughter)
   4. Nachle Sabari – age: 1 (daughter)

A 1. Yisrael Sabari – age: 19 (husband)
   2. Miriam Sabari – age: 21 (wife)
   3. Shimon Sabari – age: 3 (son)
   4. Levi Sabari – age: 1 (son)

Third Group: Father of Yhia ibn Daoud Sabari

1 Daoud ibn Yosef Sabari – age: 80 (husband)
2 Khadia Sabari – age: 55 (wife)
3 Nadra Sabari – age: 13 (daughter)
4 Yaqub Sabari – age: 21 (son)
5 Saida Sabari – age: 16 (wife of son)
6 – ? – (Saida is pregnant)

June 3, 1991

Three days later and still no progress. I was sitting before an animated Ambassador Charlie Dunbar in the United States embassy, where the mixed report was delivered. The Yemenis were prepared in principle to publicly support the Middle East peace process. But that was only according to Iryani. We could not finalize the cable until President Salih approved—and he was on the road in Dhammar with his Interior Minister.

"We must take someone out with us!" I exclaimed. Whether it be students or a family or just a tourist. We must take advantage of this confluence of circumstances. After months of dialogue, ICROJOY must offer some accomplishments to the world, where talk is cheap. Bewildered by the impasse, I left the embassy compound bemoaning our lack of progress.

"I have good news, and I have bad news." It was Charlie Dunbar—on the telephone this time—later that afternoon. His attempts at softening the blow failed, for his bad news dwarfed the good. What exactly gratified Dunbar on this particular June day in the Yemeni capital? "Chicago is leading the Lakers 2-1 in the playoffs." And the inauspicious information? I spoke to Iryani, and the Foreign Minister has all but given up. Your chances of getting five Jews out this month are very slim; the cabinet will convene on Wednesday to debate the issue, but its decision could take at least several weeks.

"I must see Dr. Iryani again," I pleaded. "Please arrange another meeting for me." I needed to register ICROJOY's protest and stress the urgency of the situation. Meanwhile, other concerns were weighing on my mind, and they revolved around ICROJOY's invited guest, the man who was serving as our secretary for Mission V. From the minute we landed in Sanaa, he had behaved oddly, acting aloof and uncooperative, and frequently disappearing in the capital city without my permission. He pumped me incessantly for his phone messages, which Dalia had promised to convey from New York. Something was wrong with the guest, and a strange telephone call from Dalia seemed to confirm this. "Watch the typewriter," Dalia told me mysteriously, "watch the typewriter." We suspected that the phone lines in both my hotel room in Sanaa and our apartment in Washington Heights were tapped; thus Dalia talked in code. "Watch the secretary" is what she really meant: watch him carefully, tell him little, don't take him anywhere.

My suspicions were confirmed the next night, when a Mukhabarat squad entered my room in the Taj Sheba and suddenly interrogated me about our secretary: Who is this man? His behavior is bizarre. Why do we see him roaming around the city by himself? Why have we spotted him in Bab-el-Yaman? My conversation with Dalia had obviously been deciphered.

"He's a good man," I lied. "He works with us as our secretary by recording and writing. There's nothing wrong." But I later learned the precise nature of the problem, and how my family had stumbled upon it. In order to retrieve the man's messages, my son Arik would call his answering machine daily. And shortly after we departed for Yemen, Arik had accidentally retrieved a message the secretary had failed to erase: a message from Yossi ben Aharon, the director of Prime Minister Yitzhak Shamir's office. So Dalia had been right; ICROJOY's secretary, was, in fact, working for the Mossad. Israeli intelligence had planted him in order to monitor our activities, even though I was willingly supplying it with honest information. This could have imperiled our group had Yemeni intelligence sniffed a Mossad informant in our midst. Indeed, the Mukhabarat was suspicious. So I cut off contact with the man, blatantly ignoring him, and he could not help but note my new attitude. Ostracized by the rest of the group, he wanted to leave Yemen as soon as possible.

The most portentous event to which the secretary was not invited occurred late on Sunday, June 2, an afternoon that would erase cultural barriers like no other episode in years of Track II diplomacy. What had begun as an innocent gesture the week before—my offering Dr. Iryani a recording of Shoshana Tobi's songs—became an opportunity to forge a profound bond with the Yemenis. On Saturday night the Foreign Minister called me at the hotel and invited Shoshana Tobi to perform at a concert. Naturally I agreed. I immediately called Saada and told the delegation to return at once to the capital.

At 3:00 p.m., Sunday afternoon, an army van packed with paratroopers bearing Kalishnikovs pulled up in front of the Taj Sheba. Yosef, Lester, Shoshana, and I climbed aboard, leaving the secretary behind all alone; Joel Kirschner of the Joint Distribution Committee had returned to New York days earlier. Shoshana, alive with nervous exhilaration, clutched her tambourine and drums as we sped toward Hadda, an exclusive suburb of the capital, and a beautiful villa therein.

When we arrived, young girls in white greeted us with flowers. Removing our shoes and ascending to the second floor, we found ourselves in a magnificent *mafraj* brightened by rosy light pouring through stained-lass windows, furnished with the finest rugs and pillows. Atop those rugs and pillows reclined Sanaa's intelligentsia, men cloaked in white *galabiyas*, chewing qat, smoking cigars. Dr. Iryani. And the mayor of Sanaa. And the Ministers of Information, Interior, Tourism, and Culture, the army generals, the businessmen—all eagerly waiting Shoshana's arrival. Yemen's famous national singer, seventy-year-old al-Harithi, was there too. On a brilliant September day in 1962, al-Harithi had intoned his hours-old country's national anthem in Sanaa's Independence Square. Now, he and his country's leaders, were to enjoy a concert featuring melodies of the Yemeni Jews.

"Sit down and chew some qat," Charlie Dunbar had advised me. I did as he said and began to chew qat, but didn't much like the taste of the bitter green leaves. Don't insult your hosts, Dunbar had insisted: at least pretend to chew. I enjoyed some light conversation with government ministers, their cheeks bulging with qat. Then Dr. Iryani introduced Shoshana Tobi as an expert in the art of ancient Yemeni women's songs, and she mesmerized the elated audience for two hours, warmly chanting Arabic lyrics—and at one point Hebrew words—swaying along with her rhythmic cadences. She and al-Harithi sang together the tunes of their common heritage. And I introduced the concert's final ballad . . .

The author of its words was a seventeenth-century Jewish poet and kabbalist, I said, but he is also national figure of yours. Shalom Shabbazzi was born and buried in Taiz. He composed his masterpieces in Arabic and Aramaic and Hebrew. And one of his most popular songs is called "Qat and Coffee":

A quarrel had begun
Between Coffee and Qat
Tell us, they challenged me,
Which of us you prefer.

It was Qat who spoke first:
Choice are my leaves
And precious, too.
Proudly my shrub
Raises its head
On Mount Sabor

And it is there
The nightingale will build her nest
And hide her eggs
In crevices
Of ruined walls.
Perched on my branch,
She sweetly sings
Her song at night.

Now it was Coffee's turn:
I am the early morning glory
Brightening the start of each new day.
It is Shazli
To whom I owe my reputation . . .

Qat and coffee dissent but must live in peace, I told the Yemeni dignitaries in the *mafraj*. We human beings, though we often differ, must learn to live in peace. Witness how the poem closes:

Now came my turn:
You give me equal joy,
I long for both of you.
To each of you I owe
A vote of gratitude.
Yet I extend this praise
To wine, enjoyed with friends.
To comfort, to console
Is my, the poet's, role.

And now, my worthy friends,
Let's drink to fellowship,
And let us spend the time
With poetry and songs.

All discord be dismissed.
Thanks be and praise to God.

Lord, grant your Salem peace
And keep him from all ills.

Shoshana Tobi, a tiny five-year-old when the Magic Carpet whisked her away, was delivering the most meaningful performance of her life. And when she finished, the awestruck men of her birthplace heaped accolades upon her. The very next day, we got a call from Yemen's state-owned television station: Would Shoshana be willing to perform and be interviewed on TV? It was a stunning development, the first time a Jew would appear on Yemeni national television. I was very cautious, though, and requested a meeting with the interviewer before acquiescing to the ground-breaking offer. At 8:00 p.m. Monday evening, June 3, el-Dahabani, the program's director, entered the Taj Sheba's lobby in an immaculate suit. "These are the conditions," I began. There must be no politics, no questions concerning Israel, no probes into our delegation's activities in Yemen. My name must not be uttered during the course of the interview; it must be a strictly cultural event. El-Dahabani agreed to the conditions and invited Shoshana to a taping session at Yemeni National Television Studios on Tuesday morning. That night, sleep eluded Shoshana.

I stood behind the camera on Tuesday morning, watching the two and a half-hour taping session. Twenty-five producers and crew members joined me in front of the monitors and watched Shoshana Tobi delicately respond to el-Dahabani's often-difficult queries. Then Tobi took to the stage with her voice and timbrel, and overwhelmed everyone in the studio with stirring renditions of ancient Yemeni and Jewish favorites. My name was mentioned once near the end of the taping, and I was described as the leader of Shoshana's delegation. But the true purpose of our mission was not revealed. We were simply visiting the isolated Jews of Yemen. Six weeks later, after our return to New York, Shoshana Tobi's performance was broadcast to Yemen's television viewers, and it was rerun soon hereafter, and then rerun again. With some song and dance, we had bridged cultural gaps that were in reality quite narrow. Later on, there would be another TV special featuring Shoshana Tobi along with the nation's top female Muslim singer, a-Tawila.

That afternoon, ICROJOY went shopping in Sanaa. Thirty desks and thirty chairs later, the new Jewish school in Raida owned enough furniture to get off the ground. Said Nahari and Moshe Dahari Halla accompanied us as we combed the capital city for more equipment for the soon-to-be-constructed school building, and sent the fruits of our labor in a rented truck to Suq-el-Jadid and storage in Nahari's mud-walled home. No longer would Raida's schoolchildren sit on the dusty floor, cross-legged at the knees of their teachers.

June 5, 1991
"There is a cabinet meeting scheduled for tomorrow," Charles Dunbar told me in his embassy residence at 10 a.m. The message was clear: we would be unable to leave on our scheduled Lufthansa flight on Thursday, June 6. We would have to remain in the country until Sunday, June 9. I was furious at the delaying tactics adopted by the Yemenis, and expressed my anger to the ambassador. It was the first and last time unpleasant words were exchanged between us. "I'm not sure we can stay past June 6," I argued. The Yemen government had taken several weeks to approve five passports, and I was growing impatient as the tension mounted. In order to assist ICROJOY, Dunbar had already postponed his return to the United States, even though his son's college graduation was fast approaching. He could not abandon his post at such a crucial juncture, for Dr. Iryani, during one of their meetings, had indicated that the Yemenis were ready to publicly declare their support for the Israeli-Palestinian peace process.

Yhia Yitzhak Nahari and a Mukhabarat man entered the lobby of the Taj Sheba at 12:00 noon, carrying five shopping bags bulging with wrinkled, worn-out bills. They had been to Raida to find Yhia ibn Daoud Suberi's cache, the secret stash hidden long ago in the crevices of the Nahari home by the shrewd old man. His horde of one-, five-, ten-, twenty-, and fifty-rial bills had not seen the light of day in at least a decade. Horrible inflation of the rial had depreciated the value of Suberi's hidden treasure, though. We counted the bills for two hours in my hotel room: 73,000 rial, once a sizable sum, now worth slightly over $2,000. I signed a receipt in front of the Mukhabarat man. Five thousand rials were immediately returned to Nahari as payment for the honest man's time and effort.

But Suberi had also begged me to recover his long-lost account from the Central Bank of Yemen. Those funds were the *mu'allem's* real treasure, for he had wisely made his deposits in dollars, not rials. The Central Bank account represented Suberi's investment in the future. And as Suberi's wrinkled rial bills lay strewn across my bed, the telephone rang: This is Dr. Iryani's office. We have located the money of Yhia ibn Daoud Suberi in the Central Bank, across the street from you. Omar will deliver it to you in twenty minutes. Please wait in your hotel room. Omar, it turned out, was a senior bank officer sporting a regal white *galabiya* and an ornate *jambiya* that gleamed in the light. Lester, Yosef, and I watched in amazement as the officer presented me with a check in the name of Yhia ibn Daoud Suberi— for $32,000—at my request to be claimed at Morgan Trust in New York, the Central Bank's financial correspondent in the United States. I thanked Omar and sat down on the bed in disbelief, my trembling hand clutching the life's savings of a man from the valley of Damt.

June 6, 1991
Thursday morning, the day we were scheduled to leave Yemen. But we would not be leaving Yemen on June 6. George, the Taj Sheba's concierge, was busy converting three Thursday-night Lufthansa tickets into Sunday-morning Air France tickets. Unaware of our change in plans, Binyamin Khubani called me from Saada to bid us farewell and again plead to be taken to America, if not now, at least the next time we were in Yemen. Then Ida Zareb called, and I asked him to come from Saada to Sanaa. We had to discuss the vindictive practices of the Habib brothers, and the vicious family feud which was threatening our mission. Indeed, at that very moment, Said Habib was standing in front of the Taj Sheba. He had planted himself there to watch our every move, and refused to leave until ICROJOY abandoned its plans to take Ida Zareb to the United States. Habib did not seem to work at anything, yet he was able to support his large family. "How does he manage it?" I wondered, and eventually found out. Said Habib was connected with the Mukhabarat, I was told. According to the Jews who told me this, he was an informer and a spy. That's how the Mukhabarat knew so much about the Jewish

community, I realized. This was more than a mere family feud. This was a concerted Mukhabarat effort to hamper our progress.

At 1:00 p.m., Ida Zareb arrived at the Taj Sheba and entered through a back door to avoid his enemies, who were standing about in front. Zareb was not helpful. If I can't come with you, he exclaimed, I will go to Dr. Iryani myself and involve a sheikh from the north! I looked at Yosef desperately. If the Foreign Minister is harassed by individual Jews, our progress will be retarded, not hastened. If you don't come with us this time, I told Zareb, I promise you can come by yourself in one month's time. Someone will meet you in Frankfurt. Although Zareb acquiesced, bending to pressure from an antagonist dismayed me.

Meanwhile, Mission V was not coming to a close so soon. Brad Hanson, the embassy's information officer, dropped by the Taj Sheba and informed us that our departure would have to be delayed again— until Wednesday, June 12. Chances for processing the passports by Sunday were slim. And Charles Dunbar could impart little definitive detail. By chance I spotted the American ambassador in the Taj Sheba lobby at 8:45 p.m. attending a reception for President Ali Abdullah Salih, and he related a conversation between Dr. Iryani and John Kelly from State. Kelly, Assistant Secretary of State for Near Eastern Affairs, was not satisfied with the language of Yemen's declaration on the peace process, but nevertheless tried to talk the Foreign Minister into letting ICROJOY leave Sunday with the Jewish students—a crucial gesture if PL–480 was to be renewed. The delays were occurring in the Interior Ministry, not the Foreign Ministry, said Dunbar. At 11:00 p.m., a disgruntled ex-ICROJOY secretary and a cheerful Shoshana Tobi left for Sanaa International Airport. The guest did not utter a peep the entire flight to New York. With Joel Kirschner already gone, the ICROJOY delegation, original consisting of six members, was now reduced to three: Lester Smerka, Yosef Levy, and myself. And we knew not when our return to New York would come.

June 7, 1991
There was a battle brewing among the government ministers of Yemen this Friday afternoon. At 1:30 p.m., Charles Dunbar revisited

the Taj Sheba to deliver another update: Abdul Aziz al-Ghani, the Prime Minister, was very interested in the five Jews. And the head of the Communist party had stated, "If there is freedom of travel for Muslims, there must be for Jews as well; they, too, are citizens." But Dr. Iryani had not attended the most recent cabinet meeting, as he had been busy composing Yemen's peace process declaration. Regarding freedom for the Jews, "there might be a delay," Dunbar said.

"We will stay here forever if we have to!" I exclaimed. We must finalize this release, we must take advantage of this moment in history.

"Don't worry, Hayim," the ambassador replied. "We can really move mountains." Dr. Iryani had agreed in principle to freedom of travel for the Jews. His secret declaration meant that any Yemeni Jew could approach the Interior Ministry and obtain a passport in order to leave the country—like any Muslim. But of course the approval of President Salih was pending. Iryani's agreement in principle gave us a glimmer of hope as the Sabbath approached.

June 8, 1991

Exactly twenty-four hours later, Dunbar was once again standing in the Taj Sheba lobby updating us, delivering the most momentous news in ICROJOY's existence. The President and the Prime Minister are in agreement, he said. They are prepared to secretly declare freedom of travel for the Jews of Yemen. Jews will be able to leave Yemen for the first time since 1962. They can go as tourists and businessmen and emigrants, and will be free to go directly to any country but Israel. But regarding your three students and two visitors, he added, you will not be able to leave with them on Sunday. That humanitarian gesture must first be reconfirmed by Salih. There are sheikhs and fundamentalists in the government who resent the move, Dunbar explained. Iryani is granting too many concessions to the Jews, they say. We must be patient while he convinces his colleagues that this new policy will do no harm.

We could not leave Yemen without first breaking the ice. That afternoon, two of our Sunday Air France tickets were exchanged for Thursday Lufthansa tickets, our return to New York delayed once again. But Lester was a businessman and had already sacrificed weeks of profit for the Jews of Yemen. After the Sabbath, Lester headed for the airport. And then there were two.

June 9, 1991
Waiting patiently in the Taj Sheba for that crucial telephone call from Iryani. But the call did not come. Instead, Yhia ibn Daoud Sabari arrived to discuss his family's release. He begged us to bribe Said Habib to stop fomenting anger and trouble. Habib had actually visited Iryani, Sabari reported. And then Sabari offered two more disturbing tidbits: During his Saturday night drive from Saada to Sanaa, there had been a car accident, and now an Arab neighbor was threatening to cut off poor Yhia's fingers if the damages were not paid. Secondly, Massoud Zindani's wife was on the verge of giving birth. He had decided to remain in the country, as his economic situation was difficult and he had to earn some money. But Zindani's inclusion in our mission was crucial for symbolic reasons; a reunion with his two sisters in Israel would work wonders in the eyes of Congress. So I parted with more of our limited funds. Into Sabari's outstretched hand went $250 for Massoud Zindani—"he *must* come"—and $350 for Sabari's Arab neighbor, to preclude any friction between the Arabs and Jews of Saada. And finally to Sabari went the private telephone number of Bruce Strathearn in the United States embassy. He will be your liaison in Sanaa, he will help you leave Yemen when the proper time comes.

The Amlah region, near the Saudi Arabian border in the arid, northernmost region of Yemen, lies a full nine-hour drive from the capital. On Sunday afternoon, Yosef and I were paid an emotionally exhausting visit by Yhia Zareb and his son from impoverished Amlah. The emaciated son was one of eight children. I was moved greatly by their financial plight, and parted with another $200—again in violation of ICROJOY's policy—before opening up our meat and offering some to the famished pair. And then we made up sandwiches for their long trip home. Yosef Levy escorted the Zarebs downstairs, and then headed for Said Habib in order to deliver a severe, well-deserved tongue-lashing.

Our final visitor of the day was a haggard Ambassador Dunbar, who entered my room in the Taj Sheba at 8:10 p.m. and found me in conversation with Abdul Rahman, the Mukhabarat man. I politely asked Abdul Rahman to leave the room and he complied.

"ICROJOY is history," Dunbar announced bitterly.

"Don't worry," I consoled him. You must understand, I said, we will tell Iryani about the tremendous pressure waiting in the wings from America's Jewish organizations and the Hunt Oil people. But Dunbar was too depressed. There was no more leverage, no amount of cajoling and coaxing that would free the Jews of Yemen. The Yemenis' delaying tactics were winning. Our time had run out.

"I've been in Yemen for three years! And this is what I've achieved?" Dunbar concluded his comments with some very undiplomatic language. Meanwhile, the Taj Sheba lobby was teeming with Arab journalists pestering Yosef Levy with intrusive questions, demanding an interview with Hayim Tawil. The reporters had spoken to Said Habib. Tawil and Levy are Zionist agents, he had told them; they want to take all the Jews out of Yemen. Levy narrowly escaped a major confrontation, and Dunbar, a very troubled man, disappeared into the night.

But twenty minutes later, the outlook suddenly turned rosier. Soon after leaving the Taj Sheba, a cheerful Dunbar called my room and asked me to call Iryani at home. Dunbar and Iryani had just spoken, and the Foreign Minister had sounded more promising. Confused, I called Iryani at home at 8:45 p.m., whereupon the Foreign Minister promised "not to disappoint me." If you stay until Sunday, you can take five Jews out, Iryani said. My response was not very gentle: I'm not sure we'll be able to stay until Sunday. We have our own lives and schedules to manage. We need action now.

To end the paralysis, we decided to bring some more pressure through a deception coordinated by Dalia. Assuming that someone was recording my conversations, I received three "surprise" telephone calls in the ICROJOY suite at the Taj Sheba. One was from Jack Nasser, a wealthy Syrian philanthropist speaking in a clear Arabic, another from Albert Reichman, the Canadian real estate magnate, and the third from Stephen Solarz, the Brooklyn Congressman. Each caller told me that he was considering the purchase of the entire Jewish populace of Yemen, at $50,000-$100,000 a head. Money is no object. Present the offer to the Yemeni government, Hayim. Tell them we are serious. We hoped the phony offers would be leaked to the Arab media and disseminated to the world, thereby adding to pressure on the Yemeni government, assailing it from another side. In retrospect, however, no hoaxes were necessary.

June 11, 1991
Wednesday, shortly after dawn. Charles Dunbar explained his new strategy for breaking through the gridlock: a telephone conversation between Presidents Bush and Salih to repair the damage and smooth over the differences. But according to Richard Schifter in Washington, a dialogue with the Yemeni President was not high on Bush's list of priorities, especially in the wake of the Persian Gulf War. And besides, $5 million of PL–480 aid had already been claimed by another country. In Washington, Benjamin Gilman was trying to get Bush to talk with Salih. Andrea Farsakh was trying to convince the Hunt Oil people to heap pressure on the Yemenis. And in Sanaa, Iryani was stewing over George Bush's snub of his President. Nevertheless, a decision regarding the release of five Jews was expected on Thursday.

As another day began, the publicity stirred up by Said Habib intensified. Yosef and I were now Zionist spies hiding out in the Taj Sheba. Leaving our room meant confronting hordes of reporters and photographers. Trapped in the hotel, I spoke with Dalia in New York, appointing her the new ICROJOY spokesperson. I then spent the day calling Debbie Bodlander in Benjamin Gilman's office, Stanley Roth in Stephen Solarz's office, Michael Van Dusen in Lee Hamilton's office. You must persuade Bush to talk to Salih! Meanwhile, Dalia took to the typewriter. She became our lobbyist, and immediately mailed out a missive to our friends in Congress, Mel Levine, Alfonse D'Amato, Stephen Solarz, and Benjamin Gilman.

Following the statement issued by Dr. Hayim Tawil on June 12, 1991 from Sanaa, Yemen, I would like to reiterate ICROJOY's position.

First, let me state that we understand the position and the ill feelings of the administration toward the Yemeni government. However, when the moment arrives and 1500 human beings can be saved from bondage, politics must be put aside temporarily, allowing the voice of humanitarian reasoning to be heard and prevail.

For thirty years the government of Yemen did not even consider letting any Jew leave the country. Allowing the Jewish community the Freedom to Travel is the most bitter pill that the administration can force the Yemenis to swallow! It is this administration that at the present time has the upper hand, not the other way around. Our position to the Yemeni government is: if you want aid, let the people have the Freedom to Travel!

It is in the greatest honor, at this historical breakthrough that ICROJOY requests your support in trying to assist the 1500 Yemeni Jews to gain the elementary human right of Freedom to Travel.

The Jewish community of the free world will be ever so grateful.

Sincerely,
Dalia Tawil
    Acting Chairperson

George, the concierge, was hard at work again, converting our Thursday-night Lufthansa tickets into Sunday-morning Air France tickets. Would it be the final exchange? Would the five Jews be released at last?

Charles Dunbar did not seem to think so. Al-Ashtal, Yemen's ambassador to the United Nations, was objecting to the sanctions the Security Council had imposed on Saddam Hussein. That would not sit well with Washington. But there was little more that Dunbar could do. After all, he would be U.S. ambassador to Yemen for only six more hours. And according to Dalia, our congressional friends in Washington were locked in a fierce budget battle; the Jews of Yemen were no longer on the top burner. At 1:15 a.m., Dunbar stopped by the Taj Sheba for the last time on his way to Sanaa International Airport. Our separation was an emotional one, and tears filled the ambassador's eyes as I thanked him profusely for three years of conscientious work. With that, Charles Dunbar left Yemen forever.

June 13, 1991

The private Mercedes of Foreign Minister Abdul Karim al-Iryani pulled up in front of the Taj Sheba, and a stately chauffeur opened the door for Yosef Levy and me. Twenty minutes later, we were entering Iryani's villa and being escorted into a room with the Foreign Minister, his aides, and one of his scholarly brothers; Iryani's wife was never present at any of our meetings, as it is not customary for Muslim women to appear in public. Once again we discussed famous archaeological finds, including the Himyaric inscriptions for which Yemen's beige earth is recognized by scholars. Then the Jews. After being here for so long, I stressed, we must leave with five Jews on Sunday. Iryani reiterated his condition: that the Jews not go to Israel. And then I heard him utter the following words: "In principle the Yemeni government has decided to grant freedom of travel to the Jews of Yemen." Moreover, he said, in October or thereabouts, the Sabari family would be allowed to go to the United States, after I had clarified the matter with the American government. Gratefully, I handed the Foreign Minister the passport applications for the Sabari family. And the five passports for the students? They will be ready on Saturday night. I refused to breathe a sigh of relief, not would I until seated on a plane bound for New York with Yemeni Jews at my side. Meanwhile, I stayed a while, enjoyed a smoke with Iryani's brother, who had just returned from Syria with a carton of foreign cigarettes, and acknowledged a secret victory.

June 15, 1991

Shabbat once again in the well-appointed Taj Sheba, and the most stressful Day of Rest in my life. Yosef Levy and I, all that remained of an ICROJOY delegation that had once numbered six, were scheduled to depart on the 1:00 a.m. Air France flight early Sunday morning with four Yemeni Jews—Massoud Zindani, Moshe Sabari, Daoud Katabi, and young Menahem al-Garni—but the passports were not yet in our hands, and as each day ebbed the probability of opening the doors for Yemeni Jewry seemed further reduced.

Jewish tradition equates freeing a captive with saving a life; I was therefore obliged to use the telephone on Shabbat. At 10:30 a.m. I called Bruce Strathearn, holding down the fort at the United States embassy until the new ambassador arrived in August, to inquire about the passports. Strathearn promised to contact the Interior Ministry and Dr. Iryani at the Foreign Ministry. For the next five hours, I heard nothing. Yosef and I paced the length and breadth of increasingly claustrophobic Room 212, unable to eat or read.

At 3:00 p.m. I called Strathearn again, and learned that Iryani had just called the embassy and asked if the passports had arrived there; they had not. Apparently, our precious documents were floating somewhere in the Interior Ministry, a government department considerably less than enthusiastic about Iryani's deal with America. By 6:00 p.m., our most recent Lufthansa tickets had been converted into Air France tickets, but there were still no passports.

Six hours to go, the Shabbat over. Strathearn called me with an update: our passports were sitting on the desk of a clerk in the Foreign Ministry, but he didn't know which one. There was a reception that night for Sanaa's diplomatic community at the British ambassador's residence. He said he would call me from there.

Four hours until the flight, and my nerves were completely shot. Desperate, I dialed Dr. Iryani's home number, but the Foreign Minister was not there. That's when I heard a knock at the door. A delegation of Jews from Raida had arrived to send off its native sons. Massoud Zindani, persuaded by ICROJOY's financial aid, had left his pregnant wife to join us for the trip. Moshe Sabari and Daoud Katabi were ready to embark on their landmark journey. Menahem al-Garni, the teenage son of Mori Yaish, had come with his father and sat on the bed, suitcase in hand, in nervous anticipation. Said Habib was there, too, along with Ida Zareb, his sworn enemy.

At 10:00 p.m., Strathearn and Brad Hanson, the embassy's information officer, entered Room 212 bearing a package of five passports and wearing grim looks on their tired faces. I tore open the package with great fervor and rifled through the documents, and nearly had a heart attack. Menahem al-Garni's passport was not among them! In its place was the passport of Salem Bashari, a Saada man who had initially declined our invitation, then had changed his mind, but had been told it was too late. For some reason, I was now holding Bashari's passport in my hand. Bashari was seven hours to our north in Saada, and we were leaving in three hours.

I was relieved to get four passports—the fourth was for Ida Zareb to be used in one month's time—but dismayed at the mix-up in the Interior Ministry, unsure whether it was a deliberate or unintentional misunderstanding. I called Dr. Iryani to thank him profusely for his valiant efforts, promise there would be little publicity in the United States, and inform him of our problem. The Foreign Minister was aware of the situation. I'm sorry, he said, but it's too late to change anything. Everything is closed for the night. Then I turned to Mori Yaish and Menahem al-Garni, still sitting patiently on the bed, and delivered the tragic news: No, you will not be going to America tonight, you are not escaping Yemen tonight, you are not experiencing exodus tonight, please forgive me.

Moist drops began trickling down Menahem's olive cheeks, and soon he had buried his face in his father's chest, unable to control the childlike bawling, unable to stop the flow of tears. And the crestfallen father began crying, and soon Yosef and I joined them in their misery. But you will come soon, Menahem. We will get you out. You will walk in the Holy Land one day.

My last minutes in Sanaa were thus moments of revelry and melancholy. We rejoiced at having broken the ice, and lamented the passport complication, and heaved sighs of relief. At midnight, Yosef and I entered the departures terminal at Sanaa International Airport with three men wearing *galabiyas* and *kuftas*, long *peyot* dangling from the sides of their heads. Massoud Zindani and Moshe Sabari were wearing cheap rubber sandals; Daoud Katabi had draped a tallit over his outfit. We had purchased gray sports jackets for the three to wear upon landing, but the Western garments only made them look more ridiculous to the gawkers we encountered. A stopover in Paris, and then we landed in New York. Dalia, Lester Smerka, Shlomo Grafi, and Stewart Ain, a reporter from the *Jewish Week,* greeted the three newcomers. Overwhelmed by their first plane trips and the size of the arrivals building, the three Yemenis bravely emerged into the sunshine, quite aware that they were stepping into history.

Chapter Thirteen

FROM SANAA TO JERUSALEM

July 1, 1991

A white minibus, transporting ten El Al passengers who had recently deplaned at Kennedy Airport, turned precariously into the hairpin curve that is Exit 17N of the Southern State Parkway and entered the village of West Hempstead, deep in the heart of Long Island's bucolic suburbia. It weaved its way down tree-lined Hempstead Avenue, past the church, the duck pond, the Carvel, then made a right on Oakford Street, coasted by the split-ranches, colonials, and capes, and came to a halt before the home of Shlomo Grafi.

An eerie silence, punctured only by the occasional psalm uttered by a particularly elderly passenger, had pervaded the half-hour ride from Kennedy. David Shuker, accompanying the families for whom he had fought, stared solemnly out the tinted window. Hinda Zindani, sitting across from her sister Saada, dabbed her eyes incessantly, a wad of used tissues hidden in her fist. Bill Wolf, ICROJOY's friend from Arizona, was on board with Moshe Atzar, the friend of Pierre Goloubinoff and uncle of Moshe Sabari. Dalia, up front, kept an eye on the new arrivals. All the travelers that summer morning had healthy, olive-toned skin that revealed their Middle Eastern origins, and they were nervously anticipating their encounter with the three men inside the house in West Hempstead.

Massoud Zindani, age thirty-seven, Moshe Sabari, twenty-two, and Daoud Katabi, fifty-seven, had been cooped up in the home of Shlomo Grafi since their mid-June arrival. Yes, there had been that landmark afternoon in Washington when coffee was drunk in the offices of Benjamin Gilman, when the Congressman had revealed a personal side, discussing the misfortunes of oppressed people throughout the world and mourning the loss of Esther, his young daughter, whose life had been cut short years earlier. There had been the greetings from State Department diplomats, the White House encounter with Richard Haas of the National Security Council, the visits to Stephen Solarz and Michael Van Dusen. And there had been the side trip to Crown Heights and the Lubavitcher Rebbe, the gazing at Manhattan's huge skyscrapers. But this was truly the day for which the three Yemenis had pined: the moment when their visitors from Israel would arrive. Not just any visitors, but blood relatives caught in political crossfires, wars of words, with whom the lines of communication had been severed decades ago.

Inside, a powerful Yemeni beat blared from Shlomo Grafi's loudspeakers. My son Arik, camera in hand, stood at attention. Naamah Nahami, Daoud Katabi's older sister, swathed in flowing red and gold garments, gingerly descended from the minibus first, the tears already streaming down her cheeks. Now she was in the foyer, and then in the living room, and finally there was Daoud, standing between Yosef Levy and myself, no longer a lithe, young thing, but a distinguished man replete with full white beard and black peyot. Had the years been kind or cruel? It did not matter. Daoud Katabi was in the arms of his sister, and she was crying, and she was grasping him so firmly that the white material wrapped around his head began unraveling.

Hinda Zindani, in a black dress and white hat, entered next and scanned the busy room. *Where is he?* There were too many people in the room. Looking back and forth, back and forth. *Which one is my brother, where is he?* But then a lean, tanned face that resembled hers appeared, a middle-aged man in a brown sport-jacket, a black and maroon head covering, a scrappy black beard, a gentle smile. Massoud?

Hinda could not speak, but it did not matter, because no words could have captured her emotions. Instead, she pounced on her brother, buried her head in his chest, and wailed, releasing the years of separation, the years of frustration, of fruitless fighting. Mother and father and my other brothers are still in Yemen, but Massoud is here. Massoud simply beamed, his eyes rising toward the ceiling in an expression of sublime gratitude. Soon Saada Zindani found her brother and sister and embraced them, and it did not matter anymore that strangers were swirling about and Arik was snapping photographs and the reunion was being recorded. I looked at Yosef Levy and acknowledged his wide grin, sharing the satisfaction.

Hinda could not stop sobbing, so Massoud forced her onto a couch and made her come up for air. Saada rested her head on her brother's broad shoulder, and when asked to speak declined: "I have no strength, no strength." Instead, we settled in the living room and sang. Young Moshe Sabari huddled in a corner with his uncle from Israel, Daoud Katabi sat with his sister. We brought out a shofar and Massoud blew it, producing the beautiful, low sounds that herald redemption. There was Yemeni line dancing to a tinny beat. And with much catching up to do, the rest of that summer day in West Hempstead was spent lounging on the grass, enjoying the curative company of flesh and blood. It was also my turn to meet the family members from Israel whom I had purposely avoided for three years in order to preserve the strictly American aura of ICROJOY.

They came in the afternoon. Seven or eight Hasidim, distinctive in their peyot, beards, black garb, pacing the sidewalk in front of the Grafi home as if staking it out, but making their presence known; our surprise visitors belonged to the Satmar sect, specifically the offshoot known as Neturei Karta. They had come to Long Island to spy on the organization that had brought out three Yemeni Jews. ICROJOY had broken Neturei Karta's monopoly on dialogue with the Yemeni government, loosened the shackles of the Jews of Yemen, and was helping to increase the population of the State of Israel. Neturei Karta wanted access to the Yemenis, but we wouldn't hear of it. I immediately called the State Department and Benjamin Gilman's office in Washington, and a police car was sent to the address. As the officers ordered the Hasidim to keep off the property, Neturei Karta charged ICROJOY with keeping the three Yemenis in West Hempstead against their will, holding them hostage to our political and financial desires, denying them religious freedom.

So to Officer Barnes, a stern Nassau County policeman, I had to explain that Massoud, Moshe, and Daoud were here of their own volition, that they were beneficiaries, not prisoners, of ICROJOY, that Neturei Karta was a rabidly anti-Zionist group that wanted no Jew to leave Yemen.

"Wait, is this an Arab group?" Officer Barnes interrupted.

"No, a Jewish group," I answered. But we have the approval of the State Department. Here's our stationery, with Benjamin Gilman and Stephen Solarz and Alfonse D'Amato and Elie Wiesel on the masthead. Officer Barnes, after meeting the "three musketeers," was satisfied by my explanation. Neturei Karta, furious, left West Hempstead without being granted access to the Yemenis. Hours later, a letter was mailed to a certain address in the nation's capital:

CENTRAL RABBINICAL CONGRESS OF THE U.S.A. AND
CANADA
85 Division Avenue
Brooklyn, NY 11211
384-6765

July 1,1991
President George Bush
The White House
Washington, D.C.

Mr. President

It is with the utmost responsibility and seriousness that we are writing to you about a matter that concerns us very much.

We have become aware that at certain levels the U.S. government has used its prestige and influence with the Republic of Yemen, to allow a number of their Jewish citizens to come visit our country.

We believe that the U.S. government took this action on the basis of information received from and on behalf of a group of individuals who call themselves The International Coalition for the Rescue (Revival) of the Jews of Yemen. This group (or groups) led some officials to believe that the Jews are lacking religious/human rights in Yemen.

To begin, we want to state very frankly and solemnly, that the Jews of Yemen enjoy all religious, civil, and human rights as any other citizens of Yemen and we can attest to the very well-known fact, that the Republic of

Yemen has gone out of its way on many occasions to assist Rabbis of our organization to visit Jews in some of the remotest mountain villages. Yemen is a superb example of how Jews and Muslims can live together in peace and tranquillity enjoying all rights and freedoms as in the U.S.A.

When some leading Rabbis of our organization went to visit the three Yemeni Jews in Long Island they were not permitted to speak to these people privately nor were they permitted to take any of the three visitors to a synagogue to pray or even walk with them outside of the premises where they are being kept. On two of these occasions the Yemeni Jews told them, that they were being scared and they cannot move out of the house where they are being kept and held under "house arrest."

We will not permit this situation to go unchallenged. It is a farce and travesty of all human and basic rights to bring three people to our shores on the false pretenses of "freedom of travel," human rights, or to "study," and then to have them locked up in individual homes of a "select" group who are using and abusing these helpless and poor people for their own political and fundraising purposes and not permitting them to see any Jews not to their "hosts" liking.

We are sending this note to you now, in order to make it perfectly clear, that we will not countenance such behavior and will not remain silent.

Respectfully yours,

Rabbi Y. Gruber

Executive Director

Neturei Karta's letter found its way to the desk of a seething Richard Schifter, who promptly ignored it. We had won the State Department's allegiance through honesty, persistence, and patience; Neturei Karta's tactics were not about to supplant us. Schifter was disgusted by the vitriol being spouted. I could forgive Neturei Karta for its politics, but not for its cruel denial of communication, the years it could have delivered news and greetings to grieving relatives in Israel. They were there first; ICROJOY did not have to be the organization that opened the channels of communication.

The Satmar Hasidim, undaunted, flexed their political muscles to win access to the three Yemenis. The Hasidic stronghold called New Square lies across the Hudson River to the northwest of New York

260 • Operation Esther

City, in Rockland County, and the Congressman representing Rockland County on Capitol Hill is one Benjamin Gilman. A politician must always display fealty to his constituents, especially the ones that keep re-electing him. So on a Sunday morning one week later, a minivan bound for New Square departed from West Hempstead with my extreme reservations, ferrying Dalia, Mrs. Grafi, Debbie Bodlander from Gilman's office, Massoud Zindani, Moshe Sabari, and Daoud Katabi to a date in New Square. The Satmarers the three Yemenis met with besmirched ICROJOY's reputation and intentions, but they resisted all attempts to turn them, and then returned to West Hempstead.

When mid-July arrived, the fact that our three guests were but visitors to America hit home. The three students, sent temporarily to the United States for religious training, had enjoyed their month away and needed to return to their families in Yemen. icrojoy's objective now became the permanent release of a complete family, in accordance with the new "freedom of travel" provision. We would work family by family. Hinda and Saada Zindani, the Katabis and the Sabaris returned to Israel, praying that they would someday see their loved ones in the Holy Land. Taphat and I accompanied the students to Frankfurt, where they boarded a Sanaa-bound plane, now comfortable with the concept of human flight, undaunted by vast airport terminals and beef Wellington in tiny, double-wrapped aluminum trays.

Massoud, Moshe, and Daoud evaporated into the throng of Arab travelers and German businessmen, and we boarded another flight to the Middle East. Slightly over three hours later, the Lufthansa jet was landing in Tel Aviv and I was eyeing my old friend, the bust of Ben-Gurion, in front of the customs building. It took several days of goading from David Shuker before I agreed to meet with a senior Mossad man in my father's home in Jerusalem. When I reproached his agency for endangering my life and the lives of the delegation members by planting a member of Israeli intelligence in ICROJOY's midst, the official turned pale. Then I set out to recover from Mission V. After all, this was my summer vacation, my time with father and siblings. But before inaugurating the repose, there was some unfinished business to execute—in Netanya, the spectacular seaside resort town.

"Mori Hayim is here to see you, Mori Hayim is here!" Shalom Suberi was telling his father as I entered the Netanya apartment along with Arik and Taphat and Yosef Levy. Yhia ibn Daoud Suberi, his eyes long ago dimmed, could not see me, but reached out to touch my face and bless me, chirping merrily, basking in the presence of his visitors. The first sight of the *mu'allem* in the Holy Land, rather than in a dusty Raida hut or a Washington Heights apartment, overwhelmed me. David and Shoshana, the other two Suberi children, also stood by their newfound father's side; I had asked them to witness the presentation: "Dr. Tawil is in Israel," Shalom Suberi had told them mysteriously. "It is very important to be here." But even Shalom could not understand why.

The old man was greeting his friends Arik and Taphat, playing their hand games, when I asked for silence. "I have an announcement to make," I told the room, Yosef Levy's smile almost betraying me. "I have your father's money."

Unable to speak, Shalom and David and Shoshana just stood there. Arik snapped photographs as I produced two checks from my bag, the first for $2,000 from ICROJOY payable to Yhia ibn Daoud Suberi, the second a Morgan Trust check in the amount of $32,000 payable to Yhia ibn Daoud Suberi. The cache from the Nahari home in Raida, the shrewd U.S. dollar deposit in the Central Bank of Yemen. The dazed Suberi children looked from the checks to their father, then back to the checks, sensing the wisdom of the ancient man whose shriveled appearance belied extraordinary acuity. I wanted no more family feuds, so Shalom accepted the checks on behalf of his father, brother, and sister, and signed a receipt to that effect. My promise to the *mu'allem* had been kept.

In late July, in a mud-walled house baking in the Saada heat, a healthy daughter was born to Massoud Zindani. She was named Esther, after a girl from New York whose life had been cut short, the daughter of a prominent Congressman.

December 23, 1991

Frankfurt's bustling Rhein-Main Airport at the height of the holiday travel season does little to soothe the nerves. But there, in an observation lounge, Yosef Levy and I stood, examining the writhing human mass that raged below, looking out for a distinctive cluster of sojourners. A jet originating in Sanaa had recently landed, and the Sabari clan of Saada was scheduled to emerge into the terminal at any moment. The Sabaris would be arriving with all their worldly possessions; they were leaving the Republic of Yemen for good, granted a permanent exit with no restrictions, the first true beneficiaries of freedom of travel.

During Mission V, Yemen had granted its Jewish citizens the right to leave the country. Dr. Iryani, the Foreign Minister, had uttered the words in my presence. But after ICROJOY's three students returned to the Arabian Peninsula, the release of Yemeni Jewry proceeded at an excruciatingly torpid pace, with each emancipation proving a fight. Thus, the past five months had been spent lobbying in Washington, where ICROJOY visited the offices of Richard Schifter and other consistent allies. We met Arthur Hughes, the new ambassador to Yemen, and bid farewell to Andrea Farsakh, the officer on the Yemen desk, about to depart for her next assignment in the embassy in Algeria. We dutifully compiled lists of names and places, recorded the personal tragedies of each family, and many Yemeni Jews established blood links with current citizens of Israel. And there had a been a productive meeting with the new Assistant Secretary in the Bureau of Near Eastern and South Asian Affairs, Edward P. Djerejian. An Armenian-American fluent in Arabic, Djerejian had previously served as U.S. ambassador to Syria. Until his nomination to serve as ambassador to Israel, Djerejian would nurture ICROJOY's every move for the next two years. To our State Department partners we presented carefully compiled lists of names, specifically those of the sizable Sabari family, arranged in three divisions. In turn, Arthur Hughes became familiar with the Jews of Yemen, a people with whom his superiors in Washington seemed to be preoccupied. All of ICROJOY's allies pressed the Yemenis on the human rights issue, and written reminders arrived on the desk of His Excellency Mohsin al-Aini, ambassador of the Republic of Yemen, from Congressmen Lee Hamilton, Benjamin Gilman, and Stephen Solarz.

It was with equal measures of enthusiasm and reserve that

ICROJOY pressed for Yhia ibn Daoud Sabari and his family. Yhia, the fifty-year-old patriarch, was an intelligent and charismatic man, a bona fide leader of Saada Jewry who performed circumcisions and marriage ceremonies. Yhia was an activist, too, unafraid to approach the Interior Ministry for passport applications. But there had been a money dispute with local Arabs, death threats, the scent of a mercy case. So when Andrea Farsakh called my Yeshiva office to say, "They can come," I breathed a sigh of relief, and made plans to meet the first contingent of Sabaris in Frankfurt. Arthur Hughes would send Yhia money for Western pants and shirts for himself, fifteen-year-old Salem, and thirteen-year-old Yehudah.

A full half-hour after the last Sanaa passengers disappeared into the Rhein-Main commotion, with no sign of the Sabaris, Yosef glanced at me nervously. Yosef had returned to Sanaa in November but had failed to obtain the passports. His applications had been refused at the Interior Ministry. His presence in Yemen had coincided with the arrival of Neturei Karta and an Italian-Jewish delegation. *Where are they?*

Suddenly, an announcement from the Lufthansa desk and "Hayim Tawil" being paged. We raced to the gate, and there they were, the nine exotic-looking Sabaris sitting cross-legged on the floor in robes and veils and *kuftas* and *peyot*, confused and disoriented, receiving harsh stares from other passengers. At Yhia's side lay his nuclear family's worldly possessions, a few meager shopping bags stuffed with tattered clothing and little else. The Sabaris were famished but elated to see us. There was no problem with their German transit visas, the documents allowing them to stay in Frankfurt overnight before heading for New York tomorrow. Just a severe language barrier and the fear of being abandoned in a giant, terrifying airport.

In the airport Sheraton that night, we fed Yhia, his wife Hamama, and their seven unmarried children, then bathed the youngest ones in a hot bathtub for the first time in their lives. We put them to sleep on real mattresses: Tomorrow, my children, you will be in America.

In the final hours of December 24, the 747 carrying the first Jewish family to leave Yemen since 1962 taxied to a stop at Kennedy Airport. From the nearly abandoned terminal the family was driven northwest through New York City, across the George Washington

Bridge into New Jersey, and deposited in front of a nondescript house in Teaneck. The Sabaris spent two weeks in the basement of the suburban Habad-owned home, laying low, as advised by ICROJOY.

Rabbi Weiss, a member of the Lubavitch sect, and his family gave generously of their time, striving to make the Sabaris feel comfortable. To help them battle the tedium, Yosef Levy provided free lessons for the children, and I stopped by daily to deliver gifts, food, and good wishes. But a cellar is no place for people accustomed to open, arid expanses. Imprisonment beneath Teaneck in the dead of winter soured everyone's mood. "I must get out!" Yhia Sabari hollered early into his second difficult week in America. Who could argue? We were waiting for the arrival of the final two contingents of the Sabari clan: Yhia's two married sons and their young families, our old friend Moshe Sabari among them, and Yhia's elderly father and the remainder of the family. They would all fly to the Holy Land together, but until then ICROJOY had to change its base of operations.

In mid-January, the nine Sabaris again traversed the George Washington Bridge, bypassing Manhattan's skyscrapers, speeding toward their Long Island destination. Shlomo Grafi's home in West Hempstead would become the Sabari's for the first five months of 1992. With time the restrictions eased. West Hempstead's Jewish community noted the dark-skinned family parading by on Shabbat in its peculiar garb, its schoolchildren long remembered the strange students with the jet-black hair and peyot who attended several classes at the Hebrew Academy of Nassau County, its residents would be told they were playing host to remnants of glorious Yemeni Jewry. To the Grafi home ICROJOY sent a private tutor who taught the children some basic English and marveled at their grasp of the Torah, their ability to recite its verses from memory.

During this time, Yosef Levy was in Yemen again on his seventh trip to the Republic. Dalia Smerka went with him, and she walked the same narrow streets of Sanaa's Ga-el-Yahud where her grandparents had lived until their departure for Palestine in 1915. Yosef's tasks in Saada and Raida were educational: the training of teachers and the renting of school buildings. He ran Shabbat services, attended a wedding and a circumcision, and met a sheikh with four wives and twenty-five children. The Jews of Yemen were excited. Many had seen Shoshana Tobi's performances on television. More had heard that the first family was out, waiting in America to be joined by others.

But enduring for months as a transient, counting down the days, awaiting the rest of one's family, can disturb a person's equilibrium, make him crotchety and hypersensitive. On February 17, the tension in the Grafi house increased when Yhia's married daughter arrived with her husband, and the husband was none other than Said Habib, our nemesis from the Taj Sheba. It was obvious how Habib, certainly a collaborator with the Yemeni government, had won his freedom, even without American influence. His visa stamp bore the words, "Under the full responsibility of the Central Rabbinical Congress of the U.S.A. and Canada." Nevertheless, I had flown to Frankfurt to greet him, cradling the Habibs' month-old infant on the plane trip back, watching the four other children explore the aisles. The argumentative Habib agitated an already delicate situation by threatening to flee ICROJOY's protection or return to Yemen.

In March, the State Department informed us that the rest of the Sabari family was coming. Yosef and I flew to Frankfurt to meet Moshe and Yisrael and their wives and children, but the group never exited from the plane; the Sabaris had boarded a jet in Sanaa only to be forcibly removed under the pretext of some document problem. There will be no more problems, the American embassy in Sanaa assured me. We promise they will be on the flight to Rome tomorrow. So Yosef and I flew to Rome. But the Sabaris did not appear at Leonardo da Vinci Airport the next day either, again encountering some emigration trouble. Yosef and I returned to New York empty-handed.

The house truly became a tinderbox in April when the remainder of the Sabari clan finally arrived: Moshe with his wife Bardaqusha and two daughters, Yisrael with his wife Miriam and two sons, Daoud—the grandfather—with his wife Khadia, daughter, married son, daughter-in-law, and grandchild. There were now twenty-two Sabaris and seven Habibs living in cramped conditions in West Hempstead, preparing themselves mentally for the Holy Land, uniting to stage a Passover seder during this rest-stop on their road to freedom.

May 1992 indeed arrived—not nearly soon enough—and then it was time to pack up the few belongings and board the plane for Tel Aviv, to complete a personal journey that had begun in 1991, and to begin to close a chapter that most thought had been completed in 1950. The Magic Carpet was about to fly again.

Their Yemeni brothers and sisters four decades earlier had landed on barren tracts of land in a young, sparsely populated country recovering from its bloody War of Independence, struggling to create a viable government and economy. The sight that greeted the newly arriving Sabaris beyond the Tel Aviv tarmac was of a modern international airport anchoring a sprawling urban expanse, the State of Israel, that had sprouted in forty-four years. From the airport, the Sabari clan was escorted to the Oshiut absorption center in Rehovot, near the large Yemeni community of that city, welcomed home with open arms.

Yosef Levy, the grandson of the Chief Rabbi of Yemen, returned to his native Sanaa an eighth time, to meet with American embassy officials, and to deliver packages and goodwill to the Jewish communities of the north country. Levy was our "man on the ground," ICROJOY's soldier in the trenches, handling the Jews' crises until their freedom came. My presence in Yemen was no longer necessary; with freedom of travel declared in principle, the struggle had become a logistical one: How does one secure a passport? Who will trickle out, and when? For months at a time there was no exodus from Yemen. The burdens of familiarity with Yemeni culture and love for Yemeni Jewry belonged to Yosef. His massive accomplishments were detailed in a report for the State Department.

OPERATION ESTHER

An Ongoing Jewish Education Program in the Republic of Yemen
1992-1993

In the past three years, ICROJOY has entered Yemen eight times. The Jews of Yemen were supplied by ICROJOY with most of all their educational material. Hundreds of prayer books, bibles with medieval commentaries, five scrolls of the Torah, one hundred pairs of tefillin, prayer scrolls, as well as hundreds of small talitot. For the rabbis of the communities, they have received ten volumes of Shulchan Aruch (Jewish laws). In May of 1991, ICROJOY set up an organized educational program for the Jewish students in Yemen.

It is estimated by ICROJOY with a precise census, which was taken in the last three years, that there are approximately 1000-1100 Jews left in Yemen. A heavy percentage of this number being school-age children from the ages of three to fifteen.

The Jews of Yemen are mainly concentrated in three geographical locations in the northern part of Yemen. 1 - Raida and its vicinities, approximately one and a half hours north of Sanaa. 2 - Saada and its vicinities, six hours north of Sanaa. 3 - Hidan Asham, three and a half hours on a dirt road northeast of Saada, adjacent to the Saudi Arabian border.

Raida:

In May-June 1991, with the consent of the Yemeni government and the local sheikh Harash, a school and a mikvah was built in the village of Suq-el-Jadid. Thirty chairs and desks were bought for use of the students in the school. Two Jewish teachers were hired: Rabbi Said el-Nahari and Rabbi Salem Sleiman (both teach biblical and Jewish studies). In Suq-el-Jadid, we have approximately 28 students.

Saada:

Traditionally, and especially in the rural part of northern Yemen, students did not go to school. Instead, they studied at home with their fathers. In January-February 1992, an historical breakthrough occurred. For the first time in the history of education for the Jews of Yemen, a center of education was established in the city of Saada.

At the center of the city, ICROJOY rented a house which included five large rooms, from the famous influential Sheikh Mujali. Students are being driven every morning from the following places: Ghuraz, Asahen, and Bukah. Six teachers were hired: Rabbi Said Zareb, Rabbi Sleiman Sabari (both teach biblical Jewish studies), Idia Zareb, Binyamin Hubani (both teach modern Hebrew), Salem Zindani, and Yosef Atzar (both teach Jewish law and customs).

In the Saada school we have approximately fifty students.

Hidan Asham:

In January–February 1992, a school was established for the first time in Hidan Asham, which is heavily populated with Jews. Four Jewish teachers were hired for the program: Rabbi David Faiz, Yosef Shetari (both teach biblical studies), Salem Jeredi (modern Hebrew), and Hayim Faiz (Jewish law and customs). In Hidan Asham there are approximately sixty students, under the supervision of Sheikh Asurabi.

Daily Schedule:

7–8 a.m. –	Morning prayers
8–9 a.m. –	Breakfast
9–11 a.m. –	Biblical and Jewish studies
11–11:30 a.m. –	Recess in the courtyard
11:30 a.m.–1 p.m. –	Modern Hebrew
1–2 p.m. –	Lunch
2–3 p.m. –	Jewish Law and Customs
3–4 p.m. –	Thirty minute recess.
4–4:30 p.m. –	Afternoon and evening prayers.

The students are divided into two groups: ages 4–8 and 9–13. Each student is responsible for one hour of homework per day. During ICROJOY's last trip to Yemen, for a period of two weeks/five hours a day, Mr. Joseph Levy trained the teachers. The training consisted of teaching skills pertaining to subjects of Jewish studies.

The children attending Levy's schools were highly photogenic. As the number of reporters and photographers traveling to the north country multiplied, the images of Jews unchanged by the millennia appeared alongside news accounts worldwide. Eliav Sela, irked by the slow progress, continued to plant false accounts of forced conversions in the Israeli media. His assertions appeared around the same time as other patently false news items, most notoriously one that graced the front page of London's *Sunday Times,* to the effect that the Israeli government was planning a secret military operation to airlift hundreds of trapped Jews out of Yemen. The *Times* article was vehemently denied by Israeli officials in *Maariv* and *Yediot* and the

Jerusalem Post. It precipitated an embarrassing public feud between Ariel Sharon and Yitzhak Shamir.

Finally, on April 28, 1992, I read with pride in the *New York Times* that "Syria informed the United States over the weekend that it was lifting a travel ban on its 4,500 Jewish citizens, the State Department announced today. Most of them are expected to leave. If they do, there will be no more significant Jewish populations left in the Arab world, outside of Morocco. The move by Syria constitutes a fundamental shift in policy toward its Jewish citizens." The reverberations of Operation Esther were apparently being felt elsewhere in the Arab League.

March 3, 1992
The news from the nation's capital was not propitious for ICROJOY: Assistant Secretary of State for Human Rights and Humanitarian Affairs Richard Schifter tendered his resignation today. After six years the time had come to "move out." The departure of our primary Washington confederate created a protection vacuum for ICROJOY, and an unprecedented opportunity for the Mossad. Schifter's retirement from the State Department therefore coincided with earnest Mossad efforts to wrest control of the rescue operation from us. The Israeli government, as it had demonstrated at Ben–Gurion Airport when Yhia ibn Daoud Suberi arrived, coveted the credit for delivering the Jews of Yemen. Israel had gone about this casually at first, by smearing my name in private, by softly pressuring Washington to sever its ties with ICROJOY. Yossi ben Aharon, Yitzhak Shamir's chief of staff, had called Washington to complain: We don't want to work with Hayim Tawil, he's too independent. Get rid of him. But Richard Schifter had stood firm and resisted, publicly designating Tawil's organization the exclusive representative of the Jews of Yemen during a speech to the Conference of Presidents of Major Jewish Organizations on the topic "Jews in Arab countries."

But now Schifter was gone, and the Mossad wanted *its* people visiting the Jews of Yemen, handling the travel documents, arranging each family's exodus. There was really no more to be done in Washington; diplomatic pressure had already been successfully applied.

ICROJOY's supreme goal—opening the doors—had been accomplished. Now, only the task of physically relocating the Jews remained. So the Mossad adopted a "divide and conquer" strategy. Lester Smerka and Yosef Levy, too intimately associated with my name, were never approached, but Shlomo Grafi was lured away from us. As an Israeli citizen not carrying an American passport, the frustrated Grafi had been unable to participate in our missions to Yemen. He wanted a place in the sun and got it. Grafi was put on the JDC's payroll and began sending unqualified, unprepared emissaries to Yemen to process passports—not under the auspices of ICROJOY.

I observed the hostile takeover of the rescue business but offered no resistance. It would have been foolish and fruitless to protest a JDC move initiated by the Mossad; the organization had been funding our valuable projects and activities for three years. Besides, ICROJOY's real goal had been achieved; passports were mere technicalities. Better to quit while ahead, I thought, than to submit to others' orders and become a Mossad puppet.

The importance of political neutrality when dealing with the Yemenis—so crucial in winning freedom for the country's Jews—was lost on the JDC. Though an obviously Zionist enterprise, it would attempt to foster a relationship with a Yemeni government officially at war with the State of Israel, and would work with an American diplomatic establishment in Sanaa that was not enamored of ICROJOY's successors. David Shuker and the families he represented wrote an impassioned letter to Prime Minister Rabin, demanding that ICROJOY remain the sole surrogate of the Jews of Yemen. But the Prime Minister never saw their note: it was stopped by Shimon Sheves, his chief of staff, before it reached the Prime Minister's desk.

Courted by Mossad men in a Tel Aviv restaurant, my wife Dalia rebuffed their attempts to take over the operation. Seated with Avigdor Kahalani and Shlomo Gal, with David Shuker present, she read from a prepared statement.,

I was advised to keep silent and keep this to myself. But if I had kept it all to myself, ICROJOY would never have been born. My husband is a man who despises attention, and he knew that public service involves much filth and aggravation. But I recognized his connection to the cause and pushed him into it. ICROJOY was founded in blood, the blood of my husband, the sacrifices of my two children. Therefore, I have earned the right to protest when I see the injustice being done to us in Israel… Shlomo Gal gave an explicit order to the Joint Distribution Committee in New York to deny Yosef Levy and Lester Smerka another trip to Yemen; two others were sent in their stead. Sirs, in the span of five years we strove with all our might, heart and soul, to produce fruit, and Shlomo Gal came along and turned the tables on us. I will not allow this to pass in silence.

But Dalia's biting words fell on deaf ears; it was really too late. Four years of pro bono work and not even a thank-you letter from the major Jewish organizations or the Israeli government. With no remorse I watched ICROJOY slowly fade into nonexistence, its role becoming increasingly irrelevant. Born at a precisely defined moment, in an austere conference room at Stern College, on an extraordinarily frigid winter's evening in 1988, ICROJOY has never been officially interred, its hour of expiration never solemnly marked and filed away.

Of the original group, only Yosef Levy continued returning to the southern tip of the Arabian Peninsula; in the end he would travel to Yemen a total of twelve times. It did not faze Yosef to work for the JDC or any other organization. His obligations lay toward the needy Jews of Yemen, who revered him for his warmth, his sacrifice. And Levy's presence in Yemen—his obsession with actualizing our diplomatic coup—proved critical. Freedom of travel may have been declared, but Yemen was a bureaucratic nightmare, with the Interior Ministry procrastinating the passport process. Aided by Ambassador Hughes and John Lister, second secretary at the U.S. embassy, Levy navigated the system. Along the way, he was imprisoned three times, on each occasion falsely accused of owing large sums of money to Sleiman Habib, the belligerent Jew. In Yemen, the mere allegation of being a delinquent debtor is grounds enough for incarceration. Groups sniffing the residual odor of ICROJOY still sought to impede Yosef Levy, to delay the exodus of the remnant.

Jews did not gush forth from Yemen as they had decades earlier, soaring above desert landscapes in cargo planes. Each family experienced its own difficulties, its own delays at the Interior Ministry, and its own series of flights on commercial airliners. Our rescue operation inspired no romantic visions, produced no magnificent footage for the evening news. It simply reunited families, slowly but surely. For some, however, the process required acceleration and the inclusion of their own names. The Yemeni Federation contacted Senator Alfonse D'Amato, and on July 22, 1992, citing the danger to the survival of Yemen's dwindling Jewish community, he sponsored Senate Resolution 325, calling upon Yemen to allow the Jews free and full emigration:

> Now it is time that the Jews held hostage by the government of Ali Abdullah Salih be freed. The approximately 1500 Jews of Yemen suffer much like the Jews of Syria, except that some of the Syrian Jews are now being freed. For the Jews of Yemen, centuries of civilization have been allowed to pass by, and their living conditions are deplorable, rivaling a previous millennium.

D'Amato added a threat: "That government must pay the diplomatic and economic price." I read the smug press release from D'Amato's office with dismay. The Yemenite Jewish Federation craved the credit for redeeming Yemeni Jewry, just another organization trying to score political points through the Jews of Yemen. True, their departure was proceeding at a snail's pace, but to intimidate was to imperil the process. Thanks to swift intervention by Benjamin Gilman, Michael Van Dusen, the Israeli embassy, and the State Department, D'Amato's imprudent bill was decapitated before coming to a vote. ICROJOY had learned early on that Ali Abdullah Salih was a sensitive human being quite hostile to public censure of his policies. D'Amato handled Ali Abdullah Salih the same way Neturei Karta handled ICROJOY; both succeeded in jeopardizing progress, not producing any fruit. D'Amato's was the wrong way to hasten the exodus.

The right way involved quiet, behind-the-scenes negotiation. Van Dusen advised ICROJOY to contact the venerated Washington law firm of Baker & Botts, founded by the Secretary of State's grandfather. In order to win the legislative support of Congress, Yemen needed to rehabilitate its image. It had scheduled multiparty parliamentary elections for April 1993, but lacked the knowhow to curry favor with Washington's elite, so as to reclaim its respect after the Gulf War. So we fashioned a relationship between the powerful public relations concern and the Yemeni government, which retained Baker & Botts to lobby for Yemen on Capitol Hill. B. Donovan Picard, a Baker & Botts attorney, devised a strategy for parading Yemen's accomplishments down Constitution Avenue. According to Picard and other Baker & Botts experts, the experiment of creating a democratic form of government faced two principal obstacles: a severe economic crisis and subversion from Saudi Arabia, which in actuality had precipitated the economic crisis by flooding Yemen with refugees. Saudi Arabia had also lobbied vigorously against the extension of financial assistance to Yemen by other Arab states and international financial institutions. According to Picard, it was time for the United States to reconsider its position on foreign aid to Yemen, and to stop discouraging the World Bank and other institutions from granting multilateral loans and aid to Yemen.

Yemen deserved American aid now. It had granted 60,000 Somalian refugees the rights of asylum and employment in 1992. It had adopted a democratic form of government, participated in the Middle East peace process, championed a market-based economic system, and invited foreign investment. And yes, there was that favorable human rights record: it had released the Jews of Yemen. Picard's professional marketing strategy helped rehabilitate Yemen's image. Yemen reciprocated by eliminating delays in the Interior Ministry; the trickle of departing Jews became a steady, significant stream of emigrants.

These Jews, too, lugged their possessions on their backs as did their forefathers before them. They arrived in Sanaa from Raida, and from the Amlah, and from sun-beaten outposts in wadis and valleys all along the uncharted Saudi Arabian border to the north. They came from the district of Hidan Asham, and from the villages of al-Shaghadra and Beit Harash, and from the sheikh-ruled Hashid region. They vacated their two-story houses and abandoned their shops in the suqs of al-Hajjar and Ghuraz and Arhab. The families we had grown to love, the Basharis and Khubanis and Marhabis, in colorful *galabiyas*, with black *peyot* and olive faces. Said Zareb, seventy, came with Masudah, his wife, sixty-eight. The elderly, feeble parents of Massoud and Hinda and Saada Zindani came, landing joyfully in the modern Holy Land, emerging from the pages of the Bible. Ruma Sabi, seventy-five, came with his brother Said, seventy-three. Yaakov Hamami, sixty, and his wife Hawida, fifty-eight. Yhia ibn Said Irgi, sixty-five, his brother Salim, eighty, Salim's wife, Shameh bint Irgi, seventy-five. The entire Boni clan of Ghuraz: Sleiman, his two parents, two wives, and eight children. The Katabi clan from the Shaaf in Hidan Asham: Daoud, his wife Rumah, his daughter Gusna, an epileptic. Then the married children: Yhia and Lawza, Yosef and Naama, little Bracha and Jamla . . .

As they left, conditions for those remaining improved dramatically. With the opening of the gates came a change in attitude and atmosphere, respect for the Jews.

Some of the departing Yemenis never made it to the Holy Land. With the International Coalition for the Revival of the Jews of Yemen out of the picture, with Operation Esther expired, others had begun to influence the Jews of Yemen. I would read in London's *Jewish World*:

> Little Moshe was shouting "Gib mir, Gib mir" ("Give me, give me," in Yiddish), as he chased a ball amid a crowd of youngsters outside an ultra-Orthodox Jewish school in Clapton, in London's East End. He looked different from the others, with his long braided peyot and dark skin, but he appeared at ease and was obviously enjoying the pick-up game of soccer.
>
> Only a few months ago, 8-year-old Moshe was living in a mud house in Saada, a village in Yemen, over 100 kilometers away from the capital Sanaa. Emigration restrictions against Jews had been relaxed, and his father, who made necklaces to be sold in the Sanaa marketplace, was preparing to leave for Israel, where he and his wife have many relatives.
>
> Then, Moshe recalls, two men dressed in strange black clothes and wearing large black hats arrived at his house and talked for hours with his

father and mother. After the visit, the plans were changed. London, not Jerusalem, would be their destination. Moshe heard of other families in the village who were also changing their plans in the wake of the visit. His friend Yaakov told him he too had been about to leave for Israel with his parents and six brothers and sisters. But the two men had persuaded them they should head for New York instead.

In Israel you will be persecuted, Yemeni Jews were being told. They will cut off your peyot, make the women wear indecent clothes. A tragic piece of history now used to manipulate prospective arrivals. Yemeni Jewry had been reduced to three hundred, but politically motivated forces still groped for its allegiance. But once you've returned to normal family life with wife, daughter, and son, there is little more you can actuate. When you're living in Apartment 24B on Bennett Avenue, not Room 212 of the Taj Sheba, your sphere of influence has been substantially reduced.

There was a wooden chair and a naked table that had stood vacant for three years on the fifth floor of the Yeshiva University library. Once, half-hidden behind the leather-bound tomes, the lexicons, cuneiforms and manuscripts, the binders and the notepads, a man with hair considerably darker than mine had scribbled the microscopic marginal notes, using the multicolored pens and pencils in the cup, sipping the coffee from the jar of crystals. Once, that professor had contributed to scholarly journals. He had devoted his energies to the students in his classroom, though occasionally lapsing into talk of Himyaric inscriptions, tombs and tablets, the treasures buried beneath Middle Eastern sands. He was captivated, as well, by his mythic heritage, by the citadels of piety and erudition born in the land of his grandparents, the culture inherited by his father, Yosef, and his mother, Esther. And he was only minding his own business when the call came. He didn't even know there were Jews left in Yemen.

Shoshana Tobi performing traditional songs at the home of Abdul Karim al-Iryani.

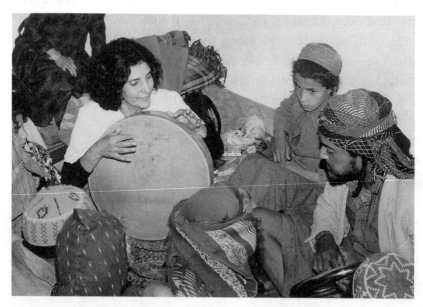

Shoshana Tobi with tambour.

David Ransom   David Shuker

Mike van Dusen with the three students, Summer 1991.

The three students with Richard Haas at the White House, Summer 1991.

Three students with Benjamin Gilman

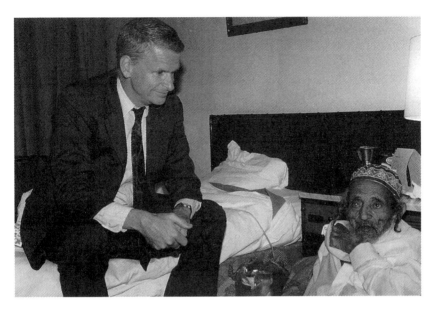

Charles Dunbar with Yhia ibn Daoud Suberi in hotel room,
September 1991.

Shalom Suberi and Yhia ibn Daoud Suberi on plane, September 1991.

Hayim Tawil and Yosef Levy with Ambassador Arthur Hughes, 1992.

Hayim Tawil and Yosef Levy with Assistant Secretary in the Bureau of Near Eastern and South Asian Affairs, Edward P. Djerejian, 1992.

Abdul Karim al-Iryani shaking hands with Hayim Tawil.

Yehudah Tzadok with Yosef Levy, 1990.

Massoud Zindani, Moshe Sabari, and Daoud Katabi arriving at Kennedy Airport, June 1991.

Massoud Zindani, Dalia Tawil and the Lubavitcher Rebbe, July 1991.

Epilogue

In 1996, ICROJOY began to document Operation Esther with video interviews of its main participants. Excerpts from some of these interviews are presented below.

RICHARD SCHIFTER
(Former assistant Secretary for Human Rights and Humanitarian Affairs)

The United States has, I would say, during the last twenty or so years, made it its business to concern itself with the effective application if Human Rights principles, everywhere in the world.

The efforts in Human Rights were initiated in the first place in the Congress in the early seventies, when actually, the State Department was opposed. What happened in the Carter administration is that the administration then aligned its policy with that of the Congress, and it has been U.S. government policy ever since.

~

The Human Rights bureau, when I was its head, would meet with American citizens who were interested in Human Rights and we would discuss issues with them. Therefore, it was not in any way unusual for me and my colleagues to meet with persons who were interested in the Human Rights of the Jews of Yemen, particularly the right to leave.

What is needed to succeed in a matter of this kind is to proceed thoughtfully, rationally, deliberately, but also persistently. There's no need to pound the table or anything like that. There are some groups that will insist that the government of the United States make public statements to condemn one practice or another. There are situations when that is necessary and then you do it. There are other situations when you can accomplish more by what is sometimes referred to as quiet diplomacy.

~

I believe an important point to keep in mind, is that once the United states government puts an issue on its agenda, in dealing with a country, that country then has to take that interest of the United States government into account. What happened in 1989, was that an issue which was out there, which had not previously been on the bilateral agenda in terms of dealings between Yemen and the United states, was placed on the agenda and that meant that now the government of Yemen had to deal with it.

~

They were very strongly anti-Zionist, and they did not want the Jews to immigrate to Israel. These were, orthodox Jews who I suppose believed that the state of Israel is an abomination, that tried to prevent the government of the United states and ICROJOY and all the rest of us who were involved in this matter from succeeding.

~

It was basically left to me to make the decision as to whom the government of the United States would recommend under the circumstance. I reached the conclusion that ICROJOY and Dr. Tawil were people who, in my judgment could be most effective in that regard, and I discussed that question with my colleagues in the State Department and with key members of Congress who were interested, and concerned about this issue, and it was agreed, and we let everybody know . . . get together and work through ICROJOY.

And that is what happened.

~

In the case of the Jews of Yemen, the right to leave was denied. And the fact that the government turned around, the government of Yemen turned around on that question, and ultimately granted Jews in Yemen the right to leave and for that matter to return, was indeed an important step, another recognition internationally, of basic principles of human rights.

DAVID RANSOM
(Former Head of Arabian Peninsula and former U.S. Ambassador to Bahrein)

They couldn't leave. It was denied, a right that other citizens of Yemen received unquestioningly from their government.

~

My first post in the Foreign Service, in 1966, was in Yemen. I had become aware of the existence of a remnant community of Jews living in a sea of Muslims, in the northern part of Yemen. In fact, during that period we urged the Yemeni government to allow these Jews to have some contacts with brethren outside, and the Yemeni government actually arranged for such contacts with a group of American Jews who were anti-Zionist.

I went back to Yemen in 1975, and then I renewed my contact with this issue, in a very interesting way.

I used to spend a lot of time traveling around Yemen. On one trip in the remotest part of Yemen, where I don't think anybody like me had ever been seen before, a man came running out of his house, stopped us, and he said, "khutab!" "khutab!" It made no sense to me because this word means books. I suddenly realized that he was a Jew, looking for books that had been promised by the group that had been in touch with him before. They hadn't been delivered. I went to see the Foreign Minister, and I said, You've got to do something about it. You cannot deny these people the basics of their religious experience. You wouldn't deny a Koran, even if he was in jail And yet these people who are some of your citizens in a Republic, cannot get the Torah. That's wrong. And the Foreign Minister agreed. He wasn't prepared, however, to go beyond the contacts that had been established with this one group.

The issue was largely left there until I got back to Washington and became head of the Arabian Peninsula desk.

~

The Yemenis were reluctant. They were worried about criticism at home, they were worried about criticism from their neighbors, they were worried about criticism in the broader Arab context: that Jews left and went to Israel.

~

There were two issues that had to be thought through, if we were going to be of any assistance to Yemeni Jews. The first was, to consider the position of Yemen and what its political dilemmas were. It resided between the most radical left-wing government in the Arab world, the people's Democratic Republic of Southern Yemen, and the most conservative and Muslim government, the Kingdom of Saudi Arabia. It could expect criticism on both sides, and it didn't want it.

But it also wanted a relationship with the United States, and the issue for us was whether our efforts to help improve the human conditions of Yemeni Jews, in particular their right to leave the country if they wished, was going to use our improving relationship to good advantage, or whether it was going to be an issue that frustrated and crippled our efforts to expand this relationship.

~

It's fair to say that there were divisions of opinion in the American Jewish community and Congress over how to perceive this issue, how vigorously, how confrontational. And we were beset by groups who wanted us to turn this into another case of getting the Felasha out of Ethiopia or the Jews out of Russia, where it was a bruising experience.

Frankly, what we did in talking to all these groups was to insist that there would only be one group that worked with us to propose a strategy, and to work closely with us in trying to bring this about.

~

Hayim Tawil spoke the language of sweet reason and of collegial cooperation. And it made all the difference in the world for him to go in and say, "I don't want to embarrass you, I don't want to demand, I don't want to threaten you, and I want you to be able to do this for your own reasons and make it a success." And that is the way it worked out, and it finally did work out. I remain convinced that if we had gone in and demanded of the Yemenis, that they do this and that, and demean them for not respecting this basic human right of emigration, we would not have had any success, no matter how long we pursued the tactic.

~

And Professor Tawil emerged, almost out of no place, as a man of reason, and of sweet cooperation, and of steely principal

~

Throughout that visit, everywhere he went he heard not only about the cooperation that we had in the area of aid, and the cooperation in the area of diplomacy and in security, but the cooperation in the area of the expanding efforts of Yemen to establish a democracy and improve human rights, and to provide all citizens of Yemen with the same opportunity to emigrate if they wished. He heard about that on the hill, he heard about that in the oval office from the President. This was not too small an issue to raise for the President of the United States, and I think the Yemenis were impressed. I think he decided that this was something that was more important than he had understood. Not the actions of a small foreign group working through the United States but a reflection of our own character and interests.

~

When we finally had a success, and the first Yemeni Jew was allowed to leave, to be reunited with his family, I was elated in ways that I really didn't anticipate. It was a professional and I think a diplomatic achievement. I'm always glad when those things happen, but I felt a rare euphoria when we did something that was not only difficult, but very good. And I still feel that.

~

In the world of diplomacy, good deeds have a terrible way of producing punishing effects. But in this particular case it worked. And I can only ascribe it to a great deal of good luck, and a great deal of great people, and it makes me very pleased and it makes me think that we better take on these difficult and interesting tasks wherever we find them.

The United States has, I would say, during the last twenty or so years, made its business to concern itself with the effective application of Human Rights principles, everywhere in the world.

The efforts in Human Rights was initiated in the first place, in the Congress, in the early Seventies, when actually, the State Department was opposed. What happened in the Carter Administration is that the Administration then aligned its policy with that of the Congress, and it has been U.S. government policy ever since.

CHARLES DUNBAR
(Former U.S. Ambassador to Yemen)

They were denied communication with the outside world.

~

It was viewed, I think, in the U.S. government as something that was a very long-term question, and one that simply needed to be managed rather than to be actively worked on.

~

First and foremost, I think the Yemeni government, like most other responsible Yemenis, generally wanted to see the Yemen Jews get a fair shake within the country. They were respectful of human rights, and were indulging in a limited experiment in democracy, and wanted to be able to show that all Yemenis were equal.

But the Yemeni government had a very unpleasant relationship with Israel, and made no bones about the fact that like other Arab states, it was at war with the State of Israel, and made no bones about the fact that it objected to the law of return, and did not want to strengthen the State of Israel by allowing Yemen Jews to return and thereby increase the size and presumably the power of the State of Israel. It was said to be a matter of principle

~

The question was raised in Congress with President Salih, and he was asked about the travel of Yemen Jews, and he responded that all Yemenis were free to travel. And this was the position that he took, increasingly in his public pronouncements, a position that didn't square entirely with the way things were on the ground in Yemen.

~

I think that the Yemenis became, to a certain extent, prisoners of their own rhetoric. They had said everybody should be able to travel, and they needed to deliver on that. I think also it became easier for them in kind of a perverse way, once the Saudis publicized the travel of Yemen Jews, including the travel of Yemen Jews to Israel, as they did in an effort, I believe, to embarrass the government of Yemen, I think it became easier for the Yemenis to say, oh well, it's been publicized by the Saudis, we've taken whatever licks we're gonna take, because the Arab world did not rise up in condemnation of this action.

~

It was a fascinating and intense negotiation. There was often humor in it because of the care with which the Yemen government in general, and Dr. Abdul al Karim al Iryani in particular, approached the matter, and the rhetorical positions various parties had to take. But it was one that I found extremely rewarding, and was very pleased to have been able to play a role in. I think this is actually one diplomatic problem that has been resolved, and those, unfortunately, are few and far between, and I was very much pleased to be able to take part in it.

~

We began to feel that we were actually going to be able to do some good in the world. Any American has a concern for human rights, and for bettering the lot of their fellow human beings, and it began to look as if we were going to be able to do this. And it's something that I can look back on my time in the State Department as one of the most positive experiences of my career.

STEPHEN J. SOLARZ
(Former Congressman for Brooklyn, N.Y.)

Congress has an important role to play in the formulation and implementation of American foreign policy. There are many benefits, which other countries want from the United States, which can only be obtained with the approval of the Congress. So I have found, over the years, that very often one is able to advance the cause of human rights around the world by making it clear to foreign governments that their hopes for a better relationship with the United States would be enhanced if they are prepared to address our concerns about the human rights of their own people.

~

I went to Yemen years ago in order, primarily, to meet with the Jewish community in that country. Unfortunately, however, when I met with Yemeni officials and asked them for permission to visit with the Jewish community, they flatly turned me down. They never really made it clear why they were refusing to give me permission, but my impression was that they were concerned that a visit by an American congressman to the Jewish community in their country might generate concerns among the more rejectionist elements in the Arab world in general, and among the PLO in particular. But now, for a variety of reasons, they appeared willing to let me go, and so I undertook, once again, to visit that country.

~

Professor Tawil reached me through a very simple method. He called me on the phone and he arranged to see me and, particularly since the cause on whose behalf he was coming was close to my heart, I was quite eager to see him.

There is no question that my concerns were fully shared by the administration at the time. There were people like Dick Schifter, our Ambassador in Yemen, others in the Department of State who saw, in the plight of these people, an opportunity to use the influence of the United States for constructive purposes.

~

He very graciously offered to help facilitate the visit and to arrange for me to meet with people in the Jewish community when I was there, to provide interpretation services which obviously would be necessary once I did get there, and to assist in other ways as well. I must say that I don't think that this mission could have succeeded, it might not even have been able to have gotten off the ground, without his help.

~

I arrived one week after the Iraqi invasion of Kuwait, under circumstances where the government of Yemen, unlike Egypt, Saudi Arabia, Syria, and other Arab countries, was supporting Saddam Hussein And indeed, I had previously arranged to go from Yemen to Iraq, where I was supposed to meet with Saddam, but decided that it would be utterly inappropriate for me to meet with the butcher of Baghdad while he was in the process of digesting his ill-gotten gains in Kuwait. So I canceled my visit as a small gesture of opposition to what he had done.

~

I was deeply moved when I saw the community for the first time. I felt as if I had stepped in the pages of the Bible. These people dressed the way they did in those days, they lived the way people did in those days, and so it was a very moving, indeed an extraordinary experience, and of course I was aware that they were the reminiscence of a flourishing community, most of which had long since gone to Israel. But these people had been left behind under

286 • *Operation Esther*

circumstances where I had reason to believe that they would very much have liked to depart as well. And so there was an acute sense of the difficulty of their circumstances and of their existence and of their hopes to be able to build a better life for themselves and their children and their families in a land where they would be far freer than they were at that time in Yemen.

MICHAEL VAN DUSEN
(Staff Director of the House Foreign Relations
Committee on Europe and the Middle East)

Several members of Congress and staff were very interested in the Jewish minorities throughout the Arab world. The two that were the focal point of concern were the Syrian Jewish community and the Yemeni Jewish community. Many individuals came to the United States Congress seeking help. Many organizations did. We looked upon this in the 1980s as an issue that had to be resolved if you were going to have stable, long-term, improving relations with the United States, and we certainly saw it as a compliment of American oil company involvement that we resolve other outstanding bilateral issues of which this was certainly one of them.

~

Congress has many levers when it looks at a situation like this. One is sort of Track I diplomacy. To use our contacts with the Yemeni Ambassador to try and improve the situation, to have members visit the country and to bring up the issues directly with the government. Another is for Congress to promote Track II diplomacy. Track II diplomacy, at its core, means that private individuals get involved in a foreign policy issue to supplement, compliment, and work the Track I diplomacy ultimately. The goal of both Track I and II diplomacy is to resolve a problem. Track I is an official track. Track II can involve people outside of government that can say things, do things, meet with people, travel places, often at a time when it is much more difficult for officials to do it.

Of course ICROJOY was the kind of Track II diplomacy that can be successful in solving a discrete problem. So it became, in effect, a partnership where people operating on Track II came and worked with Congress and the State Department, and we were all working together.

~

I consider this a real success story and its a success story because it succeeded without a lot of publicity. It's a success story because it shows how Track II diplomacy can help the United States help solve an international problem.

ABDUL KARIM AL-IRYANI
(Foreign Minister of Yemen)

Yemen has always been a State with traditional boundaries, with cultural civilizations that goes back more than three thousand years ago, and throughout history, Yemen has always been united either by rulers who rule from Sanaa or those that rule from Taiz, and the real division took place in the last century, but Yemen has never been separate in the real sense that they will diverge politically or culturally.

~

The political leaders of both countries at that time only responded to the desire of the people for reunification, which took place on the twenty second of May, 1990.

~

This request had been put, even before Dr. Tawil came, by the United States government. We received an appeal from James Baker to the President to permit Yahai Sabari, he was about eighty years old, to travel. We took it as a Human Rights and Constitutional Right for those people to travel.

In the sixties Egyptian forces were in Yemen, during the tensions of the 1967 war, it became just a policy, without any written law, that the Jewish community in Yemen would not be given passports or the right to travel. But the appeal by the US and the visit by Prof. Tawil and his group opened our minds to this right of these people to travel.

~

At that time, another Jewish organization, which is known not to be in favor of the travel of the Jewish families, called Neturie Karta, they would come and make fuss and shout – why do we allow Prof Tawil to take these out.

The Neturei Karta is an organization that, I understand, doesn't believe the Messiah has come to create the State of Israel.

~

Professor Tawil's quiet manner was very helpful in facilitating the passport issue and the travel

~

It was not any more a secret. We did not need too much discretion by then because the decision was that the constitution of the Yemen Arab Republic at the time makes it a full right of every citizen to travel. There was no pressure whatsoever to allow Jewish families to travel wherever they wanted. No Arab States came and protested. Actually Syria followed suit immediately, when they found what we are doing.

So it was not any more difficult. The first few cases were difficult, but then it became easy.

HAYIM TAWIL

After working for five years, very hard, all the members of ICROJOY, and especially myself, as the chairman of the organization, all the reward was that I was able to fulfill a great deed. I always was taught by my father: To redeem a person in captivity, be it a Jew or a gentile, is like to redeem the whole world. And this was really a great salvation. And a great mitzvah, a great deed of releasing the prisoner. In Hebrew we call it *pidyon shevuyim*, which means releasing of prisoners from captivity. To let them live a free life, in a free society, with all the dignity that God bestowed upon us, from the human rights point of view.

Appendix

DOCUMENTS

COMMISSION ON
SECURITY AND COOPERATION IN EUROPE
237 HOUSE OFFICE BUILDING ANNEX 2
WASHINGTON, DC 20515

(202) 225-1901

22 March 1989

Ms. Laurie Johnson
Room 4224 — NEA/ARP
Department of State
2201 C. Street, NW
Washington, DC 20520

Dear Ms. Johnson,

I would like to bring to your attention the case of Yehia Ben Dawoud Sabari, a Yemeni Jew who raises a most distressing allegation in a letter recently secreted from the Yemen Arab Republic. I am enclosing Mr. Sabari's letter, a response by the Y.A.R. ambassador to another letter raising concern over the right of Jews to emigrate from North Yemen, and a letter whose contents we are considering transmitting to President Saleh, perhaps in the form of a "Dear Colleague".

Secretary of State Baker's response to my letter of January 24 states that the Embassy in Sanaa is attempting to substantiate allegations of mistreatment of Yemeni Jews. I hope that Mr. Sabari and other parties involved in this case could be contacted as soon as possible to avoid what might become a life threatening situation. I would also hope, in light of Ambassador Alaini's contention that Jews are free to emigrate, that local queries be made concerning allegations to the contrary, and a response be forwarded to my office as soon as possible.

Given the isolation and complex situation surrounding the Jews of Yemen, I understand the difficulties involved in substantiating allegations and gathering reliable information. I do, however, feel that Mr. Sabari's and other previously raised cases should be given prompt attention given their seriousness.

Should you need further information concerning Mr. Sabari's case or others, please contact Mike Amitay at 225-1901. Thank you for your assistance.

Sincerely,

DENNIS DeCONCINI

cc: William Wolf, Hayim Tawil, David Golan

Congressional Human Rights Caucus
Washington, D.C. 20515

CO-CHAIRMEN

Congressman Tom Lantos (CA)
1707 Longworth Building
Washington, D.C. 20515
(202) 225-3531

Congressman John Porter (IL)
1501 Longworth Building
Washington, D.C. 20515
(202) 225-4835

EXECUTIVE COMMITTEE

Gary L. Ackerman (NY)
Les Aspin (WI)
Ben Blaz (Guam)
Beau Boulter (TX)
Jack W. Buechner (MO)
Tony Coelho (CA)
John Conyers, Jr. (MI)
Joseph J. DioGuardi (NY)
Robert K. Dornan (CA)
Dante B. Fascell (FL)
Thomas M. Foglietta (PA)
Benjamin A. Gilman (NY)
Paul B. Henry (MI)
John R. Kasich (OH)
Ernest L. Konnyu (CA)
Mickey Leland (TX)
Sander M. Levin (MI)
Thomas J. Manton (NY)
Matthew G. Martinez (CA)
Raymond J. McGrath (NY)
John R. Miller (WA)
Stephen L. Neal (NC)
Nancy Pelosi (CA)
Peter W. Rodino, Jr. (NJ)
Charles Rose (NC)
James H. Scheuer (NY)
Gerry Sikorski (MN)
Fofo I. F. Sunia (Am. Samoa)
Frank R. Wolf (VA)
George C. Wortley (NY)

OFFICE

House Annex II, Room 3??
Washington, D.C. 20515
(202) 226-4040

April 18, 1989

SPECIAL ORDER: PERSECUTION OF JEWS

Dear Colleague:

Sundown on April 19th begins Passover. This week-long holiday, recognized as the "Festival of Freedom," marks the exodus of enslaved and oppressed Jews from Egypt who were led by Moses to freedom in Canaan. Their strength and courage serves as an inspiration, even today, to Jews who still suffer from anti-Semitism.

The Congressional Human Rights Caucus will call a Special Order on Wednesday, April 26, to recognize the thousands of Jews around the world who remain oppressed and denied their basic religious rights and human dignity. Make no mistake, Jewish persecution continues.

> ETHIOPIA - Approximately 12,000 - 15,000 Jews suffer from family separation, forced population transfer, restrictions on religious rights and expression, and denial of the right to emigrate.

> SYRIA - Over 4,000 Jews are refused emigration and treated as second-class citizens. They undergo constant surveillance, arbitrary arrests, torture, restricted travel rights, random night searches of their homes; and killings by secret police.

> YEMEN - Approximately 4,000 Jews are victims of targetted killings, unlawful arrests, detention without trial, mail censorship, travel constraints and restrictions on emigration.

> USSR - Among the 2,000,000 Soviet Jews, many are arbitrarily denied the right to emigrate, religious freedom and cultural expression, and anti-Semitism has resulted in desecration of Jewish property and threats of pogroms.

We encourage you to join us on the House Floor at the end of business on April 25th for this timely Special Order, or to submit statements for the Congressional Record. If you plan to participate or if you need additional information, please have your staff contact Alex Arriaga or Karen Muchin at x6-4040.

Cordially,

Tom Lantos
Co-Chairman

John Porter
Co-Chairman

One Hundred First Congress

Congress of the United States
Committee on Foreign Affairs
House of Representatives
Washington, DC 20515

May 2, 1989

The Honorable James A. Baker, III
Secretary of State
Department of State
Washington, D.C. 20520

Dear Mr. Secretary:

We write to express our concerns about the plight of the Jewish community in the Yemen Arab Republic (North Yemen). Although the State Department reports that there are approximately one thousand Jews living under this repressive regime, independent sources suggest that as many as several thousand Jews still reside in the northern area of the country.

The Subcommittee is receiving information that Jews in North Yemen are increasingly harassed and persecuted. Reportedly, North Yemen authorities have denied the Jewish community's basic human rights including the right to emigrate, the right to free speech, and the right to practice Judaism. In light of these reports, we respectfully request that you instruct a U.S. official in our Embassy in Sanaa to visit the region in which the Jewish community resides. We feel such a visit would be essential to our understanding the difficulties in confronting the Jewish community in this predominantly Moslem society.

We greatly appreciate your consideration of our request.

Sincerely,

Gus Yatron
Chairman
Subcommittee on Human Rights
and International Organizations

Doug Bereuter
Ranking Minority Member
Subcommittee on Human Rights
and International Organizations

United States Department of State

Washington, D.C.   20520

MAY 31 19

Dear Mr. Yatron:

I am responding to your letter to Secretary Baker of May 2, 1989, concerning the situation of the Jewish community in the Yemen Arab Republic. I am providing the same reply to Congressman Bereuter.

The Department of State has long maintained a strong interest in the status of Jewish communities in various Arab countries, including Yemen. Officials in the Department and at our Embassy in Sanaa are gathering detailed information on the Yemeni Jewish community so that we can make as accurate an assessment as possible of the current situation. Due to the unique nature of Yemen's traditional society, the lack of a centralized structure in the Jewish community and the isolation of rural areas, including those where most Jews live, this collection of information has been a time-consuming process. Embassy officials have visited areas where Yemeni Jews reside and will certainly do so again, to the extent that this may be helpful in ascertaining the situation.

We are aware of reports that several thousand Jews reside in Yemen. After serious consideration of the available information, we continue to believe the best estimate for the size of the Jewish population in Yemen is approximately 1000 people. Yemeni Jews are able to practice their religion in private and instruct their children in the tenets of the faith. They can own property and work in businesses. In general their economic and health conditions are comparable to those of their Muslim neighbors. In those areas where they live, however, matters of justice and welfare are affected by tribal as well as formal government structures. Like all Yemeni citizens, Jews do face some restrictions on free speech, as our Country Human Rights Report mentions.

The Honorable
    Gus Yatron,
        House of Representatives.

We also are concerned about reports that Yemeni Jews are subject to discrimination and harsh treatment. We have been looking into such reports, including allegations of rape, forced conversion to Islam and forced marriage to Muslims, but so far we have not been able to verify them. We are still exploring the question of the right of Yemeni Jews to travel outside Yemen and emigrate. While Yemeni authorities will not permit Yemeni citizens to travel or emigrate to Israel, we do know that there has been some temporary travel by Yemeni Jews within the Arab world.

Once we believe we have an accurate assessment of the status of the Yemeni Jewish community, I can assure you that we will consider carefully what course of action might be called for on the part of the U.S. government.

Sincerely,

Janet G. Mullins
Assistant Secretary
Legislative Affairs

One Hundred First Congress

Congress of the United States

Committee on Foreign Affairs

House of Representatives

Washington, DC 20515

August 14, 1989

Dr. Hayim Tawil
Chairman
International Coalition for the
  Rescue of the Jews of Yemen
150 Nassau Street
Suite 1238
New York, New York 10038

Dear Dr. Tawil,

I wanted to follow up on our two meetings and conversations about the situation in North Yemen and the status of the Jewish community in that country.

You should know that we want to be helpful and that we remain available to write letters for you or to speak with Ambassador al-'Ayni or others about the general situation or about specific humanitarian cases.

I trust that you will stay in touch and will keep the subcommittee informed of your activities. I would also hope that we can make some progress in the months ahead.

With best regards,

Sincerely yours,

Michael H. Van Dusen
Staff Director
Subcommittee on Europe
  and the Middle East

DANIEL P. MOYNIHAN
NEW YORK

405 LEXINGTON AVENUE
NEW YORK, NY 10174

United States Senate
WASHINGTON, DC 20510

November 13, 1989

Dear Dr. Tawil:

I am delighted to learn of your historic trip to Yemen.
Your mission appears to have made a most remarkable
breakthrough in reviving the long dormant ties between
Yemenite Jewry and their brethren throughout the world.

It is a considerable honor to be associated with this
important humanitarian effort.

I look forward to continuing to work with the Coalition
in the future.

Sincerely,

Daniel Patrick Moynihan

Dr. Hayim Tawil
Chairman
International Coalition for the Revival of the Jews of Yemen
150 Nassau Street   Suite 1238
New York, N.Y. 10038

ASSISTANT SECRETARY OF STATE
WASHINGTON

November 28, 1989

Dr. Hayim Tawil
Chairman
ICROJOY
150 Nassau Street, Suite 1238
New York, New York 10038

Dear Dr. Tawil:

Your very kind letter of October 25, 1989, has just reached me. (The mails at the State Department are, I am afraid, not fully reliable.)

It was very kind of you to write me as you did. My view of the matter is that you, above all, deserve the credit for what has already been accomplished. I know, too, that a great deal will be accomplished in the future for the Jews of Yemen because of your dedication and your extraordinary ability to navigate through very difficult waters.

Let me also use this opportunity to express to you my gratitude for sending me your most interesting book.

With all good wishes,

Sincerely,

Richard Schifter
Bureau of Human Rights
and Humanitarian Affairs

ASSISTANT SECRETARY OF STATE
WASHINGTON

January 4, 1990

Ms. Sara Dahari Haiby
2185 Bolton Street
Apt. 1F
Bronx, NY 10462

Dear Mrs. Haiby:

Thank you for your letter regarding your trip to Yemen and your concern about your cousin, Moshe Dahari-Hallah, who is in need of medical treatment.

As you know Dr. Tawil has been a very important part of efforts being made to improve travel and communication between the Jewish Yemeni community and Americans. He is fully aware of your concerns and can keep you fully apprised of his travel plans.

We believe that the government of the Yemen Arab Republic views favorably further travel by your cousin to other Arab states for medical treatment. At this point, travel to Amman or Cairo appears possible. In light of this, your best course of action is to identify in those cities medical facilities capable of diagnosing and treating Mr. Dahari-Hallah's disability.

In order to come to the United States, your cousin will require, in addition to a U.S. visa, an exit visa from the Yemen government. Details for facilitating such travel to the United States have not as yet been worked out, nor has a timetable been established. We hope however, that this year we will see the start of travel between the two countries.

Sincerely,

Richard Schifter
Bureau of Human Rights
and Humanitarian Affairs

STEPHEN J. SOLARZ
13TH DISTRICT NEW YORK

COMMITTEES

FOREIGN AFFAIRS
CHAIRMAN, SUBCOMMITTEE ON ASIAN
AND PACIFIC AFFAIRS

JOINT ECONOMIC COMMITTEE

PERMANENT SELECT COMMITTEE
ON INTELLIGENCE

MERCHANT MARINE AND FISHERIES

Congress of the United States
House of Representatives
Washington, DC

WASHINGTON OFFICE
1536 LONGWORTH HOUSE OFFICE BUILDING
WASHINGTON, DC 20515
(202) 225-2361

DISTRICT OFFICES
532 NEPTUNE AVENUE
BROOKLYN NY 11224
(718) 372-8600

619 LORIMER STREET
BROOKLYN NY 11211
718) 706-6603

356 COURT STREET
BROOKLYN NY 11231
718) 802-1400

January 18, 1990

The Honorable Richard T. Crowder
Under Secretary of Agriculture for
International Affairs and Commodity Programs
Department of Agriculture
Independence Avenue
Washington, D.C. 20250

Dear Secretary Crowder:

I recently learned that a $15 million program to provide feed grains to the Yemen Arab Republic will soon be under consideration by the Agriculture Department and other agencies of the government. Given the upcoming visit of President Ali Abdullah Saleh to Washington, in which the subject of how the United States can assist the Yemen Arab Republic in its development efforts will be a major item on the agenda, I hope favorable consideration of this modest, yet desperately needed, program can be expeditiously given.

The visit of President Saleh, whose government has already cooperated with the U.S. in many important ways, offers us the opportunity to expand to even greater levels the cooperation we have received from North Yemen. It is clear that their needs are pressing. The Yemen Arab Republic is a very poor country, saddled with a burgeoning population and desperate development needs. I understand that the slight income from petroleum sales that it now has may begin to decline in the next three to four years, which will undoubtedly have a highly detrimental impact on the already severe foreign exchange crisis the government is facing.

It is my further understanding that the feed grains in this $15 million program would be destined for one of the few promising sectors of the North Yemen economy, a growing poultry industry which, if given the necessary "seed money", has the potential to provide future markets for U.S. commodities.

Clearly, the combination of factors involved at this time -- the desire of the United States and the Yemen Arab Republic to expand cooperation on many different issues, the upcoming state visit of President Saleh, and the significant impact this modest program can have for a promising sector of the economy of North Yemen -- all speak strongly in favor of this program. I hope will give it your most sympathetic consideration.

Sincerely,

STEPHEN J. SOLARZ
Chairman
Subcommittee on Asian and
Pacific Affairs
House Foreign Affairs Committee

SJS:pr

One Hundred First Congress
Congress of the United States
Committee on Foreign Affairs
House of Representatives
Washington, DC 20515

January 22, 1990

His Excellency Ali Abdallah Salih
President of the Yemen Arab Republic

Dear Mr. President:

We would like to express our deep appreciation for the gracious and courteous humanitarian assistance that you, Foreign Minister Iryani and your government have extended to Dr. Haim Tawil and his colleagues during their two recent visits to the Yemen Arab Republic.

The open distribution of religious articles brought by Dr. Tawil to the Jewish community in Yemen reflects well on our two countries' shared commitment to freedom of religious expression. We hope that this cooperation can continue and can be expanded. Your help and support in enabling this cooperation is deeply appreciated.

In this regard, we wish to enlist your support: to allow Yehia ibn Daoud Suberi to travel to the United States and see family members; to expand student exchanges to include members of the Yemen Arab Republic's Jewish community; and to enable the Jewish community to obtain better medical care and greater access to postal and telephone communications.

We view these as important humanitarian issues and believe we can work together to improve conditions for this community within the context of our improving bilateral relations. Yemen is an important country in the Middle East and for the United States. Your visit is a signal of this and we are confident that our ties can continue to expand to our mutual benefit.

January 22, 1990
Page 2

We appreciate the opportunity to meet with you and wish you and members of your delegation a pleasant and successful visit to the United States.

With best wishes,

Sincerely yours,

Lee H. Hamilton
Chairman
Subcommittee on Europe
and the Middle East

Benjamin A. Gilman
Ranking Minority Member
Subcommittee on Europe
and the Middle East

Stephen J. Solarz
Chairman
Subcommittee on Asian
and Pacific Affairs

Mel Levine
Member of Congress

ASSISTANT SECRETARY OF STATE
WASHINGTON

March 9, 1990

Professor Hayim Tawil
Chairman, ICROJOY
159 Nassau Street
Suite 1238
New York, New York   10038

Dear Dr. Tawil:

Thank you very much for your letter of March
1, 1990 and the enclosure.

I hope we can soon follow up on our
discussion regarding the Federation. I hope we
can, as they say, make lemonade of the lemon.

Sincerely,

Richard Schifter

Richard Schifter
Bureau of Human Rights
    and Humanitarian Affairs

One Hundred First Congress
Congress of the United States
Committee on Foreign Affairs
House of Representatives
Washington, DC 20515

March 12, 1990

Dr. Haim Tawil
Chairman
International Coalition for the
  Revival of the Jews of Yemen
150 Nassau Street
Suite 1238
New York, New York 10038

Dear Dr. Tawil,

Thank you for your letter of March 1st. I appreciated your comments.

I also appreciate your efforts to keep us informed of developments concerning the Yemeni Jewish Community. I am hopeful that following President Saleh's visit there will be positive steps taken to help the community and to resolve the issues of most concern to you. I want you to stay in touch with me and Mike Van Dusen regarding what happens. If more followup is needed, it will be done.

Thanks again for your letter.

With best regards,

Sincerely,

Lee H. Hamilton
Chairman
Subcommittee on Europe
  and the Middle East

SENT BY:Xerox Telecopier 7020 ; 6-14-90 ; 2:35PM ;   2022265551-   ;# 2

DANTE B FASCELL, Florida
  Chairman

LEE H HAMILTON, Indiana
GUS YATRON, Pennsylvania
STEPHEN J. SOLARZ, New York
GERRY E. STUDDS, Massachusetts
HOWARD WOLPE, Michigan
GEO. W CROCKETT, JR., Michigan
SAM GEJDENSON, Connecticut
MERVYN M. DYMALLY, California
TOM LANTOS, California
ROBERT G. TORRICELLI, New Jersey
LAWRENCE J. SMITH, Florida
HOWARD L. BERMAN, California
MEL LEVINE, California
EDWARD F FEIGHAN, Ohio
TED WEISS, New York
GARY L. ACKERMAN, New York
MORRIS K UDALL, Arizona
JAMES McCLURE CLARKE, North Carolina
JAIME B FUSTER, Puerto Rico
WAYNE OWENS, Utah
HARRY JOHNSTON, Florida
ELIOT L. ENGEL, New York
ENI F.H. FALEOMAVAEGA, American Samoa
DOUGLAS H. BOSCO, California
FRANK McCLOSKEY, Indiana
DONALD M. PAYNE, New Jersey

  JOHN J. BRADY, JR
    Chief of Staff

WILLIAM S. BROOMFIELD, Michigan
  Ranking Minority Member

BENJAMIN A. GILMAN, New York
ROBERT J. LAGOMARSINO, California
JIM LEACH, Iowa
TOBY ROTH, Wisconsin
OLYMPIA J. SNOWE, Maine
HENRY J. HYDE, Illinois
DOUG BEREUTER, Nebraska
CHRISTOPHER H. SMITH, New Jersey
MICHAEL DeWINE, Ohio
DAN BURTON, Indiana
JAN MEYERS, Kansas
JOHN MILLER, Washington
DONALD E. "BUZ" LUKENS, Ohio
BEN BLAZ, Guam
ELTON GALLEGLY, California
AMO HOUGHTON, New York
PORTER J. GOSS, Florida
ILEANA ROS-LEHTINEN, Florida

  STEVEN K. BERRY
    Minority Chief of Staff

One Hundred First Congress
Congress of the United States
Committee on Foreign Affairs
House of Representatives
Washington, DC 20515

May 24, 1990

His Excellency Mohsin A. Alaini
Embassy of the Republic of Yemen
Suite 840
600 New Hampshire Avenue, N.W.
Washington, D.C. 20037

Dear Mr. Ambassador,

We write to follow up on our letter to President Salih of January 22nd concerning humanitarian issues involving the Jewish Community in Yemen.

We appreciated the opportunity to meet with President Salih during his visit to Washington and we felt that his visit was an important signal of the importance we attach to furthering U.S.-Yemeni relations and of the increasingly crucial role the Republic of Yemen is playing in the region. The recent successful unity talks attest to the pivotal role played by Yemen.

Given the discussions we had and the progress we achieved, we frankly do not understand and are disappointed that several steps we discussed in January have not been taken. Dr. Haim Tawil will be taking another humanitarian trip to Yemen in June, we understand, but there has not been any action on the agenda we discussed.

In this regard, we hoped then and still hope now to enlist the support of your Government: to allow Yehia ibn Daoud Suberi to travel to the United States and see family members; to expand student exchanges to include members of the Yemen Arab Republic's Jewish community; and to enable the Jewish community to obtain better medical care and greater access to postal and telephone communications.

We view these as important humanitarian issues and believe we can and should work together to improve conditions for this community within the context of our improving bilateral relations. We also view these steps as reasonable. We are not asking your Government for extraordinary concessions or to provide special permissions for travel or for study abroad that are not available to other Yemeni citizens or generally available to all citizens in other Arab countries in the region.

May 24, 1990
Page 2

We appreciate your consideration of this matter and hope we can effect these humanitarian steps soon.

With best regards,

Lee H. Hamilton
Chairman
Subcommittee on Europe
 and the Middle East

Sincerely,

Benjamin A. Gilman
Ranking Minority Member
Subcommittee on Europe
 and the Middle East

Stephen J. Solarz
Chairman
Subcommittee on Asian
 and Pacific Affairs

Mel Levine
Member of Congress

```
MAILGRAM SERVICE CENTER
MIDDLETOWN, VA. 22645
28AM
```

```
4-0072735209002 07/28/90 ICS_IPMBNGZ CSP JFKB
1 7183324938 MGM TDBN BROOKLYN NY 07-28 1015A EST
```

```
MOSES SHARABI
2063 E 22 ST
BROOKLYN NY 11229
```

THIS IS A CONFIRMATION COPY OF THE FOLLOWING MESSAGE:

FRB TDBN BROOKLYN NY 72/68 07-28 1015A EST
INT DR ARIANI
MINISTER OF FOREING AFFAIRS
SANA (YEMEN)

WE HAVE LEARNED FROM TAIZ THAT CONSTRUCTION WORK IS ABOUT TO BE
PERFORMED TO ENLARGE A SCHOOL AT ALSAWANI. SUCH CONSTRUCTION WILL
DESTROY THE GRAVE OF SALAM SHABAZI. AS THIS GRAVE IS NATIONAL YEMEN
HOLY SITE OF IMPORTANCE TO ALL YEMNIES WE URGE YOUR INTERVENTION TO
PREVENT SUCH DESTRUCTION. THANK YOU IN ADVANCE FOR YOUR EFFORT.
    DR HAIM TAWILI AND COLEAGUES

10:09 EST

MGMCOMP

To reply by Mailgram Message, see reverse side for Western Union's toll-free numbers.

MAILGRAM SERVICE CENTER
MIDDLETOWN, VA. 22645
28AM

4-0075115209002 07/28/90 ICS IPMBNGZ CSP JFKB
1 7183324938 MGM TDBN BROOKLYN NY 07-28 1020A EST

MOSES SHARABI
2063 E 22 ST
BROOKLYN NY 11229

THIS IS A CONFIRMATION COPY OF THE FOLLOWING MESSAGE:

 FRB TDBN BROOKLYN NY 96/91 07-28 1020A EST
INT MR ABDU NUAMAN
MAYOR OF TAIZ
TAIZ (YEMEN)

WE HAVE LEARNED FROM TAIZ THAT CONSTRUCTION WORK IS ABOUT TO BE
PERFORMED TO ENLARGE A SCHOOL AT ALSAWANI. SUCH CONSTRUCTION WILL
DESTROY THE GRAVE OF SALAM SHABAZI. AS THIS GRAVE IS NATIONAL YEMEN
HOLY SITE OF IMPORTANCE TO ALL YEMNIES WE URGE YOUR INTERVENTION TO
PREVENT SUCH DESTRUCTION. THANK YOU IN ADVANCE FOR YOUR EFFORT.
QUOTE OUR CABLE SENT TO DR ARIANI, MINISTER OF FOREIGN AFFAIRS. ANY
ADDITIONAL HELP YOU CAN PROVIDE WILL BE APPRECIATED. BEST OUR
REGARDS.
 DR HAIM TAWILI AND COLLEAGUES

10:14 EST

MGMCOMP

To reply by Mailgram Message, see reverse side for Western Union's toll-free numbers.

BENJAMIN A. GILMAN
22d District, New York

FOREIGN AFFAIRS COMMITTEE

SUBCOMMITTEES
EUROPE AND MIDDLE EAST
(RANKING MINORITY MEMBER)
INTERNATIONAL OPERATIONS

POST OFFICE AND CIVIL
SERVICE COMMITTEE
(RANKING MINORITY MEMBER)

SUBCOMMITTEE:
INVESTIGATIONS

SELECT COMMITTEE ON
NARCOTICS ABUSE AND
CONTROL

SELECT COMMITTEE ON
HUNGER

VICE CHAIRMAN,
TASK FORCE ON
AMERICAN PRISONERS AND
MISSING IN SOUTHEAST ASIA

Congress of the United States
House of Representatives
Washington, DC 20515-3222

August 20, 1990

His Excellency Mohsin A. Alaini
Embassy of the Republic of Yemen
600 New Hampshire Ave., N.W. Suite 840
Washington, D.C. 20037

Dear Mr. Ambassador:

I am writing to follow up on earlier correspondence regarding
humanitarian matters involving Jewish citizens of Yemen. I learned
a few days ago from Dr. Haim Tawil of his return to the United
States with Moshe Dhahari Halla, who was seriously injured in an
automobile accident and who was interested in receiving permission
to leave Yemen temporarily for medical treatment in the United
States.

I was informed that Moshe Dhahari Halla has been admitted to
a hospital in New York, and is undergoing the required treatment.
For this to have been arranged while Dr. Tawil was in Yemen
recently is indeed appreciated, and I wanted to thank you for your
kind assistance in this humanitarian effort. Please convey my
personal thanks to President Salih and Foreign Minister Iryani for
their assistance as well.

It is hoped that this recent action signals the onset of the
resolution of a number of humanitarian issues relating to the
Jewish community of Yemen, to the satisfaction of all interested
and involved parties.

With best wishes,

Sincerely,

BENJAMIN A. GILMAN
Member of Congress

PLEASE REPLY TO:

WASHINGTON OFFICE:
2185 RAYBURN BUILDING
WASHINGTON, DC 20515-3222

DISTRICT OFFICE:
44 EAST AVENUE
P.O. BOX 358
MIDDLETOWN, NY 10940-0358

DISTRICT OFFICE:
223 ROUTE 59
MONSEY, NY 10952-3498

DISTRICT OFFICE:
32 MAIN STREET
HASTINGS-ON-HUDSON,
NY 10706-1602
TELEPHONE (914) 478-5550

S/S 10/29 at 1530PM

NEA

United States Department of State

Washington, D. C. 20520

October 24, 1990

ACTION MEMORANDUM

SECRET (With SECRET/EXDIS Attachment)

TO: The Secretary

THROUGH: P - Robert Kimmitt

FROM: NEA - John H. Kelly

SUBJECT: Messages of Appreciation to Yemeni
         Foreign Minister and Deputy Prime Minister on Yemeni
         Jews.

ISSUE FOR DECISION

    Whether to send messages of appreciation to the Yemeni
Foreign Minister and Deputy Prime Minister for their assistance
in two humanitarian cases involving Yemeni Jews.

ESSENTIAL FACTORS

    Yemeni Foreign Minister Al-Iryani and Deputy Prime Minister
Abu Shuwarib were instrumental in obtaining permission for two
Jews to depart Yemen. The first came to New York for surgery
and returned to Yemen, and the second, a very elderly man, was
reunited with his family in New York after a separation of
forty years. Both cases, and particularly the second, had been
the focus of strong Congressional interest.

    These messages will indicate to the recipients the
importance we attach to the welfare of the Jewish community in
Yemen, and our desire for continuing cooperation with the
Yemeni Government in trying to improve the conditions of that
community. President Bush has sent a message of appreciation
to Yemeni President Saleh on this issue. This was appropriate,
since the decisions could not have been made without Saleh's
approval. However, we think it also important to acknowledge
the key roles played by the Foreign Minister and Deputy Prime
Minister.

ORIG TO
EXDIS
FILES
COPIES:
S
D
P
C
S/S
S/S-S
TMA
TMB
S/S-O
HA
NEA
RF/CWA

RECOMMENDATION

    That you approve the attached cables.

Approve____RHK____   Disapprove_____

OCT 29 1990

SECRET (With SECRET/EXDIS Attachment)

OUTGOING TELEGRAM

DEPARTMENT OF STATE

AUTH JAB DRAFT
CLEAR 1 RMK 2
3 RS 4 DLM 5 MM
6 SS 7 SSO 8

DECLASSIFIED

SECRET

NEA/ARP:AMFARSAKH:AMF
10/16/90 76571 SEARPGEN 2157
S: JABAKER

NEA/ARP: DRKEENE   NEA: DLMACK
NEA: JHKELLY   HA: RSCHIFTER
P: RKIMMITT ,C:MFOULON,   S/S: EMCKUNE
S/S-O: RMANZANARES,

IMMEDIATE   SANAA

IMMEDIATE   TEL AVIV, JERUSALEM

EXDIS

E.O. 12356: DECL: OADR

TAGS: PREL, PHUM, YM, IS, US

DEPARTMENT OF STATE		IS/FPC/CDR (AW) Date. 5/4/93
(X) RELEASE	(X) DECLASSIFY	MR Cases Only:
( ) EXCISE	( ) DECLASSIFY	EO Citations _____
( ) DENY	IN PART	
( ) DELETE Non-Responsive Info		_____ TS authori
FOIA Exemptions _____		( ) CLASSIFY as ( ) S or ( ) CO
PA Exemptions _____		( ) DOWNGRADE TS to ( ) S or ( ) CO

SUBJECT: MESSAGE FROM THE SECRETARY TO DEPUTY PRIME
MINISTER ABU SHAWARIB ON YEMENI JEWS.

1. SECRET ENTIRE TEXT.

2. PLEASE TRANSMIT THE FOLLOWING MESSAGE FROM SECRETARY
BAKER TO DEPUTY PRIME MINISTER ABU SHAWARIB THANKING ABU
SHAWARIB FOR HIS ASSISTANCE IN HELPING THE YEMENI JEWISH
COMMUNITY. NO SIGNED ORIGINAL TO FOLLOW.

3. BEGIN TEXT.

DEAR SHAYKH MUJAHID:

I WOULD LIKE TO EXPRESS MY PERSONAL APPRECIATION FOR ALL
YOUR ASSISTANCE WITH TWO HUMANITARIAN CASES WHICH WERE
RAISED DURING PRESIDENT SALEH'S STATE VISIT TO WASHINGTON
LAST JANUARY. AS YOU KNOW, MOSHE DHAHARI-HALLA UNDERWENT
A SUCCESSFUL OPERATION IN NEW YORK IN AUGUST AND IS NOW
BACK WITH HIS FAMILY IN YEMEN. MUALLIM YAHYA TSABARI WAS
REUNITED WITH HIS FAMILY IN NEW YORK IN MID-SEPTEMBER. I
UNDERSTAND THAT WITHOUT YOUR HELP THESE EVENTS WOULD NOT

UNCLASSIFIED

SECRET

SECRET   PAGE 2

HAVE TAKEN PLACE.

I HOPE THAT THESE AUSPICIOUS EVENTS WILL SIGNAL THE
BEGINNING OF AN EVEN CLOSER COOPERATIVE RELATIONSHIP
BETWEEN OUR TWO COUNTRIES ON THIS AND OTHER IMMEDIATE
ISSUES OF HUMANITARIAN CONCERN.   OUR EMBASSY IN SANAA
LOOKS FORWARD TO CONTINUING TO WORK WITH YOU ON SUCH
MATTERS.

SINCERELY YOURS,

JAMES A. BAKER, III

END TEXT. YY

SECRET

DEPARTMENT OF STATE

AUTH <u>JAB</u>   DRAFT<u>AMF</u> 49
CLEAR 1 <u>DRK</u> 2 <u>DLM</u>
3 <u>RS</u> 4 <u>RK</u> 5 <u>MM</u>
  7 <u>SE</u> 8 <u>SSO</u>

SECRET

DECLASSIFIED

NEA/ARP:AMFARSAKH:AMF
10/19/90 76571 SEARPGEN 2186
THE SECRETARY

NEA/ARP: DRKEENE ,C:MFOULON,   NEA: DLMACK
NEA: JHKELLY   HA: RSCHIFTER
P: RMKIMMITT   MMALINOWSKI
S/S:EMCKUNE   S/S-O:RMANZANARES

IMMEDIATE   SANAA

IMMEDIATE   TEL AVIV, JERUSALEM

EXDIS

E.O. 12356: DECL: OADR

TAGS: PHUM, PREL, YM, US

DEPARTMENT OF STATE	IS/FPC/CDR CWN Date. 5/4/95
(X) RELEASE (X) DECLASSIFY	MR Cases Only:
( ) EXCISE ( ) DECLASSIFY	EO Citations _____
( ) DENY IN PART	
( ) DELETE Non-Responsive Info	_____ TS authority to.
FOIA Exemptions _____	( ) CLASSIFY as ( ) S or ( ) C OADR
PA Exemptions _____	( ) DOWNGRADE TS to ( ) S or ( ) C OADR

SUBJECT: MESSAGE FROM THE SECRETARY TO FOREIGN MINISTER
AL-IRYANI ON YEMENI JEWS.

1. SECRET ENTIRE TEXT.

2. PLEASE DELIVER THE FOLLOWING MESSAGE FROM THE SECRETARY
TO FOREIGN MINISTER AL-IRYANI ON THE SUBJECT OF YEMENI
JEWS. NO SIGNED ORIGINAL TO FOLLOW.

3. BEGIN TEXT.

DEAR DR. AL-IRYANI:

I WOULD LIKE TO EXPRESS MY PERSONAL APPRECIATION FOR ALL
YOUR ASSISTANCE WITH TWO HUMANITARIAN CASES WHICH WERE
RAISED DURING PRESIDENT SALEH'S STATE VISIT TO WASHINGTON
LAST JANUARY, AND WHICH YOU HELPED TO BRING TO A
SUCCESSFUL CONCLUSION. AS YOU KNOW, MOSHE DHAHARI-HALLA
UNDERWENT A SUCCESSFUL OPERATION IN NEW YORK IN AUGUST AND
HAS RETURNED TO YEMEN. MUALLIM YAHYA TSABARI ARRIVED IN
NEW YORK IN MID-SEPTEMBER AND WAS REUNITED WITH HIS FAMILY
THERE.

DECLASSIFIED

SECRET

SECRET   PAGE 2

DECLASSIFIED

I HOPE THAT THESE AUSPICIOUS EVENTS WILL SIGNAL THE
BEGINNING OF AN EVEN CLOSER COOPERATIVE RELATIONSHIP
BETWEEN OUR TWO COUNTRIES ON THIS AND OTHER IMMEDIATE
ISSUES OF HUMANITARIAN CONCERN.

SINCERELY,

JAMES A. BAKER, III

END TEXT.   YY

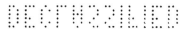

SECRET

United States Department of State

Washington, D.C. 20520

November 13, 1990

TO WHOM IT MAY CONCERN:

At the request of my much admired friend, Professor Haim Tawil, I am pleased to write about my cooperation, over a period of almost two years, with ICROJOY, an organization which has been concerned with creating better fraternal links between American and Yemeni Jews.

In an effort which required political sophistication, sensitivity, firmness, great energy and some real personal risk, Prof. Tawil was magnificent, gaining not only the confidence of ranking officials in the Department of State but also of the government of the Yemen Arab Republic.

The effort which ICROJOY mounted was multilateral, requiring endless contacts between groups and officials who did not always see eye to eye on tactics or even ends, but Tawil -- by simple force of character, by unimpeachable good will, by charm and scholarship and good sense, won the support and applause of all the key groups.

ICROJOY melded its concerns with those of the existing diplomatic situation and put forward programs and agendas which were the basis for unprecedented successes in dealing with an isolated and uncertain community of Jews who had long been out of touch with their brothers in America. Contact and communication, travel and education, aid and comfort were pressed by ICROJOY and the selfless Professor -- who took on in these tasks a public role which was, for him, new and daunting. Tawil never faltered and never complained, and posed to my mind a splendid example of an American who sets out to do privately good works which governments cannot always manage.

I worked with Tawil and his compatriots closely and always enjoyably and while my tasks have shifted now to another area, I am delighted to provide my own testimony on the estimable efforts of ICROJOY.

Sincerely,

David M. Ransom
Director,
Office of Southern European
Affairs

BENJAMIN A. GILMAN
22D DISTRICT, NEW YORK

FOREIGN AFFAIRS COMMITTEE
SUBCOMMITTEES
EUROPE AND MIDDLE EAST
(RANKING MINORITY MEMBER)
INTERNATIONAL OPERATIONS

POST OFFICE AND CIVIL
SERVICE COMMITTEE
(RANKING MINORITY MEMBER)

SUBCOMMITTEE
INVESTIGATIONS

SELECT COMMITTEE ON
NARCOTICS ABUSE AND
CONTROL

SELECT COMMITTEE ON
HUNGER

VICE CHAIRMAN,
TASK FORCE ON
AMERICAN PRISONERS AND
MISSING IN SOUTHEAST ASIA

Congress of the United States
House of Representatives
Washington, DC 20515-3222

December 3, 1990

Dr. Hayim Tawil
International Coalition for the Revival
of the Jews of Yemen
150 Nassau Street   Suite 1238
New York, New York   10038

Dear Dr. Tawil:

As the year draws to a close, permit me to take this opportunity to commend you and ICROJOY for the successful efforts undertaken this year on behalf of the Jewish community of Yemen. Certainly, we have reason to be pleased.

Promoting and preserving the unique cultural and religious heritage of Jewish Yemenis remaining in Yemen is a high priority of mine. You can be certain of my commitment in future endeavors.

I look forward to working with ICROJOY in the months and years ahead, and hope for the day when the Jewish community of Yemen will be able to reunify with family members abroad at will.

With best wishes for future successes,

Sincerely,

BENJAMIN A. GILMAN
Member of Congress

BAG/db

PLEASE REPLY TO:

WASHINGTON OFFICE:
2185 RAYBURN BUILDING
WASHINGTON, DC 20515-3222
☒ TELEPHONE (202) 225-3776

DISTRICT OFFICE:
44 EAST AVENUE
P.O. BOX 358
MIDDLETOWN, NY 10940-0358
☐ TELEPHONE (914) 343-6666

DISTRICT OFFICE:
223 ROUTE 59
MONSEY, NY 10952-3498
☐ TELEPHONE (914) 357-9000

DISTRICT OFFICE:
32 MAIN STREET
HASTINGS-ON-HUDSON,
NY 10706-1602
☐ TELEPHONE (914) 478-5550

PRIORITY   CONFIDENTIAL   INCOMING

                DEPARTMENT OF STATE   EXCISE
                   ARA/NEA REARCS

PAGE 01   TEL AV 02474 271308Z   014624   S091226   TEL AV 02474 271308?   014674   S091226
ACTION: IS (02)

INFO: NEA (02) RA (01) MRA (01) PR (01) YE (01) ARPD (01)?
------------------------ 27/1314Z A3 HS   (TOTAL COPIES: 039)
ACTION NEA-00

INFO LOG-00 ADS-00 ANAE-00 CIAE-00 DODE-00 DS-00 HA-09
      INRE-00 INR-02 NSAE-00 NSCE-00 PA-01 PM-00 PRS-01
      P-02 SCT-03 SP-00 SS-00 USIE-00 /023W
      ------------------46BD5C 271314Z /49

P 271256Z FEB 91
FM AMEMBASSY TEL AVIV
TO SECSTATE WASHDC PRIORITY 1292
INFO RUFHJU/AMCONSUL JERUSALEM
AMEMBASSY SANAA

C O N F I D E N T I A L TEL AVIV 02474

E.O. 12356:DECL: OADR
TAGS: PHUM, PREL, IS, YM   MFA DOUBTS SELA'S CREDIBILITY
SUBJECT: ISRAELI PRESS REPORT ON YEMENI JEWS   --------------------------

REF: STATE 58948

1. (C) SUMMARY: THE ARTICLE CITED (REFTEL) DID INDEED
APPEAR IN THE FEB. 19 ISSUE OF "YEDIOT AHARONOT" AND WAS
EXPANDED UPON IN CONVERSATIONS WE HAD WITH THE
INTERVIEWEE, ELIAV SELA. AN MFA OFFICIAL TOLD US SELA'S
INFORMATION IS NOT TO BE TRUSTED. END SUMMARY.

2. (U) POST HAS LOCATED THE TWO-PARAGRAPH STORY
ENTITLED "DOZENS OF JEWS IN YEMEN BEATEN BECAUSE OF GULF   BROWN
WAR" IN THE FEB. 19 EDITION OF "YEDIOT AHARONOT" BY ZVI
ALOUSH (REFTEL). A TRANSLATION FOLLOWS:

3. (U) BEGIN TEXT. "DOZENS OF JEWS IN YEMEN HAVE BEEN
CRUELLY BEATEN BY EXTREMIST ARABS DUE TO THE WAR IN THE
GULF. ELIAV SELA FROM ARAD, AN ACTIVIST ON BEHALF OF
YEMENITE JEWRY, LEARNED OF THIS DURING THE WEEK.

   THE JEWS LIVE IN THE DISTRICT OF HABAYDAN, NEAR TO
YEMEN'S BORDER WITH SAUDI ARABIA. THE INCIDENTS BETWEEN
ARABS AND THE JEWS OCCURRED CLOSE TO THE END OF
DEMONSTRATIONS BY YEMENIS IN SUPPORT OF IRAQ. ELIAV
SELA REPORTS THAT IT IS KNOWN FOR SURE THAT TWO JEWISH
WOMEN, AGED ABOUT 60, WERE SEVERELY BEATEN AND INJURED.
ACCORDING TO WITNESSES, ONE OF THEM DIED FROM HER
INJURIES." END TEXT.

                        CONFIDENTIAL

PRIORITY

████████████████████████
CONFIDENTIAL

OUTGOING 3

DEPARTMENT OF STATE
ARA/NEA REARCS

R

PAGE 01   STATE   058948   230238Z   S028698
ORIGIN: YE (01)

INFO: ARPD (01) IS (02) NEA (02) PR (01)
       ------------------- 23/1534Z A4 YC   (TOTAL COPIES: 007)
ORIGIN NEA-00

INFO LOG-00   ADS-00   CIAE-00 AMAC-01 DODE-00 HA-09   INRE-00
      INR-02   NSAE-00 NSCE-00 PM-00   P-02   SP-00   SS-00
      /018R

DRAFTED BY: NEA/ARP: AMFARSAKH: AMF
APPROVED BY: NEA: DKURTZER
NEA/ARP: DRKEENE   NEA/IAI: KMCKUNE
NEA: DLMACK
         ---------------4543A9 230238Z /38

P 230238Z FEB 91
FM SECSTATE WASHDC
TO AMEMBASSY TEL AVIV PRIORITY
AMCONSUL JERUSALEM
AMEMBASSY SANAA

Φ PHUM
Jews

C O N F I D E N T I A L STATE 058948

E.O. 12356: DECL: OADR
TAGS: PHUM, PREL, IS, YM
SUBJECT: ALLEGED ISRAELI PRESS REPORT ON YEMENI JEWS

1. CONFIDENTIAL ENTIRE TEXT.

2. A VERY RELIABLE SOURCE PHONED THE YEMEN DESK ON
FEBRUARY 21 TO REPORT THAT THE FEBRUARY 19 EDITION OF
YEDIOT AHARONOT PUBLISHED AN ARTICLE BY REPORTER TZVI
ALOUSH ALLEGING ATTACKS ON JEWS IN YEMEN PRECIPITATED BY
THE GULF CRISIS.

3. THE REPORT, BASED ON AN INTERVIEW WITH ELIAV SELLA, A
MEMBER (PERHAPS A LEADER) OF A YEMENI ORGANIZATION IN
ISRAEL, CHARGED THAT THERE HAD BEEN A PRO-IRAQ
DEMONSTRATION IN A TOWN NORTHWEST OF SA'ADAH IN YEMEN
RECENTLY, AFTER WHICH A MOB ATTACKED YEMENI JEWS AND
SEVERELY BEAT TWO ELDERLY WOMEN ONE OF WHOM DIED AS A
RESULT OF HER INJURIES.

4. FOR TEL AVIV: DEPARTMENT WOULD GREATLY APPRECIATE
EMBASSY EFFORT TO LOCATE THE ARTICLE AND CABLE A
TRANSLATION TO US ASAP.

5. FOR SANAA: AS WE HAVE HAD SEVERAL INQUIRIES ABOUT THE
EFFECT OF THE GULF CRISIS ON THE JEWISH COMMUNITY
RECENTLY, WE WOULD APPRECIATE ANY INFORMATION YOU MAY HAVE
ON THE SUBJECT. EAGLEBURGER

CONFIDENTIAL

IMMEDIATE ░░░░░░░░░░░░░░░░░░░░░░░ R- INCOMING ⌐

CONFIDENTIAL

DEPARTMENT OF STATE
ARA/NEA REARCS

PAGE 01   SANAA 02462 181333Z   001728   S052649   SANAA 02462 181333Z   001728   S052649
INFO: YE (01) ARPD (01) IS (02) NEA (02) RA (01)
------------------------ 18/1357Z A3 HS   (TOTAL COPIES: 001)
ACTION HA-09

INFO LOG-00 ADS-00 AMAD-01 NEA-00 SSO-00 /011W
------------------73675A 181334Z /38

O 181334Z JUN 91
FM AMEMBASSY SANAA
TO SECSTATE WASHDC IMMEDIATE 5276
INFO AMEMBASSY TEL AVIV

C O N F I D E N T I A L SANAA 02462

E.O. 12356: DECL: OADR
TAGS: PHUM, YM
SUBJECT: ICROJOY'S FOURTH VISIT TO YEMEN

REF: A) SANAA 2437; B) SANAA 2468; C) SANAA 1826

1. CONFIDENTIAL - ENTIRE TEXT.

2. SUMMARY: RECENTLY CONCLUDED ICROJOY VISIT TO
YEMEN MADE CONSIDERABLE PROGRESS IN ADVANCING THE
GROUP'S AGENDA OF IMPROVING THE QUALITY OF RELIGIOUS
LIFE AND RELAXING RESTRICTIONS ON FOREIGN TRAVEL FOR
YEMENI JEWS. DELEGATION ENJOYED UNPRECEDENTED ACCESS
TO FOREIGN MINISTER AND ATTRACTED CONSIDERABLE LOCAL
AND SOME INTERNATIONAL PRESS ATTENTION. END SUMMARY

3. A FIVE MEMBER DELEGATION FROM THE INTERNATIONAL
COALITION FOR THE REVIVAL OF THE JEWS OF YEMEN

(ICROJOY) HEADED BY COALITION CHAIRMAN DR. HAYIM
TAVIL VISITED YEMEN MAY 23 TO JUNE 16. THIS WAS THE
FOURTH IN A SERIES OF VISITS WHICH BEGAN IN OCTOBER
1989. MEMBERS OF THE GROUP TRAVELED TO SA'DAH,
AMRAN, AND RAYDAH TO VISIT THE LOCAL JEWISH
COMMUNITIES, ACQUIRE LAND AND ARRANGE FOR
CONSTRUCTION OF A SYNAGOGUE AND RITUAL BATH IN
SA'DAH, AND TO PREPARE TRAVEL DOCUMENTS FOR A NUMBER
OF YEMENI JEWS INTENDING TO TRAVEL ABROAD.

4. THE DELEGATION MET WITH FOREIGN MINISTER
AL-IRYANI SEVERAL TIMES DURING THEIR STAY, FORMALLY
IN HIS OFFICE AND INFORMALLY AT HIS HOME. DURING ONE
MEETING, A TRADITIONAL YEMENI AFTERNOON SOCIAL
SETTING, A YEMENI-AMERICAN WOMAN MEMBER OF THE
DELEGATION SANG A NUMBER OF TRADITIONAL SANANI
SONGS. THE PROFESSIONAL ETHNO-MUSICOLOGIST'S
PERFORMANCE WAS WELL RECIEVED BY THE FOREIGN
MINISTER'S GUESTS, WHO INCLUDED SENIOR GOVERNMENT
OFFICIALS. YEMEN TV SUBSEQUENTLY INTERVIEWED THE
ARTIST AND TAPED HER PERFORMANCE FOR LATER BROADCAST.

5. IN ADDITION TO THE UNPRECEDENTED ACCESS TO THE
FOREIGN MINISTER, ICROJOY'S FOURTH VISIT TO YEMEN
BROKE NEW GROUND ON ANOTHER FRONT. THE LOCAL AND
INTERNATIONAL PRESS REPORTED ON THE PRESENCE IN SANAA
OF ICROJOY AND OTHER INTERNATIONAL JEWISH GROUPS
(REFS A AND B). WHILE THE PRESS ATTENTION IS AT
LEAST PARTLY DUE TO THE FACT THE ICROJOY DELEGATION
STAYED AT THE MID-CITY TAJ SHEBA HOTEL, WHERE THE
PRESENCE OF SMALL GROUPS OF YEMENI JEWISH TRAVELERS

ATTRACTED CONSIDERABLE ATTENTION, THE ROY APPEARS TO
BE TAKING A MUCH MORE RELAXED ATTITUDE TOWARD
VISITING JEWISH DELEGATIONS. IN MID-MAY FM AL-IRYANI
ADMITTED TO PROVIDING AN OFFICIAL VEHICLE FOR A VISIT
OF JACQUES UNGER, A SWISS NATIONAL MARRIED TO AN
ISRAELI OF YEMENI JEWISH ORIGIN. UNGER'S STAY IN THE

TAJ SHEBA ALSO DREW SMALL CROWDS OF YEMENI JEWS TO THE
HOTEL'S LOBBY AND ENTRANCE AREA. RMUREH KARTA RABBI
YUSSEF BECHER ALSO MET WITH THE FOREIGN MINISTER AND
OTHER ROYG OFFICIALS (REF'C) DURING HIS APRIL-MAY
VISIT TO YEMEN.

6. WHILE ICROJOY WAS NOT ABLE TO FINALIZE TRAVEL
ARRANGEMENTS FOR ALL THE YEMENIS IT EXPECTED TO
ESCORT TO THE U.S. FOR STUDY, MEDICAL TREATMENT OR
FAMILY REUNIFICATION, IT DID SUCCEED IN OBTAINING
FIVE PASSPORTS FOR JEWISH TRAVELERS AND ESCORTED
THREE OF THE TRAVELERS TO THE U.S.

7. ICROJOY ALSO MADE CONSIDERABLE PROGRESS ON LARGER
ISSUES. THE ROYG HAS AGREED TO THE CONSTRUCTION OF
SYNAGOGUES AND RITUAL BATHS IN JEWISH COMMUNITIES IN
THE NORTH; ICROJOY-SPONSORED RABBIS WILL BE ABLE TO
COME TO YEMEN TO TEND TO THE JEWISH COMMUNITY'S
EDUCATIONAL NEEDS. MOREOVER, THE ROY APPEARS TO HAVE
ACCEPTED "IN PRINCIPLE" THAT THE ROY CONSTITUTION
GRANTS YEMENI JEWS THE RIGHT TO TRAVEL ABROAD LIKE
OTHER YEMENI CITIZENS. STRATHEARN

⌀ PHUM
Jews

IS/FPC/CDR CWN Date: 5/4/95

MR Cases Only:
EO Citations

TS authority to.

( ) S or ( ) C OADR
( ) CLASSIFY as
( ) DOWNGRADE TS to ( ) S or ( ) C OADR

DEPARTMENT OF STATE

(X) RELEASE   (X) DECLASSIFY
( ) EXCISE   ( ) DECLASSIFY
( ) DENY   IN PART
( ) DELETE Non-Responsive Info
FOIA Exemptions
PA Exemptions

CONFIDENTIAL

BENJAMIN A. GILMAN
22d District New York

FOREIGN AFFAIRS COMMITTEE
SUBCOMMITTEES
EUROPE AND MIDDLE EAST
(RANKING MINORITY MEMBER)
INTERNATIONAL OPERATIONS

POST OFFICE AND CIVIL
SERVICE COMMITTEE
(RANKING MINORITY MEMBER)

SUBCOMMITTEE
INVESTIGATIONS

SELECT COMMITTEE ON
NARCOTICS ABUSE AND
CONTROL

SELECT COMMITTEE ON
HUNGER

VICE CHAIRMAN,
TASK FORCE ON
AMERICAN PRISONERS AND
MISSING IN SOUTHEAST ASIA

Congress of the United States
House of Representatives
Washington, DC 20515-3222

June 27, 1991

His Excellency Mohsin A. Alaini
Embassy of the Republic of Yemen
600 New Hampshire Avenue, N.W. Suite 840
Washington, D.C. 20037

Dear Mr. Ambassador:

Earlier this week I had the pleasure of meeting the three individuals who accompanied Dr. Hayim Tawil upon his return from the Republic of Yemen recently. It was certainly a gratifying experience, and I look forward to seeing them again soon.

I was also pleased to learn that the President's Council has recommended the adoption of a freedom of travel provision for all of Yemen's citizenry. I would appreciate it, however, if we could meet in the near future to discuss the specifics of this new law, and its implementation in the coming weeks and months.

Moreover, I have expressed my interest and support to the appropriate officials regarding $5 million in PL480-Title I assistance to the Republic of Yemen. I hope that continued positive developments in humanitarian matters, as well as other issues of concern such as arms control and the quest for peace in the Middle East, will succeed in overcoming the current tension between our two nations.

Should a meeting in the next few weeks be feasible, please have your office contact Deborah Bodlander of my staff at 226-0165.

With best wishes,

Sincerely,

BENJAMIN A. GILMAN
Member of Congress

PLEASE REPLY TO:

WASHINGTON OFFICE
2185 RAYBURN BUILDING
WASHINGTON DC 20515-3222
☐ TELEPHONE (202) 225-3776

DISTRICT OFFICE
44 EAST AVENUE
P O BOX 358
MIDDLETOWN NY 10940-0358
☐ TELEPHONE (914) 343-6666

DISTRICT OFFICE
223 ROUTE 59
MONSEY NY 10952-3498
☐ TELEPHONE (914) 357-9000

DISTRICT OFFICE
32 MAIN STREET
HASTINGS-ON-HUDSON
NY 10706-1602
☐ TELEPHONE (914) 478-5550

THIS STATIONERY PRINTED ON PAPER MADE OF RECYCLED FIBERS

PRIORITY

▲▲▲▲▲▲▲▲▲▲▲▲▲▲▲▲▲▲▲▲▲▲▲
CONFIDENTIAL

R - INCOMING 16

DEPARTMENT OF STATE
ARA/NEA REARCS

PAGE 01 OF 02 SANAA 02437 00 OF 02 171438Z   000100   S036496
ACTION: YE (01)

INFO: ARPD (01) IS (02) MIL (01) NEA (02) RA (01)
------------------------ 17/1622Z A3 YC   (TOTAL COPIES: 005)
ACTION NEA-00

INFO LOG-00 ADS-00 AMAD-01 CIAE-00 DODE-00 HA-00   INRE-00
      INR-01 NSAE-00 PA-01 PRS-01 RP-10 SP-00 SR-00
      /026W
------------------72F949 1715242 /49 44

P 171431Z JUN 91
FM AMEMBASSY SANAA
TO SECSTATE WASHDC PRIORITY 5255
INFO USIA WASHDC PRIORITY 7867
AMEMBASSY TEL AVIV

C O N F I D E N T I A L SANAA 02437

USIA FOR FERNANDEZ

E.O. 12356: DECL: OADR
TAGS: PHUM, YM, US, IS
SUBJECT: INTERNATIONAL PRESS ON YEMENI JEWS AND FM'S
DENIAL OF FALASHA-TYPE EVACUATION

REF: SANAA 2428 (NOTAL)

1. (C) SUMMARY: THE INTERNATIONAL PRESS HAS PICKED
UP ON REPORTS IN LOCAL PAPERS CLAIMING THAT AMERICAN
JEWISH DELEGATIONS HAVE VISITED YEMEN TO ORGANIZE A
FALASHA-TYPE EVACUATION OF YEMENI JEWS. IN
RESPONSE TO A POTENTIALLY EMBARRASSING AFP REPORT OF
ROYG-JEWISH NEGOTIATIONS, THE ROYG FOREIGN MINISTER

ISSUED AN OFFICIAL DENIAL OF ANY AGREEMENT ON THE
TRAVEL OF YEMENI JEWS TO ISRAEL TO A STRINGER OF
AL-HAYAT PAPER (LONDON-BASED). AT THE SAME TIME, THE
OFFICIAL DAILY HAS FOR THE FIRST TIME OPENLY
CRITICIZED PRIVATE PAPERS FOR THEIR COVERAGE OF THIS
AND OTHER CONTROVERSIAL ISSUES. END SUMMARY.

2. (U) AN AFP ARABIC WIRE SERVICE STORY OF JUNE 15TH
REPORTED THAT AN AMERICAN JEWISH DELEGATION VISITING
SANAA HAS BEEN ATTEMPTING TO ARRANGE THE EVACUATION
OF THE YEMENI JEWISH COMMUNITY TO ISRAEL. QUOTING
FROM TWO LOCAL ARTICLES IN AL-SAHWA (THE AWAKENING)
ISLAMIC WEEKLY AND AL-TAJAMU (THE GATHERING) (DETAILS
TO FOLLOW IN SEPTEL), THE WIRE STORY STATED THAT
WHILE THE DELEGATION WAS OSTENSIBLY IN SANAA TO
ARRANGE TO BUILD A JEWISH CULTURAL CENTER FOR THE
YEMENI JEWS, IT WAS NEGOTIATING WITH THE FOREIGN
MINISTER TO HAVE THEM TRAVEL TO ISRAEL. THE REPORT,
FILED BY THE AFP CORRESPONDENT IN SANAA, SAYS THAT
HAYIM TAWIL, A MEMBER OF THE DELEGATION, WAS
CONTACTED BY TELEPHONE ON SATURDAY, BUT REFUSED TO
COMMENT ON THE PURPOSE OF THE DELEGATION'S VISIT
OTHER THAN TO SAY THAT IT HAD A NUMBER OF PURPOSES
AND THAT NOTHING HAD BEEN SETTLED WITH THE YEMENI
AUTHORITIES.

3. (U) THE REPORT GOES ON TO QUOTE FROM THE AL-SAHWA
ARTICLE WHICH REPORTED THAT JOSEPH BECKER, WHO CAME
TO YEMEN IN A JEWISH DELEGATION EARLIER THIS MONTH,
PAID 600,000 DOLLARS TO PREPARE THE WAY FOR THE
TRAVEL OF YEMENI JEWS TO ISRAEL. THE AFP REPORT ALSO

STATES THAT THE AL-SAHWA ARTICLE WAS UNSOURCED. THE
REPORT CONCLUDES BY MENTIONING A SECOND YEMENI
ARTICLE IN AL-TAJAMU, THE WEEKLY PARTY PAPER OF THE
YEMEN GATHERING FOR REFORM, WHICH ALSO CLAIMED THAT

SANAA 02437 00 OF 02 171430Z   000100   S036496
THE AMERICAN DELEGATION WAS SEEKING TO GET ROYG
PERMISSION FOR YEMENI JEWS TO TRAVEL TO ISRAEL.

4. (U) IN RESPONSE TO THE THE AFP STORY, THE MINISTER
OF FOREIGN AFFAIRS, DR. ABDUL KARIM AL-IRYANI, GAVE
AN INTERVIEW WITH THE LOCAL STRINGER OF AL-HAYAT
NEWSPAPER, ABDUL RAHMAN AL-HAIDERI, DENYING THAT
THERE HAS BEEN ANY DEAL TO LET THE YEMENI JEWISH
COMMUNITY TRAVEL TO ISRAEL. THE REPORT WAS
FRONTPAGED ON THE JUNE 16TH ISSUE OF AL-HAYAT UNDER
THE HEADLINE: "AMERICAN JEWISH DELEGATION IN SANAA;
OFFICIAL DENIAL OF ANY EVACUATION." THE ARTICLE
REPORTS THE OFFICIAL YEMENI DENIAL OF THE DETAILS OF
THE AFP REPORT AND THE CLAIMS OF THE ARTICLES WHICH
APPEARED IN THE TWO YEMENI PAPERS. THE FOLLOWING ARE
BLOCK QUOTES FROM THE AL-HAYAT ARTICLE.

5. (U) BEGIN QUOTES:
AN OFFICIAL SOURCE IN SANAA CONFIRMED YESTERDAY THAT
A DELEGATION OF AMERICAN JEWS OF YEMENI ORIGIN IS
VISITING YEMEN CURRENTLY ON A MISSION CONNECTED TO
THE BUILDING OF A TEMPLE AND RELIGIOUS BATH IN THE
REGION WHERE JEWS RESIDE. THIS SOURCE DENIED
ABSOLUTELY WHAT WAS PUBLISHED IN TWO YEMENI PAPERS
ABOUT AN EVACUATION OF YEMEN JEWS TAKING PLACE NOW ...

THIS SOURCE STATED THAT HAYIM AL-TAWIL, WHO

REPRESENTS AN ASSOCIATION OF AMERICAN JEWS OF YEMENI
ORIGIN IN NEW YORK, HAS BEEN VISITING YEMEN TO
CONFIRM THAT YEMENI JEWS ARE PRACTICING THEIR
RELIGIOUS OBSERVANCES FREELY, AND THAT (THE PURPOSE
OF) HIS LATEST VISIT IS TO SIGN A CONTRACT WITH A
BUILDER TO BUILD A TEMPLE AND BATH IN (THE TOWN OF)

RAIDA ... AND HE REQUESTED FROM THE YEMENI
AUTHORITIES PERMISSION FOR TWO STUDENTS TO STUDY IN
NEW YORK.

... JOSEPH BECKER WHO REPRESENTS NATUREI KARTA, WHICH
IS AN ASSOCIATION OPPOSED TO ZIONISM AND DOES NOT
PERMIT THE IMMIGRATION OF JEWS TO ISRAEL. BECKER HAS
VISITED YEMEN MANY TIMES SINCE THE SEVENTIES WITH THE
APPROVAL OF THE YEMENI GOVERNMENT AND WITH THE
RECOMMENDATION OF THE PALESTINE LIBERATION
ORGANIZATION ... IT IS KNOWN THAT THE YEMENI
CONSTITUTION DOES NOT PERMIT DISCRIMINATION BETWEEN
CITIZENS FOR REASONS OF RACE, RELIGION OR ORIGIN.

FOR THE FIRST TIME SINCE YEMEN UNITY OCCURRED AND THE
PUBLISHING OF DOZENS OF PRIVATE NEWSPAPERS, THE
OFFICIAL DAILY PAPER, AL-THAWRA, DIRECTED CRITICISM
OF A NUMBER OF PARTY PAPERS IN A PROMINENT PLACE ON
ITS BACK PAGE UNDER THE HEADLINE, "A NECESSARY
WORD." THE PAPER SAID YESTERDAY: "WE HOPE FROM THE
HEART THAT THE PARTY PAPERS WHICH ATTEMPT TO POISON

YEMENI RELATIONS WITH NEIGHBORING COUNTRIES HAVE A
CLEAR VIEW OF THE FUTURE OF THESE RELATIONS IN ORDER
THAT THERE BE JUSTIFICATION FOR THESE DETRIMENTAL
ACTIONS.
END BLOCK QUOTES.

6. (U) THE AFP REPORT HAS APPARENTLY STIRRED UP SOME
INTEREST AMONG THE INTERNATIONAL WIRE SERVICES. THE
EMBASSY WAS CONTACTED YESTERDAY BY THE ASSOCIATED
PRESS OFFICE IN MANAMA AND ASKED TO COMMENT ON THE

IMMEDIATE

▪▪▪▪▪▪▪▪▪▪▪▪▪▪▪▪▪▪▪▪▪▪▪
CONFIDENTIAL

INCOMING 21

DEPARTMENT OF STATE
ARA/NEA REARCS

PAGE 01   SANAA 03059 280950Z   021198   S010598   SANAA 03059 280950Z   021198   S010598
ACTION: YE (01)

DECLASSIFIED

INFO: ARPD (01) NEA (02) IS (02) RA (01) MRA (01) PR (01)
------------------------ 29/1018Z A3 HS   (TOTAL COPIES: 0091
ACTION NEA-00

INFO LOG-00   ADS-00   AMAD-01   CIAE-00   DODE-00   HA-09   H-01
      INRE-00 INR-01   L-00   NSAE-00 NSCE-00 PA-01   PM-00
      PRS-01   P-01   SP-00   SSO-00   SS-00   USIE-00   /022W
      ------------------02A665 280951Z /12

O 280948Z JUL 91
FM AMEMBASSY SANAA
TO SECSTATE WASHDC IMMEDIATE 5604
INFO AMEMBASSY TEL AVIV

C O N F I D E N T I A L SANAA 03059

FOR NEA AND HA

E.O. 12356: DECL: OADR
TAGS: PREL, PHUM, XF, US, YM
SUBJECT: SALEH'S STATEMENT ON TRAVEL OF YEMENI JEWS

REF: 90 SANAA 6768

1. CONFIDENTIAL - ENTIRE TEXT.

2. IN A LENGTHY WIDE-RANGING INTERVIEW WITH ITALIAN
TELEVISION MONTE CARLO (SIC) PUBLISHED IN THE
GOVERNMENT DAILY "AL-THAWRA" JULY 18, PRESIDENT ALI
ABDULLEH SALEH TOLD INTERVIEWER THAT YEMEN'S
CONSTITUTION GUARANTEES YEMENI JEWS THE SAME RIGHTS
GRANTED TO OTHER YEMENIS INCLUDING ALL POLITICAL AND

SOCIAL RIGHTS.

3. INFORMAL EMBASSY TRANSLATION OF THE INTERVIEWER'S
QUESTION AND SALEH'S ANSWER AS PUBLISHED IN
"AL-THAWRA" FOLLOWS:

Q: STATISTICS INDICATE THAT THERE IS A JEWISH
COMMUNITY IN YEMEN AND THAT THEY DESIRE TO EMIGRATE
TO ISRAEL. IS IT TRUE THAT YOU DO NOT PERMIT THEM
FREEDOM OF CHOICE?

A: FIRST, IT IS NOT TRUE THAT WE HAVE AN SMALL
COMMUNITY. WE HAVE YEMENI JEWS, THEY ARE YEMENI JEWS
IN THEIR COUNTRY. IT IS NOT TRUE THAT THEY WANT TO
EMIGRATE OR DEPART BECAUSE THIS IS THEIR COUNTRY,
THEIR FIRST COUNTRY IS YEMEN AND THE CONSTITUTION
PROTECTS THEM AND GUARANTEES THEM ALL RIGHTS ENJOYED
BY OTHERS. THE YEMENI JEWS ENJOY COMPLETE POLITICAL
AND SOCIAL RIGHTS AND CIVIL RIGHTS.

3. COMMENT: SALEH'S REMARKS AS REPORTED IN THE JULY
18 "AL-THAWRA" CONSTITUTE THE FIRST PUBLIC
PRONOUNCEMENT THAT YEMENI JEWS ENJOY A CONSTITUTIONAL
RIGHT TO TRAVEL THAT WE ARE AWARE OF. SALEH WAS
ASKED A SIMILAR QUESTION ABOUT THE STATUS OF YEMENI
JEWS IN A TELEVISED PRESS INTERVIEW IN SEPTEMBER 1990
(REFTEL). HIS ANSWER THEN OVERSTATED THE RIGHTS OF
YEMENI JEWS TO TRAVEL AND DID NOT LINK THE CIVIL
RIGHTS OF YEMENI JEWS TO THE ROY CONSTITUTION. SINCE
THAT TIME, A FEW MORE YEMENI JEWS HAVE TRAVELED
ABROAD AND THE GOVERNMENT HAS EXPLICITLY STATED, IN

PRIVATE, THAT YEMENI JEWS ENJOY THE SAME
CONSTITUTIONAL RIGHT TO TRAVEL AS OTHER YEMENIS.
STRATHEARN

IMMEDIATE ■■■■■■■■■■■■■■■■■■■■■■■ CONFIDENTIAL ℞ INCOMING 17

DEPARTMENT OF STATE
ARA/NEA REARCS

PAGE 01   SANAA 03757 310737Z   033146   S001289   SANAA 03757 310737Z   033146   S001289
ACTION: YE (01)

INFO: ARPD (01) IS (02) RA (01)
-------------------- 31/1118Z A4 NW   (TOTAL COPIES: 005)
ACTION NEA-00

INFO LOG-00 ADS-00 AID-00 AMAD-01 CIAE-00 DODE-00 ANHR-01
      EB-00   HA-09   H-01   INRE-00 INR-01   IO-19   LAB-04
      L-00   NSAE-00 NSCE-00 OIC-02   OMB-01   PA-01   PM-00
      PRS-01 P-01   RP-10   SCT-03   SIL-00   SNP-00 SP-00
      SR-00   SSO-00 SS-00   STR-18   TRSE-00 T-01   USIE-00
      /086W
                ------------------8F7C6E 310737Z /38

O 310736Z AUG 91
FM AMEMBASSY SANAA
TO SECSTATE WASHDC IMMEDIATE 6003
INFO AMEMBASSY TEL AVIV

C O N F I D E N T I A L SANAA 03757

FOR NEA AND HA

E.O. 12356: DECL: OADR
TAGS: PREL, PHUM, XF, US, YM
SUBJECT: VICE PRESIDENT AL-BIDH COMMENT ON STATUS OF
--   YEMENI JEWS

REF: SANAA 3059

1. CONFIDENTIAL - ENTIRE TEXT.

2. GOVERNMENT-OWNED DAILY "AL-THAWRA PUBLISHED
AUGUST 24 AN INTERVIEW WITH VICE CHAIRMAN OF THE

PRESIDENTIAL COUNCIL ALI SALEM AL-BIDH. THE
INTERVIEW WAS CONDUCTED IN LONDON BY A REPORTER FOR
THE ARABIC LANGUAGE NEWSPAPER "AL-ARAB". IN THE
INTERVIEW AL-BIDH COMMENTED ON THE STATUS OF YEMENI
JEWS. THE VICE PRESIDENT EITHER WAS UNAWARE OF THE
TRUE GEOGRAPHIC DISTRIBUTION OF YEMENI JEWS, PERHAPS
DUE TO HIS YEARS OF ISOLATION FROM THE YEMENI JEWISH
COMMUNITY AS A CITIZEN/OFFICIAL OF THE PEOPLES
DEMOCRATIC REPUBLIC OF YEMEN, OR WAS MISQUOTED.
WHILE AL-BIDH'S COMMENT BREAKS NO NEW GROUND, WE
REPORT THE VICE PRESIDENT'S REMARKS FOR THE RECORD.

3. INFORMAL EMBASSY TRANSLATION OF THE INTERVIEWER'S
QUESTION AND AL-BIDH'S ANSWER AS PUBLISHED IN
"AL-THAWRA" FOLLOWS:

Q: SOME PRESS REPORTS MENTION THAT A YEMENI JEWISH
BUSINESSMAN SEEKS TO TRANSPORT YEMENI JEWS IN
EXCHANGE FOR USD 50,000 THOUSAND (SIC) FOR EACH JEW.
CAN YOU COMMENT ON THESE REPORTS?

A: IN FACT WE HEAR ABOUT THINGS WHICH DO NOT EXIST.
I AM AWARE THAT THERE ARE YEMENI JEWS LIVING IN THE
RAYDAH AREA. THEY ARE YEMENIS, THEY DON'T FACE ANY
SPECIAL PROBLEM. WE DO NOT CONSIDER THEM A PROBLEM,
FOR THEY ARE YEMENIS PRACTICING THEIR JEWISH
RELIGION. A YEMENI NEWSPAPER INTERVIEWED ONE OF
THEM. I HAVE NO COMMENT ON THESE REPORTS EXCEPT TO
SAY THE REPUBLIC OF YEMEN'S ARAB CHARACTER IS OBVIOUS
TO ALL. END TEXT

STRATHEARN

CONFIDENTIAL

ROUTINE |||||||||||||||||||||||| $\cancel{R}$ INCOMING 44

CONFIDENTIAL

DEPARTMENT OF STATE
ARA/NEA REARCS

RESULT OF COOPERATING WITH FOREIGN JEWISH GROUPS AND
THE U.S. ON THIS ISSUE. AL-MUSTAQBAL ALSO RAISED THE
SPECTER OF YEMENI JEWISH EMIGRANTS SERVING AS ISRAELI
SOLDIERS. THE ARTICLE ENDED BY STRESSING, AS DID
PRESIDENT SALEH (REFTEL) THAT YEMENI JEWS ARE YEMENIS
AND ENJOY THE SAME RIGHTS TO TRAVEL ABROAD AS OTHER
YEMENIS.

5. COMMENT: THE AUTHOR'S SOURCE, MR. HABIB, AND/OR
OTHERS WAS REASONABLY WELL-INFORMED ABOUT THAT LAST
ICROJOY VISIT. THE ARTICLE NOTES THAT TAWIL REQUESTED
PERMISSION FOR SOME YEMENI JEWS TO TRAVEL AND CLAIMS
THAT ICROJOY REQUESTED THAT A "MR. ZINDANI" BE ALLOWED
TO LEAVE, BUT THAT ZINDANI "WAS HESITANT". THE
ARTICLE ALSO NOTED THAT "AL-QATABI" AGREED TO TRAVEL.
STRATHEARN

F 311232Z JUL 91
FM AMEMBASSY SANAA
TO SECSTATE WASHDC 5653
INFO AMEMBASSY TEL AVIV
AMCONSUL JERUSALEM

C O N F I D E N T I A L SANAA 03125

SUBJECT: YEMENI PRESS REPORT ON YEMENI JEWS

REF: SANAA 3059

1. SUMMARY: YEMENI WEEKLY "AL-MUSTAQBAL"
ACCOUNT OF ICROJOY DELEGATION'S MAY VISIT TO YEMEN
IMPLIES ROYG SUCCUMBED TO U.S. POLITICAL AND ECONOMIC
PRESSURE TO ALLOW THE VISIT AND PERMIT YEMENI JEWS TO
TRAVEL. THE ARTICLE ALSO PROVIDES SELECTIVE INSIGHTS
INTO YEMENI JEWISH ATTITUDES TOWARD IMMIGRATION. END
SUMMARY.

2. THE JULY 21 EDITION OF YEMENI WEEKLY
"AL-MUSTAQBAL" INCLUDED AN ACCOUNT OF AN ATTEMPT BY
YEMENI JOURNALIST MOHAMED ABDULLAH AL-ASAR TO
INTERVIEW VISITING ICROJOY REPRESENTATIVES DR. HAIM
TAWIL AND YUSEF LEVY. WHILE MUCH OF THE ARTICLE IS
BOMBASTIC AND CONVEYS A CONTRIVED SENSE OF INTRIGUE,
THE ARTICLE DOES OFFER INSIGHTS INTO THE ATTITUDES OF
YEMENI JEWS AND MUSLIMS TOWARD JEWISH IMMIGRATION.
POST IS POUCHING A COPY OF THE ARTICLE AND A ROUGH
TRANSLATION TO NEA ARP. MAIN POINTS OF THE ARTICLE
FOLLOW.

3. JEWISH ATTITUDES TOWARD ICROJOY AND
IMMIGRATION: A YEMENI JEW NAMED SAID HABIB,
APPARENTLY UNHAPPY WITH ICROJOY ACTIVITIES IN YEMEN,
WAS THE OSTENSIBLE SOURCE OF MUCH OF THE ARTICLE.
HABIB REPORTEDLY SAID YEMENI JEWS HAD REQUESTED
ASSISTANCE FROM THE ROYG SO THEY WOULD NOT HAVE TO
RELY ON ASSISTANCE FROM FOREIGN JEWISH GROUPS AND HAD
ASKED ROYG FONMIN AL-IRYANI TO END VISITS OF FOREIGN
JEWISH DELEGATIONS. HABIB WAS QUOTED AS SAYING THESE
DELEGATIONS WERE "TRAFFICKING IN MEN". ACCORDING TO
HABIB, YEMENI JEWS DO NOT WISH TO LEAVE YEMEN AND
WOULD NOT ALLOW ANY JEW WHO DID LEAVE TO RETURN.
NONETHELESS, HABIB ADMITS IN THE ARTICLE TO ASKING THE
ICROJOY DELEGATION TO "TAKE ME WITH YOU" DURING HIS
NEXT VISIT.

4. "AL-MUSTAQBAL'S" RESPONSE:
CRITICIZED THE ROYG FOR ALLOWING

5. JEWISH DELEGATIONS TO INTERFERE IN INTERNAL
YEMENI MATTERS AND IMPLIED THAT SUCH VISITS WERE A
QUID PRO QUO FOR ECONOMIC ASSISTANCE. THE ARTICLE
WENT ON TO PREDICT THE ROYG WILL SUFFER POLITICALLY
BOTH INTERNALLY AND AMONG OTHER ARAB STATES AS A

[handwritten: OPTION Jews /AF - another spin]

CONFIDENTIAL

IMMEDIATE

ACTION

▪▪▪▪▪▪▪▪▪▪▪▪▪▪▪▪▪▪▪▪▪▪▪▪

CONFIDENTIAL

DEPARTMENT OF STATE
ARA/NEA REARCS

~R~ INCOMING 19

PAGE 01   SANAA 03656 261355Z   023744   S012190
ACTION: YE (01)

INFO: ARPD (01) NEA (02) RA (01) MRA (01) IS (02) PR (01)
                    ------------ 26/1420Z A4 HS   (TOTAL COPIES: PGS)
ACTION NEA-00

INFO LOG-00 ADS-00 AID-00 AMAD-01 CIAE-00 DODE-00 ANHR-01
      EB-00   HA-09   H-01   INRE-00 INR-01   IO-19   LAB-04
      L-00   NSAE-00 NSCE-00 OIC-02   OMB-01   PA-01   PM-00
      PRS-01 P-01   RP-10   SCT-03   SIL-00   SNP-00   SP-00
      SR-00   SSO-00 SS-00   STR-18   TRSE-00 T-01   USIE-00
      /086W
                    ------------8D2BBB 261355Z /38

O 261355Z AUG 91
FM AMEMBASSY SANAA
TO SECSTATE WASHDC IMMEDIATE 5968
INFO AMEMBASSY TEL AVIV

C O N F I D E N T I A L SANAA 03656

FOR NEA/ARP AND HA

E.O.: 12356: DECL: OADR
TAGS: PHUM, PREL, SCUL, YE
SUBJECT: SHOSHONA TUBI PERFORMANCE TELEVISED

1. CONFIDENTIAL - ENTIRE TEXT.

2. SUMMARY: YEMEN TV AUGUST 25 BROADCAST MUSICAL
PERFORMANCE OF U.S. CITIZEN YEMENI JEW WHO HAD
VISITED YEMEN IN MAY-JUNE 1991. THE PROGRAM MADE A
POSITIVE IMPRESSION ON THE YEMENIS WE HAVE SPOKEN TO
AND SEEMS TO HAVE EVOKED FAVORABLE MEMORIES OF YEMENI

JEW-MOSLEM RELATIONS. END SUMMARY

3. DURING MAY-JUNE 1991 VISIT OF INTERNATIONAL
COMMITTEE FOR THE REVIVAL OF THE JEWS OF YEMEN
(ICROJOY) DELEGATION, SHOSHONA TUBI (YEMENI NAME
SHAMA' TAYBI), AN ACCOMPLISHED SINGER-MUSICIAN AND
MEMBER OF THE DELEGATION, WAS INVITED TO YEMEN
TELEVISION STUDIO TO TAPE AN INTERVIEW/PERFORMANCE OF
YEMENI ARABIC AND HEBREW SONGS FOR BROADCAST AT AN
UNSPECIFIED LATER DATE. THE INTERVIEW/PERFORMANCE
WAS AIRED AFTER THE EVENING NEWS AUGUST 25.

4. THE INTERVIEW BEGAN WITH THE IDENTIFICATION OF
MS. TUBI AS A YEMENI JEW WHO HAD LEFT SANAA AT AGE
FOUR IN 1948 AND WAS NOW SETTLED IN THE U.S.
PICTURES OF MS. TUBI AND HER FAMILY AT THE TIME OF
THEIR DEPARTURE WERE DISPLAYED, AS WERE OTHER
PICTURES OF MS. TUBI IN HER TRADITIONAL YEMENI
WEDDING OUTFIT AND HER SON AND DAUGHTER IN
TRADITIONAL DRESS APPARENTLY PERFORMING TRADITIONAL
DANCE. BETWEEN SONGS, THE MALE YEMENI INTERVIEWER,
WHO WAS OBVIOUSLY ENJOYING THE SONGS AND DISCUSSION,
ASKED QUESTIONS THAT FOCUSED ON MS. TUBI'S TIES TO
YEMEN AND THE LINKS OF YEMENIS (JEWS AND MOSLEMS) IN
THE U.S. AND "PALESTINE" TO THEIR HOMELAND.

5. THE INTERVIEWER ASKED IF MS. TUBI HAD ENCOUNTERED
PROBLEMS IN RETURNING TO YEMEN AND SOUGHT HER
COMMENTS ON THE STATUS AND CONDITIONS OF YEMENI
JEWS. IN EACH INSTANCE, MS. TUBI RESPONDED DEFTLY
BUT WITH FRANKNESS. THE ROYG HAD NO REASON TO BE

DISPLEASED WITH HER ANSWERS AND NO EDITING OF THE
INTERVIEW OF THE DISCUSSION PORTION OF THE PROGRAM
WAS NECESSARY OR APPARENT.

6. OUR SAMPLING OF YEMENIS WHO SAW THE ONE HOUR
TWENTY MINUTE SHOW, "AN EVENING WITH AN ARTIST"
INDICATES MS. TUBI'S PERFORMANCE WAS VERY WELL
RECEIVED. VIRTUALLY ALL YEMENIS WE HAVE TALKED TO
EXPRESSED PLEASURE WITH THE INTERVIEW/PERFORMANCE AND
SEVERAL RECALLED WITH FONDNESS YEMENI JEWISH
NEIGHBORS WHO LEFT WITH OPERATION MAGIC CARPET. A
NUMBER HAVE ASKED IF WE HAVE RECORDINGS OF THE
PERFORMANCE AND ONE NEWSPAPER EDITOR ASKED TO BE
INTRODUCED TO MS. TUBI.

7. COMMENT: "EVENING WITH AN ARTIST" APPEARS TO
HAVE STRUCK A CHORD WITH YEMENIS. OBVIOUSLY THEY
ENJOYED HEARING AN EMIGRANT YEMENI JEW SAYING NICE
THINGS ABOUT YEMEN AND YEMENIS AND TOOK PRIDE IN
HEARING AND SEEING AN ACCOMPLISHED "YEMENI" ARTIST.
WE ARE STILL TRYING TO DETERMINE IF THE ROYG HAD A
HIDDEN AGENDA IN AIRING THE PROGRAM NOW. STRATHEARN

Opium Jews (handwritten annotation)

CONFIDENTIAL

ROUTINE

ACTION

∎∎∎∎∎∎∎∎∎∎∎∎∎∎∎∎∎∎∎∎∎
UNCLASSIFIED

INCOMING 14

DEPARTMENT OF STATE
ARA/NEA REARCS

ℝ

DECLASSIFIED

PAGE 01   SANAA 03548 201224Z   015263   S031381
ACTION: YE (01)

INFO: ARPD (01)   RA (01)   IS (02)
         ------------------ 20/1245Z   A4   HS   (TOTAL COPIES: 005)

ACTION NEA-00

INFO   LOG-00   ADS-00   AID-00   AMAD-01   CIAE-00   DODE-00   EB-00
       HA-09   H-01   INRE-00   INR-01   IO-19   LAB-04   L-00
       NSAE-00   NSCE-00   OIC-02   PA-02   PRS-01   P-01   RP-10
       SIL-00   SP-00   SR-00   SS-00   STR-18   TRSE-00   USIE-00
       /079W
                 ------------------8AF577 201224Z /38

R 201223Z AUG 91
FM AMEMBASSY SANAA
TO SECSTATE WASHDC 5903

UNCLAS SANAA 03548

E.O. 12356: N/A
TAGS: PHUM, YE
SUBJECT: YEMENI GOVERNMENT REFUSES "ZIONIST"
-          OFFER TO HELP YEMENI JEWS

GOVERNMENT DAILY "AL THAWRA" PUBLISHED A SHORT
ITEM ON THE BACK PAGE OF ITS AUGUST 20 EDITION
STATING THAT THE ROYG HAD REFUSED AN OFFER BY
UNIDENTIFIED U.S. "ZIONIST" GROUPS TO PAY A
MONTHLY STIPEND TO ASSIST YEMENI JEWS.
ACCORDING TO THE ARTICLE, THE ROYG CONSIDERED
THE OFFER INTERFERENCE IN YEMEN'S INTERNAL
AFFAIRS.   STRATHEARN

Φ PHUM
Jews ✓

Do we know anything more?
OtL

DEPARTMENT OF STATE	IS/FPC/CDR *CIDN* Date *5/4/95*	
(X) RELEASE ( ) DECLASSIFY	MR Cases Only:	
( ) EXCISE ( ) DECLASSIFY	EO Citations _____	
( ) DENY IN PART		
( ) DELETE Non-Responsive Info	_____ TS authority to.	
FOIA Exemptions _____	( ) CLASSIFY as ( ) S or ( ) C OADR	
PA Exemptions _____	( ) DOWNGRADE TS to ( ) S or ( ) C OADR	

DECLASSIFIED

UNCLASSIFIED

EMBASSY OF THE
UNITED STATES OF AMERICA

December 20, 1991

The Immigration Inspector
Immigration and Naturalization Service

Dear Sir or Madam:

The persons listed below have been issued non-immigrant
visas by the American Embassy in Sanaa, Yemen. Their
visas were incorrectly annotated concerning the sponsoring
organization in the United States. The correct annotation
should read: "sponsored by the International Committee
for the Rescue of the Jews of Yemen" (ICROJOY). We
understand that two members of ICROJOY will be
accompanying these travellers through customs and
inspection formalities.

The travellers are:

Yahya Daoud Sabari
(children)
Azra Yahya
Belqis Yahya
Salem Yahya
Azri Yahya
Yahya Yahya (correct as given)
yohuda.
Hamama Yahya Dawod
(children)
Saied Yahya
Shamaia Yahya

Saied Yahya Habib (father)
Haida Yahya Dawod (mother)
(children)
Libya Saeed
Amrica Saeed
Alamania Saeed
Warda Saeed

Thank you for your assistance.

Sincerely yours,

John L. Lister
Second Secretary
American Embassy, Sanaa

United States Department of State

Assistant Secretary of State for
Near Eastern and South Asian Affairs

Washington, D.C. 20520-6242

Dr. Hayim Tawil
Chairman ICROJOY
150 Nassau Street
Suite 1238
New York, New York 10038

Dear Dr. Tawil:

On behalf of the Department of State, I would like to thank you
for your letter of June 24, 1992, expressing ICROJOY's
appreciation for the Department's efforts in behalf of the
Yemeni Jews.

As you and I discussed in June, the United States Government is
committed to continuing its dialogue with the Government of the
Republic of Yemen on the status of the Jewish community in
Yemen. We continue to encourage the Government to ensure that
all its citizens enjoy the rights of full citizenship
guaranteed under the Yemeni Constitution, including freedom of
travel. In this regard, we will continue to work closely with
representatives of the Jewish community in the United States.

We are happy that thirteen Sabari family members have recently
been allowed to travel to be reunited with family members
outside Yemen. We hope to see more Jewish citizens follow
suit. I assure you that assisting ICROJOY and the Amercian
Jewish community in their humanitarian efforts to help Jewish
citizens of Yemen remains an important priority for the United
States Government in its relations with Yemen.

Sincerely,

Edward P. Djerejian

RICHARD SCHIFTER
4520 EAST-WEST HIGHWAY
SUITE 200
BETHESDA, MARYLAND 20814

PHONE: 301/652-4288
FAX: 301/656-3681

November 9, 1992.

Dr. Hayim Tawil
ICROJOY
150 Nassau street, Suite 1238
New York, N.Y. 10038

Dear Dr. Tawil:

Thank you very much for your kind recent letter.

Let me use this opportunity to extend my thanks to you for the outstanding work done by you on behalf of the Jews of Yemen during my tenure as Assistant Secretary of State for Human Rights and Humanitarian Affairs. Into a situation in which there was turmoil and confusion as to the role to be played by interested American Jewish organizations you brought order and coherence. Your work was highly regarded by the United States Government, both by the State Department and by members of Congress. The authorities of the Government of Yemen also came to respect you as a person on whose word they could rely.

Most importantly, you brought hope and contacts with the outside world to the Jews remaining in Yemen and helped some of them leave that country. Your knowledge, your gentle approach and your tact made it all possible. All those concerned with the fate of Yemen's remaining Jews and more broadly all those concerned with the cause of human rights are indebted to you for taking on this difficult task and for accomplishing so much.

Please accept my very best wishes.

Sincerely,

Richard Schifter

LEE A. HAMILTON, INDIANA
Chairman

SAM GEJDENSON, CONNECTICUT
TOM LANTOS, CALIFORNIA
ROBERT G. TORRICELLI, NEW JERSEY
HOWARD L. BERMAN, CALIFORNIA
GARY L. ACKERMAN, NEW YORK
HARRY JOHNSTON, FLORIDA
ELIOT L. ENGEL, NEW YORK
ENI F.H. FALEOMAVAEGA, AMERICAN SAMOA
JAMES L. OBERSTAR, MINNESOTA
CHARLES E. SCHUMER, NEW YORK
MATTHEW G. MARTINEZ, CALIFORNIA
ROBERT A. BORSKI, PENNSYLVANIA
DONALD M. PAYNE, NEW JERSEY
ROBERT E. ANDREWS, NEW JERSEY
ROBERT MENENDEZ, NEW JERSEY
SHERROD BROWN, OHIO
CYNTHIA A. McKINNEY, GEORGIA
MARIA CANTWELL, WASHINGTON
ALCEE L. HASTINGS, FLORIDA
ERIC FINGERHUT, OHIO
PETER DEUTSCH, FLORIDA
ALBERT RUSSELL WYNN, MARYLAND
DON EDWARDS, CALIFORNIA
FRANK McCLOSKEY, INDIANA
THOMAS C. SAWYER, OHIO
(VACANCY)

MICHAEL H. VAN DUSEN
Chief of Staff

BENJAMIN A. GILMAN, NEW YORK
Ranking Republican Member

WILLIAM F. GOODLING, PENNSYLVANIA
JIM LEACH, IOWA
TOBY ROTH, WISCONSIN
OLYMPIA J. SNOWE, MAINE
HENRY J. HYDE, ILLINOIS
DOUG BEREUTER, NEBRASKA
CHRISTOPHER H. SMITH, NEW JERSEY
DAN BURTON, INDIANA
JAN MEYERS, KANSAS
ELTON GALLEGLY, CALIFORNIA
ILEANA ROS-LEHTINEN, FLORIDA
CASS BALLENGER, NORTH CAROLINA
SARA ROHRABACHER, CALIFORNIA
DAVID LEVY, NEW YORK
DONALD A. MANZULLO, ILLINOIS
LINCOLN DIAZ-BALART, FLORIDA
EDWARD R. ROYCE, CALIFORNIA

RICHARD J. GARON
Republican Chief of Staff

One Hundred Third Congress

Congress of the United States
Committee on Foreign Affairs
House of Representatives
Washington, DC 20515

March 17, 1993

His Excellency Mohsin A. Alaini
Ambassador
Embassy of the Republic of Yemen
Suite 705
2600 Virginia Avenue, N.W.
Washington, D.C. 20037

Dear Mr. Ambassador:

We write to thank you and your government for the latest developments concerning the Jews of Yemen and your allowing additional families to travel freely abroad.

It is indeed an encouraging sign for us here in the United States as well as for democracy in the world at large. This important humanitarian policy of the Yemeni government is noted by many of us in Congress and is a step which will help improve our bilateral relations. Other steps you had taken were all important, including: Yemen's favorable performance supporting U.S. relief efforts in Somalia; the signing of the convention on the prohibition of the development, production, stockpiling, and use of chemical weapons, and on their destruction; the resolving of Yemen's border dispute with Oman; and the ongoing serious border negotiations with Saudi Arabia.

We understand Yemen expects to hold multi-party parliamentary elections on April 27, 1993, with full participation for Yemeni citizens, regardless of race, creed or gender. Such successful elections would be an affirmation of Yemen's status as a democratic nation in the Middle East. We urge your government to continue to grant complete freedom of travel with no restrictions whatsoever to all Yemenis, including the indigenous Yemeni Jews, following the upcoming elections.

March 17, 1993
Page 2

We appreciate your consideration of this letter and hope we can continue to work together on these issues.

With best regards,

Sincerely,

Benjamin A. Gilman
Ranking Republican Member

Lee H. Hamilton
Chairman

LHH/MVD:kpw

Bibliography

Ahroni, Reuben. "Tribulations and Aspirations in Yemenite Hebrew Literature." *HUCA* 49 (1978), 267–294.

———. "The Theme of Love in Yemenite Hebrew Literature." *HAR* 4 (1980), 1–13.

———. "From Bustan al-'Uqul to Qissat al-Batul: Some Aspects of Jewish-Muslim Religious Polemics in Yemen." *HUCA* 52 (1981), 311–360.

———. *Yemenite Jewry: Origins, Culture, and Literature.* Bloomington, 1986.

Barer, Shlomo. *The Magic Carpet.* New York, 1952.

Brown, William R. "The Yemeni Dilemma." *Middle East Journal* 17 (1963), 349–367.

Daum G. Werner. *Yemen: 3000 Years of Art and Civilization in Arabia Felix.* Innsbruck and Frankfurt am Main, 1988.

Dunbar, Charles, "The Unification of Yemen: Process, Politics and Porspects," *Middle East Journal* 46 (1992), 456–76.

Goitein, S. D., ed., *From the Land of Sheba: Tales of the Jews of Yemen,* trans. Christopher Fremantle. New York, 1947.

———. "The Jews of Yemen." In *Religion in the Middle East,* ed. A.J. Arberry. Vol. 1, 226–235.

———. "The Social Structure of Jewish Education in Yemen." In *Jewish Societies in the Middle East: Community, Culture and Authority,* ed. Shlomo Dreshen and Walter P. Zenner, 211–233. Washington 1982.

Halkin, Abraham, ed., *Moses Maimonides' Epistle to Yemen,* trans. Boaz Cohen. New York, 1952.

Marks, Paul F. *Bibliography of Literature Concerning Yemenite-Jewish Music.* Detroit, 1973.

Neubauer, A. "The Literature of the Jews of Yemen." *JQR* 3 (1891), 604–621.

Nini, Yehudah. *The Jews of the Yemen, 1800-1914*. Chur, 1991.

Parfitt, Tudor. *The Road to Redemption : the Jews of the Yemen, 1900–1950*. Leiden, 1996

Pritchard, James B. ed. *Solomon and Sheba*. London, 1974.

R.B. Serjeant and Ronald Cock. ed. *San'a: An Arabian Islamic City*. London, 1983.

Tritton, A. S. *The Rise of the Imams of Sanaa*. London, 1925.

van Beek, Gus W. "Frankincense and Myrrh." *BA* 23 (1960), 70–95.

Wenner, Manfred W. *Modern Yemen 1918–1966*. Baltimore, 1967.

Index

A

Abdu, Miriam, 188, 191
Abdul Aziz, 138, 189, 227
Abdul Rahman, 235, 249
Abdullah, 188, 191
Abed, son of Sheikh Asurabi, 168–169, 196
Abushwareb, Mujahid, 123, 193, 195–197, 206, 211–212
Adani, R. Shlomo, 15
Aharon, Hayim, 71
Ahmad, 18
Ahmad bin Hassan ibn al-Imam al-Qasim, 13
Ahmed, the embassy driver, 227
Ain, Stewart, 254
Alaini, 173
al-Aini, Mohsin, 63, 125–127, 186, 262
Al-Ashtal, 251
al-Baidh, Ali Salem, 183
al-Garni, Menahem, 234, 252–253
al-Garni, Mori Yaish, 38, 43, 234
Algemeiner Journal, 151
al-Ghani, Abdul Aziz, 40, 71, 247
al-Hadrani, Ibrahim, 71
al-Harithi, 241
al-Iryani, Abdul Karim, 39, 41, 43, 100, 126–127, 129, 138–139, 147, 150, 152–154, 161–162, 169–170, 173, 178, 184, 188, 196–197, 211, 219, 224, 228–230, 233, 237–241, 244–247, 249–250, 252–253, 262
al-Kibsi, Ibrahim, 40
al-Mutawakel, Yhia M., 40
Aloni, Shulamit, 157–158
al-Shajeini, Ahmed, 100
al-Thawr, Ali, 40
al-Uthrub, Ali, 40

American Council to Save Yemenite Jewry, 62, 77, 104
American Jewish Committee, 76, 107
American Jewish Congress, 80, 98
American Jewish World, 151
American Sephardic Federation, 117, 129, 178–179
Amitai, Yaakov, 201
Amitay, Mike, 106, 109
Amos, 135, 150, 235
Anti-Defamation League, 98, 107
Aref, son of sheikh of Ghuraz region, 196
Argaman, David, 186
Arusi, Ratzon, 184
Aryeh, 61
Association for the Advancement of Culture in Israel, 71
Asurabi, Sheikh, 168, 196, 227, 268
a-Tawila, 243
Atzar mother, 57
Atzar, Afyah, 55
Atzar, Miriam, 18, 50
Atzar, Moshe, 18, 49, 55, 57, 67, 72–73, 75, 84, 124, 255
Atzar, Salem ben Yousef, 230
Atzar, Yosef, 267
B
B'nai B'rith, 107
B'nai B'rith Messenger, 151
Bacher, Yosef, 78, 164–165
Baker & Botts, 273
Baker, James A., III, 63, 111, 128, 213, 225, 231–233
Barnes, Police officer, 257
Baron, Jeffrey, 169
Barr-Nea, Sir Moshe, 79, 88–91, 98–99
Bashari family, 274

Bashari, Salem, 253
Bayer, Abraham, 80, 99, 219
Bedar, Hamoud, 71
ben Aharon, Yossi, 150, 240, 269
Ben Avraham, David, 50, 54, 58, 67, 70, 83
Ben-Gurion, David, 134
Ben-Shalom, Ovadiah, 71
bint Irgi, Shameh, 274
Bodlander, Debbie, 224, 250, 260
Boni family, 274
Boni, Sleiman, 274
Boni, Yhia, 28–29
Boston Jewish Advocate, 62
Bush, George, 170, 173, 211, 225, 231–232, 250, 258
C
Canadian Jewish News, 62, 151
Canon, Morris, 200–201, 203
Carlebach, R. Shlomo, 83–84
Carter, James Earl, 41, 115–116, 179
Changeux, Simone, 48
Cohen, Shalom, 67
Cohen-Avidov, Meir, 69
Committee for the Jews of Yemen of America, 178
Conference of Presidents of Major Jewish Organizations, 98, 269
Crowder, Richard T., 173
D
D'Amato, Alfonse, 103, 155, 250, 258, 272
Dahari Halla, Amram, 112
Dahari Halla, Hamida, 112
Dahari Halla, Hayim, 143, 148–149, 153
Dahari Halla, Moshe, 143, 148–149, 153, 155, 161, 164, 192, 195–197, 200–201, 203–206, 209, 212, 229, 232, 234, 244
Dahari Halla, Salem Ben-Yehudah, 112, 128
Dahari Halla, Sarah, 93, 111, 124, 127–128, 130, 132, 137, 139, 141–143, 148–149, 155, 160–161, 163–164, 168, 192, 195
Dahari Halla, Yagov, 112
Damari, Shoshana, 117
Dar, Raya, 37
DeBelle, Georgia, 148, 150, 163–164, 169, 192

DeConcini, Dennis, 63, 103–104, 106
Demjanjuk, John, 61
Djerejian, Edward P., 262
Dulzin, Arie, 71
Dunbar, Charles, 122–124, 145, 147, 163–164, 169, 171, 173, 185, 191, 197, 205–206, 208, 210, 219, 223–224, 227–230, 232–233, 237–238, 241, 244, 246–248, 250–251
E
Eban, Abba, 67
el-Dahabani, 243
Eli, Ovadiah, 101
Elliott, Deborah, 210
England, Bernard, 104
Exxon Corporation, 120
F
Faiz, Hayim, 268
Faiz, R. David, 268
Faiz, Sleiman, 168, 171, 191, 193, 235
Faiz, Yakub, 93
Faiz, Yhia, 235
Farouk (friend of William Thomas), 38
Farsakh, Andrea, 215, 219, 250, 262–263
Fisher, Jane, 106
G
Gadi, 135, 150
Gal, Shlomo, 151, 270
Gamliel, Aryeh, 100–101
George, the concierge, 245, 251
Gephen, Barbara, 95–96, 98
Gephen, Doug, 95–96, 98
Gilboa, Moshe, 71
Gilman, Benjamin A., 103, 155, 173–176, 186, 219, 224–225, 229, 231, 250, 255, 257–258, 260, 262, 272
Gilman, Esther, 256
Goldin, Harrison, 196
Goldstein, Robert M., 72
Golon, Anne, 48
Golon, Anne & Serge, 48
Golon, David, 45
Goloubinoff, Cohi, 49, 81–82, 94, 103, 216
Goloubinoff, Pierre, 45, 48–54, 59–61, 76, 81, 84, 94–95, 98, 106–107, 109, 118, 121, 124, 127, 130, 132, 134–136, 216–218, 255
Goloubinow, Sergei Petrovitch, 47

Goloubinow, Vsevolod Sergeivitch, 47–48
Grafi, Shlomo, 66–67, 77–78, 80, 82, 89–
  90, 92, 98–99, 102, 104, 109, 118, 124,
  127, 130, 254–256, 264, 270
Graham, Robert, 103
Grama, Israel, 178
Greater Phoenix Jewish News, 77, 81, 151
Grossman, Haika, 68
Grove, Neil, 82
H
Haas, Richard, 256
Habib family, 265
Habib, Said, 235, 237, 245, 248, 250, 253,
  265
Habib, Sleiman, 235, 237, 245, 271
Hadad, Arik, 184
HaLevi, Yhia Yitzhak, 131, 139
Halla, Avraham Yitzhak, 93
Halla, Salem, 127
Halla, Yehudah, 39
Halla, Yhia Yehudah, 93
Halpert, Shmuel, 158
Hamad-a-Din, Ahmad, 7, 16, 19, 105
Hamad-a-Din, Yhia, 16, 131
Hamami, Daoud, 45, 50, 53–58, 203
Hamami, Hawida, 274
Hamami, Yaakov, 274
Hamilton, Lee H., 107, 173–174, 176,
  186, 224, 250, 262
Hammer, Zevulun, 67
Hanson, Brad, 169, 196, 253
Harash, Sheikh, 267
Hassan (friend of William Thomas), 38
Hassan, Ahmed, 152–153, 169–170
Hebrew Immigrant Aid Society, 82
Herzl, Tova, 67
Herzog, Chaim, 71
Hibshoosh, Yehiel, 28, 154
Hillel, Shlomo, 67
Hubara, Varda, 160, 163, 168
Hughes, Arthur, 262–263, 271
Hunt Oil Company, 120, 162, 179, 226,
  249–250
Hussein, Saddam, 107, 171–172, 184, 187,
  194–195, 205, 225, 232, 251
I
Irgi, Salim ibn Said, 274
Irgi, Yhia ibn Said, 274

J
Jeredi, Salem, 268
Jerusalem Post, 61, 77, *269*
Jewish Agency, 17
Jewish Chronicle, 151
Jewish Defense League of Israel, 71
Jewish Federation, 81
Jewish Floridian, 151
Jewish Ledger, 151
Jewish Monthly, 83
Jewish Observer, 151
Jewish Press, 71
Jewish Telegraphic Agency, 82, 90, 151
Jewish Times, 151
Jewish Week, 254
Jewish World, 151, 274
Johnson, Laurie, 104, 106–107, 109, 118,
  121–122, 124, 136, 150, 189, 204, 215
Joint Distribution Committee, 77, 98–99,
  156, 226, 240, 271
K
Kach, 71
Kadi, Tzemah, 186–187
Kahalani, Avigdor, 150, 184, 214, 217, 270
Kahanamen, Rav, 69
Kahane, Meir, 68, 71
Kapeliuk, Amnon, 51
Katabi family, 260, 274
Katabi, Bracha, 274
Katabi, Daoud, 93, 252–257, 260, 274
Katabi, Gusna, 274
Katabi, Jamla, 274
Katabi, Lawza, 274
Katabi, Naama, 274
Katabi, Rumah, 274
Katabi, Yhia, 274
Katabi, Yitzhak, 67
Katabi, Yosef, 274
Kelly, John H., 211, 246
Khamis, Muhammad, 39, 41
Khubani family, 274
Khubani, Binyamin, 234–235, 245, 267
Khubani, Yosef, 93
Kimmitt, Robert, 211
Kirkpatrick, Jean, 113
Kirschner, Joel, 225, 227–228, 233, 240,
  246
Kramer, Ken, 40

L
Lamm, Norman, 179
Lane, George, 33–36, 40
Levi, Yitzhak, 158
Levine, Mel, 63, 103, 107, 109, 174–176, 186, 250
Levinsky, Akiva, 71
Levy, Janice, 132
Levy, Yosef, 2–5, 130–132, 136, 140–141, 144, 160, 163, 168, 170, 188–190, 195–198, 205–210, 217, 225, 227–228, 230, 233, 235, 240, 245–246, 248–250, 252, 254, 257, 261–266, 268, 271
Li, Ahai, 214
Lichtblau, George, 82
Lieberman, Joseph, 121
Lister, John, 271
Lubavitcher Rebbe, 79, 134, 256
M
Maariv, 184, 217, 223, 268
Maimon, David, 60, 184
Maimonides, Moses, 12, 198
Mansura, Shalom, 26–27
Marhabi family, 274
McHenry, Donald, 40
Melamed, Avraham, 77
Milo, Ronnie, 222
Missouri Jewish Post & Opinion, 151
Mizrahi, Eliezer, 157
Mori, Boaz, 103, 130, 132, 137, 141, 147, 160
Mossad, 52, 60–61, 134–136, 150–151, 218, 235, 240, 260, 269–270
Mouse, Mickey, 120
Moynihan, Daniel Patrick, 103, 155
Mujali, Sheikh, 267
Mustah, Mustah, 17–18
Mutaher, Abdul Rahman, 233
N
Nahami, Naamah, 256
Nahari, Said, 244, 267
Nahari, Sleiman, 192
Nahari, Yhia Yitzhak, 165, 168, 171, 191–193, 229, 244
Najjar, Elisha, 178
Nasser, Gamal Abdul, 29–30
Nasser, Jack, 249
National Geographic, 83

National Jewish Community Relations Advisory Council (nacrac), 80, 98–99, 219
National Security Office, 34, 114, 147, 172
Neturei Karta, 56–57, 60, 70, 78, 96, 117, 129, 153, 164–165, 177, 220–221, 228–229, 235, 257, 259, 263, 272
New York Jewish Week, 82
New York Post, 178
New York Times, 195, 269
Nicolsky, Count, 46
O
Omar, 245
Omari, Ahmed, 71
Operation Magic Carpet, 1, 3, 14–15, 17, 19, 25, 29–30, 50, 57, 62, 65, 68, 81, 83, 89, 93–94, 127, 130–131, 157, 159, 210, 218, 226, 243
Operation On Eagles' Wings, 14, 159
P
Peres, Shimon, 54, 67–68, 72, 74
Philadelphia Exponent, 63
Picard, B. Donovan, 273
Pollak, Isaac, 96–98
Pollak, Ovadiah, 97
Public Committee for Yemeni Jewry, 61, 65, 67, 70–71, 73–74, 76–77
R
Rabin, 270
Rajah, 192–193, 195, 208–210
Rajeh, Al-Kathi Ghalib Abdullah, 71
Ransom, David, 4, 118–119, 121–122, 124–125, 150, 173, 179, 215
Reagan, Ronald W., 42
Reichman, Albert, 249
Rosenberg, Dvora, 62
Roth, Michael, 109
Roth, Stanley, 196, 224
Roth, Stephen, 250
Rubin, Dr., 213
Ruma, Said, 274
S
Saadiah Gaon, 10, 12
Sabari family, 252, 260, 262–265
Sabari, Balqis, 237
Sabari, Bardaqusha, 238, 265
Sabari, Daoud, 265
Sabari, Daoud ibn Yosef, 238
Sabari, Dhabia, 76

Sabari, Ezra, 238
Sabari, Ezri, 238
Sabari, Hamama, 237, 263
Sabari, Hawida, 76
Sabari, Khadia, 238, 265
Sabari, Levi, 238
Sabari, Miriam, 238, 265
Sabari, Moshe, 55, 230, 233, 238, 252–255, 257, 260, 264
Sabari, Nachle, 238
Sabari, Nadra, 238
Sabari, R. Sleiman, 267
Sabari, Said, 238
Sabari, Saida, 238
Sabari, Salem, 237, 263
Sabari, Shimon, 238
Sabari, Yaqub, 238
Sabari, Yehudah, 237, 263
Sabari, Yhia, 238
Sabari, Yhia ibn Daoud, 75, 82, 90, 212, 237–238, 248, 263–264
Sabari, Yisrael, 238, 265
Sabi, Ruma, 274
Salih, Ali Abdullah, 34, 40–41, 51, 96, 120, 139, 149, 154, 156, 172, 174, 177–179, 183–184, 186, 190, 199, 205, 211, 225, 231, 237–238, 246–247, 250, 272
San Diego Jewish Times, 63
Scheuer, James, 104, 111, 121
Schifter, Richard, 4, 112–118, 121–122, 124–125, 129, 155, 176, 220–221, 228, 232, 237, 250, 259, 262, 269
Schneider, Michael, 156, 226
Schultz, George, 74, 113
Sela, Eliav, 222, 268
Sentinel, 63
Serels, R. M. Mitchell, 89, 92
Shabbazzi, Shalom, 31, 58–59, 83, 105, 133–134, 138–139, 142, 145, 153, 188, 191, 201, 241
Shabbetai Zevi, 13
Shalamish, Abdallah, 71
Shamir, Yitzhak, 54, 67, 72–74, 150, 184, 240, 269
Shapiro, Saadia M., 102, 104
Sharabi, Moshe, 188–189, 191, 196–197, 205
Sharansky, Natan, 99

Sharon, Ariel, 269
Shetari, Yosef, 268
Sheves, Shimon, 270
Shuker, David, 61, 63, 65–68, 70–76, 78–80, 82–84, 88–90, 92, 98, 100, 124, 184, 218, 255, 260, 270
Shuker, Naomi, 65
Sleiman, Nahari, 209
Sleiman, R. Salem, 267
Smerka, Dalia, 160, 200, 264
Smerka, Lester, 92–93, 99, 104, 106, 109, 111, 118, 124, 129–130, 133, 135, 160–161, 163, 168, 178, 188–189, 191, 196–197, 205–210, 217, 227–228, 233, 240, 245–247, 254, 270–271
Solarz, Stephen J., 104, 107, 155, 173–174, 176, 186, 189–190, 192, 194–199, 224, 231, 249–250, 256, 258, 262
Soloveitchik, Hayim, 103
Stein, Hava, 46
Steinhardt, Michael, 133, 156
Strathearn, Bruce, 192, 196, 208–209, 227, 248, 253
Strauss, Annette, 179
Strauss, Robert, 179
Suberi, David, 17, 143, 203, 216–217, 261
Suberi, Doron, 214, 217
Suberi, Eyal, 214, 217
Suberi, Shalom, 17, 24–26, 55, 124, 143, 203, 214–217, 261
Suberi, Shoshana, 17, 143, 203, 216–218, 261
Suberi, Yhia ibn Daoud, 16–17, 19, 26–28, 38–39, 42, 66, 139, 143, 154, 164, 170, 176, 192, 203–211, 213, 215–219, 229–230, 244, 261, 269
Sunday Times, 268
T
Tadmur, Gidon, 74
Tawil, Arik, 94, 98, 213, 239, 256–257, 261
Tawil, Dalia, 88–89, 92, 94, 98, 103, 129, 133–136, 213, 215, 217, 227, 239–240, 249–251, 254–255, 260, 270
Tawil, Esther, 275
Tawil, Taphat, 94, 98, 213, 260–261
Tawil, Yosef, 87, 275
Tawili, Bracha, 15
Tawili, Hayim, 15

Tawili, Said, 15
Tawili, Yhia, 15
Tawili, Yosef, 15
Terrell, DuWayne, 23–30, 32–34, 36–42, 49–50, 59, 66, 78, 136, 191, 203, 215, 234
Terrell, Mr. & Mrs. Samuel, 35
Terrell, Samuel, 37, 40
Thomas, Kim, 31, 34, 40
Thomas, William, 31, 33–34, 36, 38–41
Tobi, Shoshana, 226–228, 231, 233, 240–241, 243, 246, 265
Tzadok, Yehudah, 140, 145, 206–207
Tzur, Yaakov, 68
V
Van Dusen, Michael, 107–109, 121, 124, 175, 224, 250, 256, 272
Vessey, John, 33–34, 39
von Schwarzburg-Sondershausen, Gunther Friedrich Karl II, 46
W
Washington Post, 177
Wassilkovsky, Alexander, 47
Wassilkovsky, Seraphina, 47
Wechsler, Michael, 200, 203
Weinstein, Peter D., 102
Weisberger, Tova, 104, 124–126, 130, 132, 137, 139, 141–142, 149, 152
Weiss, Rabbi, 264
Wiesel, Elie, 103, 258
Wolf, William J., 61–63, 77–78, 81, 104, 109, 118, 255
World Union of Jewish Students, 84, 107
Y
Ya'avetz, Mori, 18–19
Ya'avetz, R. Ovadiah Yaakov, 67, 78
Yaish, Mori, 39, 253
Yarimi, Yhia, 59
Yarimi, Zohorah, 59
Yatron, Gus, 121
Yedid, Mordehai, 82
Yediot Aharonot, 51, 53, 93, 223, 268
Yemenite Jewish Federation, 117, 178, 272
Yerimi, Yaakov Salah, 207
Yerimi, Yosef Salah, 207
Yisrael Shelanu, 186
Z
Zahavi, Tzion, 67
Zareb, Ida, 230, 233, 235, 237, 245, 253, 267
Zareb, Saada, 60
Zareb, Said, 267, 274
Zareb, Yhia, 248
Ze'evi, Rehavam, 159
Zindani, Esther, 261
Zindani, Hinda, 1, 5, 72, 124, 233, 255–256, 260, 274
Zindani, Massoud, 1, 5, 230, 233, 248, 252–257, 260–261, 274
Zindani, Saada, 233, 255–256, 260, 274
Zindani, Salem, 267
Zipporah, 69